Praise for Roger Kahn's *A Season in the Sun*

"For baseball's characteristic stories—anecdotes and lore the game is rich with—Roger Kahn is best of all, with his sweet ear for the cadence of baseball talk. . . . Take Roger Kahn's *A Season in the Sun* down from the bookshelf to hear the soft baseball voices repeating old games in your ear, stories for summer nights or for long winters away from the diamond and the green."—*New York Times Book Review*

"A time capsule of the '70s as well as a prescient look at what the game would eventually become."—*USA Today Baseball Weekly*

The Roger Kahn Reader

The Roger Kahn Reader

Six Decades of Sportswriting

Roger Kahn

Edited and with an introduction by Bill Dwyre

University of Nebraska Press | Lincoln and London

Library of Congress Control Number: 2017043085

Set in ITC New Baskerville by Mikala R Kolander.

To Mark Roberts, in friendship

His soul had arisen from the grave of boyhood, spurning her grave-clothes. Yes! Yes! Yes! He would create proudly out of the freedom and power of his soul, as the great artificer whose name he bore, a living thing, new and soaring and beautiful, impalpable, imperishable.

§ JAMES JOYCE

Contents

Part 3. Changing Times

Preface

Roger Kahn

I am not certain that there are hard-and-fast rules for collections, beyond the overriding and defining one: provide good reading.

Some editors believe that collections sell best when they have a single theme, say feminism, or Babe Ruth, or egg-white omelets. Among these monothematic enterprises is one with much better substance than title: *Tennis and the Meaning of Life*, edited by Jay Jennings. Here we encounter the formidable and seductive Joan Dunn in a lilting poem by the English laureate John Betjeman (1906–84). It is called "A Subaltern's Love Song."

> Miss J. Hunter Dunn, Miss J. Hunter Dunn,
> Furnish'd and burnish'd by Aldershot sun,
> What strenuous singles we played after tea,
> We in the tournament: you against me!

Miss Dunn wins the set. She also ends up in the arms of the subaltern amid mushroomy, pinewoody, evergreen smells. That last excerpt takes us closer to the essence of life than does even the finest topspin lob. (But enough exposing the secrets of my game.)

All too frequently, single-topic anthologies simply run out of good writing on their single topic. Jules Tygiel's *Jackie Robinson Reader* includes some wonderful stuff and some writing that is rather less than wonderful. There are not that many outstanding pieces on the man. Most of my own favorite collections are multithemed, reflecting the author's or editor's varied interests. I particularly like Otto Friedrich's *Grave of Alice B. Toklas: And Other Reports from the Past.* Friedrich begins with his search for the burial site of Toklas, Gertrude Stein's lover, who encouraged Friedrich when he was a young novelist. The gatekeeper at Pere-LaChaise cemetery in Paris has never heard of Toklas. He offers instead to guide Friedrich to the burial plot of Edith Piaf. *Grave* ranges from Wagner's *Parsifal* to a memoir of Friedrich's friendship with the late James Baldwin. I'd suggest, on behalf of the cause of varied themes, that a reader who doesn't care about Toklas, *Parsifal*, Jimmy Baldwin, or Otto Friedrich is all the poorer.

Another personal favorite is Eugene McCarthy's *No Fault Politics: Modern Presidents, the Press and Reformers.* McCarthy had a gift of being serious and funny simultaneously, as when he wrote that the first President Bush did not even take responsibility for his running mate. He treated Dan Quayle as a kind of accident or an act of nature—something found on the doorstep one morning.

I've enjoyed a number of collections consisting of short takes from daily and weekly journalism. The title of an assortment of John Lardner's *Newsweek* columns draws a smile: *Strong Cigars and Lovely Women.* Ah, if that truly were the essence of a writer's life. Dave Anderson, the *New York Times* columnist, gathered Red Smith's pieces on the deaths of many people that Smith cared about—Honus Wagner, Bill Tilden, Joe Louis—creating an attractive and moving volume, *To Absent Friends.* Even when considering death, Smith was consistently a cheerful man.

Jimmy Cannon's brothers, Jack and Tom, gathered much of Cannon's best newspaper work into a collection called *Nobody Asked Me, But . . .* The title comes from a signature opening for a particular genre of Cannon columns:

"Nobody asked me, but . . . people who crush cigarettes in butter plates ought to be barred from every restaurant in town."

"Nobody asked me, but . . . anyone who can drink whiskey out of a paper cup qualifies for Alcoholics Anonymous."

"Nobody asked me, but . . . if Howard Cosell was a sport, it would be Roller Derby."

In a deeper vein, Cannon's "The Ernest Hemingway I Knew" should hang in a hall of fame for newspaper writing. "Death assumed many shapes in the novels of Ernest Hemingway," Cannon begins. "It was the foul breath of a hyena, or a heavy emptiness squatting on the chest, or a puff of wind blowing across a summer's day, or a leopard lying frozen in the snows of a high mountain. But death, as I think of my friend and the foe that obsessed him, becomes a sniper in a tree.

"It always kept him within range."

Imagine. This passage appeared first on the back page of a raucous tabloid.

While gratifying in many ways, my own adventures with collections have been a bit mixed. After the success of *The Boys of Summer*, first published in 1972, I prepared a five-part collection, broadly sport, culture, crime, farewells, and politics. The publisher issued a four-part collection. We don't want the politics, an editor said. Politics dates. He would not budge, and it took me ten years to think of the appropriate answer: Of course politics dates. When it does, we call it history. That book was titled *How the Weather Was*, which comes from a Hemingway passage. The good and the bad, the ecstasy, the remorse and sorrow, the people and the places, and how the weather was. If you can get so that you can give that to people, then you are a writer.

Nineteen years later another publisher asked for a collection. This time the editor—a darned good one—insisted that the work have one theme only: sports. That became *Games We Used to Play*. The general response was enthusiastic. "A big canvas covered with style and grace," wrote Heywood Hale Broun. But I found the ground rule of "sports only" to be limiting.

Almost fifteen years after that, I was wooed by an academic who wanted to publish an anthology called *Curveballs and Culture*. I resisted that pomposity, but when the title changed to *Beyond the Boys of Summer*, I more or less let the academic take over. This collection drew praise from such varied readers as Bill Walton and Gay Talese, but much of the work consisted of excerpts from my other books, most of which are easily available at stores or through the internet. Mark Roberts, a young film producer from the Bay Area, suggested quite a different idea for the book you are now reading, a collection of pieces not readily available elsewhere.

Even before the advent of the internet, the number of newspapers and general magazines published in America had been declining steadily and, for those who care about reading and writing, alarmingly. There are by far more dead newspapers than living ones.

The first factor certainly was radio, with television hard on its heels. If you were listening to Jack Benny or the Lone Ranger, you probably were not simultaneously leafing through the pages of *Collier's* or even Hearst's tawdry *New York Journal-American*. Along with other intellectuals of the 1920s and '30s, my parents expressed concern that Americans were losing the reading habit. (One hears similar complaints today.) By "reading habit" the intellectuals presumed an intelligent, some would say elitist, pursuit. Dime-store novels, with their Indian fighters, torn bodices, and successful little orphans named Annie, did not qualify as the stuff of real reading. That term was reserved for such as Joyce, Hemingway, Dante, and Aeschylus. Hack stuff can be entertaining and occasionally has some cultural impact, but it is not art.

Television continued the electronic attack on reading, winning ever more advertising dollars away from publications and criminally assaulting English. Fortunately, a hard core of Americans—some estimate it at 5 percent of the populace—still reads the classics crafted by Homer and Shakespeare and Whitman and such gifted contemporary writers as Don DeLillo, Donald Hall, and Harold Pinter. So the good news, among all the disheartening reports, is that patient, real reading refuses to die.

Dr. James Gates, the librarian at the Baseball Hall of Fame, tells me he has never read a well-written sports story on the internet. Jim's point is unassailable. While the internet obviously uses words, it is not really about writing. Flash, cash, dash, and gash summarize the internet, which has popularized such terms as "upskirt" and "nip-slip." That is not necessarily bad per se. Shakespeare and Chaucer had rollicking bawdy moments, and I still smile at Joyce's comment on libido in his native land: "Ireland sober is Ireland stiff." What the internet lacks is a sense of style. But it is young and may discover the wonders of good writing in a few centuries.

The demise of general magazines collapsed the market for short stories. True, the old *Saturday Evening Post* bought some terrible fiction. Otto Friedrich, who edited the magazine in its late years, believed that the worst was "Impersonation," by Clarence Buddington Kelland. The story begins: "Garland Lee owed much of her glamorous success to the fact that she looked like the wholesome girl next door."

Kelland, Friedrich wrote in a dry comment, had been selling fiction to the *Post* for forty years without intruding on posterity.

But if the *Post* printed trivial work by Kelland, it also published powerful short stories by John O Hara and Isaac Bashevis Singer and, long before that, in 1914, Ring Lardner's classic baseball yarn *You Know Me Al.* Here is a sample of the way in which Lardner, in the *Saturday Evening Post*, captured the sense of distant dugouts:

Terre Haute, Indiana, September 6

FRIEND AL: Well, Al old pal I suppose you seen in the paper where I been sold to the White Sox. Believe me Al it comes as a surprise to me and I bet it did to all you good old pals down home. You could of knocked me over with a feather when the old man come up to me and says Jack I've sold you to the Chicago Americans.

I didn't have no idea that anything like that was coming off. For five minutes I was just dum and couldn't say a word.

Ever since, people have speculated: Upon whom was Jack Keefe (the ballplayer/letter writer) based? Lardner never said. My guess is that Jack is an old-time ballplayer sui generis, a portrait fashioned from the diverse semiliterate characters Lardner encountered along the baseball trail.

In researching *A Flame of Pure Fire: Jack Dempsey and the Roaring Twenties,* I immersed myself in the sports pages published before and during the 1920s. There lay a general level of newspaper writing that has not since been matched. Besides Lardner, some of the practicing sportswriters were Grantland Rice, Heywood Broun, and Sheriff Bill McGeehan. Each was a journalistic Olympian. (Bat Masterson also wrote sports back then. As a journalist Bat was an excellent pistol shot.)

On old vanished newspapers the *Chicago Inter-Ocean* and the *New York World,* people were encouraged to write as well as they could, without much hindrance from copy editors, and their gifts carried them variously into poetry (Rice) and short stories (Lardner and Broun). Other short-story masters of the period (who also worked in journalism) were Hemingway and F. Scott Fitzgerald. The so-called golden age of sport, now mostly famous for Dempsey, Rockne, and Babe Ruth, was also a golden age of writing, with short fiction and journalism overlapping.

But first there had to be a market. Hemingway, Fitzgerald, and Lardner made handsome sums selling what they wrote, moving with the demand between fiction and nonfiction. As magazines folded over the decades, it became harder and harder to sell a short story. With a woeful market, the short-story form itself began to wane. Families used to have regular gatherings after dinner where members read aloud to one another—not only short stories but narrative poetry and novels. Few families have group readings in this era of 52-inch HD LCD screens.

Between them, the *Saturday Evening Post* and *Collier's* bought about three hundred short stories a year for fees that began at $1,500. I remember Robert Frost talking about the importance of markets. "Some say," he told me, "do you write for yourself entirely? I say, do you mean for the waste basket?"

No.

The death of so many newspapers created the one-newspaper town, or the one-significant-newspaper town, throughout America. Many of these papers do excellent work, but essential competition from other newspapers is gone. With that, humility seems to have fled. Have you tried lately to get an important correction into a major American newspaper? The experience tends to be both unpleasant and futile. As one of my friends on a huge monopoly paper puts it, "With nobody chasing us, the arrogance around our shop is higher than ever. If, as happened every so often, I made a mistake in the pages of the *Herald Tribune*, no reader had to plead with me to publish a correction. Those brash tabloids, the *Daily News* and the *New York Post*, corrected me as soon as possible, often with raucous glee."

My comments here are something more than simplistic longing for good old days that glitter more in retrospect than in reality. As Red Smith remarks in my 1979 interview with him for *Esquire*, old newspaper staffs consisted in part of numbers of illiterate bums. Well into the 1940s, newspapers demanded that Major League teams pay the travel expenses of their baseball writers, from spring training through the World Series. Every ballclub served the writers free food and drink before, during, and after games. In that climate the reporters were compromised, and a lot of their stuff read like press releases. You got no sense from the old sporting press of Christy Mathewson's cold arrogance, or Babe Ruth's alcoholism, or (except for Stanley Woodward's great scoop on the failed 1947 players strike) the ordeal of Jackie Robinson.

In the stories that follow, written across five decades, my first effort was always to set events and characters down as they truly were in a manner that was neither compromised nor cruel. I was fortunate in having such colleagues as Smith at the *Herald Tribune* and John Lardner at *Newsweek*, and fortunate too in working for such protean editors as Woodward and Otto Friedrich.

One of the side benefits of a writer's life—fringies, Billy Jean King calls them—is that you get to meet prominent people who have read your stuff. I have been charmed across the years by Hillary Clinton, Rudy Giuliani, and Bushes I and II. No one possessed greater charm than Ronald Reagan. One day in the 1980s, President Reagan arranged a meeting at the Waldorf Towers on Park Avenue. He wanted to talk a little baseball. I wanted my daughter, Alissa, to have a chance to meet a sitting president.

After a pleasant forty minutes, Reagan's chief of staff approached and said quietly, "You have another appointment, Mr. President." He did indeed. He was to mediate a session on a nuclear-coexistence treaty between seething representatives of India and Pakistan.

"Don't you have one more baseball story for me?" the president asked.

I told him about the time Sam Snead took batting practice against a Yankees right-hander named Bob Grim. The pitcher threw nasty low sliders, and Snead didn't come close. Then, relenting, Grim threw a chest-high, medium-speed fastball. Snead hit that pitch a long way to left-center.

Casey Stengel poked me in the ribs and said, "Imagine that. A golfer who's a high-ball hitter."

Reagan laughed, straightened his shoulders, and headed for huge oak doors behind which the Asian emissaries were waiting. But he looked back just before the doors opened, and if I read his eyes correctly, the president would have preferred talking more baseball. I called one word to him: "Peace."

Ronald Reagan called one word back to me: "Tryin'."

I cherish the memory, but that is not my only point here.

As I wrote all the stories that follow, I was tryin'.

Introduction

Bill Dwyre

My assignment was to go to the ice cream store and pick out the best flavors. Taste them all, I was told, and then bring back about three-quarters of what you sampled in those big buckets, under the glass. Just the best of the best.

And so, in *The Roger Kahn Reader,* you get chocolate vanilla swirl, butter pecan, and raspberry mint. Kahn has no bad flavors, but some melt on the tongue so perfectly that they can't be resisted.

This collection is to be cherished and revisited often. Great sportswriting can be magical and spell-binding, a sensory treat for a reader. Kahn's always was, and it still is.

Sportswriting is also becoming an abandoned literature. Phrase-making and insightful storytelling are being squeezed out by tweets and texts and internet deadlines, mostly directed by people whose priorities put corporate profits before literary journalism, resourceful reporting, and inspiring analysis.

Kahn writes that Joe Black's "on-field manner is as tough as his off-field manner is gentle."

He reminds us that Clem Labine pitched a shutout the day before Bobby Thomson hit his "shot heard 'round the world," and that Labine also pitched a shutout the day after Don Larsen's perfect game.

Kahn describes the attractive shortcomings of Ebbets Field and later mourns its loss: "Its architecture suggested a mail-order tool shed. . . . It was a ballpark. Not a stadium or a superdome or a multisport arena. A ballpark, bad for football, unsuitable for concerts, unthinkable for track."

And then, when the Dodgers moved from Brooklyn to Los Angeles: "The soul of Brooklyn shriveled and was lost when a baseball franchise moved and the wrecking ball ravaged Ebbets Field."

Few have captured the souls and personalities of baseball players as effectively as Kahn. He writes that Bob Gibson grew up in a house with seven people and four rooms, and "it was there that a rat bit one of his ears." He quotes another star pitcher of the era, Warren Spahn, as saying, "Home plate is seventeen inches wide. All I asked for were the two inches on each corner. The hitters could have the thirteen inches in between. I didn't throw there."

No sport is free of his flair for memorable summation. "The tradition of powerhouse football at Notre Dame," he writes, "traces at least to 1905, when the Irish eased past American Medical College, 142–0."

He describes hockey player Guy Lafleur as a precious national asset in Canada, "like the oil fields of Alberta or the restaurants of Montreal." And he describes the year when Canadian prime minister Pierre Trudeau had to hand out the champions trophy of the Canada Cup to the Soviets by saying that Trudeau was properly poised and diplomatic, "but the smile was funereal and forced."

The content herein is much more than just bats and balls and jockstraps. There is certainly sociology. Kahn relates this conversation with manager Charlie Dressen:

Kahn: "How do you feel about Negroes in baseball?"

Dressen: "Can they hit, throw, and run? That's all I want to know."

Kahn says he took inspiration from his father, who told him that "you could enjoy Dodgers baseball and Paul Robeson's concerts equally, if with different sensibilities."

Readers of *The Roger Kahn Reader* need just one sensibility: an appreciation for masterful manipulation of words.

The Roger Kahn Reader

Part 1

An American Tragedy

1

A Death Without Sunlight: Jackie Robinson Jr.

Esquire, November 1971

Young Jack had difficulties finding a comfortable place within and outside of his famous family. In time he went to Vietnam as an infantryman, turned on to heroin, died young. The story his platoon mates tell is stark.

I begin this collection with this work because our country has slipped into a pattern of ill-defined, semiconstant, probably needless and unquestionably murderous wars: Korea, Vietnam, Iraq, Afghanistan to name four, excluding deadly brevities in Granada, Somalia, and Bosnia. I hope that this examination of one forgotten death spurs the outrage that it merits.

This poem is a death chant
and a gravestone and a prayer for young Jackie Robinson
who walked among us with a wide stride
moving moving moving
through blood and mud and shit of Vietnam.
Moving moving moving
through blood and mud and dope of America.

Ethridge Knight, who himself is recovering from heroin addiction, had written these words through tears and reworked the lines many times and now . . . he bowed his large dark head and showed them deferentially. Ethridge is groping back toward manhood at Daytop in Seymour, Connecticut, the institution where young Jackie Robinson tried to make himself whole in the brave late years of a brief life. . . .

Knight, a published poet, is a resident of Daytop. He has stopped taking drugs, but he has not yet reached confirmation, the day when he is pronounced competent to reenter the world beyond. His judges, the people who run Daytop with some professional psychiatric consultation, are all former skin-poppers and mainliners. Junkies.

"Thanks, Ethridge," said Jimmy DeJohn, black-goateed and squat as a linebacker. He is an assistant director of Daytop and twenty-four years old. "You can go back to work." Ethridge drifted off soundlessly. "We don't talk about Jackie too much with the residents," DeJohn said. "It upsets them. They can't hear it."

Summer sat on the Housatonic River and on the valley cottages where one finds the pallbearers for Jackie Robinson Jr.—careworn George Tocci, Eddie Brown, eight years a Marine, and Jimmy DeJohn, who was married in a Catholic church last fall with young Jack as best man. "A few people were surprised to see a black guy best man at an Italian wedding," he said, "but the maid of honor, who was white, was proud to walk down the aisle of St. Margaret Mary's with someone that fine. And I was damn proud." Jimmy shook his head.

The summer day and death talk made incongruity. Nearby field corn had grown man high and in the river, beyond the curving blacktop, someone had anchored a jump and you could hear the skiers on the water, their voices exultant in youth. Summer and death and youth and death: an equation reason cannot solve.

The death facts may be stated simply. On June 17, 1971, at about 2:30 a.m., Jackie Robinson Jr. was found dead in the remnant of a yellow MG. He had driven off the Merritt Parkway at such high speed that the car, which belonged to his brother David, demolished four heavy oak guard posts. The engine came to rest a hundred feet from the chassis, which looked like a toy car bent double by the hammer of a petulant child. Only wire wheels remained intact. Police theorized that death was instantaneous. The coroner fixed cause as a broken neck. David Robinson identified the car and his brother's body. Jackie Robinson Sr., fifty-two, broke the news to his wife, Rachel, an assistant professor of psychiatric nursing at Yale.

Newspapers filled their obituaries with fragments of a molten life. The late Mr. Robinson, wounded in action in Vietnam, was the son of the first Negro to play in the Major Leagues. After his discharge the younger Robinson was twice arrested on charges growing from heroin addiction. Later he was said to have ceased using drugs. At the time of his death, he was employed as assistant regional director of Daytop, Inc. Police found neither drugs nor evidence of continuing drug use on the corpse.

"We both came in here September 1968," said Jimmy DeJohn, "which made us close. And we were dope fiends and we licked it together. He was interested in philosophy and helping street people and he was getting to be some speaker. That's what he did. Spoke. His dream was having his own community center in some bad ghetto."

The Daytop centers—there are only two—attack addiction through self-confrontation. The approach echoes Jung, who spoke of destruction and rebirth, and even shadows Socrates in the agora, speaking his willingness to die many times. Withdrawal from heroin, say Daytop people, is not physical torture. It produces sweating, restlessness, and the symptoms of intestinal flu for seventy-two hours. But the idea of convulsing spasms and shrieking agony is decried as the stuff of bad Sinatra pictures and of people who lean on bad Sinatra pictures to cop out. (Withdrawal from barbiturate addiction—heroin is a narcotic—is described as another problem, truly hideous.)

The addict entering Daytop quits cold. His system recovers quickly, but it takes a year or even two to make an emotional adjustment. A Daytop resident lives in a dormitory with others and plants corn, works lathes, writes poems. Part of the day is given to talk, in which one is encouraged, figuratively whipped, to face himself. Images shatter. People cry. Although the cure ratio is 80 percent, it is not a gentle place. Young Jackie Robinson ran no gentle road to find Daytop.

He was born in 1946, after the thrilling season when his father broke through baseball's cotton curtain on the way to becoming a Brooklyn Dodger. In succeeding years little Jack became a darling of the Dodgers' entourage. I have before me a *Life* magazine photograph taken by Nina Leen that shows Jackie sitting on a tricycle before a Brooklyn stoop-front. His father looks on with intent pride; Rachel, his mother, contains her smile, as is her way. The little boy is wearing a white playsuit. Perched surely, no hands, he drinks a glass of milk. It is a pretty picture suggesting contentment, but at the time it was taken people still chuckled as they remembered a remark by the politician Al Smith. The only trouble with kittens and pickaninnies is that they grow up.

As young Jackie Robinson moved past three-wheelers, black resistance formed, rising against bigotry. The point, an arrow of dark fire, was Jackie's father. The big man beat off mixed hatred and scorn: beanballs, obscenities, a too-small salary, a righteous, condescending press. But after he had broken through, Alan Paton made a pilgrimage to shake big Jack's gnarled hand. Earl Warren sprawled in a private box at Ebbets Field, sipping a drink and cheering my fellow Californian. Two years after that Earl Warren's court struck down school segregation.

When I was traveling with the Dodgers in 1953, Jackie Robinson remarked that he missed being home and the chance to watch his children change day by day. In 1955 he built an estate in a corner of North Stamford, Connecticut, where until then blacks had come only as servants. This must have been a paradoxical boyhood for young Jackie, pampered by strangers, attacked by bigotry once removed, with an adoring father who went away every other day (it seemed) to play in St. Louis, Cincinnati, or Pittsburgh. Still, when the father retired from baseball in 1956, young Jackie cried.

With adolescence, disaffection entered. Young Jack performed poorly in junior high school and went off to prep. He dropped out and enlisted in the army. He wanted to achieve discipline, he said.

In Vietnam he became a good rifleman. Once as his platoon sat panting on a hummock near Pleiku, he heard a sound and turned and fired a burst from his M-14. Two Vietcong fell dead. A third crawled into undergrowth. The men of the platoon rushed up and slammed his back and yelled, "Nice shooting, Jackie." He nodded and walked slowly to the corpses. He was surprised that they were younger than himself.

Later the platoon was pinned, and as mortar fragments fell some men began to cry in panic. Fragments killed the soldier next to Jackie, who himself took shrapnel in the hip. Afterward he put down the incident as "the time I got shot in the ass." But it was in Vietnam that he first turned to heroin.

"When he came to Daytop he was very inward," Jimmy DeJohn said, "and he had hang-ups. He knocked his own family as cliché middle class. I'm middle class myself. I grew up next to a golf club outside Hartford. I started drinking cough syrup with codeine and getting stuff out of Darvon pills when my father died, but that's another story and you came to talk about Jackie."

DeJohn, Tocci, Brown, and I were sitting in a bare office at Daytop. Above DeJohn a sign hung, white paint on brown wood: J. Robinson.

"From when he was night mayor," Tocci said. "The staff man in charge late is the night mayor. He seemed to like that when he had kicked the dope and started working here. That was the sign we hung when he was night mayor. *J. Robinson, Night Mayor of Daytop.*"

"A good ballplayer," DeJohn said. "Batted lefty. He hit a softball a helluva way. But he didn't like it. After him and me was making progress and going places, people who met him said, 'You're the ballplayer's son.' He'd say, 'Baseball's not my thing.' Then he'd say, 'Don't use the whole name. Just introduce me as Jackie.'"

"The street people got to be his thing," Tocci said. "He'd go to Hartford, Waterbury, New Haven, where there were bad slums, and tell them about staying away from heroin and about Daytop."

"No shirt and tie like at home," DeJohn said. "He wore dashikis. Still, he always had good communication with his mother."

"Did he talk to you about his time in Vietnam?"

"I was there," Eddie Brown said. "Long time back. '65. They had us fighting with World War II gear. . . . You got to go on these missions, search and destroy, you get high. Booze, hash, whatever. Grass got me a dishonorable discharge. Now when Jackie told me about shooting this burst and finding out he'd killed people who were just kids, I asked him what he thought. He said he thought nothing. He made his mind go blank." . . .

"Mr. Robinson was very nice to us," DeJohn said. "He had us over to his estate and football's my bag and he reached into his trophy case and took out a white football a lot of people had signed. This musta been some kind of an award."

"Before baseball he was a star running back," I said.

"I told him we couldn't use that one, but Mr. Robinson wanted us to go ahead. And before we were through kicking it around, every signature was rubbed off. Mr. Robinson laughed and said he was just happy to see young people playing ball around his house."

"Did Jackie come to appreciate what his father had done in baseball?"

"Not really," DeJohn said, "but he was coming to appreciate him as a man."

"He found out his dad didn't always have the good life," Tocci said, "that when Mr. Robinson was young his people were so poor dinner would sometimes be a sugar sandwich."

"That started things opening," DeJohn said. "It got better and better between him and his dad, and last year Mr. Robinson had a party for Daytop and he and Jackie hugged each other."

"Wonderful people," Tocci said.

"Jackie won this great victory over heroin," DeJohn said, "and we used to talk—like I say we're both twenty-four—about the greater victories ahead."

On his funeral day, June 21, the coffin had stood open. The family had abandoned the suburbs for the services and chosen Antioch Baptist Church on Greene Avenue in Brooklyn. . . . "In Memoriam," said the program, "Jack Roosevelt Robinson Jr., 1946–1971." . . .

I looked at the leonine head of the young man newly dead. His beard was trimmed. For an instant I allowed myself to consider what was locked within the skull: Gibran and Herbie Mann and racism and the faces of teenaged Asians killed in battle and the narcosis of heroin and the shock of withdrawal and a father's hug. And then I would not let myself think that way anymore.

The family was escorted to their pews at 1:15. Rachel Robinson, who had mixed martinis with exquisite care when last we saw her, was clinging to another of her children. Two men had to support Jackie Robinson, most powerful of base runners. He was crying very softly for his son, his head down so that the tears coursed only a little way before falling to the floor.

A solo flute played "We Shall Overcome." A chorus from Daytop sang "Bridge Over Troubled Water" and "Swing Low, Sweet Chariot." . . . David Robinson, who is nineteen, walked to the pulpit with a wide stride and read a eulogy for his brother. David had written it in a single afternoon and pleaded with his father to be allowed to speak it.

"He climbed high on the cliffs above the sea," David called in a resonant tenor, "and stripped bare his shoulders and raised his arms to the water, crying, 'I am a man. Give me my freedom so that I might dance naked in the moonlight and laugh with the stars and roll in the grass and drink the warmth of the sun. Give me my freedom so I might fly.' But the armies of the sea continued to war with the wind and raced through the stones and mocked his cries, and the man fell to his knees and wept. . . . He rose," David's voice called from the pulpit, "and journeyed down the mountain to the valley and came upon a village. When the people saw him, they scorned him for his naked shoulders and wild eyes, and again he cried, 'I am a man. I seek the means of freedom.'

"The people laughed, saying, 'We see no chains on your arms. Go. You are free.' And they called him mad and drove him from their village. The man walked on, eyes red as a gladiator's sword, until he came to a stream where he saw an image, face sunken in hunger, skin drawn tight around the body.

"He stood fixed on the water's edge and began to weep, not from sorrow but from joy, for he saw beauty in the water, and he removed his clothing and stood naked before the world and rose to his full height and smiled and moved to meet the figure in the water, and the stream made love to his body, and his soul cried with the ecstasy of being one." . . .

David's strong voice rose and choired, "He laughed, for he felt the strength of the stream flowing through his veins, and he cried, 'I am a man,' and the majesty of his voice was heard above the roar of the sea and the howl of the wind, and he was free." . . .

I saw Jackie Robinson after the services, white-haired, dry-eyed, and sure as when he doubled home two runs, walk among street people outside church, talking perhaps of the hell of heroin, touching and being touched, and I thought how proud his firstborn son would have been, not of the ballplayer but of the man, had he lived, if only the insanity of the present had given him a chance.

Part 2

When Eisenhower Reigned

2

Joe Black's Odyssey

New York Herald Tribune, June 8, 1952

This was my first baseball column in the Trib. *A column, as opposed to a news story, meant at least two things: the paper published your picture, and Red Smith was getting a day off.*

From Plainfield, New Jersey, to Brooklyn runs some twenty-five miles, barely far enough to give a seasoned commuter time to list half the shortcomings of railroads, buses, and highways. But Joe Black, a better pitcher than a commuter, turned the journey into an odyssey by making stops in Cuba, Venezuela, Baltimore, Montreal, and St. Paul before he reached the rosy-tinted land across the river.

In place of the one-eyed gods and murderous vixens who kept the plot moving in Homer's epic, baseball players peopled Joe's journey. It will never be required reading for high-school freshmen, because, among other reasons, there was no blood or thunder anywhere along the way.

Instead, to hear Black tell it, making the Dodgers' pitching staff was a task as pleasant as it was circuitous. From the Plainfield High School counselor who advised Joe to go to a Negro college because "I didn't know enough about my race," to men like Preacher Roe and Chuck Dressen, who gave him tips that made his curveball big league, Joe has found people willing to go out of their way to help him.

When you meet him it isn't hard to understand why. As soon as he talks or smiles he makes a friend, and more often than not, when Joe Black talks, smiles follow.

"When I first started playing in the Negro leagues . . . I figured I was a shortstop. I started hitting, and the pitchers started curving me.

After a little while the manager came to me and said, 'Son, maybe you can pitch.'"

"Are you a hitter, Joe?" someone wanted to know.

"I'm a swinger," Black announced.

"How'd the pitching go?"

"The first seven men I faced struck out," Joe said, "but those next eight guys, well, they didn't all hit the ball over the fence; some of them hit it against it. I didn't finish the start."

He finished others, though. He has the big-league hatred of losing, and his on-field manner is as tough as his off-field manner is gentle.

When Black played football for Morgan State College, he was a back on offense but an end on defense by his own request. "I'd get tackled when I ran," he explained, "but I never had much chance to do any tackling of my own. I wanted to hit the other fellows as hard as they were hitting me, so I moved up to end."

Joe kept moving up when he finished his war-interrupted studies at Morgan State and graduated with a working knowledge of psychology. He taught school for a while in Baltimore but found the classroom a little cramped for his six-foot-two-inch frame. Before that he played winter baseball in Venezuela, and by 1950, when he went to play ball in Cuba, he was established as a pitcher. The Dodgers signed him in October, and he spent time with farm teams in Montreal and St. Paul. It was in the Brooklyn organization that Joe found a happy ending to his wanderings.

Jackie Robinson broke through the color line only five years before Black entered organized ball, but a century of progress had been made.

Looking backward, Robinson insists it wasn't so difficult, but when he was asked if any International League clubs gave him trouble, he rattled off three in no time at all. And opposing Major Leaguers like the Philadelphia Phils' Lee Handley and Hank Greenberg, who apologized for bigots on benches, were so few that each one of them stands out in Jackie's memories.

Black, at twenty-eight a veteran of little more than one full season in organized baseball, found virtually no incidents marring his days, so the one unpleasant experience he had stands out in his memory.

"Some Buffalo player was really vicious," Black recalled, "and got me as sore as I've ever been. I was with Montreal then, and after the game, as we were walking to the clubhouse, I was right behind him, but he didn't know it. He had a bat in his hand and said to the guy ahead of him that he'd like to break it over my head. I told him to go ahead and try, but they grabbed me before anything started.

"I was waiting for him next time we played Buffalo, and sure enough he came around. He wasn't looking to fight, though. He said he was sorry and stuck his chin out and told me to belt him because he had it coming. That was the end of it, and that was the only time there was any trouble."

"The progress has been tremendous," Robinson commented. "Democracy working, that's what it's been."

And at the same time, Black, whose great relief pitching has been a big factor in the Dodgers' success so far, has made tremendous personal progress since he first started wandering from Plainfield. He has moved to Brooklyn now, married a young schoolteacher, and is settling into life as a Brooklynite and as a big leaguer. "It's kind of nice around here," he says. "I think I'll stay."

3

What White Big Leaguers Really Think of Negro Players

Our Sports, June 1953

This story was written at the request of Jackie Robinson for a magazine he and I started almost sixty years ago. I spoke with scores of baseball people, and Robinson followed the results intensely. We were both pleased with what I heard.

In the space of three days last March, morale on the Brooklyn Dodgers traveled a complete cycle. On a Thursday white and Negro players operated together in perfect harmony. On Friday there was apparent trouble. And on Saturday the confusion was over, and the harmony was more harmonious than ever.

Believe it? Or does the story sound too simple and too pat to be true? The way to find out is to study those three March days from a day-to-day perspective.

On Thursday, March 19, Jackie Robinson played third base for the Dodgers and Junior Gilliam started at second. Where there had been two Negroes in the Dodgers' daily exhibition-game lineup—Robinson and Roy Campanella—there now were three. And one white Dodger was out of a job.

When you consider the Dodgers generally model race relationships over the years, that situation does not seem to hold the seeds of tension. Chuck Dressen, the Dodgers' manager, saw nothing explosive in the lineup switch. "That's my strongest team," he said. "I think Gilliam's gonna be a star. You know Robinson. This way we'll get more hitting than we would if Robinson stayed at second and Billy Cox stayed at third.

"Sure," he admitted, "Cox will field better at third than Jackie. But not so much that it'll make a difference."

To Dressen, hitting and fielding were the only matters worth consideration. A midwestern Catholic who remembers the Ku Klux Klan's strongest days, the manager has given bigotry no sanction ever since he met the hooded hoodlums.

But to a few other Dodgers, another point was worth consideration.

A Negro wearing the uniform of the Dodgers' St. Paul farm club walked past the Brooklyn bus after the switch had been announced. "Hey," said a Dodger, "how come that guy isn't on our club?"

"It's all right to have Negroes in the game," another Dodger granted, "but now they're taking over."

"I don't know how Billy Cox feels," said a third, "but I wouldn't want a nigger to take my job." . . .

Two newspapermen overheard the remarks. The reporters knew that Cox was upset not by racial questions per se but by the fact that he'd lost his starting position at third base. They knew that sympathy for Cox and the tasteless remarks of a few Dodgers might fuse into a raw and ugly situation. They knew, too, that if they wrote of racial tension, Dodgers officials and other newspapermen who did not have the story might go to extremes to deny the report.

The reporters considered the situation and decided to write. Their stories appeared in the *New York Herald Tribune,* a widely respected conservative newspaper, and the *Daily News,* a tabloid selling about two million copies a day, the largest circulation in the nation.

As soon as the papers hit the newsstands of New York, telephone calls began streaming into the Dodgers' hotel in Miami and the club's permanent spring training base at Vero Beach. As soon as the phone calls began, denials followed. . . . Buzzie Bavasi, the Dodgers' personable vice president . . . spent Friday morning talking to groups of players. Then he announced: "There is no racial tension on this club. A few remarks have been made, sure. But they were jokes, not anything to take seriously." Another Dodgers official insisted that the whole thing was caused by newspapermen who were looking to make a story.

A number of Dodgers ballplayers expressed surprise that anyone could think there was tension on the club, much less write it. By Saturday the general feeling was that the remarks had been exaggerated and misunderstood. And besides, they had never been uttered. But no matter how hard and how often denials were declared, the truth is that the remarks were uttered. They were not mouthed as jokes. They were neither misunderstood nor exaggerated.

Is it possible, then, that in 1953—seven years after baseball's color line was shattered—Negro ballplayers have not been accepted?

Is it possible that there remains a great undercurrent of resentment that has yet to come to the surface?

Is it possible that beneath all the new expressions of brotherhood lie the old feelings of bigotry and intolerance?

Is it possible that the position of Negroes in America's national game has still to be finally resolved?

A flip answer would be a wrong answer because this is not a flippant situation. Baseball has traveled a long way down the road to brotherhood, and a handful of bigots can no more stop the advances to come than they can turn back the ones accomplished. The bigots are being beaten, and the most encouraging fact is that only a handful of them are left.

Although the thoughtless remarks some Dodger made about Junior Jim Gilliam were not exaggerated, some fans exaggerated the number of thoughtless Dodgers.

Of the forty men on the Brooklyn squad when the March incident happened, three were guilty of speaking out of turn. Thirty-seven were not. That's a pretty good percentage of right-thinking men.

Carl Erskine, the trim right-hander, explains his feelings this way: "You couldn't dream up a better group of people than the fellows on this club. I've made a lot of friends in baseball, but few closer than Jackie Robinson. The day I joined the Dodgers a kid trying to get along, not knowing anybody, Jack came over to me. He put his arm around me and wished me luck. Sure he's a great ballplayer, but he's more than that. He's a great friend."

Carl Furillo, the muscular right fielder, wasn't sure about Negroes in 1946. He listened to some bigots, and he had his doubts. Ask Carl today and he'll tell you: "What difference does it make what a guy is? If he's a good guy and he can play ball, I want to play on his team."

Grill Dressen and you'll hear a manager who thinks right.

"How do you feel about Negroes in baseball?"

"Can they hit, throw, and run? That's all I want to know."

"Do Negroes create any special problems for you as a manager?"

"Not a one. As long as I've been managing the Dodgers, there hasn't been any trouble. And there isn't gonna be, either."

"How about those fellows who popped off?"

"There are stupid guys in every business. Some fellows will always complain about one thing or another."

"What about the lingering feelings of white supremacy? What will happen when your best team consists of five Negroes and four whites?"

"Then that's the way it'll be. The nine best guys will play, and anyone who doesn't like it can quit. But they won't quit, and they'll start to like it when they see the Negro ballplayers getting them into the World Series and making an extra five thousand bucks."

Essentially Dressen is both candid and correct. There isn't any Negro problem on the Dodgers. All that leaves to check is the rest of the big leagues.

A good deal of bench-jockeying still resounds with racism. Unfortunate as that may be, it's baseball. Joe DiMaggio, probably the greatest player of his time, was called "Dago" by his own teammates. He was Big Dago. Phil Rizzuto was Little Dago. Not socially acceptable, but as Jim Turner, the Yankees' pitching coach, says, "Don't confuse big-league ball with a fucking garden party. Because it isn't. It fucking is not."

Dizzy Dean of the St. Louis Cardinals busied himself during the 1934 World Series by bellowing, "Hey, Moe," at the great Detroit slugger Hank Greenberg. Over the seven games, Greenberg led both team in runs batted in. In 1939, when I was eleven year old, I sat in the center-field stands at Ebbets Field behind a solid outfielder named Goody Rosen. Suddenly a fan waved his beer bottle and bellowed, "Hey, Jewboy. Go home and eat your matzos." Rosen never turned. He responded by scratching his butt.

The theoretical idea behind bench-jockeying is to stir anger, rage so blind that the victim strikes out or throws a home-run ball. You don't have to like such tactics, but you do best to accept them. They exist and don't mean much except that grown men play tough baseball and the stakes are high. . . .

Players off the field, in calm moments, seem to me to fall broadly into three groups. Most players think right. To the vast majority of big leaguers, color is secondary to ability. Eddie Stanky's Cardinals needled Robinson and Joe Black sharply last year, but here's what Eddie says when wearing street clothes: "I played with Robinson on the Dodgers and Monte Irvin, Willie Mays, and Hank Thompson on the Giants. How'd we get along? Fine. I'd say my relationships with all the Negroes I've played with have been 100 percent pleasant. Don't mind what I say during a ball game. I want to win, and sometimes I get rough. But Robinson does too, you know. It's part of the fiercely competitive side of baseball."

The second group consists of doubters. There are a few on each team. "Sure," they say, "it's okay to have Negroes in the game, but the thing is going too far. In ten years there won't be any jobs for white players. It's okay to have Negroes, but there ought to be a limit."

Above all else, fear motivates the doubters. They're usually athletes who hang in the big leagues by their thumbs. One push and they go back to East Podunk. They're a little frightened, a little insecure, a little stupid, and a small minority themselves.

After the doubters come the out-and-out bigots. They are there but hard to find. Ballplayers don't launch tirades against Negroes anymore. So the handful of men who believe baseball stopped being baseball when Jackie Robinson hit his first home run for the Dodgers keep their beliefs to themselves. . . .

For the surest sign of baseball's progress, you do well to visit the Deep South. Come to Vero Beach, Florida, where the Dodgers organization practices equality without advertising and laughs in the face of Jim Crow. . . .

"There's the dining room," Walter O'Malley says, pointing to a large room behind screen doors. "Our Negro players and our white players eat in there, side by side. This is Florida, but you couldn't tell it."

"See the four boys playing cards over there," he continues, indicating a group at a table in one corner of the main hall. "Two white boys and two Negroes at the same table in Florida. Look at the gang around the piano. We aren't boasting about this; we don't ask for credit. We run our organization the right way, and you see what we think is right.

"There are the barracks," O'Malley adds. "Negro boys and white boys under the same roof in Florida. The other day we had some electricians in from Melbourne to fix the lights in our new stadium. They worked a long day. When they were through it was late, and I asked them if they wanted to sleep over. . . . They asked me if they'd have to sleep under the same roof with the Negro players, and I told them, 'Of course.' They said they couldn't. What did I tell them then? You couldn't print it."

As he said, O'Malley wasn't boasting. But the Brooklyn boss, one of baseball's most powerful magnates, tipped the game's hand. The national sport is showing the way to the nation. More and more clubs are hiring Negro players; more and more parts of the country are seeing that white and Negro can live and work together and even become friends.

There may be a few more bad moments like the one the Dodgers suffered last March before baseball's last racial incident is over. But for every moment of tension, there'll be a thousand hours when democracy is quietly in action.

Are there still bigots in baseball?

A few, but they're hiding under their beds.

4

The Twilight of the Gods

Sports Illustrated, September 20, 1954

Casey Stengel's proud Yankees, playing at a clip that had won them five world championships, went into Cleveland and met a better team—the 1954 Cleveland Indians, who did not "choke up."

"Attention, please!" boomed the impersonal voice of the loudspeaker at Cleveland's Municipal Stadium, breaking in on the second game of the Indians' Sunday double-header with the New York Yankees. "Today's paid attendance is 84,587, the most that ever saw a regular season Major League game." The crowd applauded but quieted down when the speaker boomed again. "Attention, please. Today's attendance, including passes, is 86,563, the most that ever saw a Major League game." This time the crowd was permitted to cheer its own magnificence without interruption.

This impressive compliment fully digested, the largest crowd that ever gathered to watch a baseball game went back to the fascinated contemplation of what had brought most of them to Municipal Stadium in the first place—the Cleveland Indians' effective demonstration that they are a better team than the five-time world champion New York Yankees. As drama, it might very well have been titled "The Twilight of the Gods." While a band played brassily in left field, the Yankees followed Thor and Wotan into eclipse.

The inevitable end of the champions did not dull the spectacle. The Yankees died hard, and Cleveland watched with deep-grained satisfaction. Yankees manager Casey Stengel chose one of his best, twenty-five-year-old left-hander Whitey Ford, to pitch the first game. Cleveland's Al Lopez reached into his deep bin of pitchers—richest in baseball—and picked right-hander Bob Lemon, winner of twenty-one games this year. For a while, until Ford wrenched his shoulder with a side-arm throw, it was a pitchers' game: 1–1 in the sixth. Then Casey Stengel called on Allie Reynolds, thirty-seven, once the possessor of the most effective fastball in the league.

THEY NEVER HAD A CHANCE

Al Rosen, third baseman for the Indians, stepped to the plate. He was a college boy when Allie Reynolds was a Major Leaguer. With two men on base, he hit a slider into right-center field. The ball skipped past Mickey Mantle for a two-base hit and two runs scored. After that, Bob Lemon never gave the Yankees a chance. At the end of the first game the score was 3–1 for the Indians, and the Yankees were seven and a half games out of first place.

Stengel had lost with his best. For the second game he turned to an old Yankees castoff—Tommy Byrne, the thirty-four-year-old left-hander who had been hurriedly called in from Seattle only ten days before. Against him Al Lopez sent Gus Wynn (20-11 for the season). Wynn throws every known pitch, including a wildly breaking knuckleball, and in the first inning Yogi Berra, the Yankees' catcher, hit one of them into the upper right-field stands for a two-run homer.

The Yankees held on until the fifth. Then the Indians caught up with Tommy Byrne. Wynn singled, rookie Al Smith singled, and hard-hitting Bobby Avila, the league's likely batting champion, singled again. Home came Wynn, barely safe under a high throw from the outfield. "Just missed him," said a Yankee on the bench.

"He threw it bad," muttered Casey Stengel, sensing catastrophe. "Too high to be cut off."

Stengel was right, as usual. Another hit, a double by Wally West-lake, sent two more Indians home. After that, the Indians left it to Gus Wynn, and in the fading light he almost seemed to toy with the world champions. After the first inning, the Yankees got only one hit, and that was a bunt.

Casey Stengel was not through. He called on Enos Slaughter, the old Cardinal, to pinch-hit in the ninth. Slaughter let a knuckleball sweep by for the third strike. Now came Mickey Mantle, the twenty-two-year-old picked to replace the great Joe DiMaggio. Mantle struck out, for the one hundredth time this season.

STRIKE-OUT NO. 12

Finally it was the turn of Yogi Berra, the twenty-nine-year-old gnome around whom the Yankees of 1955 can hope to rebuild. A home run would have tied the score, and Yogi had hit twenty this season. But Gus Wynn had given up his home run for the day. The Yankees' catcher swung mightily and became his twelfth strike-out victim.

Some of Wynn's fellow Indians hugged him as he walked from the pitcher's mound. Others turned and shouted, "Choke-ups!" in the direction of the Yankees' bench.

No one had taunted the Yankees in this manner for years, but the Indians had full right to their moment. For three years in a row they have finished second to the Yankees. They have heard, for the three years, the intolerable chant that they were the ones who choked up in the pennant stretch. This spring, the Indians' captain, Al Rosen, took up the "choke-up" charge in an exasperated declaration: "We don't lose to the Yankees because we choke up. We lose to the Yankees because they're a better team."

But the fans of Cleveland, some of whom had come from hundreds of miles, were gentle. There was little booing of the dying gods. Most of them knew that the 1954 Yankees were finishing one of their best seasons. At week's end, and with eleven more games to play, the world champions had won ninety-five games. In most seasons that many victories would have won the American League pennant (see table). But this time even the Yankees seemed to sense that time had run out on them. They tried to joke about it before the double-header.

In the morning, as buses and trains and planes poured fans into Cleveland, the Yankees ate breakfast at the Hotel Cleveland.

"Did you come to bury us?" Jerry Coleman, an alert infielder, asked a visiting writer from New York.

"The slowly dying Yankees," Charlie Silvera, substitute catcher, read aloud from a local newspaper. "The slowly dying Yankees," he repeated. "Very funny."

Stengel's Big Six

In six years as manager of the Yankees, Casey Stengel has won five world championships. This year, ironically, the Yankees have played at a better clip than ever. Yankees victories (with 11 games to play) as compared with their full-season totals in the past:

	Won	*Lost*	*%*
1954	95	48	.664
1953	99	52	.656
1952	95	59	.617
1951	98	56	.636
1950	98	56	.636
1949	97	57	.630

Cleveland, with 104 victories, 40 losses, was .722 this week. If the Indians maintain this pace in their remaining 10 games, they will win the pennant with the highest average in American League history.

"I defy anyone," manager Casey Stengel barked, "to say this team ain't worth a quarter. I don't want to blow up another club because the race is still going, you can be sure, and we get paid to win, not blow up other clubs, but Cleveland has played tree-mendous and we been trying to catch 'em, so how can you say our team ain't worth a quarter?"

Around the batting cage before the game the Indians matched the Yankees' edginess with nonchalance. "It's not rough," said Bobby Avila. "All year we play, now we play. We play okay."

NO HAND-HOLDING

Said Al Lopez: "I don't have to go in there to talk to my players and hold their hands. We've got players now who like to play. They know what's going on. I don't have to go in there and talk to them like they were children."

After the double-header was over, Casey Stengel was still giving out his own brand of unpunctuated chatter. "I ain't conceding," he said, "but they won because they got amazing pitching like I have never seen in six years in the league and they was well-managed and they won all those games from those other clubs which makes me wonder why some of those other clubs that is always worrying about the Yankees this the Yankees that don't get the idea and start worrying about themselves."

5

Baseball 1954

Sports Illustrated, **October 4, 1954**

For the fans it was a season of vivid moments, while the impersonal scorebooks wrote a story of their own.

> It was the best of times, it was the worst of times, it was the age of wisdom, it was the age of foolishness, it was the epoch of belief, it was the epoch of incredulity, it was the season of Light, it was the season of Darkness, it was the spring of hope, it was the winter of despair . . .

No one ever accused Charley Dickens of being a baseball writer, but give or take a few Victorian adjectives, Old Chuck might almost have been telling "A Tale of Two Boroughs" last week.

In darkest Brooklyn the New York Giants sent Sal Maglie, the blue-jowled right-hander, against the Dodgers. The Giants needed one game to win the National League pennant. Maglie, aging, backsore but courageous, had been winning needed games all season. This time he started slowly, walked two in the first inning. Then he threw a double-play ball to Duke Snider. Then he never gave the Dodgers another chance.

At Ebbets Field the fans of Brooklyn hooted Maglie. Sal had heard— and ignored—their hoots before. Between innings Maglie rushed to the Giants' clubhouse so that a trainer could knead the twisted muscles in his back. On the field he relentlessly bent his curveball past Dodgers bats.

In the ninth inning Maglie snapped one final curve, and Roy Campanella drove it slowly to the mound. Maglie clutched the ball, ran toward first base, and tossed to Whitey Lockman. Lights went out all over Brooklyn. Manhattan, from Toots Shor's bar to Tallulah Bankhead's dressing room, rejoiced.

Lockman, ball in glove, jumped at Maglie and landed halfway up the tired pitcher's frame. It was a scene that will be remembered when baseball fans turn back their albums to the season of 1954.

In Milwaukee another picture will haunt memories: the brilliant Bobby Thomson stretched out in the sand of a training camp infield at St. Petersburg, Florida. Back there in March even the most sanguine of Milwaukee rooters suspected that their pennant chances lay with Thomson in the dust at second base. The Braves, without the slugging outfielder until August, finished third.

There were other scenes that will be remembered and embroidered during the chilly winter months by baseball fans who live to relive baseball. Ted Williams of the Boston Red Sox broke a collarbone on his first spring training day and did not return until May. With a metal pin holding the broken bones together, Williams played both games of a double-header in Detroit and lashed eight hits, including two home runs, in nine turns at bat.

"It hurt like hell," Williams said.

"When they take that pin out," said the Yankees' Casey Stengel, "I want it. Wanna stick it into a coupla my guys."

HIGH ABOVE BIG KLU

On a May afternoon in St. Louis the Cardinals' Stan Musial, uncoiling from his frightening crouch, pounded five home runs during a double-header with the Giants. On a September day in Brooklyn, Ted Kluszewski, his shirtsleeves cut off at the shoulders and his biceps casting a shadow over the mound, hit just one. It was his forty-ninth of the season.

High in the stands when the Reds' Kluszewski homered, when Maglie pitched, sat an official scorer. Nobody took his picture or marveled at whatever biceps he had. No one fought to shake his hand or to get his autograph. As usual over the scheduled 1,232 games of the 1954 season, the scorer just sat and kept score. But at the end of the season last Sunday the scorer's books told stories, too.

After eleven years, after twelve years, after thirteen years, the figures said, three of the biggest stars in baseball had grown dim. With Yankees shortstop Phil Rizzuto, thirty-six, it was a case of slower reflexes, a higher arc on his throw to first base, and finally, near the end of the season, eyeglasses. Rizzuto's batting average sagged to .194, lowest of any Major League regular.

With Preacher Roe, thirty-six, the Dodgers' best left-handed pitcher, it was a curveball breaking less sharply, a slider forgetting to slide. Three years ago Roe won twenty-two, lost three. In 1952 he won eleven, lost two. Last year he won eleven, lost three. In 1954, the scorebook reported impersonally, Preacher Roe won three, lost four.

The scorebook told more subtly of Allie Reynolds, thirty-six-year-old Yankees right-hander. Reynolds's back gave out, but the records showed that he still won eleven and lost four for the year. The records showed, too, that Reynolds, once a man annoyed because he could not pitch every day, won only three games after July.

Some of the figures in the scorebook will help when it comes time to pick baseball's Most Valuable Players. They showed that Willie Mays had won the National League batting championship in his first full season with a mark of .345. They showed that Mays was third in runs scored with 119, first in triples with 13, second in total bases with 377, and first in slugging percentage with .667.

They revealed that Kluszewski's forty-nine home runs made him the first Cincinnati player to lead the Majors in home runs since a worthy named Fred Odwell hit nine in 1905. And they showed that Kluszewski's forty-nine were only three homers less than the entire roster of Baltimore Orioles hit all year.

The Dodgers' Duke Snider fulfilled his long-predicted promise by hitting .341 with forty home runs. Stan Musial continued to surpass reasonable promise by batting .330, fourth best in the league. In his twelve full seasons, Musial has always been among his league's six top hitters, with six firsts, two seconds, two thirds, a fourth, and a sixth in 1947 when he was suffering from chronic appendicitis.

LAST ON MERIT

The pitching statistics showed that Bob Lemon had won twenty-three games for Cleveland, beating Baltimore, Philadelphia, Boston, Detroit, and Washington a total of eighteen times. Lemon matched teammate

Early Wynn with twenty-three victories, matched Washington's Bob Porterfield with twenty-one complete games. Both figures were league highs.

The scorebooks showed that Bobby Avila, the Indians' second baseman, had been the most significantly improved hitter. His .341—a big jump for a man who had never done better than .305—had won him the batting championship. The books also showed that Cleveland's Larry Doby had hit thirty-two homers to win the title in his league.

Recorded figures will help to decide the Rookies of the Year. The Yankees' Bob Grim was the first twenty-game-winning freshman since 1948. The Indians' Don Mossi had an earned run average of 1.94, or only slightly more incredible than his teammate Ray Narleski's 2.22. The Cardinals' Wally Moon hit .304, stole eighteen bases. The Cardinals' Joe Frazier collected twenty pinch hits.

Usually, team averages were a fair reflection. The Indians set an American League record with 111 victories, and their pitching staff compiled an earned run average of 2.79, best since that record began in 1930.

The Yankees set a league record for victories by a second-place team (103) and led in batting and runs scored.

The Baltimore Orioles scored fewer runs, hit fewer home runs than any other team in the Majors. The Baltimore Orioles finished seventh only because . . .

The Philadelphia Athletics, with the lowest team batting average in the Major Leagues (.235), were worse.

The Giants, first National League team to jump from the second division to the pennant since the 1934 Cardinals, were baseball's finest opportunists. The scorebooks showed that the Giants pinch-hit ten homers, three more than any other team in history.

The Pittsburgh Pirates, by way of confirming general manager Branch Rickey's statement that the team was last on merit, finished last in the National League in batting, pitching, fielding, homers, runs, and, for good measure, stolen bases.

A NONSTATISTICAL PHENOMENON

Much of the space in the scorebooks was oddity material.

Murry Dickson won a great deal of sympathy in 1952 when he lost twenty-one games with the last-place Pirates. Dickson was traded last winter to the vastly superior Philadelphia Phils. This year with the vastly superior Phils, Dickson lost twenty.

Mike Garcia, one of Cleveland's best pitchers, uses a fastball as his best pitch. Most home runs are hit off fastballs, but Garcia, in 257 innings, allowed just six home runs.

Robin Roberts, possessor of one of the best fastballs in the game, led the National League with twenty-three victories. But Roberts also led in home-run balls. He threw thirty-six.

Bill Bruton stole thirty-four bases for the Milwaukee Braves. As a team, the champion Giants stole twenty-nine, the champion Indians thirty.

Milwaukee's fans, who give their players everything from Cadillacs to sausages, supposedly give the Braves strength through ardent home-town cheering. The scorer, smiling pleasantly, noted that Milwaukee won forty-three games at home but won forty-six away from home.

None of these statistics in the scorebooks altered the two big ones— the Giants and Indians won pennants. No statistic was much help in remembering Sal Maglie pitching with a twisted back or Ted Williams slugging with a pin in his shoulder. Nor, for that matter, could any statistic explain the phenomenon of Willie Howard Mays Jr.

No scorer's book could contain Willie Mays. He jumped at you, larger than life on the field, the way he did one brisk September night when Willie's Giants were still struggling for the pennant.

Robin Roberts was to pitch against the Giants, and in September races the sight of Roberts heightens the tenseness and the weariness of ballplayers.

While other Giants sat stiffly on the bench and waited for the game to start, tense, weary Willie Mays propped an empty ice bucket on a bat rack, took his glove from his pocket, and began a makeshift game. Willie tossed his glove at the bucket, and someone else tossed it back. Mays laughed when the glove went into the bucket and glowered when it missed.

Like the scorers' books, Mays was telling a story. "Baseball," Willie Mays was saying in the tension of September 1954, "is fun."

6

Here's Tap Day

Sports Illustrated, November 22, 1954

Major League Baseball's annual ritual for drafting minor leaguers, with memory tests for the tappers.

A joint ordeal is scheduled this Monday with Major League officials and baseball writers battling for the role of star sufferer. The officials will meet at New York's Biltmore Hotel to start the annual "draft" of talent from the minor leagues. Each official has received, and presumably studied, a sixty-nine-page list of draftable players prepared by the commissioner's office. The draft tests each official's ability to remember and to choose. It combines the main features of a final examination and tap day.

When Monday wanes and the draft is ended, the reporters' anguish starts. The newsmen will be required to write as many as one thousand words on the enlistment of such players as George Schmees, outfielder. Schmees, the No. 1 draft choice in 1951, became famous as soon as his selection was announced.

"Who's Schmees?" shouted a puzzled newspaperman.

"God bless you," said his neighbor. That was George Schmees's moment in the sun. He failed to make the St. Louis Browns' outfield, turned to pitching, and was traded to Boston. There he couldn't make the Red Sox' pitching staff. Schmees was back in the minors again the following summer. He is eligible to be drafted again Monday.

The draft and the draftees in it are not what they used to be, as Ty Cobb might say. The bargains are harder to come by, but that the draft has survived at all is remarkable. It began in the late nineteenth century, and today not much is heard of early contemporaries of the draft such as the Open Door Policy, Tony Pastor's, and the battleship *Maine.*

The actual process of drafting entails simply selecting players from a list. Major League teams pick and minor league teams yield the contracts of players for a sum fixed by baseball law. The sum varies from $15,000 for Pacific Coast League draftees to $2,000 for Class D ballplayers.

No more than one man may be drafted from any one team, and the clubs make their picks in reverse order of the season standings. The leagues alternate first pick annually, and on Monday the Kansas City X's, successors to last-place Philadelphia Athletics, will make the opening choice. Then the Pittsburgh Pirates, last in the National League, choose. So it goes until the New York Giants have picked, and then the whole thing starts over again until everyone has made all the choices he wants or all the Major League rosters have reached the forty-player limit.

The original idea of the draft resembled the original idea of the hammer lock. In the nineteenth century the Major Leagues forced a draft upon the minor leagues to keep the line clear between Major and minor. The theory was to prevent a minor league club from keeping good young ballplayers until they had become great young ballplayers and given, say, East Walla Walla a "minor league" team of Major League caliber.

The theory proved practical, and the draft was a pillar of baseball's complex structure until Branch Rickey, perhaps the most practical man in baseball history, hit upon something that replaced the old pillar with a new one. Rickey took thought one night and invented the farm system.

Today nearly every minor league team works with a Major League team. Some are owned outright; others are tied to big brother by working agreements. Most of the standout players in the Majors today are products of the farm system. When Rickey built the great St. Louis Cardinals teams of the 1930s, he built them with farm products. Dizzy Dean was one. Joe Medwick was another. A trend was established, and current Major Leaguers from Stan Musial to Willie Mays are up from the farms.

On their way up, promising young players are protected from the free-for-all of the draft by a thoughtful network of contract options. A player on a Major League roster can be optioned to a minor league team three times and remain immune to draft. The best youngsters are almost always covered by these options. Nonetheless, bargains are occasionally found in the yearly draft. Oversights, mistakes, and sheer luck all work to produce surprises. No baseball man will take the draft lightly on Monday.

Considered strictly as an investment, it is doubtful if anything short of a uranium strike ever exceeded the return the Philadelphia Phils got for $7,500 in the 1931 draft.

The Phils made their investment when they tapped Al Todd, a catcher, from Dallas. Todd played with the Phils for four seasons, hit .318 once, and was traded to the Pittsburgh Pirates for two players. . . .

One of the two ex-Pirates, pitcher Claude Passeau, stayed with the Phils for four years and was traded to the Chicago Cubs for an unannounced sum of cash and three more players. . . .

One of the three ex-Cubs, pitcher Kirby Higbe, was traded to the Brooklyn Dodgers for another three players and an announced $100,000. . . .

One of the three ex-Dodgers, catcher Mickey Livingstone, was traded to the Cubs for pitcher Bill Lee. . . .

Lee was sold in 1945 for $7,500, and the Phils had their original investment back. They also had a great deal more.

Returns on the $7,500 draft of Todd totaled use of ten players for periods up to four years each, plus an unannounced sum plus $100,000.

It isn't likely that a capital gain like Todd will be drafted Monday. Nor is it likely than an organization will slip as the New York Giants once did and allow a name like Hack Wilson to appear on the list. Wilson, drafted by the Cubs in 1925 after the Giants thought they had him safely hidden, hit fifty-six home runs five seasons later.

Yet on the 1954 list there may be someone who doesn't belong, who's too good, who should have been covered up but wasn't. It's a long list. Between now and Monday, lights will burn late in Major League offices.

Baseball's Best Bargains in Draft

Year	Player	Drafted by	From	Highlights of careers after draft
1904	Branch Rickey	Chicago, AL	Dallas	Hit .239 over 4 seasons, became executive, reached top
1911	Jim Bagby Sr.	Cincinnati	Hattiesburg	Won 25 games for Cleveland in 1917, won 129 games in career
1917	Jimmy Dykes	Philadelphia, AL	Gettysburg	Spent 15 seasons with A's, played 22 years, managed in 17
1923	Red Lucas	Boston, NL	San Antonio	A pitcher, he set record for lifetime pinch hits—107
1925	Hack Wilson	Chicago, NL	Toledo	Holds NL homer record (56) and baseball RBI mark (190)
1927	Lefty O'Doul	New York, NL	San Francisco	Hit .353 over 7 seasons, led NL in 1929 and in 1932
1931	Al Todd	Philadelphia, NL	Dallas	Caught in NL for 11 seasons, hit .318 once (see story)
1933	Bob Newsom	St. Louis, AL	Los Angeles	In 17 seasons after draft, won 211 games and lost 219
1936	Debs Garms	Boston, NL	San Antonio	Sold to Pirates in 1939, led NL batters in 1940 with .355
1937	George McQuinn	St. Louis, AL	Newark	A first baseman, he led league in fielding 4 times, hit .276

Year	*Player*	*Drafted by*	*From*	*Highlights of careers after draft*
1938	Hugh Casey	Brooklyn	Memphis	Ace reliever, set Series record with 6 appearances in 1947
1941	Sal Maglie	New York, NL	Buffalo	Clutch pitching ace on two pennant winners, has .699 pct.
1942	Nels Potter	St. Louis, AL	Louisville	Ace hurler of only Browns pennant winner ever, won 19 in 1944
1946	Ferris Fain	Philadelphia, AL	San Francisco	Twice won batting championship, has played in 5 All-Star Games
1946	Gus Zernial	Cleveland	Atlanta	Has hit 152 home runs, mark sixth among active AL players
1950	Harry Dorish	Chicago, AL	Toronto	Finished 4 good seasons as reliever, with 3.07 ERA
1952	Dave Jolly	Boston, NL	Kansas City	Became a top relief pitcher last season, winning 11, losing 6

7

Forget Something, Boys?

Sports Illustrated, December 20, 1954

---

*The desperate plight of the minor leagues was a backdrop for the
annual Major League meeting in New York. But the rulers of baseball
dealt with trivia, ignored the minors, and went home.*

Eleven floors above the conference room in New York's Hotel Commodore, where the rulers of Major League Baseball met last week, a troubled man named George Trautman sat in his bedroom and talked. On his dresser was a bottle labeled:

DORMIN

For the Relief of Insomnia

George Trautman's trouble and his insomnia stem from a common source. Trautman is president of the National Association of Professional Baseball Leagues—the minors.

For two days Major League magnates talked of expansion, of new cities, of California gold. The American League set up a committee to see what can be done, over the next year or two, about adding teams on the Pacific Coast. The National League, confident that it has a foot in the California door already, kept its counsel.

The minors? They were mentioned at the meetings. The Major Leaguers agreed to invest a bit more money in clubs with which they have working agreements—and from which they draw nearly all their talent. The Majors refused to vote a ban on telecasting or broadcasting their games into minor league cities. "We couldn't," one magnate explained confidentially. "Restraint of trade."

Before the 1954 Major League meetings began, the fast-folding minor leagues were baseball's most pressing problem. When the meetings were over, the minors remained baseball's most pressing problem.

"Sure," said an angry minor league official as he prepared to head home, "the magnates haven't done much in fifty years. You can't expect them to do anything in two days."

After more than fifty years of meeting, the Major Leagues' winter session has come to resemble, in broad outline, a convention of the American Dried Fruit and Pecan Nut Packers Association. There are industry-wide problems to be faced, and the captains of industry sit at conference tables apparently facing them. This year baseball's captains actually faced very little.

On the first day of the meetings—Monday—the American and National Leagues met separately. The American League launched a study of expansion. The National League voted to bar press photographers from working on the field during games and dealt with matters of similar moment.

CHATTER IN THE LOBBY

Tuesday the leagues met in joint session and spent the morning voting down the minor league request that TV and radio be limited. The owners began leaving town Tuesday afternoon.

Some player trades had been made. With so many baseball men so close together, trades invariably evolve. While the owners met in conference rooms, managers and lesser officials spilled into the lobby, talking baseball and setting up deals as they stood under team flags displayed by the Commodore in honor of the clubs that stop at that hotel on trips to New York during the season.

But the story of the Major League meetings was not, as it has been in other years, somewhere in the lobby. It was not, as it has been, in the conference rooms. It was not even in George Trautman's suite. Rather, the story unfolded in many places—a story of baseball galloping off in two directions at one time.

The minor leagues are vanishing. Twenty-six leagues have disappeared since 1949, the minors' peak year, and holes have opened in the U.S. baseball map like the holes in a well-aged chunk of swiss cheese.

There was the Mountain States League and the Central League, the Inter-State League and the Sunset League, the Lone Star League, the New England League, and, to break the meter, the KOM League (Kansas, Oklahoma, Missouri) and the Wisconsin State League. All have blown away. With them have gone some of baseball's notable minor league towns: Sheboygan, Wisconsin; Nashua, New Hampshire (where the Dodgers' battery of Don Newcombe and Roy Campanella broke into organized baseball eight years ago); Ponca City, Oklahoma; Flint, Michigan; Zanesville, Ohio. They get baseball only by radio and TV now.

Meanwhile the Major League owners talk of spreading talent, already spread thin, still further.

That's pretty much what George Trautman discussed while the rulers of baseball discussed other things eleven floors below. "We have not yet met present conditions with progress," Trautman said. "That's the trouble."

It is possible the collapse of so many minor leagues is a reflection of a change in American habits—a preference for network TV talent to minor league baseball talent. If that be so, then only direct Major League subsidy can enable the minors to survive and preserve the present structure and caliber of baseball. Without subsidy, all that can be asked is neat chisel work on minor league monuments by the man who carves "Requiescat in pace."

According to Trautman, neither a chisel nor a subsidy is needed. "We just have to make our product more attractive," he said.

"After the war," Trautman explained, "we had our boom. At one time there were fifty-nine minor leagues. That's more than there should have been because we got careless. Almost any eight men who came to see us with cities got a league. We didn't consider financial stability. That's one thing we're paying for now."

Trautman thinks the situation will get better as more draftees are released—2,300 minor leaguers are now in the service. He thinks a flaw that is correctable exists in those leagues that include both local independent franchises and Major League farm clubs because farm clubs often have far better players and produce lopsided races. He points to surveys proving—surveys always prove—that people outside Major League areas are still interested in minor league baseball. He points to enlightened minor league promotion, to destruction of the myth that minor league players starve, to better-balanced leagues, all as potential steps in the right direction.

"Out yonder," Trautman said, pointing west, "the minor leagues are reaching a point where they're going to be more successful. There's better promotion right now, and more hustle by the clubs to get out the fans. That'll make the leagues go."

Anyone with the faintest interest in the preservation of baseball must hope that Trautman is right. Unfortunately, the magnates did nothing more than hope, either.

Trautman and the minors have been left to shift for themselves. It looks like a banner year for the makers of DORMIN—For the Relief of Insomnia.

8

New York Proudly Presents

Sports Illustrated, September 27, 1954

In the spring, when New York's Giants were ending a series of twenty-one exhibition games with the Cleveland Indians, someone asked Al Lopez to sum up the Giants' pennant chances.

"They have a good eight men," the Cleveland manager said quickly. "A real good eight men."

"And the pitching?" Lopez was pressed.

"They have a real good eight men," he repeated.

A few days ago when the Giants were about to clinch the National League pennant, Gary Schumacher, an erudite man who works in the Giants' front office but speaks with a Brooklyn accent, was asked to sum up the reasons why his team had won.

"The pitchin'," he said. "It was consistently brilliant. In fifty-six games the other clubs got two runs or fewer. That's the basic strength."

Last spring Lopez's opinion was sound. In fact, it was shared by every baseball man who watched the Giants and manager Leo Durocher launch what sportswriters liked to call "the year of atonement" for the dreary fifth-place finish in 1953. This fall, Schumacher's statement is irrefutable. Pitching is the Giants' basic strength, but unpredictability is the Giants' basic characteristic.

First, of course, there is Willie Mays, the wondrous boy of twenty-three who plays center field as no Giant ever played it before him. Willie is alive and bubbling and in love with baseball. He catches "doubles" in stride, strains a little catching "triples." While Willie is not yet ready for baseball's Hall of Fame, he is surely the best defensive center fielder in the game.

For half a season Willie hit home runs at one of the fastest clips in history. Then he stopped hitting homers, but his batting average climbed to over .340. No one, least of all Willie, knows how or where Willie Mays is going to hit.

But from the start everyone, most of all the Giants' pitchers, knew that Mays would catch everything catchable. "It's gonna be easy with him out there," said Marv Grissom, a thirty-six-year-old pitcher who possessed no great distinction when he first saw Mays last spring. "All you got to do is make 'em hit the ball in the park. Willie will catch it anywhere." Then Grissom, helped equally by a newly developed screwball and by suddenly strong defense, became an outstanding relief pitcher.

Where Mays, returned to the Giants last March after two years in the army, has been the sensation, Johnny Antonelli, a tall, serious, young left-handed pitcher, has been the quiet hero. The Giants acquired Antonelli from the Milwaukee Braves in a winter trade for outfielder Bobby Thomson and got in him a pitcher of promise but no proved merit.

At seventeen Antonelli had been given a bonus of $65,000 to sign with the Braves, but until this year his best effort was a 12-12 season in 1953. Frank Shellenback, a fatherly man who serves as pitching coach for the Giants, took Antonelli in hand, shortened his pitching stride, improved his control, and helped make him a twenty-game winner.

Antonelli is a good bet to start the first game of the World Series. Sal Maglie, a nerveless veteran right-hander, is the best choice to start the second. Last year Maglie seemed through, undone by a back ailment. Last winter he went to a chiropractor and showed up in the spring with a rubber lift, an eighth of an inch thick, which he placed in the heel of one shoe.

"My pelvis is tilted," Maglie explained. "The lift evens up my legs." There was some scoffing, which ended when Maglie pitched strongly all spring, then went on to regain most of his old effectiveness.

Behind the tutored Antonelli and the tilted Maglie is Ruben Gomez, a perfectly healthy Puerto Rican right-hander who was earlier rated the Giants' best pitcher but has dropped back to No. 3 because of Antonelli's development and Maglie's recovery. Hoyt Wilhelm, a knuckleballer, is the only other Giants pitcher who looks like a Series factor.

He shares the relief pitching with Grissom. Beyond these five pitchers there is little mound strength.

Defensively the infield is steady. Whitey Lockman at first, captain Al Dark at shortstop, and Hank Thompson at third are all competent fielders. Davey Williams at second is outstanding. Lockman, Dark, and Thompson are tough hitters; Williams has been in a season-long batting slump.

For years Wes Westrum, the top catcher, has been in a batting slump—now regarded as permanent—but his fine receiving and excellent handling of pitchers makes him a good choice to do most of the work in the Series.

Don Mueller, the right fielder, hits well over .300 and fields adequately without fuss. Monte Irvin, the left fielder who hit .458 in the 1951 World Series, has suffered through a bad season at bat. Jim (Dusty) Rhodes, a weak-fielding free-swinger, probably will share left with Irvin.

THE ASSET CLEVELAND HASN'T GOT

It may not mean much, but the Giants won thirteen of their twenty-one spring games with Cleveland. What means more is that the two clubs have been making spring tours for years and know each other as well as any World Series rivals ever have.

The Giants know they will be underdogs. They are not one of the all-time great clubs, although Durocher says they are better than the '51 team that came from nowhere to overtake the Brooklyn Dodgers in a playoff. Their strength is pitching and clutch dramatics.

A year ago Durocher gambled constantly and finished nowhere. This year he has managed conservatively and let the players themselves produce the excitement. A large block of experts conceded the 1954 National League pennant to the Brooklyn Dodgers last January, so for the Giants this has been a stimulating year. Let the experts pick Cleveland—and Cleveland pitching—if they want to. The true Giants fan knows his team has got some pitching too. Moreover, he points hopefully to an asset Cleveland hasn't got.

"Mays," the Giants fan says. "Willie Mays."

9

1 . . . 2 . . . 3 . . . 4 . . . & Bingo

Sports Illustrated, October 11, 1954

Baseball experts gave the Giants only a slim chance to beat the Indians, but the Giants amazed the experts, the fans, and undoubtedly themselves. Everything Leo Durocher tried worked.

Only once during the New York Giants' annihilation of the Cleveland Indians did Al Lopez, the Cleveland manager, permit himself the luxury of rage.

For four days Lopez suffered in reflected humiliation while the Giants swept the 1954 World Series from the Indians, four games to none. The sweep was an achievement baseball men had insisted was impossible. Bookmakers admitted it was possible but rated the possibility at 22–1. Yet as the incredible victimized him, Al Lopez remained soft-spoken save for a single interlude after the second game when Early Wynn failed, when the Indians' attack failed for the second time, and when ultimate defeat became a clear and present danger.

Reporters were admitted to the visitors' clubhouse at the Polo Grounds five minutes after the second game ended. They gathered in a tight circle about Lopez. There were some good questions and some bad. At first Lopez answered in whispers.

"What was the turning point today?" one reporter asked.

"There wasn't any turning point," Lopez murmured.

"There's got to be a turning point," the reporter insisted. "What was it?"

"There wasn't any, I'm telling you," Lopez repeated, breaking out of a whisper.

"Was the turning point when Doby couldn't catch that ball Rhodes hit?" the reporter persisted thickly.

"Now goddam," Lopez shouted, "what are you trying to do? Ask your questions and answer them, too? Goddam. What are you trying to do?"

When the Series ended Saturday some reporters tried to plant in Lopez's mouth more words about a turning point. With considerable difficulty synthetic quotes were created. Actually, as Lopez knew, the 1954 World Series was without one single hinge. There were a great many points at which things turned against the Indians. To equate one against the other is to equate the destructiveness of a teaspoon against a tablespoon of uranium.

The first game, which the Giants won 5–2, was a turning point because it had been generally assumed that Bob Lemon, Cleveland's starting pitcher, was stronger and better than the Giants' Sal Maglie.

The second game, which the Giants won 3–1, was a turning point because it had been generally assumed that Early Wynn, pitcher of three two-hit games in September, was unbeatable in a clutch.

The third game, which the Giants won 6–2, was a turning point because it had been generally assumed that the Indians were waiting to sandbag the Giants at Cleveland's Municipal Stadium.

The fourth game, which the Giants won 7–4, was a turning point because it had been generally assumed that the Indians would win the World Series.

In the first inning of the first game the Indians looked good. They scored two runs when Vic Wertz made the first of his eight hits, a triple to right-center field that batted in Al Smith and Bobby Avila. Then the Indians, winners of more games than any other American League team in history, went into a miniature decline and fall. The Giants tied the score in the third inning. In the sixth, with Wertz at third base, Jim Hegan bounced fiercely to Henry Thompson at third. Thompson fought the grounder with both hands until it surrendered. His throw to first base was in time by half a step.

"When that ball squirted away," Thompson said, "all I was thinking was I gotta get that son of a buck over to first base."

In the eighth inning, with two Indians on base and no one out, Vic Wertz hit a ball 450 feet, where Willie Mays caught it. Never before had so unbelievable a catch been seen and disbelieved by so many.

"Was it real?" someone asked Al Dark, the Giants' captain, later.

"It was real," Dark said, as though he had only then convinced himself.

But there was at least one more turning point in that first game. With two Giants on base in the tenth inning, a high-living southerner named Jim Rhodes pinch-hit for Monte Irvin and lifted a fly into the breeze that blew toward right field. Bobby Avila, Cleveland's second baseman, started back for the ball. A customer in the right-field stands muffed it. Three runs scored; the Giants had won.

Next afternoon at the Polo Grounds the crowd sagged below fifty thousand, and there were proportionately fewer turning points. Johnny Antonelli, the Giants' young left-hander, made his first pitch a fastball, and Al Smith, Cleveland's young left fielder, hit the fastball to the roof of the upper deck. Thereafter thirteen Indians reached base, and though none was observed biting dust, none scored, either.

Early Wynn pitched four perfect innings, then two Giants reached base and Rhodes again hit for Irvin. This time he pinch-popped a single to short center field beyond the reach of Larry Doby. The Indians were impaled on a sharp new turning point.

"He's a pretty fair hitter," said Giants scout Tom Sheehan of Rhodes.

"He's a County Fair hitter. He goes up there and swings."

Then the Series moved to Cleveland, where one store was caught with a sign showing. "Congratulations, Indians," the sign in the window read. "You're sitting on top of the world."

A BIG DEAD SALAMI

Lemon and Wynn had been beaten. Al Rosen, Cleveland's clean-up hitter, was crippled by a pulled leg muscle. Rosen sat down as Mike Garcia got up to pitch the third game. A thirty-seven-year-old veteran named Hank Majeski took over third base from Rosen. All season subs had come through for Cleveland, but by this time a great many points had turned. Majeski went hitless, Rhodes pinch-hit a two-run single, Ruben Gomez outpitched Garcia, and the Indians were down three games.

"No sense waiting for the spring," Rosen said a day later as he prepared to go back to third base. "Lemon goes fine with two days' rest," said Al Lopez when someone wondered what had become of Bobby Feller.

A small left-hander named Don Liddle held the Indians while Lemon did not go fine, and the Giants moved ahead, 7–0. Cleveland fought back too late when Majeski pinch-hit a three-run homer and when a rally knocked out Liddle for Hoyt Wilhelm in the seventh. Wilhelm stopped it, but another rally knocked him out for Antonelli with one out in the eighth. Johnny whipped a curve past Wertz's bat for a second out. With two strikes on Wally Westlake, Antonelli tossed a changeup pitch, and Westlake watched it drift over the plate. When he did so, Cleveland's hotelkeepers who had raised prices for rooms, barkeeps who had raised prices for drinks, and Cleveland's fans who had wanted to see another game on Sunday knew what the Indians knew, too. The Giants were in.

"A big dead salami!" the Giants' Joe Garagiola shouted during the clubhouse celebration. "Johnny threw Westlake a big dead salami."

"The boys did it all!" manager Leo Durocher shouted.

"Leo," said a moist-eyed reporter. "You managed great."

"The boys did it all," Durocher said in normal tones.

"World champions," Whitey Lockman, the first baseman, said quietly. "What do you know? But I bet they'd like another crack at us."

Big Jim Rhodes spoke for the majority. Big Jim stuck a cigar in his mouth. "Hey!" he shouted. "Where's the champagne?"

Afterward there came perspective, and with perspective came questions. Were the Indians' 111 victories merely the reflection of a fairly good team in a terribly weak American League? Had Rosen's leg been sound and Larry Doby's shoulder uninjured, would there have been a struggle? Or were the Giants baseball's supreme opportunists, unbeatable always in 1954 because of a Mays catch, a Thompson stop, or a Rhodes pinch-hit home run? The answers, if they exist at all, are as elusive as that single turning point the reporter tried to get from Al Lopez.

But one Giants official had all the answers he needed. "We didn't just beat Cleveland," he insisted. "We showed those Yankees up but good."

10

Glory Day in Columbus

Sports Illustrated, November 29, 1954

Ohio State turned on its historic tormentor, Michigan, and trounced the Wolverines 21–7. The victory gave the Buckeyes a Rose Bowl bid and gave the city of Columbus a night of wild singing, cheering, and celebrating.

Woody Hayes, the beefy former tackle who coaches Ohio State's football team, stamped into his office in the caverns of Ohio Stadium at 4:15 last Saturday and climbed up on a chair. "Boys," he shouted at two platoons of newspapermen, "this is how I feel." He leaped off the chair into the air and uttered a tenor shriek: "Whoopee!"

Wayne Woodrow Hayes is a massive man. When he hit the concrete floor of his office, Columbus felt a tremor. It was the city's second earthquake of the afternoon.

What prompted Hayes to leap and shriek was the first earthquake. Columbus rocked and trembled and reveled as Ohio State came from behind and defeated the University of Michigan 21–7 in a grinding, rugged game. With that single triumphant stroke the Buckeyes achieved an unbeaten season, the Big Ten championship, and an invitation to the Rose Bowl.

In Columbus the moment of victory was magic. When the outcome first became apparent during the final minutes of the game, the big crowd at Ohio Stadium broke into an exultant, rolling chant:

We don't give a damn for the whole state of Michigan
Whole state of Michigan
Whole state of Michigan
We don't give a damn for the whole state of Michigan
We're from O-HI-O

Late Saturday night as the chanted song and blaring automobile horns filled the downtown area with sound, it was clear that Columbus was stretching its magic moment into an enchanted evening.

Saturday in Columbus began with rain, wind, cold, and a Michigan team that for one quarter seemed invincible. But the elements bothered no one, and the 82,438 fans who filled the stadium were troubled mostly by remembrance of things past. Ohio State had beaten Michigan only once in its last nine tries. Michigan had laughed at Ohio State's spirit. In Columbus the blue-and-gold-clad team of Wolverines was a personification of evil.

The first time Michigan got its hands on the ball it scored. Danny Cline, a halfback also known as No. 44, carried four times on an eleven-play, 68-yard drive. The fourth time, he went 7 yards for a touchdown. Things looked bright for the forces of evil. Not until late in the second quarter could the good men of Ohio counterattack.

Jack Gibbs intercepted a pass and ran 47 yards to the Michigan 10. Coach Hayes, who had been resting his best quarterback, deliberately inserted Dave Leggett into the game and took a 5-yard penalty for an illegal substitution. Before anyone had a chance to second guess, Leggett passed to end Fred Kriss in the end zone.

Tad Weed converted, the game was tied, but the crowd's roar was almost restrained. It had been Michigan custom to wreck Ohio State with second-half power. The strutting bands at halftime did not relieve Columbus's anxiety.

When the game resumed Michigan pushed, Ohio held, Ohio pushed, Michigan held, and the third quarter waned. Then Michigan pushed and fumbled. Ohio State took over on its own 21, failed to gain, and fullback Hubert Bobo delivered a classic 80-yard punt: 40 yards straight up, 40 yards straight down. Michigan recovered the ball on the Buckeyes' 14-yard line.

Quickly the Wolverines moved to the 4. With three more carries, Cline and fullback Dave Hill rammed the ball to within a foot of the goal line. On fourth down Hill flung himself into the center of the line. The Ohio State line held fast.

That was the hinge about which the football game and the autumn season in Columbus revolved. Michigan was beatable. It took the Buckeyes just the next twelve plays to march almost 100 yards to a touchdown. They got it when Leggett threw 9 yards to end Dave Brubaker. Hopalong Cassady had set it up with a 52-yard run. Again Weed converted, and this time the crowd's roar carried with it the lust and assurance of a cheer sent up by the Praetorian Guard.

Michigan could push no more. Ohio State scored again with forty-four seconds remaining, but this final touchdown was not needed. Before the Buckeyes' final drive ended, the fans were chanting their song. Before the drive ended, programs and newspapers were torn and thrown, filling the air with king-sized ticker tape. Before the drive was over, Ohio State students lofted a banner. It read: "BEAT U.S.C. JAN. 1."

At the final whistle, Ohio State's heroes stopped playing football and began to jump up and down. Then they hoisted Woody Hayes to their shoulders and carried him into the clubhouse. They dunked him in a shower and they cheered him. Finally they let him meet the press.

For Hayes the dunking was a pleasure. He told the press that. He told them more, delivering short speeches like a man accustomed to making the dais of both a Rotary luncheon and a Kiwanis luncheon on the same day. Once a question interrupted: "What happened to change the game around from the first half to the second?"

"You can't run over a team like mine for a full sixty minutes," Hayes said.

He made more short speeches until a minor Ohio State official appeared with an insect gun full of sweet-smelling liquid. He sprayed Hayes. "It's scent of roses, Woody," cried the official. "Scent of roses for yuh, Woody boy."

"I'll say this," Hayes announced. "We plan to spend the holidays on the coast."

Back in Columbus the evening began slowly. "It's taking a while," explained the city editor of a local newspaper, "because the folks are spent."

By ten o'clock, downtown Columbus had turned vibrant. The sidewalks were jammed with shouting people. The streets were jammed with cars, and horns blared their cacophony to the skies. By midnight those few downtown residents who wanted to sleep had abandoned the idea. And always above the blare came the refrain:

Whole state of Michigan
Whole state of Michigan
We don't give a damn for the whole state of Michigan
We're from O-HI-O

Sunday morning in Columbus dawned gray and cold. An exodus began early, but at the airport there were no signs of letdown among the departing alumni though night in Columbus had run into day.

"What I liked," said a man at the airport, "was the way we won it for all those blue chips. But what I really liked was that we beat Michigan."

A lady with him chanted in a tired voice: "We're from O-hi-o."

11

Alonzo, Alonzo

Sports Illustrated, January 10, 1955

Once, when the class struggle was considerably younger than it is today, a Yale basketball team coached by Ken Loeffler traveled to Peoria, Illinois, for a game with Bradley. Yale was, of course, overmatched, and it was clear that only the greatest of orations by Loeffler could avert disaster. Fortunately, Loeffler has an oration to fit almost any occasion.

Just before the game, the little band of Elis huddled in the visitors' locker room, a mere beaverboard partition away from the room where Bradley's team was similarly grouped. Loeffler climbed a stool and, with every Yale eye upon him, inhaled, as a preface to his speech. He proceeded no further.

Before Loeffler could declaim a syllable, the voice of the Bradley coach boomed through the partition.

"Men of Bradley! Tonight you will be playing against the sons of the men who own the factories in which you will some day be working. But you are not working in them yet." . . .

Yale lost the basketball game by more points than anyone remembers, and that night in Peoria stands as the only occasion when Ken Loeffler was unable to deliver a pregame philippic.

In some thirty years of coaching, Loeffler has probably cleaved the general air with more speech than any of his rivals. That covers considerable territory, including as it does the Oxonian-accented addresses of New York's Nat Holman and the basketball-boosted-me-from-slag-heaps-to-heights style of West Virginia–born Clair Bee.

ANOTHER ORATION

Lately Loeffler has been coaching a national championship team at La Salle College and has also developed an ulcer. There was an inclination to wonder whether these recent developments had cramped the man's speaking delivery. A quick trip to Philadelphia last week ended the wondering.

At 4:30 one afternoon, the team gathered in the gymnasium for drill. Loeffler trotted out a blackboard, took some scouting records from his pocket, exacted a pledge of secrecy from a sportswriter, and began to read the report aloud and to chalk diagrams.

It was pretty dry stuff on the blackboard for a while, but soon Loeffler split his team into bad guys (without shirts) and good guys (with shirts) in the chilly gym. While the bad guys played the role of the opposition and the good guys played the role of La Salle, Loeffler drilled them all on technical basketball. Within a few minutes he was punctuating the drill with rapid, nontechnical oration.

"Alonzo, Alonzo," he pleaded to one of the good guys. "Why doncha hustle when you haven't got the ball? Didn't you hustle when you didn't have the ball in high school? No, you always had the ball when you were in high school. Well, you're in college now."

"Yods," Loeffler addressed a bad guy, "we're going to make a trip, and we can't take everybody. Fredericks will make it instead of you if you don't start to hustle like Fredericks. He's terrible, but he hustles."

"Alonzo, why doncha watch Greenberg? Look at how he's moving. I wish Greenberg had your physique, Alonzo. He'd be playing all the time."

"Gomez, you lost the ball. That's what drives me nuts. Maybe that's what you want to do."

There followed a long Loeffler sigh. "Übung macht den Meister," he muttered. "They don't understand that, but it doesn't matter. They don't understand anything I say."

So it went for a couple of hours. When the drill was over, La Salle's national champions had pretty much learned the secret maneuvers Loeffler had been working to teach.

Sometimes the players chuckled at Loeffler and sometimes Loeffler chuckled at the players. Chuckling most was Tom Gola, who, great as his potential was, must be viewed as a monument to Loeffler coaching. Gola also must be viewed as a cause of Loeffler's ulcer. He graduates in June, leaving an unpluggable gap in the squad.

"My freshman team," said Loeffler, "consists entirely of A students."

"But, Kenny," someone asked, "what do they expect you to do when Gola's gone?"

"Coach harder," Loeffler said.

In a clutch, the man can quote good chunks of Shakespeare, and next season it might be: "Alonzo, Alonzo, thou marble-hearted forward." But next season Alonzo likely will have mastered the tricks of movement Loeffler is drilling into him. Next season, or any season, nothing short of a return of the class struggle can stop Loeffler from talking his basketball teams to heights they are not good enough to reach without him.

12

Big Newk and His Psyche

Sport, **August** 1955

Before Sports Illustrated *appeared during the summer of 1954, under the dominating, some would say oppressive, influence of Henry Luce,* Sport *magazine led the field. Its longtime editor, Ed Fitzgerald, said, "I can get any writer in the country to work for me for three reasons. If he's good, I don't change his stuff. I give him an interesting choice of topics. And if he gets me a story on Tuesday, he has a $500 check on Thursday. There's not a writer in the country who doesn't need $500 on Thursday."*

This was the first of something close to forty articles I published in Sport *over the years. Don Newcombe had all kinds of baseball talent. The huge right-handed Brooklyn pitcher once started both ends of a double-header. (He split.) Early on he was projected to win thirty games. In 1956, at the age of thirty, he did win twenty-seven. Seemed mighty as a dreadnought, but within lay a delicate psyche.*

When Don Newcombe was drafted into the army in 1952, there was muttering in Brooklyn—perhaps the same sort of muttering that was heard around Fort Sumter in 1861. The talk in Brooklyn was of going it alone, of letting the rest of the United States shift for itself, regardless of how difficult that might prove to be. All that stopped Brooklyn's movement toward secession was the drafting three months later of Willie Mays. Forced to conclude that the Army of the United States was impartial and inducted Dodgers and Giants alike, Brooklyn secessionists gave up the struggle. The union, from Flatbush to La Jolla, was saved.

A little bitterness remained, though, and Charlie Dressen, managing Brooklyn in those days, was among the bitter. "Losing Newcombe is worse than losing Mays," Dressen said. "Where can you get a pitcher like that? Where can you make up those games? Let the Giants have Mays back. Let 'em have two Mayses. It's okay with me, so long as the army gives me back Newcombe."

It was not Dressen's fate ever to regain Newcombe. Last year, the gigantic pitcher was discharged and won nine games for another Dodgers manager, Walter Alston; he lost eight. Mays was discharged last year, too. He won the National League's Most Valuable Player Award, and the Giants won the baseball championship of the world.

Don Newcombe went into the army six feet four inches tall and massive enough to weigh 220 pounds, in perfect condition. He returned from the army just as big and just as strong. But although in his last pre-army season he won twenty games and led the National League in strikeouts, he was only an ordinary (9-8) pitcher in 1954. Was the difference in his arm? Quite probably it was not. More likely the difference was in his psyche.

Ever since Sigmund Freud began puttering inside human brains, psyches have become more and more popular, at least as talking points. You cannot put your finger on a psyche. Like conscience, it is hard to define. Mental life, one dictionary suggests, and this seems to be as good a definition as any. But anyone suggesting to a pitcher that a sore arm comes from an overactive psyche, a sort of hyperactive mental life, had better be prepared to run. Baseball is primarily a physical game, and an active psyche is perceived as a sign of weakness, like knees of jelly.

Partly because of this, Burt Shotton is not the most popular of all managers with whom Don Newcombe has worked. During the years that Shotton led the Dodgers, he made a career of blaming Newcombe's psyche for all of Don's spring troubles. It was standard procedure for Newcombe to retire from a few early season games because "my shoulder is tight," or "my arm won't loosen up." The sight of his stopper walking off the mound brought out the worst in Shotton. He repeatedly offered ugly comments about Newcombe's character and determination. Inevitably, some reached Newcombe's ears.

One summer during Shotton's reign Newcombe was feeling unusually fit when a friend turned to the pitcher with misplaced cheer. "See," the friend said. "There was really nothing wrong with your arm, after all. It was mostly in your mind."

Newcombe winced. "You too?" he said, in tones probably last used by Julius Caesar. . . .

"It wasn't fair to say it was all in Newk's mind or that the pain was only in his psyche," a man in the Brooklyn organization who is close to Newcombe commented recently. "Sometimes he might have magnified an ache or a pain, but whenever he complained, there always was some real pain. Any doctor could feel the tight shoulder."

At the start of the 1950 season, Newcombe's arm trouble seemed to be especially severe. In his misery, he had company. Carl Erskine and Ralph Branca had arm trouble, too. In understandable alarm, the Dodgers' front office carted all three off to see a physician who specialized in sore-armed pitchers. The physician prescribed rest for Newcombe, and two days later Don announced that he was ready.

"But you can't be ready," someone told him. "Two days isn't what he meant by rest. Your arm couldn't have cleared up that quickly."

"I'm ready," Newcombe insisted.

Word drifted up to Shotton, and Newcombe was promptly given a chance to prove his point. He failed to finish three innings and could not pitch again for more than two weeks. Whether you want to blame it on his psyche or not, Newk undeniably has a sore-arm history. It has appeared each spring and vanished with warm weather. This spring it appeared one April day after Newk tried to pitch against the Giants on a cold afternoon. It vanished, Newk says, as quickly as it came. So maybe, he figured, his psyche was wearing out.

When Don Newcombe sits half-stripped on the little stool in front of his locker in a corner of the Dodgers' dressing room, it is hard to think of this enormous man in terms of a psyche. Bugs Baer once wrote of a pitcher who was fast enough to throw a lamb chop past a wolf. Newcombe looks strong enough to throw a steak past a tiger. The first and lasting impression he gives is overpowering strength. But there is more than strength to the art of pitching, and there is more than size to Newcombe. The pitcher is a sensitive man whose life has not been without troubles. Ever since he broke into the Major Leagues, he has suffered from the recurrent sore arms. And for almost that long, the papers have been full of predictions that he was sure to win thirty games the following season.

Newk sat before his locker to receive a visitor one afternoon a few weeks ago, drinking milk from a paper container that was completely surrounded by his enormous right hand. "Sit down on this stool here," he said, motioning toward one in front of an adjoining locker. A little milk had spilled on the stool. "Watch it," Newk said.

"It's okay," I said. "My coat is old and dirty."

"I'll get a towel," Newcombe said. He extended one of his enormous arms a few yards to a trunk, grabbed a towel from the top of a small pile, and wiped the milk from the stool. "You wanna talk?" he said. He is a friendly man.

"Yeah."

"About what?" Newcombe said.

"About you. As a guy."

"Shoot," Newcombe said. "Go ahead."

"You like baseball?"

"Yup," Newcombe said.

"It is fun?"

"Fun and business both. I like it."

"Would you play if you didn't have to?"

"Sure," Newcombe said, "'less I had a real soft job in an office that paid piles of money." He ran a thumb along his chin. "Know what?" he said. "If I had an office job like that, I'd still miss baseball."

"What about pressure?"

"Well, there's pressure, sure," Newcombe said. "It's a little more on us fellers than it is on the white guys. We got to be real good, else we don't stick."

"What about people expecting big things? Does that bother you?"

"Don't bother me, no," Newcombe said. "I don't feel that from people. I feel that from me. I don't want to be watcha call mediocre. I can't be no mediocre pitcher and be happy. I'm not used to losing. I like that winner's money. You can't afford to lose. You got to produce."

On June 14, Newk was twenty-nine years old. Talk to any established Major Leaguer who is pressing or who has passed thirty, and the chances are you will find an attitude very much like Newcombe's. It is healthy and normal and wise.

"On that sore arm of yours . . ."

"Had it all the time," Newcombe said. "This is the first spring I can't remember having it."

"Did you have it when you were a boy?"

"No," Newcombe said, "but ever since I been with the Dodgers. Right here." He dug his huge left hand into a spot behind his right shoulder. "That's where I get it. Used to get it every spring. But it don't mean nothing. All pitchers get it."

Newk's psyche did not affect his arm last season any more than it did long before, when he won twenty games. Newk himself believes the problem was one of adjustment to civilian life. "In the army, they orientate you," he said. "You got to do things the army way. Forget all you ever knew. You get up the army way. You eat army, you dress army, you even got to think army. It doesn't matter about you. All they want is you to do everything army. There's not a thing wrong with the army. I mean, I lost money, but so did a lot of other fellows. It's just when you get out, you got to watcha call adjust. You got to orientate yourself outta the army. That's rough to do real quick."

In the spring of 1954 . . . Newcombe threw hard, very hard, very early. "Had that shoulder pain all year," he said. "It never went away. Used to always go away. Didn't even come this spring."

"This spring, then, was different?"

"I was back in the swing of things," Newk said. "You come back from the army, you feel like a rookie all over again. Your number is strange to you; your home, even. This spring was easy. A couple of times, I've been as fast as ever."

Years before he went into the service, one of his Dodgers teammates voiced a complaint against Newk. "Some days in this game," the Dodger said, "are easy. Then there are other days when it's rough. When it's easy, you can coast along, but when it's rough, you got to push yourself. Newk, he won't push himself. That's his trouble."

Jackie Robinson, whose tongue is easily as sharp as the tooth of a serpent, for a long time conducted a one-man needling campaign to keep Newk angry. Robinson feared that Newk, in calm moments, might not throw as hard as he could, so Jack dedicated himself to preventing the big fellow from having calm moments. One day, he needled Newk to distraction. The pitcher stepped off the rubber, turned to face Robinson, and demanded: "How can you throw hard when you can't throw hard?" Robinson subsided into silence.

Because he walks with a rolling gait that makes him look like a shuffling Sherman tank, Newcombe still creates an impression of laziness. But he works as hard and tries as hard as any pitcher on the Dodgers' staff.

When he reported to Vero Beach in spring 1954, Newcombe's weight was fine. Yet he pitched batting practice almost daily and ran endlessly under the noonday Florida sun. Partly, this was because Newk had made temporary peace with his psyche; partly, it was a matter of money.

"You seem awfully serious about pitching," someone remarked one day.

"You got to be serious after you've had a bad year like I just did," Newcombe said. "You get your pay cut and you can't wear flashy clothes and ride around in big cars. I like those big cars and those good clothes."

On Opening Day at the Polo Grounds, Newk pitched against the Giants and hit two home runs. It was a gray day, bleak and drizzly. He pitched as always, mixing curves and changeups with his fastball. He didn't finish, but the Dodgers won.

"Look at that," a baseball writer said in disgust, when one of the Giants lined a change of pace against the right-field wall. "Throwing changeups on a day this dark! Dizzy Dean wouldn't throw anything except fastballs on a day like this. A hundred fastballs and he'd be done. He'd have his victory."

But Newcombe is not Dean, and he is not Bobby Feller, and he is not Lefty Grove. He pitches a la Newcombe. "I try to keep the hitter guessing," he says. "It depends on the situation, what I throw. Campy, he calls for something, and I throw it. A lot of times, I stand there shaking my head. I'm not shaking him off. I'm just trying to keep the hitter guessing."

There is a theory that Newcombe doesn't have to bother to keep the batters guessing, that he can throw fastballs through their bats. There is another theory that his fastball doesn't hop and that it is an overrated pitch. Sometimes, Newcombe is entirely surrounded by theories. That may be when his psyche takes over.

Anyone following a policy of watchful waiting for Newcombe's psyche to flash before the public last spring had only to wait until May 5. Bright and early that morning, Don got himself suspended.

When he reported for duty on May 5, the Dodgers' pitching coach, Joe Becker, told him to pitch batting practice.

"I thought I was supposed to pitch in Philadelphia tomorrow night," Newk said.

"We've changed plans," Becker replied.

"Well, you can take those plans and—" Newcombe began his impractical suggestion.

Becker reported back to Alston, and Alston told Newcombe that if he felt that way, he best take off his uniform and feel that way at home. Newcombe did just that.

When Newcombe arrived home, a telegram was waiting. It was from E. J. "Buzzie" Bavasi, the Dodgers' vice president, and it informed Don of an indefinite suspension. That night Newk and his psyche sank together to a new low.

Newcombe obviously had made the unfortunate mistake of challenging his manager in the wrong way at the wrong time. Manager Alston, who had suffered a somewhat deserved bad press in early spring, was in no mood to receive back talk from his players.

"Maybe I was wrong," Don later confessed, "but you sit on the bench and you watch all the other guys do good and you got to figure they don't want you."

That the Dodgers both wanted and needed Big Newk quickly became apparent. After his apologies and reinstatement a day later, he was called upon for a bit of late-inning emergency work against the Phillies. He acted as if each opposing batter had signed the suspension wire. He blew them down with his pitches, not allowing a ball to be hit out of the infield. Five days later, he pitched a one-hitter against Chicago, facing only twenty-seven Cubs.

"That was the best game I ever pitched," Newk said. "I guess Bavasi was trying to get me sore. Maybe he was right."

Actually, there is one overpowering reason to believe that this season Newk is picking up his career where a New Jersey draft board left it more than three years ago. Don Newcombe was discharged from the army in 1954, but his psyche stayed behind. This year, both Newk and his psyche are pitching for the Dodgers. If the two, combined, don't win twenty games, Sigmund Freud perhaps should not have bought that couch.

[The year this story appeared Newcombe went 20-5. The following season he went 27-7. But it was all downhill after that. Following ten years in the Majors Newcombe retired with a record of 149 victories and 90 defeats and—shockingly—a World Series record of 0-4. He said all his numbers would have and should have been better, but he used to drink too much. Others, including his catcher, Roy Campanella, demurred. They said that Big Newk used to think too much.]

13

Early Wynn: The Story of a Hard Loser

Sport, March 1956

Tough, hard-throwing Gus Wynn was an affable sort who piloted his own Stinson single-engine aircraft, wrote a weekly column for a Cleveland newspaper, drove, and enjoyed good company and martinis. But when he lost, Wynn's affability was swallowed up, as if by a thundercloud.

Myths have a way of surrounding baseball people so completely that it occasionally seems as if some Great White Press Agent were guiding typewriters all across the land. We've all been told, for example, that the Giants' Horace Stoneham carries within one mortal shell all that was best of baseball's Bourbons. We've been informed that within Ted Williams's sulky exterior there thumps a heart of burnished gold. This is not to imply that all we have been told is bright and shiny. We've learned, too, that the Cleveland Indians' Early Wynn is a dreadfully mean man. . . .

"Mean" is the wrong word for the rugged Mr. Wynn. The applicable word is "tough."

Wynn's chest looks about as frail as an oaken log. He is no more than an even six feet tall, but when he is in perfect condition he weighs a thickly muscled 210 pounds. His black hair grows well down his forehead, and his deep-set eyes often appear to narrow so that his face in repose can suggest sullenness. Wynn's appearance has yet to prompt a stranger to pick a fight with him, which is remarkable because Early does not always conduct himself in the manner of a pacifist. Once he tagged an onrushing base runner in the belly with such violence that the runner fell unconscious. Another time he dropped a lighted cigarette into the jacket pocket of an unpleasant fan. Purely for fun, he decided to learn judo. None of this necessarily merits the adjective "mean." Life has been tough for Wynn, and his most strenuous actions merely indicate that he takes an understandably tough counter-view of life.

Gus, as his teammates call him, isn't sneering tough like Humphrey Bogart in the movies or bellowing tough like a drill sergeant. Rather, he is tough in the pure, and dictionary, sense of the word. Without bravado, he is "able to endure strain, hardship, or severe labor; extremely difficult to cope with." Further, his toughness is so honest that he has no need to proclaim ignorance of fear. He admits that he has been afraid of a great many different things at a great many different times. They range from airplanes in rough skies to Yogi at the bat. But whatever seemed most frightening is what Wynn fought hardest. Typically, he now carries a private pilot's license and possesses enough personal victories over Berra to satisfy even himself.

Wynn's parents split when he was still in his teens, and when they did, the only home he had known disappeared. He had hardly recovered from this blow when his first wife was killed in an automobile accident that left him with a motherless infant son. Early has learned that there are things to be afraid of in life, but because he is tough he knows that the best and even noblest way to handle fears is to fight them.

"Don't let any ballplayer tell you that there's no such thing as choking up," Wynn says. . . . "Everyone feels fear in the big ones. When we're playing the Yankees and there's a big crowd and it's late in the season, there isn't a man on the field who doesn't feel the tension. I know what it's like. I'll be pitching in a late inning to Gil McDougald or some good hitter like that, and I'll feel the fear rising up. Maybe Mantle and Berra are coming up next, and all I got is this one run to work with. I'll figure, 'Lord, I got to get this McDougald. I can't let him get on. I only got one run. If I let him get on, maybe one of these next guys'll pop one and I'll get beat.'

"I start pitching to the corner, just a little slice of the plate, and I miss one, maybe two times. And there are these big hitters coming up next. Don't let anybody tell you he don't feel fear then. Me, I got to do this." Wynn paused and heaved his chest in an enormously deep breath. "After I do that, then I'm okay," he said. "I mean, I got the fear licked after I stop and do that."

But watching the fiercely glowering Wynn at work, you see a man who appears to be no more rattled by a batter than Gargantua was awed by a banana.

In the 1954 World Series, Wynn went the way of all Indians, but before losing a 3–1 game to the Giants he was around long enough to make a decided impression on everyone. For four innings he pitched hitless ball, and late in the game when it was becoming obvious that the Giants were going to win, he fired a fastball between Dusty Rhodes's head and halo. As Rhodes twisted into the dirt, there was an awed gasp from the Polo Grounds crowd. Wynn, it was clear, had no intention of losing gracefully. . . .

Later, in the Cleveland clubhouse, visitors from the press box gathered about Al Lopez, the Indians' manager. As the losing pitcher, Wynn obviously had a story to tell, but none of the reporters seemed anxious to get it. Wynn was sitting on a little stool in front of his locker, holding a paper cup of beer in one hand and a cigar stub in the other. He was staring at the wall, totally unconcerned by what was going on around him, totally oblivious of the press, aware only that he had started and had been beaten. So the reporters stayed close to Lopez and peppered him with questions. Maybe their stories suffered, but it was safer.

I remember repeating to myself that Wynn was, after all, only a human being, then walking over to him, all alone and unarmed. When I reached him there was a need for both tact and tactics. The wrong first question might lead to a punch in the mouth. The right one might lead to a story. . . . I fell back upon sportswriting tactic 4-F, the one that calls for getting on the ballplayer's side immediately.

"Gus," I said, "the Polo Grounds sure is a lousy ballpark, huh?"

There was no reaction. Wynn continued to stare at or through the wall.

"The ballpark, Gus," I said. "What do you think of the ballpark?" This time Wynn answered.

"Horse-shit park," he said.

"That ball Rhodes hit in the fifth for the double," I said, feeling my oats. "What kind of pitch was it?"

"Horse-shit pitch," he said.

"I know, but I mean what kind of a pitch? Curve, knuckleball, or what?"

"Horse-shit knuckler," Wynn said.

Only then did he turn away from the wall. He stared straight at me and cocked the paper cup of beer. I don't remember his expression, but I do remember that I asked no further questions. Instead, I joined the group around Lopez, which was now learning that Mike Garcia was going to start when the Series got back to Cleveland and that, no, Lopez wasn't giving up, he was only two games down. Nobody bothered Gus.

Wynn loses hard. Ballplayers who lose easily spend summers scattered in towns from Shreveport, Louisiana, to Fargo, North Dakota. They rarely get to see the bigger cities, and unlike Wynn, they cannot afford to own a large home with a swimming pool, a Packard sedan, a Willys Jeep, a twin outboard motorboat, and a private airplane. Nor can they afford to send their children to prep school as Early, with the agreement of his second wife, Lorraine, has done for fourteen-year-old Joe Early Wynn. It is ridiculous, when you think about it, to regard Wynn as a mean man because he is a brooding loser. He broods simply because he knows that losing pitchers do not live as well as winners.

But this hatred of defeat is a splendid symptom of his toughness, that quality which, even more than ambition to succeed, has been the mark of Wynn's manhood. Tough ballplayers are hardly unique, but oddly enough, it was away from the ball fields last season that Wynn finally and conclusively demonstrated his complete unwillingness to yield to fear.

Wynn became a newspaper columnist last spring, and shunning all ghosts, he spent a good many hours composing lengthy, carefully reasoned articles for the *Cleveland News*. Wynn's columns ran substantially uncensored, and the results of his honest writing were not surprising. He made enemies.

J. G. Taylor Spink, publisher of *The Sporting News*, was probably the first enemy his column, "The Wynn Mill," earned for its author. Spink had devoted years to getting his weekly newspaper nicknamed "Baseball's Bible." Wynn suggested that it was more a confidential magazine because of its references to the private lives of ballplayers.

Hank Greenberg, general manager of the Indians, stopped speaking to Wynn except at public functions after Wynn wrote a number of articles on what was wrong with baseball at large and general managers in particular.

A small army of men in front offices were horrified at Wynn's insistence upon what for ballplayers was a new and startling right: freedom of the press. What made the situation particularly trying for baseball's censors was that Wynn wrote his pieces very well. Any random gathering of the collected works of Early Wynn bears this out. Here are a few of Wynn's familiar quotations, lifted from three separate columns:

> My wife has great understanding. Whenever I lose a tough one and I get home she meets me at the door and says, "The kids are asleep; your dinner is on the table; good night, honey. See you in the morning." The year I lost 19 games we had dinner together only on days when I didn't pitch.

> You can't get enjoyment out of hate. I wish I could live by this 100 percent but every fourth or fifth day during the summer, I go into a Jekyll-and-Hyde act. Every time a player gets a hit or home run off me, I get strange notions and ideas of things I would like to do to him. Then after the game I feel ashamed and think to myself, "This guy is a nice fellow and I wonder what's happening to you, Early?" So I'll call him up and invite him to be my guest at dinner and spend the evening talking shop.

> Mr. Greenberg pinned me down and insisted on knowing who my ghost writer is. I finally had to confess it is Mrs. Wynn. But here's the way it is really done: I write the column, give it to her, she corrects the spelling, censors it, rewrites it and sends it to the paper. I burn the original. That's the one you should see.

Technically, Wynn's debut as a columnist took place during the 1954 World Series, but in the beginning there was a professional ghost writer. Every World Series press box is populated with sportswriting ghosts, writing pieces that are bylined by athletes. The ballplayers are so rushed after each Series game that they have hardly a minute to spend with the ghosts, and the ghosts, even when they are able writers, are afraid to write too well because then the stories might not sound as though ballplayers had written them. The results: articles that drive strong men to the crossword puzzle.

Wynn and his ghost happened to be a rare and fortunate combination. The ghost was literate, and Wynn had something to say. The *Cleveland News* decided to use more of Wynn's opinions when the following season started and Wynn decided he would like to take a try at writing his own stuff. It took him less than one month last spring to become involved in a sort of class struggle—one that is still raging. By now Early is very nearly convinced that the pen is mightier than the beanball.

He started quietly enough in a bloodless skirmish with Lou Boudreau, manager of the Kansas City Athletics, about sign stealing. A week later he tapped Hank Greenberg lightly on the head because Greenberg had praised the restoration of the sacrifice fly as a move giving needed help to batters. Wynn wrote of a pitcher's woes, then drew blood with this conclusion: "My pal Hank Greenberg also says that pitchers dominate the salaries of the league. If so, I have been negotiating with the wrong man because all the time I thought general managers dominated the salaries."

On May 18, *The Sporting News*'s front page was filled with an article by Gerry Hern, a Boston sportswriter, about Joe Cronin, the former shortstop who is the Red Sox' general manager. Cronin told Hern that the trouble with modern players was their diversity of interests—too much play time off the diamond, too many outside jobs, too much searching for the extra dollar, too much nonsense like writing newspaper columns. Wynn, the only column-writing ballplayer alive, answered Cronin brilliantly. First, to show how his outside interests were hurting him, he pitched a one-hit shutout against the Detroit Tigers. Then he wrote a memorable Wynn Mill.

"I like baseball as a sport and as a business," he began. "I hold respect for those who played the game and are now on the executive end. You can go a long way with a man who was a star, but there is a breaking point even in a steel cable. Some people are trying to come up with a solution of what's wrong with baseball. There's been so much of it, in fact, that *The Sporting News* is beginning to look like a confidential magazine. . . . The article of Mr. Cronin's started off true to form. The first three paragraphs were about himself and the things he had accomplished. Then the next line started cutting up the players. . . . General managers all say that the ballplayers themselves are the club's best public-relations and good-will representatives. So they browbeat the player in February, agitate him in March, cut him up all summer and then expect him to go jump at the chance to go out on free public appearances to sell tickets. There has to be a certain amount of good will with the player also."

In reading Hern's article, Wynn made one error. He thought Cronin had done the writing. But the error was not what drew blood and tears from the barons of baseball. It was other statements not in error that hurt enough to drive the barons into action. Instead of acting wisely, and attempting to answer Wynn with logic, the barons acted traditionally. They tried to bully and frighten Wynn into silence.

A few days after Wynn's column appeared, a message from Will Harridge, president of the American League, turned up on the bulletin board in the Indians' dressing room under the grandstand of Municipal Stadium. The message pointed out that there was a clause in all Major League contracts forbidding players "to write or sponsor newspaper articles or magazine articles without written consent of the club." The message did not mention that the clause customarily is honored in the breach.

There are sports editors who panic when a controversial story is challenged and, taking the path of least resistance, find fault with the writer. (I worked for one of those at the *Herald Tribune,* a charming but wobbly Yale man named Bob Cooke.) Happily for Wynn, Regis McAuley, executive sports editor of the *Cleveland News,* is a man of conscience. To support Wynn, McAuley lent his hand and, more important, his typewriter. Shortly after the gag notice appeared, McAuley wrote an open letter to Harridge.

"We are permitting an employee of the *News* sports staff to play baseball in his spare time," McAuley opened with cheerful sarcasm, "and said employee was embarrassed recently by one of your directives. Now we don't have nor does our employee, Early Wynn, have a note from the Indian management saying that it is all right for him to write for our paper. But, on the other hand, neither does the Cleveland ballclub have written consent from us that it is all right for our reporter to play ball for them. Hoping that the American League will accept our arrangement with Early Wynn in the same broad-minded manner in which we accept his affiliation with the Indians, I remain . . ."

Ridicule and publicity seem to be equally effective in a battle against censorship. Whether it was Hank Greenberg who had called Harridge to demand that Wynn be silenced is a moot point, but after the publicity, it was Hank who told Wynn that he could continue writing the column. Knowledge that lawyers for the *News* were studying the legality of the contract clause in question possibly hastened the Cleveland office's decision.

Spink followed a more devious path. Early insists that he had written about *The Sporting News* in terms of "a confidential magazine" because of more than the Cronin article. In an annual poll of newspaper baseball writers, Sprink asks for selections of ballplayers to fill a wide variety of superlative categories. "Best parent" and "happiest marriage" are two that Wynn considers distinct invasions of that small area of privacy still left to professional athletes. But as soon as Spink saw Wynn use the word "confidential," he gave way to rage. According to Wynn, the publisher wired a newspaperman in Washington, where Wynn broke into the Major Leagues, offering to pay for any article about the sportswriting pitcher that was sufficiently uncomplimentary. He sent a similar request to a nonpitching sportswriter in Cleveland. Both requests were turned down.

The Sporting News then swung at Wynn with an editorial headlined: "Wynn Mill Pumps Muddy Water." In part, it read: "Wynn's slur is baseless. The 'confidential' type of publication runs to lurid sensationalism and deals to a large extent with crime and sex 'exposes.' In 69 years of publication *The Sporting News* has dealt with baseball and its best interests. We don't know how many readers are familiar with the so-called 'confidential' type of publication but it would seem that if Wynn is a reader of that kind of literature, he might spend his time to better advantage."

Wynn was startled to discover that when stung sacred cows bellow. There was a good deal of feeling in his next Wynn Mill. "Since the first time I saw my father play semi-pro ball in Alabama," Wynn wrote, "it has been my greatest ambition and desire to be a big-league ballplayer.

In my column I have tried to put the ballplayer in good standing with Joe Fan. I have tried to explain some of the things players do and the reason for doing them. In explaining, I find I have ruffled *The Sporting News'* feathers. Well, gentlemen, be my guest. When you are through with me, help us promote baseball for Mr. and Mrs. Fan, who really own the game. My Dad once told me, 'Son, don't knock a good thing, join it.' Baseball is a good thing. Frankly, gentlemen, you flatter me just to think that an uneducated ballplayer and inexperienced writer could set off such a wide-spread bomb."

It was now that Wynn's toughness began to tell. Word reached him that Spink was trying to unearth a story that would bruise, but Wynn never flinched. When the following week rolled around he pointed out proudly that writers had "refused to do Spink's knife work on me." He mused with high glee about the deflation of Spink. He laughed in print about a trap that wasn't there.

"They had a perfect story," Wynn wrote. "Here was a ballplayer squawking real loud about comments on making money on the side and all the time this ballplayer was writing on the side and getting paid for it. Boy! This would make real juicy reading, they must have thought. I had no intention of it coming out and little did they know that the full check for this writing goes to charity until they had already started to work." The charity involved is the Elks Club Building Fund in Wynn's home of Nokomis, Florida. To this day, Early has not profited from his writing, except in the artistic satisfaction of self-expression.

Wynn's sharp column produced, at last, a direct response from Spink. First Spink wired Wynn and demanded a letter of apology. "I figure he wanted that so he could use it in his paper for free," Wynn says. Next, Spink sent Regis McAuley a six-page telegram in which he denied asking writers to rough up Wynn. Then he had his attorney . . . write a full-page letter to Wynn. "An immediate retraction of your statements together with an apology to Mr. Spink is necessary," it maintained. Up to that time, Wynn had withstood pressure from the league office, his own front office, and a publisher. The lawyer's letter did not make him back down, either.

Wynn feels he won his joust with Spink by a technical knockout, because he received a wire from a reliable and veteran baseball reporter.

"Mr. J. G. Taylor Spink of *Sporting News* contacted me in regard to doing uncomplimentary piece on Early Wynn," the reporter stated. "I told Mr. Spink I would not." Wynn still has the telegram. He plans to keep it.

"Just in case Spink ever wants to make a case," he says. "We'll see who has a case." . . .

Quite probably, Early Wynn was born tough, but life has done very little to make him soft. He entered the world on January 6, 1920, by way of Hartford, a village in southeastern Alabama, which is locally famous as the site of a yearly peanut festival. Hartford is in red-clay country, and Wynn, who returns for peanut festivals now and then, remembers from his boyhood, "After a rain everyone had red clay in his car; everyone who could afford a car, that is."

Since Wynn's father, Early Sr., an auto-mechanic, had played baseball semi-professionally, young Early was encouraged to pitch from as far back as he can recall. He played mostly in the backyard of a neighbor . . . until he broke so many windows and destroyed so much shrubbery that he wore out his welcome.

At first, Early was not big for his age, but he could always throw hard. While still in his early teens, he won a job pitching for the Hartford village team, which played teams from nearby towns each summer Sunday. Wynn was fascinated by baseball, but he also liked football and some basketball.

As football halfback and safety man, he ran with good speed, and of course, he passed well. By the time Early was in his sophomore year at Hartford High School, he was expected to become a star back. Just before the season began, he was drilling hard on punt returns, and during what was planned to be his last return of the day, a tackler hit him hard and broke his leg. "My best break ever," he says, happily. "It sort of forced me into baseball."

Wynn doubts if he could ever have become an outstanding football player, but he knows that he approached high school football with much less sincerity and seriousness than that with which he now approaches each baseball pennant race. "I was rah, rah, rah," he says. "Just a kid, having fun, not caring a helluva lot whether I won or lost. My sporting blood has got thicker as the years have gone on. After all, it's an occupation now. I'd rather see young kids have less spirit to win and more will to improve. The real drive to win shouldn't come till later on. It's better to get the drive at twenty or later like I did. At twelve a kid has no business burning himself out trying too hard to win." In his extensive Little League work, Wynn tries to stress this point.

The spring after his football injury, Early left school—a move he still regrets—to attend a baseball school in Sanford, Florida. He did not plan or hope to sign a contract, since he was considering a return to high school, but he impressed two scouts with his speed and control, and his reluctance to sign worked in his favor. He was given a contract for well above the prevailing wage scale. It called for $100 a month.

At Hartford, Wynn had worked summers in a cotton gin. He handled five-hundred-pound bales of cotton, putting them on hand trucks and shoving the trucks when he was not busy at other chores like shoveling cotton seed. He earned ten cents an hour. "That's why a hundred bucks a month looked big enough to make me quit school," he explains.

Wild Bill "Raw Meat" Rogers, the Washington Senators' scout who signed Wynn, did not do so because of a curveball. Wynn didn't have a curveball. "I didn't have one till I got to Cleveland eleven years later and Mel Harder showed me how to throw one," he admits. But the fastball, a change of pace, and control were enough to get Wynn assigned to the Sanford club in the Class D Florida State League.

Early's first professional appearance was disastrous. He was summoned to relieve a wild left-hander named Pankowski after Pankowski had walked three runs home, loaded the bases, and thrown three straight balls to Bob Swift, a catcher who later played in the American League. Wynn threw two fastballs past Swift. Then he threw a third, which Swift pulled out of sight. Early had begun his professional career by throwing a grand-slam home run. Things could not get worse, and in fact, they got better immediately. During the rest of the game he struck out eleven men and pitched shutout ball.

For the rest of the season, Wynn proved that he was worth $100 a month. He appeared in thirty-five games for Sanford, won sixteen, lost eleven, and pitched 235 innings. Since the Florida State League played a five-month season, Wynn earned $500. . . .

The following year Wynn was assigned to Charlotte, North Carolina, and there he met Mabel Allman. After the 1939 season, he married her, and within two years Joe Early was born. While Joe Early was still an infant, after the 1941 season, Early and his wife went out one evening, leaving their new son with a babysitter. When they returned home Mrs. Wynn offered to drive the sitter home. Early agreed. On the way, a bus struck the car and Mabel Allman Wynn was killed. At the age of twenty-one Early was a widower. He was never the casual rah-rah boy again. He cracked the Majors with Washington that summer. One year later, in 1943, he won eighteen games.

It was while he was serving in the Army of the United States that Wynn met the woman who would become his second wife, Lorraine. They were married in 1944, when Wynn had worked his way clear up to corporal. Actually, corporal was only the last in a string of jobs that Wynn had held since the cotton-gin days of his boyhood. Off seasons, he had been a dishwasher, a short-order cook, a flunkey in an office-safe company, a clothing salesman, and a truck driver hauling high explosives for a navy ammunition dump.

With a new wife and mother for Joe Early, Wynn moved to Florida and, at the same time, began to work furiously at becoming a bigger star. "I knew if I didn't really make good in baseball, I wasn't gonna really make good at anything," he says. "I didn't have the education. What was I fit for? Pitching and manual labor."

Partially because of the enduring sour quality of the Senators, Wynn could not become a full-fledged star in Washington, but he did get his salary up to the $20,000 level before he was traded to Cleveland after the 1948 season. At Cleveland, Early seemed to get tougher and better, so of course, people concluded he had gotten meaner. The fact is, what he had gotten was a curveball.

"I'd always figured that some guys had curves and some guys didn't and I was one of the guys that didn't," Wynn says. Mel Harder, the Cleveland pitching teacher, corrected Wynn's impression. Harder showed Early that he was releasing the curve from the wrong portion of his fingers, and that was the biggest single step. "Whenever I tried to throw a curve," Wynn says of his pre-Harder pitching, "I'd come up with a nothing ball, a bad slider. So I was just throwing fastballs and changeups.

I had the knuckler, but I just threw it on the sidelines. That's another pitch I didn't really use until I got to Cleveland." Wynn won twenty games for the first time in 1951, when he was thirty-one. Along with Mike Garcia and Bob Lemon, he helped make up Cleveland's Big Three.

Garcia is a large, amiable man. His nickname, "Bear," perfectly summarizes the impression he makes: a big, friendly Yellowstone Park–type bear. Lemon, quiet and likeable, is an efficient-looking pitcher, dealing such stuff that become ground balls. Wynn, with his high, hard one and his narrow-eyed glower and his cap pulled down over his eyes, is the man who looks mean. In Cleveland, Early rapidly realized that if hitters wanted to call him mean, there was no sense in acting like a cream puff.

The time he knocked out a base runner is an example of a play that in some players might be attributed to "grit" but in Wynn is attributed to meanness. An ex-Indian had bunted toward first base, and Wynn, moving swiftly, scooped up the ball near the base line and waited for the runner to reach him. When the runner was twenty feet away, Wynn saw him lift his elbows in the start of what was to be an attempt to separate Wynn from some teeth. "Don't be silly," Wynn warned the player, or words to that effect. The elbows stayed high. Early dodged the left elbow and pushed the ball in the runner's stomach in a manner not unlike the way he had pushed five-hundred-pound bales onto hand trucks.

"I'll tell you about that," Wynn says almost apologetically. "To be real honest, I didn't have much use for that guy anyway. Whenever there were ballclub parties, he was the guy that always spoiled things. You know what I mean. Everybody would be feeling kind of happy, and we'd look up and here would be this guy trying to make somebody else's wife."

Wynn was almost as well motivated the night he slipped the lighted cigarette into the fan's pocket. After a tough loss in Detroit, he left the Sheraton Cadillac Hotel for a brooding dinner, and while alone with a glass of beer, he heard a fan he did not know bellow, "Early Wynn! Watcha doing in here drinking a beer?" The fan's speech was thick. Early realized he was drunk.

"I wanna shake your hand, Early," the fan said, walking over, "for losing that game today." Wynn offered a hand, hoping that the fan would take it and go away. He was somewhat startled when the fan clutched his right arm with a fair grip and began talking. "I saw you lose that World Series game, Early Wynn," the fan said. "What happened after those first few innings?"

"You better take your hand off my arm," Wynn said.

"You choke up?" the fan said.

"I know judo," Wynn said. "If you don't let go of my arm, I'm going to break both of yours."

The fan weaved back to his table, but he had lingered too long. When Wynn's dinner arrived, the pitcher found he had lost his appetite. "I wasn't so mad at what he said," Wynn explains. "There are a lot of drunken fans you got to put up with. But losing a game and losing my appetite in one day, that got me sore." Wynn paid his bill and got up from the table, lit a cigarette, and on the way out, dropped it into the fan's jacket pocket. "I knew the owner of the restaurant well," Early says, "so before I left I told him. I wanted him to keep an eye on that drunk to make sure he didn't burn up. Then I went back to my hotel."

If he isn't mean, neither is Wynn soft in his attitude toward pitching. "Do you find," someone asked him once, "that you get more of a charge out of winning the big ones, like beating the Yankees, than you do throwing a good game against the Orioles?"

"I find," Wynn said, "I get a charge out of pitching when I got my good stuff and my control no matter who I'm pitching against. And if I don't have it, pitching isn't gonna be any fun against anybody."

Last year Wynn started sensationally, then went into a slump after the All-Star Game. He never fully recovered from it. For a time, at the age of thirty-five, he was the best pitcher in baseball. If Cleveland is to win a pennant next season, Early had better be one of the best pitchers in baseball at thirty-six. "I'm figuring I've got two or three more good years and then maybe a couple more in relief," he says. Then, with the loyalty all the Big Three seem to feel toward each other, he adds, "And Garcia and Lemon aren't through yet, either. I don't know what Mr. Greenberg thinks, but we old boys still have a chance."

One day in his living room last winter, Wynn was talking about toughness and meanness and seriousness. He was mentioning his careless, undriven youth when the death of his first wife was suggested as a turning point in his life. Wynn admitted that he had done a lot of thinking after the tragedy.

"Was that when you realized you'd have to be tough?" the visitor asked. "Was that when you got so serious about baseball?"

Wynn sat back in his chair. "Serious about baseball?" he repeated. "I didn't get serious about baseball, I just got serious about life. And I realized that baseball was always going to be a large part of my life."

That was a summing up, and there was nothing else that had to be spoken.

[Three years after this article appeared, Wynn, by then with the White Sox, won twenty-two games and the Cy Young Award. He was then thirty-nine years old. He was inducted into the Hall of Fame in 1972 and died in 1999, a few months before his eightieth birthday. When asked once if he would throw at his own grandmother, he said, "I'd have to. My grandma could really hit the curve."]

14

The Boswells of Baseball

The Nation, September 7, 1957

A look at sportswriters and sportswriting as the craft was practiced fifty years ago.

According to a quotation that I have traced to Cato the Elder, "Some of the best and most of the worst writing anywhere is that which appears in sports sections." I think you could apply this statement equally to the collected prose of Boswell, to *Poetry Magazine*, and, with a small deletion, to the novels of Frances Parkinson Keyes. A more accurate and more pertinent view is that sportswriters are allowed to write very well or very badly with precious little risk of editing.

Most sports events start at approximately the same time, and most of the stories arrive in the newspaper office at approximately the same hour. As a result, there is rarely much chance for a quick rewrite, let alone a complete revision. Down through the years, sports-page readers have been punished with prose like this: "A lot of cuticle was removed from the Tiger hide this fair and idyllic afternoon when the Tiger football team undertook to do battle with the formidables of Notre Dame. It was a severe beating the Tigers, still in the primer stage of gridiron development, took from the Westerners. They were no match for the fast and crafty lads from South Bend, who beat them by a score of 25 to 2, while 28,000 persons saw the one-sided encounter. The Tigers still have their stadium left, though as said, they lost cuticle by the square yard."

In the third paragraph, the writer mentions that the game played was football and explains that the Tigers were Princeton's football team.

The cuticle gem dates from 1923, and although there has been improvement on a broad front since then, a regular reader will still encounter some horrible stuff. Once, not too long ago, when the New York Giants played an exhibition game in Colorado, a *Herald Tribune* baseball writer found it droll to repeatedly address his readers as Podners. He wrote and his paper published an account in which he told how in this rugged country, Podner, the Giants looked like a rugged team, Podner, and the total effect, Podner, was about as droll as a tornado.

For years, there seemed to be a belief at the Associated Press that no golfer was identifiable without an alliterative, denominative adjective. It is impossible to recall an AP golf story in which Ben Hogan was not Bantam Ben and Sam Snead was not Slammin' Sam. I knew a gallant copyreader who spent years in the sports department of a New York newspaper removing alliterative adjectives and pining for the appearance of a golfer named Xavier. Eventually he surrendered and now works in the business-news department, where, except for handling one story beginning Sly Serge Rubinstein, he reports that he has been considerably happier.

Clearly, a sports reporter writes with a minimum of restrictions. He is expected only to tell the result of the event and employ some insight in explaining how the result came to pass. Nowhere, not even on the hidebound *New York Times*, are sportswriters bound by the classic who-where-what-when-why lead. There are sound reasons for this, which are probably best illustrated through baseball.

The bare result of a ball game is not likely to be news to a fan. He has probably seen the game on television, or heard it on radio, or listened to a friend's account in the office. The newspaperman must provide more than the telecaster, the broadcaster, or the friend. Quite understandably, the baseball writer who covers 180 games a year cannot and will not write the same story 180 times. The best baseball writers search relentlessly for the unusual.

A *Daily News* baseball reporter named Dick Young has employed a technique in which he mentions the result in passing, then proceeds to the serious business of punning or whatever else his special gimmick is that day. Late in the 1950 season, Young concluded that the Dodgers were losing because of cowardice at critical moments, a trait ballplayers call choking up, in allusion to the difficulty in swallowing that often accompanies severe tension. To get his cowardice point across, Young began a story, "The tree that grows in Brooklyn is an apple tree and the apples are in the throats of the Dodgers." From the standpoint of *Daily News* editors, one sensational lead such as Young's justifies all the latitude given their sportswriters.

The danger is excess, and on the sports page excess is routine. Several years after the apple story, when the Dodgers again were slumping, Chuck Dressen, their manager, ordered several cases of liquor and thrust drinks upon his players after a game. "To relax 'em," Charlie said. Young's response was a story in alcoholic dialect with such lines as, "Wash wusha score?" It might have made a bright night club monologue, but it was impossible to follow in print the next day.

A batter can line a single to center field. He can also loop it, smash it, bash it, belt it, drill it, crack it, smack it, wallop it, larrup it, powder it, poke it, power it, conk it, rocket it, whistle it, paddle it, push it, and still have his single to center. All these descriptive verbs are acceptable to sports copy desks, and all are used by baseball writers striving for color. The football fullback can hit the line like a Roman phalanx, like a Mack Truck, like a battering ram, like a pile driver, like a block-buster, and make a first down in the sports section. Each of these images is valueless. The best of them is hopelessly vague. But all will be used as long as sportswriters insist on offering their readers fifty images a week, a chore that might have vanquished Dylan Thomas.

If the public conception of a sportswriter grappling with English is somewhat vague, theories about the life he leads are clear. "Must be gin for breakfast, Scotch for lunch, and a Copa girl to help out with the story at a late supper," friends sometimes suggested when I wrote sports for a newspaper. The drinking is optional, but a sportswriter today is far more likely to have a publicity man than a Copa girl providing suggestions for his lead. During the 1920s there seems to have been a good deal of outright corruption of sportswriters, notably by boxing promoters. There is almost no corruption through cash now, not because of any upturn in the honesty of mankind, but simply because the risks exceed any possible gains. Public relations have replaced the handouts, and again baseball, the most intensively covered sport, has set the pattern.

For years the ballclubs offered to pay all travel expenses for newspapers assigning a writer to their team. Within the last fifteen years, some—but not all—newspapers recognized the danger of this paternalistic relationship and started paying their own way. In addition, papers are allowed to buy huge allotments of World Series tickets, which are largely used by advertising salesmen but also are available to important editors and to promotion men.

On the individual level, the teams make a determined effort to please both the sports editor and the writer assigned to cover them. Would the writer like to take his family to spring training? The paper won't pay for it, but the ballclub may. Is the managing editor riding the sports department? Perhaps the club can leak a few exclusives. The "difficult" writer, the one who enjoys sarcasm, is singled out for special treatment. Two years ago Walter O'Malley telephoned three writers covering the Dodgers and suggested that they were suffering from negativity. "You and I would both do better if you wrote more positive stuff," he said, helpfully. Once, when covering the Yankees in a year when their competition was particularly weak, I began a story, "The Yankees, who looked bad losing yesterday, managed to look mediocre winning today." The next night the club publicity director invited me to his hotel room, poured a drink, and asked if I was trying to ruin baseball.

No sportswriter is trying to ruin baseball. Over the years the writers have tended sports fondly, and though they may criticize among themselves or complain in print, the outsider who dislikes sports is considered unclean, possibly leftist, and probably effeminate.

For the most part, the big-city sportswriter is an honest man, a little bored by his job, easily convinced that he should be writing something more important, but secretly snug in the field he knows best. Ultimately, he is likely to stop trying to write well and instead settle comfortably on clichés and say, as one friend said not long ago, "What do the bastards want for a hundred and fifty bucks a week? Shakespeare?"

The editors don't, the circulation men don't, and few readers are disturbed at the number of sportswriters who quit papers for jobs that pay more than $150. Those who remain, the veteran sportswriters, are the important ones. They are the best promotion force anywhere in American industry.

[My focus was on "beat" writers, which had the effect of eliminating comment on the gifted superstar columnists Red Smith, Jimmy Cannon, and John Lardner. Although Lardner was the least famous of the three, he had matchless moments. After Bill Veeck obtained a controlling interest in the perpetually inept St. Louis Browns, Lardner wrote: "Bill Veeck bought the Browns under the impression that the Browns were owned."]

15

Stan Musial Is Baseball's No. 1 Citizen

Sport, **February 1958**

One of the greatest hitters and good fellows in the history of the game.

For savaging ballplayers, gossip in 1957 scored big. . . .

I heard enough rough stuff about four of the five best percentage batsmen on Earth to draw up a handy little Knocker's Guide. It goes like this:

Ted Williams: "Will not deliver crucial hit."

Willie Mays: "Biggest showboat of modern times."

Mickey Mantle: "Hypochondriac."

Jackie Robinson: "Biggest showboat of modern times . . . and hypochondriac."

I endorse none of these statements, but each repeatedly resounded, offered with passionate intensity. Fortunately for believers in good will, the reign of rapping governs only to a point. The particular point right now is St. Louis, Missouri, because applied to Stan Musial, an obvious omission from the Knocker's Guide, the rule shatters like a belt-high curve that hangs.

Once I heard a writer say that Musial lacked fire, but since this was a direct excuse for a bad job of interviewing, it does not qualify. Another time I heard a pitcher grumble, "The umps give Musial all the close ones." Since Musial had just beaten the pitcher with a double off a two-strike pitch, this one is disallowed, too. Nobody, not even the bench jockeys, successfully knock Stan Musial. Almost nobody bothers to try. At thirty-seven, Musial, with his large grin and larger bat, stands by himself. Uniquely, he has sped up the high road to success without making visible enemies anywhere along the way.

In Donora, the grim Pennsylvania mill town where Musial grew up, local boosters claim as a title "Home of Champions." Numbers of splendid athletes have sprung, or perhaps escaped, from Donora, but the personal favorite of virtually everyone who lives there remains Musial. "Whenever the Cardinals are playing in Pittsburgh, Stan comes over," one booster reports. "He visits around, goes to the children's hospital, things like that. We're not the biggest city in the world, but he's never gotten too big not to remember us."

In St. Louis, where Musial has lived for more than ten years, idolatry has developed in a curious manner. "He's certainly the biggest hero here since Dizzy Dean," says a writer for the *St. Louis Post-Dispatch*, "but with Diz, it was quick. One big splash and a lot of stories, and he was in. With Musial, the whole thing has been slower. There was no splash. He was around and people got to meet him more and more, and they told other people what a helluva guy he was. It kept growing and building until now he could have the city if he asked for it."

When Frank Lane became general manager of the Cardinals, he arrived with a vague, professional admiration for Musial. Last year he announced, "Stan is the one ballplayer I've met who'd get me to stand on line and wait for his autograph."

"You mean his autograph on the bottom of a contract," a reporter said.

"I mean his autograph on the bottom of a scorecard," Lane corrected.

Red Schoendienst, who roomed with Musial for ten years, remembers the way in which The Man provided batting tips. "Occasionally when I wasn't hitting the ball too good," Red says, "he'd ask me if the pitch I'd swung at wasn't a bad one. He'd never tell me that it was. That was his gentle way of helping."

For himself, Musial singles out the advice of old friends as the factor behind his amiability. "All my life," he says, "I've been lucky in the people I knew. Most of the time they were people older than me. I've got opinions. Maybe some of them are rough. But from my friends, the older people with more experience, I've picked things up quicker. You know. What you say and what you never say. From older people I learned a more mature way."

The quick picture that emerges shows a man who combines a sense of loyalty with sensitivity toward others who are less gifted, plus possesses enough all-around talents to rise to the top of his profession. But it's a picture that can be studied with a shrug. The appraisal falls short by one fact.

It is difficult, immensely and endlessly difficult, to be Stan Musial. The basic virtues may fairly be taken for granted in ordinary lives, but since late 1941 Musial has been living in an extraordinary manner. As a hero, he has little privacy and less peace. As a national figure, he finds strangers are his friends. For every moment of every day he is at the mercy of the public, which can, at any moment, become merciless. And all of this, even now, is a surprise to him.

Actors are tutored by public relations agents. Presidents and queens are sealed off by Secret Service men. Ballplayers may get sporadic counsel, but for the most part they face their fans alone.

Musial came into baseball prominence after a boyhood in a small town. He came into considerable income after living among factory workers during the Depression. Yet he adjusted. There have been no tantrums, no diatribes, no little hints that, "Listen, buddy, I got it made." Rightly, the dominant image that Musial will leave behind in baseball involves the magnificent uncoiling of his swing. But the style with which he has accepted the demands of fans seems equally memorable.

One morning after a night game last summer, Musial and Del Ennis left their room at the Biltmore Hotel in New York at ten o'clock and started toward the coffee shop for breakfast.

"Hiya, Stan," the elevator man said. "You riding down?"

"I hope so," Musial said, grinning.

"Right," the elevator man said.

In the back of the car someone whispered, "That's Stan Musial."

A game in Brooklyn the night before had run for longer than three hours, and Musial was smiling on a short supply of sleep.

Three people turned their heads and gaped as Musial walked through the lobby. As he went into the coffee shop, a stranger said, "Hey, Stan, you guys gonna win today?"

"We're gonna try," Musial said, pleasantly.

A waitress seated Musial and Ennis at a table in the center of the shop. They looked at menus, and then Musial began to glance through the *New York Times*.

"Mr. Musial," said a boy of about eight, "could you gimme your autograph?"

Musial put down his paper. "What's your name?" he asked.

"Gerry Coyle," the boy said.

Musial asked if it was Gerry with a "G," then wrote a short note of best wishes. "Now," he said, "while you're here, you can get Mr. Ennis to sign, too."

"Nah," said the boy. "I don't want Ennis. Just you."

Ennis forced a smile and Musial, embarrassed, buried his face in the paper.

"Stan," a magazine photographer said, "I wonder if I could get a couple of pictures."

"Sure," Musial said. "Go ahead."

"I'll be out of your way in a minute," the photographer said. "Just sort of snapping while you eat. Could I get a shot of you reading the sports page?"

Musial thumbed through the paper until he had reached the stock market quotations. "If you can hold up," he said, breaking into his grin again. "You see, some days I got to look at this page first."

"Some days?" Ennis said. "All days."

Musial, still grinning, turned to the sports section. He got through his orange juice in style, but by the time the eggs arrived, the stranger who had greeted him had summoned the courage to come over. "Who's gonna pitch for you guys today?" he asked.

"Paper says Jones," Musial said.

"You guys oughta murder Brooklyn," the stranger said. He was a red-faced man, close to fifty. "You know," he said, "I used to play some ball myself. Couldn't pull. That was my trouble. If I coulda pulled, I mighta made it pretty big."

Between forksful of eggs, Musial said that it was tough to pull outside pitches.

"No," the stranger said. "You see, I just couldn't pull anything. Even the inside ones. It's a real tough game, baseball. You guys work."

The photographer, who was hovering over the scene, cleared his throat and glared at the stranger. "Oh, look," the man said, "I wouldn't bother you for myself, but my brother, Sam Coleman, he'd really appreciate it if you'd sign something for him."

Musial signed and the stranger left. "At least his pen didn't leak," the photographer said. Musial said nothing, did not grin, and went back to eating and reading.

By count, there were six more interruptions before Stan finished breakfast. Then at 10:40 it was time for him to run a juvenile gauntlet.

Whenever a Major League team hits a hotel on the road, one small boy digs until he has discovered the schedule of the ballplayers' entrances and exits. The small boy tells his friends, who tell theirs, the whole thing mushrooms, and when it's time for the players to leave for the ballpark a junior army sets up ambushes. Sometimes the small platoons move cautiously, but if a star emerges they charge, brandishing pens, pencils, and paper and shouting a rousing battle cry that sounds like, "Hey sign mine willya?" Musial glances out of the lobby of the Biltmore at the army deployed between him and a line of waiting taxis.

"Postcards," Musial said, "just postcards. We got to get out in time for batting practice." He stepped out of the doorway, and the small boys sprang. Within seconds they had formed a ring around him and seemed to be clawing at his trousers, his jacket, and his belt. Stan moved doggedly toward a taxicab, like a fullback driving through a midget line, clutching postcards and jamming them into his pockets. The ring moved with him, but since the lead small boy missed a tackle, Musial managed to keep his feet. The cabbie threw open a door, Musial and Ennis hurtled in. . . . But the small boys, now unable to surround Musial directly, used an old Prussian tactic and surrounded the cab.

"Come on, beat it, you crazy kids," the driver suggested. "I oughta run you down."

Musial was fielding postcards fluttering through open windows. "All right, fellas," he said. "Watch it now. We got to get going. Careful or you'll get hurt. Watch it. Watch the wheels. Come on, kids, careful."

The cab pulled away, but it ran into a traffic tie-up at once and the boys regrouped for another charge. There was one further cascade of postcards. Then the cab was off, and Musial was riding down the streets of Manhattan for a few pleasantly anonymous minutes.

"I can't figure those kids," he said. "You sign once, you sign twice, okay. But some of these kids must have fifty of them by now. I don't know what they do with them. I just keep signing."

Outside of Ebbets Field, a fresh battalion of small boys lay in wait, but the cabbie pulled very close to the rotunda entrance and Musial made his way through this mob at the cost of only fifteen to twenty more postcards stuffed into his pockets. . . .

These few rather ordinary moments out of one day, multiplied by other days and ways, supplemented by talks to business groups and attendance at public dinners with dry steak and drier speeches represent an existence that few baseball stars accept cheerfully. Musial enjoys people, conversation, and stories, so some of his public hours are quite painless. What he finds painful about public pressure, no one knows. He never talks about it. He grins for small boys, bankers, and boors with the same warmth.

Usually at the end of a season, Stan spends a few weeks relishing the solitude of hunting, and two years ago he and his wife vacationed in Nassau, where cricket wickets prevail and baseball players are left alone to fish. "It was a helluva rest," he says. But whenever Musial is thrust against the baseball masses, he accepts them as cheerfully as he accepts pitchers. This is an era when some ballplayers attempt to charge $500 to be interviewed and others view autograph hunters as an unnecessary evil. Among this common unpleasantness, Musial towers as an aristocrat.

Through his entire baseball career, Musial has studied pitchers and pitching. For one thing, he started out as a left-handed pitcher himself. For another, he has the same burning interest in the path of a pitch that king cobras have in the path of a jackrabbit. . . .

Following a tactic invented by the Light Brigade at Balaclava during the Crimean War, I employed a series of spies to provide inside information. My Philadelphia man was heard from first. "Robin Roberts refuses to discuss pitching to Stan Musial," he reported. This sounded reasonable, if not helpful.

From Milwaukee, the answer was more detailed. "Warren Spahn says he has no set way to pitch to Musial," my source began. "He says he tries to figure what his best pitch is each time he works, and that's what he wants Musial to hit at. He moves the ball around and tries not to throw the same pitch twice in a row, but when he talked I got the feeling he was guessing."

At least this was an elementary guide. I then contacted the Giants' Johnny Antonelli on my own. "Musial," Antonelli said, scowling. "You want to know about Musial? Well, he's quick. Everything about him is fast. You can see that, the way he hits to all fields. You get him out on one pitch, and he'll beat your brains out on the same one next time he comes up. There's no book on him. At least I got no book." Antonelli looked up as if for a sign of hope before continuing. "He's been hitting into more double plays lately because he's getting older," Antonelli said, "but you know he's got something like a sixth sense. Some pitchers say he can tell what pitch they're gonna throw from their windup or their body motion. At times, it's unbelievable. You got him fooled, or you ought to have him fooled, and all of a sudden you find he's guessing with you."

"Now that he's older," I asked, "can you overpower him more often with a fastball?"

"Well, I've heard guys say you should throw him fastballs," Antonelli said, "and I've heard guys say you should curve him, and I've heard guys say you should changeup. I figure I have to go fast with him. It's my best pitch and it's my style, and you have to go against Musial with your best. If I could throw great slow stuff like Stu Miller, I'd give that to him, but me, all the guys around the league, we try to get him out with our best."

Clem Labine, the Dodgers' relief pitcher, enjoyed a fair stretch of containing Musial, and I checked him to learn if he had invented a new pitch. "No," Labine said, "but for the last couple of years I've been pretty lucky against him with my sinker. I show him the curve and then I throw the sinker, low, of course, and usually outside. I think he's been trying to pull it, but I don't know. I don't want to talk too much about it. My luck could change, and I've got a big family."

Preacher Roe's technique remains the house favorite. "I throw him four wide ones," Roe once confided, "and then I try to pick him off first."

Before the 1951 All-Star Game in Detroit, Ed Lopat, a Yankees pitcher full of thought, collared Roe and said that he had discovered a guaranteed way to pitch to Musial.

"Um," Roe said, recklessly.

Then Roe and Lopat wandered toward their separate bullpens, and in the fourth inning Lopat heard a call. The first batter he faced was Musial, and the first pitch he threw was driven clear into the right-field stands.

"Hey," Roe bellowed from the bullpen as Musial loped around the bases. "I see what you mean, Eddie, but I found that way to pitch to him a long time ago, all by myself." The crowd was cheering, and probably Lopat did not hear the shout. At any rate, he didn't turn to answer. . . .

The batters who have known Musial best line up brightly to talk about the hurt he inflicts upon the common enemy.

Hank Sauer, who roomed with Musial during a short stay with the Cardinals, offers an almost mathematical analysis. "Most hitters have an alley," Sauer says. "You throw it down their alley and they kill you. A guy like me, I figure I've got one alley. Never mind where."

Sauer is usually somewhat reserved, but with Musial as a subject he chattered on quite freely. "Stan doesn't hit out of any alley. He's got a zone. His zone is the strike zone, and it covers almost everything that's good. Inside Stan's zone, he's got six or seven alleys. One alley he pulls. Another one he goes over third base. Another one he goes into left-center. It all depends on the type of pitch he gets, but he can adjust to anything anybody's gonna throw him. He'll hit any pitch where it can do the most damage. Damn it, you can't compliment the guy too much." . . .

Other hitters tend to talk in more general terms.

"He's got the quick hands and wrists," Schoendienst says, "and he picks up the flight of the ball real good."

"He has great eyes and coordination," says Whitey Lockman, who was a Cardinal long enough to be sure. "On an inside fastball that I have to hit on the hands, he moves the bat around so fast he gets the fat part of the wood on the ball."

Musial works at his hitting. In batting practice he tries to hit to left or left-center, just as he would during the game. A fair number of sluggers use batting practice as a sort of animated exercise. They call for fastballs, powder them, and beam as sunlight strikes their muscles and glances upward. Then in the game, when curveballs sneak over the outside corner, they wheel on the umpire and say, "What?"

Still, by itself, intelligent practice does not make a hitter.

Conceivably, when he is through with baseball, Musial will sit down with his friend Bob Broeg and prepare a book on the secrets of hitting .350. It could do more for young America than any work since *Forever Amber.* "He knows an awful lot," Broeg says, "but he doesn't want to tell too much about it until he's through."

One night on a train loafing from Pittsburgh to New York, Stan told me a little of what he knows. It doesn't explain a .350 hitter nor will it transform an awkward boy into a slugger. But it does reveal the depth of Musial's skill.

We were sitting in a club car, and Stan was sipping beer between brief bouts with pen and pad. It was late, and he had signed autographs for everyone in the car.

"Is the specific bat you use very important?" I began.

Musial rubbed his long chin. "I can pick up a bat right away and tell you whether it weighs thirty-three ounces or thirty-four ounces," he said. "Sure, it's important. Every bat has its own kind of feel to it."

"What do you use?"

"I got a special model. The handle comes from one they made for Mel Ott. I haven't got real big hands, and I guess Ott didn't, either. Maybe I have the smallest handle around. But the barrel is big. I took that from one they made for Jimmy Foxx. I start out the year with a bat that's thirty-four ounces. Then when it gets hot and I get weaker, I go to the lighter ones."

His coordination provides Musial with a special luxury. He can use a pipestem handle safe in the knowledge that he will hit the ball with the dynamic part of the bat. The bat was a small clue and an interesting one, but it wasn't the item I wanted to discover.

"What do you think when you step in to hit?" I asked.

"Nothing," Musial said. "I try to think of nothing. I got things on my mind the same as anybody else, but I don't want to be thinking about them when I'm supposed to be hitting."

"Well, do you guess what the pitch is going to be?"

"I don't guess," Musial said. "I know."

"You know?" I answered, nearly spilling my glass of ice water.

"I can always tell," Musial said, casually, "as long as I'm concentrating."

"By studying the rotation?"

"No, it's not the rotation," Musial said. "It's something else." Musial does not speak glibly. Now, as he talked of his craft, he tried to choose each word with particular care.

"I pick the ball up right away," he said. "Know what I mean? I see it as soon as it leaves the pitcher's hand. That's when I got to concentrate real hard. If I do, I can tell what the pitch is going to be."

"When can you tell?"

"When it's about halfway up to home plate."

Then I slipped in the $120,000 question, an evaluation based directly on Musial's overall income last year. "*How* can you tell?" I said.

"I can tell by the speed," Musial said. "Every pitcher has a set of speeds. I mean, the curve goes one speed and the slider goes at something else. Well, if I concentrate real good, I can pick up the speed of the ball about the first thirty feet it travels. I know the pitcher, and I know his speeds. When I concentrate, halfway in I know what the pitch is gonna be, how the ball is gonna move when it gets up to home plate."

Every hitter works to time each pitch, and the whole technique of fastball followed by changeup was evolved to destroy timing. But to call what Musial does mere timing would compare reasonably with calling Albert Einstein expert in arithmetic.

Musial mentally sorts the deliveries of some eighty or ninety pitchers. Allowing four pitches to each, this means that in any given season he has classified something over 320 distinct deliveries. Then, through his great coordination and eyesight, he applies the knowledge during the three-fifths of a second it takes a typical pitch to reach him from the mound. The frequent result, professor, is what we in the trade call a clean blow.

"I don't always concentrate like I should," Musial said. "Maybe twenty, thirty times a year, we're way ahead and it doesn't matter much so I just go up there and swing. I guess that doesn't sound like it would make a lot of difference, but at the end of the year when I look at my batting average and figure the times I didn't concentrate like I should, it gets me sore."

A cynic who had lived among advertising men too long insisted that Musial's revelation is simply an idle boast. "It's just to get a magazine story planted with you," he said. "Nobody could do what Musial claims." . . .

I held a consultation with the next batting expert I came across. He turned out to be Yogi Berra.

Yogi thought for a while and said nothing. Finally, running his fingers across his chin, he spoke. "Sure, it's possible," he said. "Most guys couldn't do it. I don't do it. But that guy could." Then Berra relapsed into contemplation.

On the field or off it, Stan Musial is not most guys. This is less apparent with him than with a profoundly troubled man such as Ted Williams, but it would be naive to consider Musial as someone who simply took life as he found it and by and large liked what he found. Rather, through work and native gifts, Stan has imposed his own terms upon life. He seems to be a profoundly happy man, but his happiness was a hard-bought thing. . . .

Musial struggled out of an ordinary background to become an extraordinary man.

Lukasz Musial immigrated to the United States from Poland, married an American girl named Mary, and settled down to a life of hard work in a zinc factory. The couple raised six children. Stashu was the next to last.

"He was always the nice boy he is now," says Mrs. Mary Musial. "He never sassed anybody. Ask his teachers. But he has changed. His head is still the same. It's got no bigger. But now he speaks a whole lot better than he did."

As soon as Stan's sense of balance developed, Lukasz Musial began taking his boy to the Polish National Alliance in Donora for weekly workouts in tumbling. At seven, in the backyard of the family's house on Marelda Avenue, Stan first got his hands on a bat and ball. He rejected the old games for the new and soon started daily trips into the hilly, barren area around Donora's Twelfth Street, where children played pickup games of baseball. . . .

"He was tall and lean," says Charles H. Wunderlich, who teaches gym at Donora's junior high school, "and he had the kind of grace that in sports always seems to put a boy at the right place at the right time. If he hadn't gone into baseball, he would have been a great basketball player. Some boys have it. Some don't. You know how it is. You could take one look at Stan and know that he had it." . . .

Musial finished three years of high school without taking algebra, a maneuver that must have been as ingenious as diagnosing pitches. At seventeen he was not certain what he wanted to achieve in high school, but it struck him that some time in the future his lack of algebra might be damaging.

Elementary algebra was not a requirement for graduation at Donora High, but Musial, who by this time stood six feet tall, went back to junior high school and took the course surrounded by a class full of younger, smaller students. "Most boys," says one Donora lady, "would not have risked the ridicule of their friends. Here was the measure of a champion. He dared to be different. His math teacher once told me that his friends seemed to recognize the difference, and instead of scoffing, they admired Stan for it."

Learning was encouraged in the household of Lukasz Musial. Baseball was not. Lukasz, who could not get a college education in America, placed an enormous premium upon Stashu's obtaining one. Baseball, he believed, was vaguely childish. While Musial moved ahead with parental encouragement in school, he also moved ahead, despite discouragement, in his game.

Dr. Michael Duda coached baseball at Donora High when Musial played there. "Stan had an elusive quality you can't describe," he says, "except that it's something peculiar to the great. He wanted to be a great ballplayer, and he stuck to it in the face of some pretty keen obstacles at home."

Musial was a distinguished baseball player at Donora High. "He was an outstanding hitter, and he won the batting championship and set some records at DHS," Duda recalls, "but he was a pitcher first and foremost. When he wasn't pitching, he played in the outfield. Before his senior year, he had signed a minor league contract, so that spring, when he was no longer eligible to play, he helped me coach."

Lukasz Musial was more kindly disposed toward basketball, because there lay opportunities to win a college scholarship. Stan was a superb high school basketball player with a first-rate left-handed hook shot, which in those ancient days, before the jump shot was born, was just about the last word in scoring.

In 1938, when Musial led Donora through an unbeaten basketball season, a particularly critical game loomed with Washington High School, another undefeated team, just after he had caught the flu. Musial got out of a sick bed and traveled to Pittsburgh with the team and played most of the game.

"We probably wouldn't have won it without Stan," says James K. Russell, Donora's basketball coach. "But sick or not, he did what you'd expect. He played a wonderful game." . . .

College opens horizons into exalted fields, such as engineering or law or sportswriting. Sensibly, Lukasz Musial insisted that Stashu forget professional baseball and accept a basketball scholarship at the University of Pittsburgh.

Stan preferred baseball, but he had doubts. He spoke to Dr. Duda and to Coach Russell and to another close friend, Helen Kloz, the high school librarian at Donora. Miss Kloz, as sharp a judge of baseball talent as ever hid behind the complete works of Charles Dickens, offered good advice. "Your heart is in baseball, Stan," she said, "and it seems to me you ought to follow your heart, at least for a while."

Dr. Duda suggested to Lukasz Musial that Stan had enough talent to warrant at least a try at professional baseball. But when a man named Andrew French, who managed the Monessen team in the Pennsylvania State Association, called on the Musials, carrying a contract as his card, Lukasz Musial was adamant. He parried French's pleading with a recurrent, "No!" until suddenly Stan, who was sixteen, burst into tears.

"This is a free country, Lukasz," Mary Musial said, mildly. "The boy is free *not* to go to college."

The combined impact of a woman's logic and a boy's tears vanquished Lukasz. He signed the contract for his underage son, and Stan immediately promised that he would work at a more acceptable trade during the winter. There may have been something less than free choice in the latter decision. The baseball contract called for $325 a year, and even allowing for frugality and prewar prices, this could only have meant no lunch money on weekdays. . . .

As a pitcher Musial forked no special lightning. "I remember him pitching against us in an exhibition game," says Terry Moore, the fine Gas House Gang center fielder who is now a Cardinals coach. "Johnny Mize and I hit homers off him. Fastballs. I recall saying to Mize that the kid pitcher looked like he could be a pretty good hitter."

Wid Matthews, who later ran the Chicago Cubs, was one of Branch Rickey's special trouble shooters when Musial was breaking in. "This young man," Matthews once wrote in a scouting report, "is the wildest left-hander I have ever seen."

Musial feels that the report was extreme, but from what he has seen of big-league pitching he is not certain that he could have developed sufficient control and stuff to make the Majors. "I wasn't sure in the beginning, either," he admits, "but the girl I was going to marry, Lillian, her father owned a grocery store. No matter what happened in baseball, I knew I could always get a job in the store."

What happened most significantly in the early years was a tumbling catch on August 11, 1940, a night when Musial, doubling up for Daytona Beach, a class D team, was playing center field. He caught the ball but fell heavily on his left shoulder. The shoulder was terribly bruised, and Musial tried pitching only twice more. Once he defeated Sanford, Florida, 5–4, a victory he attributed to luck and others charge up to courage. Then he pitched against Orlando and was battered. Pending a long, possibly permanent rest for the shoulder, Musial the pitcher was through.

Dickie Kerr, a former Major Leaguer who had turned the implausible trick of winning two World Series games for a team that was trying to lose (the 1919 Chicago White Sox), managed Daytona. He had developed a fondness for Musial.

"I think I better quit," Musial told Kerr. "I'm not making much money. Lillian is expecting a baby. I can't pitch."

"You can't quit," Kerr said. "You can hit. In this league, you do two jobs. As you move up, they're not going to let you waste your time sitting on the bench three days out of every four. They'll want your hitting every day. They'll keep you in the outfield."

Then Kerr rented a large house, and he and his wife invited Stan and Lillian Musial to move in as their guests. Stan did not quit baseball in 1940, and when his son was born he and Lillian named the boy Richard. Then in 1941 the pleasant land for which Stan had been waiting stretched before him. He broke down the gates with his bat.

Musial played eighty-seven games for Springfield of the Western Association in 1941 and batted .379. Then he was promoted to Rochester in the International League, where in fifty-four games he hit .326. Finally, he was promoted to the Cardinals right into the middle of a pennant race. In twelve Major League games, he drove home seven runs and batted .426.

As a rookie .400 hitter, Musial was not the impressive batsman he has become. He did not coil so severely, nor did he possess his present power. He had speed, and some of his hits were ground balls he outran. In the beginning he was rated slightly below a right-handed hitter named Erv Dusak. After Dusak hit a few doubles someone nicknamed him "Two-sack Dusak." He never became more than a journeyman.

Musial became, of course (with Rogers Hornsby), the greatest batter in National League history. He arrived as a batsman in 1943, when he hit .357, and as a slugger in 1948, when his .376 average included thirty-nine home runs. He has led the National League in batting seven times, a record, and has led the league in scoring runs five times, a record he shares. He has more extra-base hits than any other National Leaguer, and his slugging percentage represents an all-time league high for a man who has played more than ten seasons. Early next season he will collect his three thousandth hit.

Musial is the most durable player in National League annals. Last season, before he injured his left shoulder, he broke Gus Suhr's record of appearing in 822 consecutive games. Stan appeared in 895 before sitting down.

He was a fine outfielder who improved with experience, and his throwing arm, weak after the unfortunate diving catch, had a way of recovering at critical moments.

He is such a devoted team player that he follows specific patterns— when to try for three bases, when to slap a single to left—designed to fit every moment of every game.

The images and memories he has created are as bright as life in zinc mills can be dark. I like to dwell on one afternoon twelve years ago in Brooklyn when he made five hits, each with two strikes against him. I like to think of the morning when Al Barlick, the umpire, said with sincerity beyond expression, "He lets you do your job. He's a gentleman." I remember an afternoon in Miami, not far from the Daytona Beach field where he almost ended his career, when Musial, now earning $80,000 a year from the Cardinals, dived for a low line drive onto a sun-baked outfield during an exhibition game that meant little except to the people who had paid to see it. I like the way he breaks down the line for first base, a picture his current manager, Fred Hutchinson, describes best. "It's like a wounded turkey," Hutch says. "Ever see a turkey run after he's been wounded by a shotgun? He's leaning all off to one side, going like hell. That's what Stan's running makes me think of."

Most of all, I relish thinking of the time, any time, when Musial hits a home run. The stance, the uncoiling, and the bat lash provide one of the instances in which the game of baseball approaches a majesty of grace.

Musial is far from eloquent in speech, but there have been instances in which his sincerity hit home with striking force. . . .

"People ask me which manager is the best," he said, "and I always tell them it's the guy I'm playing for right now. I couldn't play right if I didn't get myself believing that. I like to play my game. Especially when I'm hitting, I don't want to be worrying about everything else. So all the men I've played for, I got myself thinking that every one of them was the best around. He could handle his job, and it wasn't for me to worry about it." . . .

Insight of a different sort into The Man today is provided by Hank Sauer. "When we were on the road," Sauer says, "we'd look for new places to eat. We'd use a Diner's Club card and ask people where the best restaurants were. Musial really knows food. He can always tell the good cuts of meat from the bad ones. In New York, we'd go to the shows. Then, when we'd get back to St. Louis, he'd always be holding open house. He has a tremendous family. I mean they're nice, the nicest family and home and wife you've ever seen. If your kids rip up something at his house, you'd give them hell and then he'd chew you out. 'Never mind what they do,' he'd say. 'Just let them alone. They're at my house, and they can do anything they want.'

"There are kids all over the place. You go to his house, and you step on kids everywhere. 'That's what my home is for,' Stan says. 'It's for kids, yours and mine.'" As much as anything else, of course, baseball is for precisely the same thing.

It will do no good to measure Stan Musial against conventional or even unconventional standards. Nothing seems to apply quite properly. There is a mystical quality about some leaders that makes other men follow them into whatever valley lies at hand. But Musial does not try to lead. He simply goes about his life as if each hour were his finest; people rush to meet him, and when they have, they find they want to know him better than they can.

Stan Musial stands off larger than life, and looking at him hard we can see everybody's dream, about baseball. We cannot finally analyze the dream and The Man. It is enough simply to know that they are there.

16

Little Nellie's a Man Now

Sport, April 1958

Nelson Fox, small, quiet, and with limited talents, comes out of central Pennsylvania and becomes a Major League All-Star second baseman.

There is a philosophy current among Major League ballplayers that I believe was first expressed by Ralph Kiner on a program sponsored by the Ford Motor Company of Detroit.

"Ralph," the Ford man began, "how come you never choke up on that big stick when you swing?"

"Because," Kiner said, truthfully, "the Cadillacs are down at the end of the bat."

"Urgg," the Ford man said, momentarily losing his poise.

Except for the announcer's career, very little was affected by the remark. People continued purchasing Fords, Kiner continued driving a Cadillac, and ballplayers continued receiving watches, checks, and hubcaps for appearing on programs sponsored by motor companies. All Ralph really did was describe a trend, but his phrasing was superb, if somewhat thoughtless. Baseball is a big business these days, and the richest payoffs—excluding pitchers—go to the boys who hit the home runs. . . .

Nellie Fox has hit exactly twenty-five home runs in his nine years in the Major Leagues, an average of fewer than three per season. And yet, although he does not drive a Cadillac, he is the owner of two expensive automobiles. Nellie can hit behind the runner, and he can bunt, and he can splatter base hits to left field. But he can't hit many home runs, and he rarely wastes his strength trying. When he does manage accidentally to pop a fair ball into the stands, it is such a special occasion that the other Chicago White Sox go out of their way not to speak to him for an inning or two. "Keeps his head from swelling," reports one of our Chicago spies.

At thirty, Fox is an old-timer's dream of a ballplayer vividly come to life. It isn't just that he doesn't hit home runs; there is more to it than that. Napoleon Lajoie didn't hit homers, either. Nellie possesses the old skills of getting on base and starting rallies and irritating the opposition. And refreshingly in this sanitary new era of Dentyne, he chews a fat wad of tobacco. He fights, and he isn't afraid of being hurt. He plays each game as if the manager were standing by with a bus ticket to South Grand Forks marked "One Way; N. Fox." He hates sympathy, and when he's cornered he will give away forty pounds to tangle with Bill Skowron at second base or five hundred syllables to out-talk Casey Stengel anywhere.

"You have to say," suggests Al Lopez, Fox's manager, "that Nellie is the hustlingest player in the league."

"He has the best attitude in the world," says Paul Richards, who managed Fox at Chicago. . . .

Baseball writers give no award to the player with the most valuable attitude. The newspapers neglect to print tables listing the five hardest hustlers in each league. . . . We check the home-run leaders and the men who have driven in the most runs, and we assume that we have surveyed all the stars.

Without ever cracking a table of sluggers, Nellie Fox has played in seven All-Star Games, and any list of the top dozen ballplayers active today should unquestionably include his name. Yet, compared to hitting a home run, the things Fox does best are subtle, and there is a general tendency to underestimate his talent.

Nellie likes to play . . . and he plays with enormous skill.

In the final week of his second year with the White Sox, Nellie was coming off a .247 season and was hitting .306. Then, during a workout, he pulled a thumb, which makes swinging difficult, particularly for thumb hitters like him.

"Look," Paul Richards said. "Suppose you just sit out the rest of the season. It means a lot to you to hit .300. It means a lot to the club, too." Richards thought a .300 hitter would help the White Sox draw.

"Nothing doing," Fox said. "I don't want to rest."

"What?" Richards demanded. "Don't you want to hit .300?"

"Yeah, I want to hit .300," Fox said. "But playing. Not sitting on the bench."

Fox played for the rest of the season. In five games, he raised his average seven points and finished at .313.

This passion for action runs through all Fox's seasons. When the White Sox trained at El Centro, California, he regularly arrived for work at 8 a.m., ran by himself until the other players appeared, and then insisted on being the last man to leave the field. Fox is small, possibly lighter than the 157 pounds he claims, and whenever it was particularly hot, Richards worried lest his second baseman melt. "Hey, Nellie," Paul would shout, "you've had enough. Go on in the clubhouse."

Fox would obey, Richards would turn to something else, and Fox would sneak back, disguised as an outfielder. . . .

Fox hustles, but he is not a fake. He proved himself finally in an exhibition game the White Sox once played in Pasadena. A sharp grounder bounding straight at him struck a stone and glanced into his face. Nellie tried to make the play, couldn't, but got the ball back to the pitcher and the game resumed. Suddenly Chico Carrasquel, the White Sox' shortstop at the time, trotted into the dugout.

"Nellie," Carrasquel said, "he hurt bad."

The trainer ran out and examined Fox. The ball had knocked out one tooth, loosened several others, and cut a lip.

"It's nothing," Fox mumbled. "I'll stay in."

The next inning, Nellie almost fainted from pain when he attempted to bat. Richards took him out and that evening suggested that he see a dentist.

"I'll last till October," Fox said. "I didn't miss the tooth when I ate tonight, so I'll wait until the season's over."

"That wasn't fake hustle," Richards says. "The kid's spontaneous. That's how he's always been. He doesn't put on any act."

Probably because his feverish desire to play seems more dramatic than his singles to center, an army of home-run worshippers assumes that combativeness is the strongest of Fox's tools. He isn't a Gehringer or Gordon or Jackie Robinson, one columnist wrote, but he may be like Eddie Stanky.

It was, I think, a thoroughly bad call. Fox is a better hitter than Stanky ever was; he is by far the best singles hitter in the Major Leagues. . . .

Over the past four years, Fox's singles totals read 167, 157, 158, 155, and he led the American League each year. Further, he is the toughest man in the Majors to strike out; over the last four years, his strikeout totals are 12, 15, 14, 13. In his entire big-league career, Fox has struck out only 123 times. (Mickey Mantle has been known to strike out 111 times in one free-swinging season.) Finally, playing at second base within spike range of every runner, Fox has pulled an iron-man stunt by playing in 772 of the White Sox' past 775 games. . . .

Although I admired him, I had never spoken very much with Nellie. For one thing, he seemed to be fairly reserved, and for another, the dialogue around the White Sox' batting cage was usually bilingual. What with Minnie Minoso, Carrasquel, or Luis Aparicio swapping straight lines, half the conversation took place in Spanish, and although I have nothing against Spanish as such, it does remind me of an unpleasant experience in high school that dragged on for two semesters. . . .

A few weeks ago, as I telephoned Fox, I was considering this reportorial failure. Here was one of the finest ballplayers around, and I hadn't really talked to him enough. I'd talked to all the home-run hitters. I'd even talked to Ted Williams when I had to. Well, next year, I resolved, I was going to look at figures on homers and runs-batted-in only after I'd first checked the singles list. . . .

When Nellie came to the telephone, he said he would be glad to see me after the hunting season. "I'm going off hunting for a couple of weeks," he said. We picked a date and agreed to meet at a bowling alley he helps operate on the highway between Chambersburg and Hagerstown, Maryland.

Outside the alley I saw a large bowling pin, but no sign blazing the name Nellie Fox. Inside, there were twenty modern alleys. . . . When Fox walked in, for an instant it was hard to recognize him. He wasn't chewing tobacco, and in his sports jacket and sports shirt he looked like a trim boy of perhaps twenty-four. I stared, and he stuck out a hand. "Nellie Fox," he said. . . . We started talking about hitting. "Paul Richards helped me," Fox said, "and Roger Cramer. I was using a thin-handled bat, but I couldn't whip it around. Cramer started me on a bottle bat like he'd used. That was the difference."

The bottle bat is a short, stubby piece of wood, very thick at the handle and quite distinct from the gracefully tapered bat most players use. Swinging the bottle bat involves a curious technique. A typically successful hitter, say Al Kaline, tries to meet the ball well off his fists, and his entire approach to batting goes on from there. Should Kaline hit a pitch at a point close to the handle of his bat, he will (a) bloop the ball and (b) wince, as stinging pain shoots through his hands. Kaline can stand a moderate distance from the plate and adjust his stride to the particular pitch. Fox, with the bottle bat, can hit a ball as close as four inches from his hands and still get enough wood behind it to single cleanly. But since the bat is short, Fox must crowd the plate to keep outside pitches within his reach.

A few enormously strong men—Al Simmons was one—have hit for power using bottle bats, but in Fox's hands the bat is roughly equivalent to a paddle. He gets it around and slaps the ball between the fielders, which is every bit as artful, if less immediately impressive, as getting a conventional bat around and trying to slug the ball through a fielder's chest.

"I don't feel it much when I hit one off the fists," Fox said. "You see, I got all that wood there."

Sitting across a coffee table, Fox still looked small. It seemed reasonable that the bottle bat demanded big hands for a proper grip. He spread his hands wide on the table. They were big and hard and horny, like a carpenter's or a laborer's. Nellie grinned. "Not bad for a little guy, right?" he said. . . .

"I guess [Bob] Lemon gives me the most trouble," he said, "or used to. He was all over, moving the ball around all the time. [Herb] Score was tough and [Whitey] Ford. Most of them like to throw up and in to me. I crowd the plate; they try to hit my thumbs. One year I got hit seventeen times. They weren't throwing at me. They were coming high and inside, and sometimes the ball got away."

"Do the runners try to get you at second base?"

Fox shrugged. "They try," he said. "People ask me how to make the double play. I tell them as best you can. It's like when people ask me how I hit the curve. I tell them not good." Fox grinned again. "I didn't start as a second baseman," he said. "I was a first baseman. Then in the minors I got shifted to the outfield, and one day they needed a second baseman, and they picked me. So, I've been learning. I'm learning all the time. How you play the hitters; there's no two alike. How you pivot on the double play; you got to beat the runner to the bag so's you can have a little time. How you move with the pitch; you see the sign, curve or fastball, and you make your move. Then maybe the ball goes the other way and you look silly. It happens."

"Who hits the toughest ball for you to handle?"

"Ted Williams," Fox said, quickly. "Everything's topped. Of course, I'm back in the outfield when he's hitting, but everything Williams hits has this spin, and it sinks on you or it comes off the ground like a bomb. After Williams, Mantle. He blasts. He's not as tough as Williams because he doesn't have the spin, but those are the two roughest guys in the league. No one else is even close." . . .

Whenever you consider the aspects of Nellie Fox's job for very long, you find yourself considering the New York Yankees. . . . The Yankees are not merely favored in American League races; they are conceded the pennant by the day spring training starts. Now, Nellie Fox is a considerable craftsman, quietly proud of his accomplishments. What was it like, I wondered, to run well in a hopeless race year after year?

Nellie considered the question for a minute, drumming his fingers on the table. Finally he said, "A ballplayer doesn't look at it that way."

"How does a ballplayer look at it?"

"We got a chance," Fox said. "We got a chance right now. We all have to have good years. The Yankees got plenty of ballplayers. All right. We got plenty of pitchers. If our pitchers and the rest of us have good years, we can beat them."

"But don't you ever feel that it's discouraging?"

"What's that?" Fox said.

"Playing the Yankees."

"I look forward to it," Fox said. "I like to play against the Yankees." He paused and then he said, "Look. I like to play ball. Everybody is in it for the money, sure, because you have to be in a business for money, like I got this bowling alley. But I look forward to every game. This is what I want to do and I'm doing it."

"Well, does the team look forward to it?" I asked. "You hear talk about choking."

"You don't choke," Fox said. "You get beat. Did the Yankees choke in the Series? They got beat by a better team. That's what happens. It isn't choking."

For a moment then, it seemed a little incongruous, sitting in a bowling alley between two towns whose combined population is a lot lower than a good crowd at Yankee Stadium, and discussing the White Sox and the Yankees.

"This must feel like a long way from the Majors," I said, "especially when it snows. Have you ever thought of moving to Chicago?"

Fox shook his head. "You seen what it's like around here?" he said.

"A little."

"Would you like to?" Fox said. "I can show you where I hunt, up on North Mountain, and the apple orchards, and the farms and creeks, and a place where some Amish people live. I'll have to take you over some dirt roads, but if you don't mind riding in a station wagon I can show you what it's like."

We started down the highway toward Chambersburg, and Fox turned off down the two-lane road to St. Thomas. "This here's all farms," he said, as we came to a rise in the road above a wide valley. "Out there," he said, pointing toward a range of hills low in the west, "that's where I hunt. A friend of mine has a stone cabin up there. You can't reach it except by jeep or tractor."

We rode past small farms for a while. "The people," Fox said, "a lot of them work in Chambersburg factories, maybe at night, and farm when they get a chance in the day. They're good people. Friendly. Nice to know. I like them."

We drove into and out of St. Thomas very quickly. "A real small town," Fox said, "but there're five different churches. We got a general store. When I get done with a season and all the excitement and I settle down and go up to the mountain hunting, it feels kind of different, kind of nice."

Fox veered off the little highway onto a bumpy road. "That's an apple orchard," he said, pointing again. "Over there's what used to be an orchard. But after the trees get old they don't bear good, and you cut them down and plant new ones. You use the old wood for fires."

It was winter and the apple trees were bare, but the afternoon was warm and the earth showed soft and rich. "Those are peach trees," Fox said. "A lot of apples and peaches around here."

He drove up to the shoulder of a mountain and parked next to a rambling two-story wooden building. "They pack apples here," he said. "I'll show you how it works."

Inside the building, the air felt cool and moist. The scent of apples was strong but not oppressive. . . . Wooden beams criss-crossed under the ceiling of the little building. The conveyor belt for apples, with its grates and chutes, immobile now, looked vaguely unreal, almost grotesque. But here Nellie Fox was at home. Just as he is at home in a crowded ballpark, leaning over the plate, his bottle bat ready to slap a slider. He is at home when he pivots around second and throws low, making a charging runner swallow a peck of dirt. But the apple factory and the sheer hills and the orchard are as much a part of the man as is baseball. . . . Fox belongs to the rolling country that lies south of the smoggy mill towns and dark mines of Pennsylvania. . . .

After we left the apple factory, Fox drove to meet his father, Jacob Fox, a foreman of carpenters who played semi-professional baseball near St. Thomas from 1917 to 1940. Jacob Fox lives in a neat frame house along the highway in St. Thomas, and when we met him he was sitting in a plush chair, fingering *The Sporting News*. The shock came when he put the paper down. In Jacob Fox's cheek was lodged a wad of chewing tobacco, just as implausibly big as the wads Nellie chews during working hours all season. The father and son look alike anyway, but the tobacco touch was something of a shock. . . .

"He started playing with a ball when he could hardly walk," Jacob Fox said. "He was always a good hitter; not a long hitter, but a good one."

"When," I asked, "did you realize your son was going to be a Major Leaguer?"

Jacob Fox laughed. "Never," he said. "I don't mind telling you I'm surprised."

"Wasn't he always way ahead of his age?"

"He was ahead, all right. In grade school he was playing with the high school boys. We wanted him to study more, but he always wanted to play ball. . . . I don't believe in forcing a boy to do anything. Just because I played ball, he didn't have to. But he loved it; he always loved to play ball. He taught himself to hit and to field and everything else."

A problem some talented young ballplayers face involves the ego. "There was a boy around here," Jacob Fox said, "who got to thinking he was better than he was. The boy had talent, but he never made it. Before Nellie started, I straightened him out. I told him, 'Do whatever the manager says. The manager is supposed to be right.' We never had any trouble with Nellie acting cocky. He never tried."

"Do you get much chance to see him play?"

"Oh, yes. I go over to Washington or to Baltimore whenever I can."

"What do you think when you see your son with a Major League ballclub?"

Jacob Fox glowed with quiet pride. "I'm just glad he's got the talent for it," he said. "I'm real glad."

Later, Nellie drove to his own home, perhaps two miles down the highway. It is a brick house, not large but adequate for Nellie and Joanne Fox and their two daughters. Nellie introduced his wife, and we started talking about the things that fans shout during a ball game. "I always have a deaf ear at the ballpark," Joanne Fox said. "You have to. You can't try to answer everybody."

Nellie invited me to take a look at his den in the basement. Downstairs, the walls were covered with trophies and pictures: Nellie with Harvey Kuenn, whom he admires; Nellie with Billy Pierce, his roommate; Nellie with Ted Williams, who he thinks is a wonderfully generous man. "He's real nice to the other players," Fox said. "He'll talk hitting with you all day long." . . .

He talked hunting for a while, gripping a gun as he spoke, and then he suggested a drive to Chambersburg for dinner. Over a steak, I asked him about hustle.

"You got to hustle," Nellie said.

"But don't you find yourself getting tired?"

"You get tired, sure," he said, "but you can't let up. There are too many other guys around. There's a lot of talent in baseball." Fox paused. "There are two things you have to keep doing," he said. "One is keep driving, the other is keep learning. When you stop doing either one, it's time to quit."

"What do you think is ahead for you?"

"Well, the bowling alley is for when I quit, but I'd like to stay in the game. Then I'd have the alley winters and baseball summers. I'd like that."

Back at the bowling alley, Nellie's partner Lucky Evertt wanted to make one point about Nellie. "The thing you should put in," Evertt said, "is that he's all real. I'm in business with him. And I know. When Nellie tells you something, you can believe it."

I left Chambersburg and reached a Major League town in five hours, which is a few years shorter than a similar trip took Fox. There was no baseball team at the high school in St. Thomas, but Nellie played town ball when he was twelve. For the high school, he played soccer. "I think I liked soccer better than baseball for a while," he says. "I was only about 130 pounds, but I liked the contact. I liked to mix it up."

Nellie was still a high school student in 1944 when he made a journey from St. Thomas to Frederick, Maryland, where the Philadelphia Athletics were training. Like the voyage of the *Bounty*, this trip has been told in many versions. A particular favorite here went like this: A few days after the Athletics opened their camp, a truck rattled into the ramshackle Blue Ridge League park at Frederick, and three people stepped out of the cab. There were a man and a woman and a moon-faced boy with a great big cigar sticking out of the middle of his features. The boy was sixteen years old. The truck was somewhat older.

Fox likes this version, too, but makes corrections. "In the first place," he says, "I wasn't riding in a truck. It was a car. And I wasn't smoking a cigar. If my dad saw a sixteen-year-old son of his smoking a cigar, he wouldn't take him to a baseball camp. He'd take him out to the woodshed for a workout."

Without the cigar and in an auto, Nellie's parents did drive him to the Athletics' camp. The year 1944 was a strange one for baseball.

Spring training took place in the North. Ted Williams was flying, Joe DiMaggio was on KP, and the Majors were populated by an assortment of inoffensive elderly gentlemen and enthusiastic children who were not old enough to be drafted. Some years, so small a boy as Nellie might be thrown back, but as soon as the 1944 A's found out that he was too young for the draft, they became interested.

"We took him to Frederick for two reasons," Jacob Fox says. "It was the nearest big-league camp to St. Thomas, and we figured Connie Mack was the sort of man we'd like to have looking after our son."

After watching Nellie put out, the Athletics signed him and shipped him to Lancaster in the Interstate League, where he broke in at first base. Then he played the outfield for Jamestown in the Pony League, and the next year—1945—he went back to Lancaster and started playing second. That season he led the league in games played, times at bat, runs, hits, and triples. He did not lead the league in home runs; he hit one, which, if nothing else, was more than he had hit the year before in eighty games. . . .

Nellie made it with the Athletics in 1949, and after batting .255, he was traded to the White Sox in October where he then hit .247. "After that, I got lucky again," he says. "They hired Richards, and he brought terrific teachers to Chicago. Those first two years were nothing. I didn't field very much better than I hit. When Richards got to Chicago, they straightened me around."

What happened was partly the result of sound coaching, partly the result of Richards's quick appreciation of Nellie's skills, and largely the result of Nellie's drive. In the spring, Roger Cramer studied Nellie at bat. "You're hitting too much off the front foot," he said. He worked on the kid's stance briefly, then handed him the bottle bat.

"You've got to fight in baseball," Fox says, "and you've got to know when to stop fighting. When they give you advice, you'd better stop and listen to them. By '51, I'd been up for two years. Suppose I'd gotten smart and told myself I didn't need coaching. You know where I'd be? I'd be out of the big leagues by now, that's where." . . .

While Cramer worked on Fox's hitting, Jimmy Adair, another coach, worked on his fielding, concentrating on the double play. According to Jackie Robinson, a second baseman can avoid being hit at second base if he reaches the bag early enough to fake. Robinson seldom was hit because, he says, he would make runners slide at his feint. Fox, who is only three-quarters of Robinson's size, does not find he can do this. "I've got no time to fake," he says. "I got to get rid of the ball as quick as I can before the runner hits me. It's a scramble when I make the double play, but I make it better now than I used to. I like that Schoendienst. I like to watch him around the bag. He moves so smooth—the best around."

Fox came out of the instruction sessions a finished ballplayer, but one who, having learned the benefits to be had from good coaching, was determined to absorb whatever additional lessons he could. By the time Marty Marion succeeded Richards as the White Sox' manager, Fox seemed—even to Marion, who knows these things intimately—a polished and versatile infielder. "He has terrific range," Marion said, "and what catches my eye is the way he handles pop flies. He's about as good at that as you'll ever see. No matter how far he's gone for a fly ball, what he gets his glove on, he'll hold."

When Al Lopez took over at Chicago, he was particularly impressed by Fox's bunting. "He didn't do it much," Lopez says, "but whenever he bunted for a base hit, he beat it out. I think the figures were nine-for-nine."

What Fox achieved then was mastery of advanced technical skills without losing his original drive.

Once in 1951, Richards recalls, he decided to rest Nellie for a few days. "He didn't sit in the dugout," Richards says. "He ran. Up and down, back and forth; for nine innings, he kept running and shouting at all the guys, cheering them and chewing them out. I took it for a couple of days. Then I had to put him back in the line-up. On the bench, he was driving me crazy."

"You've got to earn your pay," Fox says. "If you re on the bench, you've got to make some noise."

When Marion moved in, he tried to profit from Richards's experience. "It was in spring training," Marty says, "and Nellie had some kind of muscle pull. I didn't see any sense in playing him, but I didn't want to get what Richards got. So when the exhibition games were on the road, I made Nellie stay back at the hotel. When the games were in Tampa, I had him dress right after a light workout and watch the game from the stands. Then all of a sudden, the club started looking dead. It frightened me. In a couple of days I realized what it was. I was missing the racket that Fox makes whenever he's anywhere around the ball game." . . .

With the White Sox, Fox has won himself a reputation as a practical joker, which occasionally has unsettling results. Any teammate wanting to needle him has only to devise some gesture of rough humor. Fox invariably will be blamed. But it is a reputation honestly won and demonstrated most courageously one day in 1953 when the White Sox were playing the Cleveland Indians. Luke Easter, the Cleveland first baseman, was slightly taller than Ted Kluszewski but otherwise built along the same lines. Between innings, Fox, running off the field, scooped up Easter's glove and inserted a wad of used chewing tobacco in it. Then he resumed running, only faster.

When Easter stuck his huge hand into the glove, he sputtered. Then he swore. In a flash, he had eliminated four suspects and was focusing his attention on Fox.

"What the hell is this, you little gentleman?" he asked. "I oughta break your back. You try this again and I'll take you apart, sire."

Fox knows when to stop pushing a joke. He nodded to indicate that he understood and went to the water cooler.

Once, and only once, Fox used home runs to demonstrate a point. He was suffering through a batting slump early in 1955 when the White Sox were to play an exhibition game in Milwaukee.

"Maybe you need a rest, Nellie," Marion said. "Suppose you sit out the exhibition."

"I don't think I should," Fox said.

"You're entitled to a rest."

"I figure an exhibition game is what I need," Fox said. "It could be just the thing to bust the slump."

Marion compromised. He started Nellie and lifted him after a while.

Nellie grumbled for the next few days, then hit two home runs in a single game at Cleveland. "Fox," Marion announced proudly, "takes less managing than anybody else on this club."

For himself, Fox is high on Marion, and on Richards, and on Lopez. "Marty helped me around second base," he says. "Richards and Lopez play the same kind of game. They make moves, but only when they have to, only when it'll help."

It is a small irony of baseball that a player such as Fox, who could be managed by a butcher and still hit and make the plays, becomes a special favorite of professional managers. The men with temperament or problems or complexes about hitting curves always seem to represent something else. "I don't want to be around that guy," you'll hear managers say, "except when I have to. He's trouble."

Eventually, since he is smart and quick, someone is going to consider Fox as a manager. "I hope it happens," he says. "I'd like to try it, but I'm not going to let myself think about it. I'm thinking about my bowling alley. That makes more sense."

Along with the wad of tobacco and the cigars that he smokes constantly during each season, sense is a special feature of Nellie Fox. On an uncertain team in an unbalanced league, he goes about his work with hustle, because he is small, and swings for singles amid the thundering stampede for the Cadillacs parked beyond the fences. Out of this he has fashioned a special place for himself in baseball that is his own, even as Ted Williams has won his own place. For Williams, the glory comes through power; for Fox, it comes through practicing the lost arts of place-hitting and stern fielding.

It is surprising sometimes to think of the number of unhappy and disappointed men scattered through the high places on big-league baseball teams. Fox has his family and his singles, the rolling orchards and the friendly hills. . . . Boyish and cheerful, he seems to be a perfectly happy man, as happy as only a man can be who has what he wants and knows he got it for himself.

17

Rookie of the Year [Fiction]

Cosmopolitan, June 1958

A tale of a brilliant, destructive ballplayer whose drive for perfection leads him to suicide. This is the only work of fiction in the collection.

I suppose I knew Whistle Phyfe better than most, and if I had a quarter for every time someone came up to me and said, "How can you like that creep?" I'd be able to quit the newspaper and try writing stuff for television, which is where the real money is. Besides, I don't think I really liked Whistle. I admired him and I envied him and I pitied him, but how can you like a god? And that's what Whistle was, in a way. A god.

He was up there ahead of all of us, lost somewhere between Heaven and Earth. I don't know how he got lost, but I know this: anywhere Whistle traveled, he was alone. He could do one thing better than any man who ever lived, and maybe it's a silly thing, hitting a baseball, but Whistle did it with absolute perfection. There's loneliness in being perfect. First Whistle had to laugh at the imperfect guys, and then he had to laugh at what he could do, and in the end he was always laughing at himself.

Maybe you know my name. Joe Demer. I write a column for the *Standard* of New York. Every spring I make the rounds of the baseball training camps and knock out eight hundred words a day. It was in the spring eighteen years ago that I first heard about Whistle. He was a kid coming up with Chicago, and old Jack Grant, who's dead now, gave me the tip.

"Come on over to Cocoa Beach," he said, "if you want to see the greatest hitter in the world." . . .

Cocoa was all the way across Florida from St. Petersburg, where I was staying.

"Come on, yourself, Jack," I said. "It's too early for you to be boozing." That was a joke between us. Jack's club used to get so terrible, he'd have to drink in midseason to stay sane.

"Did I ever give you a bum steer?"

"No," I said.

"Well, get your tail over here. This kid was late reporting. Some trouble with his folks, or something. He just took a couple swings today, and if you show up tomorrow morning, you can be first with a helluva story."

I said I would, but I started drinking with a waitress, and I didn't get to Cocoa Beach until the next afternoon.

"You dumb clown," Jack Grant said. "The Chicago guys talked to him already. This morning he hit five straight outa the ballpark, and one went five hundred feet and knocked two coconuts off a palm. It'll be all over the papers by tonight."

"I'll settle for a New York exclusive," I said. "What's the kid's name?"

"Claude Duncan Phyfe," Grant said. "I call him Whistle. You know. Like a fife."

"Can he whistle?" I asked.

"How should I know if he can whistle?" Grant said. "He can hit. I'll take you up to his room."

Grant introduced us and told the kid he could trust me. Then he blew. That was the way Jack was if you treated him square. The kid was sitting in a chair by the window, staring at the palm trees outside the hotel. Whistle never changed much. He must have been born with that long, cold face.

"First time you've seen a palm tree?" I asked, to get him talking.

"First time I seen a lot of things," Whistle said. His grammar was pretty shaky when he started.

"You want a story?" he said. "The publicity man has it, what I hit in high school and all that. I hit pretty good everywhere I played. I'll hit good here."

"That's not the kind of story I want," I told him.

Whistle sat up straight. "What do you want?" he said.

"Something about you as a person," I said.

"As far as you're concerned I ain't a person," Whistle said. "I'm a ballplayer. That's all you got to know."

"Jack says you were late getting to camp," I said. "Rookies are usually early. What happened?"

He jumped up, and he wiped his hand across his mouth, and he charged at me. He kicked full force against the stuffed chair where I was sitting and caught the pillow about an inch from my leg. "You keep my folks out of this!" he shouted. "You worry about what I do on the goddam ball field, and you keep your nose out of my goddam life. If you don't, I don't care about Grant or anybody else. I'll knock your head through the wall."

He put his hand on my chin and shook my head from side to side. Usually I can handle myself, but Whistle's grip nearly flattened my face.

"I don't care 'bout your folks," I said, after he let go, kind of squashing out the words between my lips. "I'm learning plenty about you."

"I don't care what you learn and I don't care what you write, you son of a bitch," he said.

I've got one question I save for emergencies, like when it's late and I'm stuck for a column. "What did you dream about last night?" I said.

It was the only time I could ever con Whistle. "I'll tell you what I dreamt!" he shouted, so wild I thought his eyes would pop. "I dreamt somebody threw me a big, fat, slow curve, and there were fifty thousand people in the stands, and while I was watching the ball come up I forgot how to hit. Me, Claude Phyfe. I forgot. And I struck out, and the people started booing, and my father turned around and started beating up my mother and my mother began to cry." All of a sudden Whistle stopped, and he said very low, "You ever write that, I'll kill you."

"I'm sorry," I said, and I stuck out my hand.

"Sure," he said, and he took it. Then we started talking, and he gave me a pretty nice story about the way from the time he was six or seven he could always hit anything they threw.

I didn't see much of Whistle for a while after that afternoon in Cocoa, but I heard about him. He hit like Jack Grant said he would, and right away Chicago was a pennant contender, and some fans wanted to rename State Street Phyfe Place. But the boys in the business, the sportswriters, tabbed Whistle Phyfe as a rotten.

There's a kind of underground inside baseball. If a pitcher sticks his tongue out before he throws his curve or a batter can't hit a high, tight fastball, the news gets around the league in twenty-four hours. There's an underground in my business, too. If a guy is hard to interview, he's in trouble. The Chicago writers had wondered why Whistle was late to camp, just like I'd wondered, and he threw a few tantrums at them. Word got around that he went crazy if you asked about his folks, so naturally the fellows kept asking. Get a ballplayer raging, and you've got a story. Still, it's a miserable way to have to work, and the writers hated him.

I saw Whistle late in the season when Chicago had a big series at New York. It was during batting practice, and he was standing by himself away from the other players, who were talking to some newspapermen. He looked over at me.

"The only decent writer in the league!" Whistle shouted. He had a way of making his pronouncements loud so that they'd insult a dozen men. Then he'd pretend he didn't know they were there.

"I never write about dreams," I said. "I just use the question to keep people off balance."

"You like to have the upper hand," Whistle said.

"Don't you?" I asked.

"Hell," Whistle shouted, as though I'd said something really stupid, "I always have it."

"You're going good," I said.

"I'm swinging," he said. "I'm learning to be a hitter."

He was batting .386, better than anybody ever hit in his first year. "You're a hitter now," I said.

"I'm a beginner," he said. "I get fooled by pitches, I guess. Hitting's the most complicated business in the world, and you tell me I'm a damn hitter."

We talked a lot after that, and he gave me some columns that belong in a book of essays. He was trying to learn how to anticipate every pitch that had ever been invented by judging the speed of the ball right after it left the pitcher's hand. When he mastered this, he calculated, his only outs would be failings of the human machine. He had it worked out so that he should bat .500.

That was in his head. What the fans saw was something else. The hard, lean body would uncoil, and the power would start coming up from one ankle, through the knee, the hips, the back, into the shoulder, and then down through those tremendous arms. His wrists would whip like snakes, and those hands would make the bat speak, and it was one motion, the way a tree, rustled by the wind, moves in one motion. I don't ever say the game of baseball is beautiful, but Whistle swinging had all the beauty in the world.

He finished his first year at .378 and hit .398 the next season just before the war came. The day he left to become a flyer, Jack Grant said to me, "He's the greatest hitter I've ever seen, and he hasn't got a friend in the game."

"He rooms by himself, doesn't he?" I said. "He's aloof."

"It ain't that," Jack said, "and it ain't jealousy, either. It's that he laughs when the other guys look bad. He talks hitting with them, and he gives them every tip he's picked up, but it don't help most of them, and when they mess up, they get this laugh. Not like he's laughing at them so much. More like he's trying to pity them, and he just can't."

My bad stomach kept me out of the war, and I suppose it was because he didn't have other friends that Whistle wrote a few letters to me. They were good letters. There's one I still read.

"I go higher than larks or even eagles now," Whistle wrote. "I've got all this power in my hands, and sometimes I think I could fly off the top of the world out to where they say the sky is black. I wouldn't miss what I left behind. We all believe that we have to get killed. It's percentages, like hitting. I'm a hell of a flyer so maybe I can go up and fight seventy-five times and get away with it where most would be dead at fifty missions. But if the war lasts long enough, I'll be caught. I've got to be. It's funny, but I'm glad I'll die after eating a good breakfast. I can't control the crash, but while I'm living, I want it to be neat. Dying is something that's the same in a plane as anywhere else, and the important thing to me is living neat right up until the time the ball explodes."

Whistle came out an ace, and a lot of times he lost his plane, but he always crawled out and the parachute saved him. When he got back it was as if he'd never been away. Jack Grant was dead, and the new manager couldn't stand Whistle, so Chicago sent him to New York for two good pitchers and a center fielder who'd hit .300 in any league. It was the biggest trade in twenty years, and the day Whistle hit town he called me.

"How do you stand with the cops, Joe?" he asked. "Any drag?"

"A little," I said. "Billy Keefer, who used to be on the paper, is a deputy commissioner."

"Get us together," Whistle said.

We met in a bar near Lexington Avenue, and Billy stared at Whistle and asked for an autograph. "Can I trust this guy?" Whistle asked me.

"Sure," I said. "He's a dumb fan now, but not when he's working."

"I think something happened to my parents."

"Too bad," Billy said. "Auto accident?"

"They were in Chicago until a few months ago," Whistle said. "I sent them a check, and my mother said they were moving to New York to be near me."

"I'll bet they like to see you hit," Billy said.

"They've never been to a ball game," Whistle said.

Nobody said anything. I rattled the ice in my drink. It was small, not enough to hurt my ulcer. "If I gave you pictures of my folks," Whistle said to Billy, "could you find them and keep it out of the papers?"

"Inside a week," Billy said.

"It's a big city," I said.

"We got a lot of cops," Billy said.

Four days later a sergeant found Whistle's mother and father. Whistle telephoned and asked me to get the old man work.

"I haven't got a job for him," I said.

"Well, find one," Whistle said. "Come over with me and tell him what you can do."

It's easy to forget that some people live that way. Claude Duncan Phyfe Sr. and his wife had two rooms near the West Side docks, four flights up and no hot water. I didn't see the bedroom, but what passed for a living room, dining room, and kitchen looked as though it had been painted with soot. The mother and father sat on a straw sofa, and I sat on a straw chair. Whistle stood because there was no other place to sit except the floor.

"Howzit?" Whistle said.

"Okay," the old man said. "We're just getting situated, if you know what I mean." He was wearing old pants and a jacket that didn't match buttoned over an undershirt.

"Claude," the mother said, "you shouldn't bother with us. We're all right." I don't know what she was wearing. It was a sack. But she had Whistle's face. She looked proud.

"Mr. Demer, here, has a job for you, Dad," Whistle said. "Helping load papers for the *New York Standard*. It's eighty bucks for a five-day week."

"That's real nice of you, Mr. Demer," the old man said. "I guess Claude forgot to tell you about my heart."

"What about your heart?" Whistle said.

"I get these spells," the old man said. "Pains in my chest and in my back, and I get dizzy. I can't do no physical work, if you know what I mean."

"He gets tired easy, Mr. Demer," the mother said.

Whistle glared at his father. "We're proud of you," the old man said. "Awful proud."

"He's a fine boy," I said.

"A toast to my son," the old man said. He got up and so did the mother, and they ran an awkward race to a cupboard with the woman shouting, "No, Claude, not now!"

It may have been an accident or he may have tripped her, but anyway, she fell to one side. She squealed a little when she hit the floor, not like someone in agony but like someone who has been hurt so much that any more pain, no matter how small, is unbearable. She lay there, and the old man froze with one hand in the cupboard, and she looked at Whistle and started sobbing and talking all at once.

"Don't send us no more money, son," she said. "He takes it, and he drinks, and he's a wild man when he drinks, you know that. He keeps drinking, and he could kill me some night. He could choke me to death. Just leave us be and don't send no more money."

She was still begging when Whistle dragged me out of there. In the cab I said to him, "You need a girl."

He laughed at me. "I've had plenty of girls," he said.

"I'm talking about a girl to settle down with," I said.

"I live by myself," Whistle said.

"There's a writer who says, 'Home is where, when you want to go there, they have to take you in,'" I said. "Where do they have to take you in, Whistle? Where have you got a home?"

"Anywhere in the world I've been ever since I was a kid," he said, "there've been more people wanting to take me in than I could accommodate." He laughed again. "If you've got a cousin you want me to date, I'll take her out."

It wasn't a cousin. There was a girl on the paper named Carol Crimmin who almost reminded me of Whistle. She was tall and lean and beautiful, and there was a restlessness about her that bothered every man she knew. I sat in for a while the afternoon she and Whistle met, and in the beginning I had to do all the talking. They just kept feeling each other out with their eyes.

"I'm afraid I don't know much about baseball," she said, finally.

"Neither does Joe," Whistle said. "What do you know about?"

"A little about how to write a story."

"What about the big things?" Whistle said.

"What big things?" she said.

"How to leave neatly," Whistle said. His grammar was excellent by this time.

"I live very neatly," she said.

"But everything isn't neat," Whistle said. "What do you know about the part of life that isn't neat?"

I knew what he meant, and she must have guessed. "Different parts of life belong in different places," she said. "The couch goes in one room. The bed in another."

I took off, and nobody noticed. They were married about a month later, and Carol called me once to say thanks.

There were times when Carol struck fire, but she wasn't a god. She knew perfection from the outside better than I, but just the same it had to be beyond her. For two years the marriage went better than I would have believed. Whistle hit .410 and .408. New York won the World Series twice, and Carol even went to a dozen games. Early in the third year Whistle asked me to come home after a game, and I saw that Carol was in trouble.

"Hello, Joe," she said, and she slurred it.

"What the hell?" Whistle said. "Again?"

"Again," Carol said, with a funny nod. "Eight nights now, and I won't stop."

She had put on flesh around the cheeks. "I'll go," I said.

"No," Carol said. She reached for me, and Whistle pushed her, and we fell on the thick blue foyer carpet. I rolled away, and Carol got on all fours and shook her head from side to side.

"You're his friend," Carol said. "Tell him that a person needs to be needed. Tell him that he ought to share himself. Never needs me. Not even when—" Whistle clapped his hand over her mouth. I left. I haven't seen Carol since.

I tried to talk to Whistle. He heard me out every time, but I couldn't reach him. I don't think Carol needed much from Whistle, but the trouble was he didn't need anything from her. It was all inside himself. That machine he had inside him ran itself, and he was a whole man, without parents or children or even a woman, except sometimes. He hit well when you figured he was happy, and he hit well when you figured he was sad. Right after she divorced him he got six hits in a double-header.

After that he took up flying again. He bought a little Stetson and kept it at Teterboro over in Jersey, and every decent day he'd cruise around. He brought me along once, and we went out over the Atlantic, and he showed me a few simple spins and rolls. I don't like flying even in a four-engine plane, and when they make them with seventeen engines that still won't be enough. But with Whistle holding the stick it was different. He could fly just as well as he could hit.

"You could make a living flying," I told him.

"Sure," he said. "Maybe I should have stayed in or gone with an airline."

"Not a hitter like you," I said.

"I ought to be able to hit," he said. "I'm a grown man. The whole thing was invented for kids."

I wasn't near him the next time he flew. I've checked it, though. The temperature was 43 degrees. The wind was from the southeast at four knots an hour. The sky was clear.

He climbed to 1,500 feet, and the plane went into a spin and piled up on a field where it wouldn't hurt anybody else. Our paper wrote it up like this:

"Claude D. (Whistle) Phyfe, 34, the greatest hitter in modern baseball history, was killed yesterday when his single-engine plane crashed near Teterboro Airport, N.J. Mr. Phyfe, a World War II ace, had resumed flying only recently, and investigators believe that he lost control of his plane."

Whistle never lost control of a plane any more than he lost control of a bat. I knew the guy. I knew his reflexes. I even figure I know what happened. It wasn't Carol, and it wasn't his mother and father—it was himself alone up there. I figure he thought of himself and the place where the sky is black, and he laughed that cold, inhuman laugh. Then he kicked the stick forward and held it with both hands until the crash destroyed him.

18

How the Other Half Lives

Sport, October 1958

Traveling with the last-place Washington Senators, a team that loses four or five games a week—every week. A bit poignant, perhaps, but mostly very funny.

The office has no window, which seems funny until you remember that a few years ago the manager of the Washington Senators had no office at all. Charlie Dressen persuaded the club to build one before he left, and they did the best they could with the available space. Still, the office has no window.

The manager slumped behind his desk, below two achievement plaques, and sipped coffee out of a white porcelain mug. A baseball writer who sat facing the plaques was talking about trades the Senators might have made but didn't. Another baseball writer was telephoning a story to his paper. On the floor a radio man crouched over a portable phonograph. "Wait till you hear this," Bob Wolff, the radio man, said. "Albie Pearson, Roy Sievers, and the rest. The Singing Senators. It'll surprise you."

"The Singing Senators," said Cookie Lavagetto, the manager, grinning.

"Lumenti," Bob Addie told someone on the sports desk of the *Washington Post & Times-Herald.* "That's Ralph L-u-m-e-n-t-i, the pitcher. Yeah, they sent him out."

"I'll bet with one more first-class pitcher this club would have stayed up," Burt Hawkins of the *Washington Star* said.

"Do you mind, Cookie?" Bob Wolff said.

"No," Lavagetto said. "Hell, go ahead and play it."

"One more pitcher," Hawkins said.

The voices of the Singing Senators blared out of the phonograph with a song Bob Addie had written for their appearance on the NBC television program *Today*. They sang to the tune of "Take Me Out to the Ball Game."

We play Major League baseball,
That's the living we choose.
When we're in front we are heroes all,
But when we lose
We hear nothing but boos.
For its hit, hit, hit for the home team,
You've got to produce every day.
There are times when all of us wish
We were Garr-o-waaaay.

"Now," Wolff said, "on the next band Pearson comes in with a solo on 'Night and Day.'"

Lavagetto got up to wash his coffee mug. "Could you make it a little lower?" he said.

"What have we got now," Addie said, "the Pearson solo?"

"I mean this man's trying to phone in a story," Lavagetto said.

"Sure thing, Cookie," Wolff said. He cut the volume.

"That's it," Addie said into the phone. "Right." He hung up, looked around, and started to laugh. "What is this," he said, "a Marx Brothers movie?" Pearson's tenor carried the opening lines of "Night and Day" softly through the room.

Outside the manager's office, Ken Aspromonte went up to Lumenti. "Good luck, Ralph," he said, "and take care of that arm."

Lumenti nodded, his eyes wide, but did not answer.

"Hey, Yost," someone shouted, "there's a blonde outside wants to see you."

Eddie Yost smiled and fastened his tie. A few players standing close to him laughed. It was a hot, muggy Sunday in Washington DC, and the Senators had just lost a double-header to Cleveland.

There is only one way Major Leaguers play baseball. They play to win. They don't shout, "Pretty!" the way tennis players may after an ace, or grunt, "Nice putt," the way some golfers do. They play hard, and even if they're tired, eight teammates and the boss can jump them if they loaf. At the top, baseball is a difficult and relentless game.

The big leagues are a dozen fast-ball pitchers throwing at Mickey Mantle's bad knee and bench jockeys riding a scared rookie. They're spikes at second base, crowds jeering the man in the slump, and six managers fired in a year. They're endorsements, if you win, and annuities, if you win, and a big house with a swimming pool and bar.

The Washington Senators don't win. They lose eighty-five or ninety or one hundred games each season and drop out of the pennant race in June. As the Washington franchise exists, failure has become an unvarying condition of employment. Yet the men who play for Washington have been used to winning. As schoolboys and as minor leaguers, they wanted to win, and in fact, they did win often enough to get a crack at the big leagues. It was a long climb and for most of them a slow one, marked by good earned run averages and hits. Then, when they finally reached a pinnacle, they discovered that everything had changed.

They were good ballplayers, but now they found they were not quite as good as the men who played for Boston, Detroit, and Chicago. They were used to losing hard, because that's what they were taught and that's how they were constructed, but at Washington they lost two days out of every three. Simply to survive, they had to adjust to finishing eighth in an eight-team race, and the adjustment went against their grain. But they tried, each man seeking his own way.

"Look," says Rocky Bridges, who arrived as shortstop for a cellar club, "I'm not kidding myself. I'm not what Pee Wee [Reese] used to be. But this is a good life here. I've traveled. I never had much education. I've learned in baseball. And now in Washington, look at the things I can see, the big sights I've always heard about. When my kids get a little older, it'll be even better. On off days, I'll take them around."

"But doesn't last place bother you?"

"Sure it bothers me, but I like to play, and on the other clubs I had to ride the bench."

"I used to be platooned," says Roy Sievers, who has become a star slugger with the Senators. "Here I get into every game. I've made a name for myself. That's a big thing."

"What's the difference between first place and last place?" says Ellis Clary, a coach who played for the only St. Louis Browns team that won a pennant. "You sleep in the same hotels, you eat in the same restaurants, you play in the same ballparks, and you travel the same way. I guess I'd have to say the only difference is that with a last-place club you don't get to touch home plate as often."

"You know," says Yost, the third baseman, who has a master's degree in education, "I've always been with this club. We went pretty well a couple of years, but I can't say I miss being with a winner because I've never really been with one since college." Here Yost, who is growing bald, grins. "That was a while ago," he says. "I like the business and I like the organization. Once, maybe, before I'm through I'd like to be with a contender. You know, to sort of see how it feels. But I like it here. I feel at home."

Most players and coaches in the second division live with almost as much security as players and coaches enjoy on a contending team. The Senators finish last partly because there is no pressure from the minor leagues forcing ordinary big leaguers out of jobs. On the Yankees, where the big leaguers are more than ordinary, the pressure from below is proportionately more intense. So Herb Plews at second, pressed by no one, feels as safe as Gil McDougald, pressed by Bobby Richardson or Tony Kubek or the new face of 1959.

The difference hits the manager hardest. He may survive for several years, working diligently with inadequate material, but eventually the customers are going to grow tired, as customers of losing ballclubs always do. "Let's get some ballplayers," thousands of them demand. "Fire the manager," one of them suggests. Then the front office, which cannot afford to get ballplayers, makes one move it can easily afford. It fires the manager, with officials hinting broadly that great new days lie just ahead.

Harry Lavagetto is a baseball professional with a dark face, marked by deep lines and an expression of sorrow. He learned baseball as a game you play to win. The first time he showed up in a Major League camp, the Depression raged through the country. "I've got to make it," Lavagetto told himself, "for the money."

On his first time at bat in an intrasquad game, Lavagetto singled cleanly to right field. At first base, filled with delight, he burst into laughter. "I was a kid," he remembers, "and I was happy."

Pat Moran, a veteran who was pitching, turned red. "Laugh at me, you bush son of a bitch!" Moran shouted. "We'll see who ends up laughing, busher."

The next time Lavagetto came to bat, Moran threw four straight fastballs at his head. As he trotted to first base, Moran called after him, "You still think it's goddam funny, busher?" Lavagetto didn't answer. He had begun to understand the Major Leagues.

Later Lavagetto took signs Chuck Dressen stole and drilled critical hits during the Dodgers' drive toward the 1941 pennant. In 1947, near the end of his playing career, he hit a fastball Bill Bevens of the Yankees threw, lining it against the right-field wall in Ebbets Field. With that classic ninth-inning drive, he broke up a no-hitter and won a World Series game for Brooklyn.

These were high and serious deeds within his business, and in other ways Lavagetto learned repeatedly just how merciless the business can be. He was Dressen's lieutenant when Walter O'Malley dropped his pilot after the Dodgers won the 1953 pennant. Talk followed that Lavagetto might manage Brooklyn, but it died quickly. Outraged at the firing, Lavagetto compressed his fury into a three-word wire. It read, "Please accept resignation."

Now in his midforties, he runs a team that laughs a lot because it has to, and he has a job that depends on the play of these men who laugh. He is grayer than when he played for pennant winners, but Lavagetto still talks in a gruff, laconic way, as though words make him feel slightly uncomfortable.

"I'm just learning about managing," he says. "What have I got to be disappointed about?"

"The standings."

"I'm lucky to still be in baseball, and I'm damn glad. But isn't this different," Lavagetto says. "These guys don't loaf and, what the hell, I'm learning. I'm learning a hell of a lot of things."

The day after they lost two games to Cleveland the Senators flew to Detroit for a series with the Tigers, who had just started to roll under manager Bill Norman. It was not a cheering prospect. The Tigers were hot. The Senators, with limited power, were getting fair pitching from Pete Ramos, Russ Kemmerger, and Truman Clevenger, but their bullpen had suddenly gone bad.

They boarded a 5:30 plane at Washington National Airport. . . . While they were waiting for the pilot to start the engines, Ellis Clary began to tell about another flight. "We come into the airport and hit the runway, and I guess they were trying out a rookie pilot," Clary said. "Anyway, we bounced half as high as the Washington Monument. I called the hostess over, and I told her, 'Ma'am, I'm willing to get offa this thing, but you tell the pilot he didn't give me a sporting chance.'"

"Tell that to Courtney," someone said.

"Once we get off the ground in one piece," Sievers said, "Clint is going to be so rejoiced, he ain't gonna listen."

The plane took off in one piece, and as soon as it gained altitude the pilot made an announcement on the public address system. "We're very happy to have the Senators aboard," he said. "We want to wish them luck in Detroit. This plane is called a Stratocruiser, and down the stairway in the center you'll find a lounge. It's one of the biggest and most comfortable planes you can fly, but I'm afraid they're going to take it out of service. They've just put in coatracks for the crew, and whenever this company does something like that, you can figure they're getting ready to sell the aircraft."

"Jokes," Rocky Bridges said.

It was a warm, clear day, the sky dappled with low clouds but the air lane stretching smooth and bright. In the lounge Clint Courtney sipped a beer. "It ain't no different for me no matter where I play," he said.

"That's right," another Senator said. "That's why Bridges has to get on you."

"Who gets on me?" Courtney said.

"If he don't bear down," the other player said, "you ought to hear old Rocky call him stub-jumper. It gets Clint mad."

"Look at that cloud formation," someone said, "just outside beneath your window, Clint."

"Ain't gonna look out that goddam thing," Courtney said. "I'm a farmer. I like dirt."

The plane droned quietly at twelve thousand feet, and Courtney started discussing farming with a passenger. If the stranger knew that Courtney was a ballplayer, he did not show it. He listened attentively for a time, then got up, smiled at the bartender, and walked upstairs to his seat.

Howard Fox had chartered a bus for the long ride from Ypsilanti Airport to the Sheraton Cadillac Hotel in Detroit. The players filed on quickly, Lavagetto taking the seat behind the driver so he could count heads. Walter "Boom-Boom" Beck, a gray-haired coach who once pitched for cellar clubs in Philadelphia, was one of the last men aboard. Beck stopped at the top of the stairs and abruptly chanted: "My mother was walking around the room, / She was walking around with a broom."

He paused, then beat the air like a conductor.

"Boom, boom," came a chorus of ballplayers. "My mother was walking around the room, / She was walking around with a broom."

Again Beck signaled.

"Boom, boom," the chorus repeated, this time less boisterously.

"It's just something he sings," Burt Hawkins explained. "Nobody knows what it means. He just sings it."

"Boom, boom," Beck said and grinned and sat down. . . .

The hotel was crowded with railroad men, there for a convention. It was close to nine o'clock, Washington time, when the Senators arrived. Their rooms were ready. Most of them bought newspapers and went to bed.

Early the next afternoon the players gathered in little knots within the lobby, waiting to eat early dinners before the night game. Ed Fitz Gerald, the veteran catcher, sat on a leather couch and folded a newspaper. "It was a nice break for me to get to this club," Fitz Gerald said. He speaks quietly and listens courteously. "The Pirates had a couple of catchers ahead of me. They needed a knuckleball catcher so they had to keep Mike Sandlock. I thought I might go down to the minors, but I came here."

The Pirates, when Fitz Gerald left them, were a club that Branch Rickey described as last on merit. "Looks like I only been on last-place clubs," Fitz Gerald said. He grinned self-consciously. "But in '48 the Pirates were real close. We had a chance until September. Then the Phillies knocked us out of the race. It's a little different now, but not so much. You battle as hard. You want to get there. Sure, if you're way out in any game you get discouraged, but a club like this you figure it can get up. I mean what is it? It's good years. If we all have good years together we can get up."

Ellis Clary had come back from afternoon shopping. "I'll tell you it's more fun when you win," he said. "Win a pennant, and everything is funny. You can't hardly stop from laughing." He smiled broadly, but he was serious.

At the desk a bald-headed man was checking in. "Ain't that Leo?" Ed Fitz Gerald said.

"Sure is," Clary said. "That's Durocher, all right."

When he was finished registering, Durocher walked past the little group, striding like a man on a mission. He stared straight ahead. He did not see the last-place Senators, or if he saw, he did not notice. The old baseball man walked into an elevator without stopping to chat with the last-place baseball men.

"Wonder what he's in town for?" Clary said.

"You know him?" someone asked.

"I guess I met him a couple times," Clary said. "Guess he don't remember."

"He's working in radio," Fitz Gerald said. "He must be here on some publicity."

In a little while the players drifted off to eat. They took taxis for the short trip to Briggs Stadium, and on the field they jabbered during batting practice.

"Bet I heet one," Pete Ramos, who was to pitch, told Bob Addie. "Easy park to heet one in."

"A Coke," Addie said.

"Five peetches," Ramos said.

"Okay," Addie said.

Ramos hit the first pitch to deep left, but it was foul by a substantial margin. On the next four, he didn't come close. "Bad weend, I guess," he said.

"A Coke," Addie said.

"Hey," Albie Pearson said, "you look hung over, Sammy Champagne."

"What are you talking about?" Addie said.

"I saw you," Pearson said. "On the plane you were drinking champagne, Sammy Champagne. You're hung over."

"It was Scotch," Addie said, "and I feel fine."

"Sammy Scotch, then," Pearson said.

19

The Crucial Part Fear Plays in Sport

Sport, **August** 1959

I talk to running backs, linemen, ballplayers, and tennis stars about the fear they feel at crucial moments. Fear of fumbling, fear of striking out, and most of all fear of looking like a fool.

A few hours after the Dodgers had turned the harvest moon blue by winning the 1955 World Series from the New York Yankees, Pee Wee Reese was idling at the bar in an aged Brooklyn hotel that was the site of the official victory party. Reese had thrown out the final batter on a routine ground ball to shortstop.

"Hey, Pee Wee," said a nearby semidrunk, "what was you thinking with two outs in the ninth?"

Reese smiled benignly. "I was just hoping the next man wouldn't hit the ball to me," he said.

"Shmerf?" said the drunk, in surprise, as his beer asserted itself.

Well, there it was. Honest, intelligent Pee Wee Reese had given an honest, intelligent answer, and anyone within hearing distance could now report that a great professional had known the cold hand of fear in the clutch. But had the drunk asked the same question of a duller ballplayer, had he picked on a triumphant rockhead, things might very well have been reversed. Pinned against a stein of beer, the rockhead probably would have been the man to say, "Shmerf?"

The quick conclusion, which is that the dull athlete was not touched by fright, is careless and probably incorrect. A dull athlete might have felt far more fear than Reese did, but he could not have put the feeling into intelligible English. Emotion, not words, is the issue, and it's ridiculous to assert that you have to be smart to be afraid. I know a six-year-old shortstop, not especially precocious, who feels exactly as Reese did, every time he sees his pitcher throw the ball.

One day last spring, I was driving down a flat, narrow Florida highway to cover a sports car race at Sebring. It had been raining, and water lay in dull black puddles near the palmettos along the side of the road. The car jerked and hissed through the water as I kept it at 60 miles an hour, and I remember thinking that the men who were trying to do 120 at Sebring must be having a difficult time.

It was night when I reached the race course, and Phil Hill, a slim Californian who is accepted as the best American driver, was pacing near the pits, his driving done, his team's victory all but assured. Hill is a sensitive-looking man, just over thirty, who reads a great deal and whose musical taste runs to Beethoven.

"How was it out there?" I said.

"What kind of a question is that?" Hill said, intensely. "Can't you imagine what it was like?"

I had to admit I'd never driven a Ferrari.

"A bloody nightmare," Hill said, his face going pale. "Some courses drain. This one doesn't. Trying to control the car out there for me was like it would be for you trying to drive on ice. I was moving. There must have been five, six, a dozen times when I thought I was dead. I'd hit a puddle, and the car would start to go, and I'd be skidding toward somebody, and I'd figure this was it. It wasn't, but don't ask me how. Lord, don't ask me how I'm still alive." Hill's hands were shaking. They continued to shake, and for a time he was so wound up in tension that he was unable to stop talking.

Two years ago, before the start of an equally dangerous auto race, a reporter asked Juan Manuel Fangio, the former world champion driver, if he was thinking about death.

"Death?" Fangio said. "I only give it a quick, glancing thought."

Fangio is a phlegmatic man who once drove a bus in Argentina and who seems far less imaginative than Hill. Again the outward signs indicate that the egghead, Hill, was frightened, and the duller man, Fangio, was not. But last year, still in his prime and still a champion, Fangio quietly retired from Grand Prix racing. Despite his stolid disposition, he was afraid that matters might turn around, that Death might now give quick, glancing thoughts to Juan Manuel Fangio.

Fear strikes athletes without regard to race, creed, or intelligence. It also strikes them without regard to the actual peril in their work. For the fear athletes feel is composed of two distinct things. First, there is the fear of physical pain. Here we have auto racers afraid of auto wrecks, jockeys afraid of horses' hooves, halfbacks afraid of linebackers, batters afraid of beanballs, and swimmers afraid of the water. Then there is the fear, psychological but still real, of performing badly in front of an audience. Thus we have pitchers afraid to throw changeups, quarterbacks afraid to call their own plays, golfers afraid of the first tee, and girl tennis players afraid that their gold panties won't catch the summer sunlight.

Sometimes an athlete feels such physical fear that he cannot so much as move his head out of the way of an inside pitch. Sometimes he feels such psychological fear that he cannot pick up the sort of grounder he has handled ten thousand times before. Sometimes an athlete's fear is a combination of the physical and psychological. But at different times and in different ways, all athletes learn what it is to be afraid.

During the 1952 Olympics, Ingemar Johansson, the Swedish Tiger, was matched against the late Ed Sanders in a heavyweight bout. After a few moments of preliminary sparring, Johansson sized up his opponent and ran. He didn't actually run out of the ring, because the ropes were in the way, but he fled as best he could inside the ring, obviously terrified, until kindly Olympic officials intervened and awarded the fight to Sanders.

"Ingemar, for shame!" one Swedish newspaper headlined, unkindly. "He's worse than the British heavies," an American sportswriter said. "They always get knocked out, but at least they take a couple of punches first."

Johansson himself had no comment. Sanders outweighed him by more than twenty pounds and possessed a fierce scowl, but no losing fighter ever pleads fright. The difference between Johansson then and Johansson now is partly craft, but it is also that he has learned to control the fear all fighters feel. When Johansson is frightened these days, he punches or back-pedals or clinches or covers up. He no longer does what comes naturally, which is to run.

A jockey, to be successful, must be willing to urge his horse into potentially fatal positions. He must move up between a rival horse and the rail even though the outside horse may lunge in at any time, closing the gap. He must move between two other horses, although either may veer and cause an accident.

Some years ago, in spots of this sort, Eddie Arcaro had four spills in ten days. Each time, as he lay in the dirt, horses thundered past, their hooves knifing up clods of dirt and drumming like a charge of cavalry. "For around two weeks," Arcaro said, "I couldn't get to sleep without seeing those hooves around my head. Gradually, the fear waned. I wouldn't say I'm ever afraid of a horse now," Arcaro insisted recently. "I'm nervous about some, sure, but if I was actually afraid of one, what the hell, I just wouldn't ride him, and that hasn't happened."

Some riders become so involved with fear that they stop taking chances. In the tack room, their colleagues say simply, "He's riding like a married jock." There is no quicker way for a jockey to go out of business. He must either find a way to live with his fear or quit.

Ten days before the Army-Navy football game last fall, Red Blaik, the cool, analytical man who coached Army football for almost two decades, was holding forth on halfbacks he had known. Traditionally, Army halfbacks run with a difference—knees high, head up, driving over, around, or through the opposition. Speed, Blaik was saying, and feinting and intelligence. He was walking across a practice field where Pete Dawkins and Bob Anderson were running against a scrub line. "Watch them," Blaik said.

The backs ran hard, and after they were hit they sprang up instantly, as if unwilling to give their tacklers any more than the bare minimum of satisfaction. Another Army back was hit and limped slightly.

"All right," Blaik said, "no limping. If you have to limp, don't scrimmage. If you want to scrimmage, don't limp."

The limp disappeared in a hurry.

"Over here," Blaik said, indicating another part of the field, "is a boy with as much physically as Anderson or Dawkins. Maybe he even has more."

A jayvee halfback was plunging but not in the accepted Army style. He ran well, but just before he was hit, there was a slight but noticeable change in frame. The body tightened, stiffened, tensed, and it was clear that the back was bracing for a fall even before the lineman touched him. When a tackler missed, the back, ready to be tackled, lost a step before regaining full speed.

"Something you have to understand," Blaik said, "is that this isn't a question of courage, pure and simple. The boy could turn out to be a war hero. It's just that he doesn't like body contact. I've seen this hundreds of times, and you can nearly always tell from the beginning. Some of them do and some of them don't. A boy who doesn't like contact shouldn't play football, because he isn't going to change."

If fighters change, and jockeys change and learn to live with fear, why not college halfbacks? The answer ultimately comes down to time. Johannson was young enough to be a college student when he ran, and Arcaro, in his sleepless days, was only slightly older. A college halfback is through at twenty-two. Dealing with physical fear is a question of gradually accepting hazards, day after day, week after week, until suddenly they no longer seem dangerous. Humans are adaptable, but the adaptations require patience. One simply does not march into a battle area the first time as calmly as one does the second or third. A fighter of twenty-two is likely to be more frightened than he will be three years, or thirty bouts, later. But there is a point where things turn around, where too many years of living with fear break down human drive. Fangio reached that point before he quit. Jersey Joe Walcott fought superbly against Rocky Marciano once, but the second time he sat down promptly after a punch of indeterminate power. Walcott knew Marciano could hit. He took his second purse without a review lesson.

The path of physical fear varies with the athlete, of course, but a general pattern does exist. First, the athlete encounters fear. This may come when he is a child, or when he is older, or only after he has been hurt. Then, for a time, he is at war with himself. Are the fun of the game and the pleasure of victory worth the risk of pain? The good athlete always answers yes and sets about controlling his fear. Finally, after enough years in sports, it all gets to be too much trouble and he quits. He either sits down in the ring or he retires.

The other fear in sports, fear of failure, is less predictable, more common, less understood, more discussed, and runs into the science of psychiatry. To me it has seemed clearest in terms of poker.

Consider the frightened poker player who is dealt three kings. He blinks, his stomach talks, and he raises like a man who has been dealt a pair of deuces. It isn't purely money, for he plays with the same outrageous caution, regardless of stakes. It's chiefly that fear drives common sense out of his head.

He looks at his three kings and he considers. The man at his right is due for a straight. (No one is ever due for anything in cards. Each deal is independent of the others.) The next man seems confident. Maybe he has a full house. The dealer is smiling. He probably loaded the deck. So it goes, and eventually the man with three kings gets about half of what he would have won if he had kept his head.

The nonfrightened poker player knows that three kings will probably be good enough. He bids accordingly, and . . . the next time he has three kings he plays exactly the same way. At its worst, fear paralyzes, but rarely in sports does fright assume such proportions. What psychological fear does most frequently is block the normal reasoning process.

When Early Wynn pitches against the Yankees, he glares and knocks hitters down precisely as he would against any other team. But it is not quite the same operation. "Sometimes," he says, "when I get behind to a hitter, I figure I got to do something because here is Mantle coming up and maybe Berra and Skowron. I get behind, and I figure I can't walk this guy, and I can just feel that fear."

Wynn's solution, arrived at over the years, is to inhale mightily. "After I take that deep breath," he says, "I feel okay." The deep breath doesn't throw strikes, but it enables Wynn to forget what might happen and concentrate on the business at hand.

The best clutch ballplayer I remember was a man who suffered a nervous collapse during World War II, who jumped a team because he was homesick, and who absolutely refused to travel by airplane. His name is Billy Cox, and although there have been many better ballplayers, I can't think of anyone whose game improved so much under pressure.

Cox was a third baseman, a small, wiry man with big, bony wrists who subdued ground balls with a little scooping motion and was one of the finest fielders of his time. Before ordinary games, Cox often busied himself thinking up excuses for not playing, but whenever the Brooklyn Dodgers were faced with an important series, he was almost eager to go to work.

In the big ones, he was everywhere. He guarded the line, cut in front of the shortstop, and charged topped balls with such agility that Casey Stengel once complained during a World Series, "He ain't a third baseman. He's an unprintable acrobat." Cox was never a great hitter, but he was far better swinging in a clutch than he was when it didn't matter.

"I can't explain it," Cox once said. "My wife says I have fearless nerves. Anyway, before the big ones, I feel my nerves all tightening up, sort of getting ready. You know what I mean?"

"But what about the homesickness?"

Cox's lean face was grim. He does not usually have much to say. "I believe that everybody has some kind of problem," he said. "No matter how good a ballplayer is, there's something that bothers him. My problem was that I got lonesome on the road. It takes nerve to lick your problem, but you got to have it."

"Well, doesn't it take nerve to play in clutch games?"

"They never bothered me," Cox said. "I never got scared. The thing that bothered me was that I wanted to go home."

Stan Musial insists that no one can be afraid and play baseball well. "If you're worried about what happens when you go bad," Musial says, "you shouldn't even get in the business." Musial is calling this as he sees it, but he forgets his own outlook when he left Donora, Pennsylvania, for the great world of baseball with his wife, whose father owned a grocery.

"I'm not scared," he told a friend, "because if the baseball doesn't work out, I can always get a job in the store."

In the theater, a single term—stage fright—sums up all fear of failure. In sports, which cover so large an area and employ so varied a jargon, there are a dozen words for what is roughly the same thing. "Choke" is currently most popular.

"When I get out on the field before the opening kickoff I feel it," Randy Duncan, Iowa's great quarterback last season, has remarked.

"I can't eat breakfast that day, and when I see the crowd, I guess you could say I'm choked up. Then, on the kickoff, I have to belt someone. As soon as I block a guy hard, the fear disappears. Just body contact once, and I stop choking."

Tennis player Gussie Moran, in her greatest days, found a less taxing solution. "On the pro tour," she says, "I'd get so worried I wouldn't make a good showing, I started taking a slug of Canadian Club before each match. I got so I couldn't play at all without the slug."

The only tie between Phil Hill, trembling after an auto race, and Gussie, downing a shot before the first serve, is the fact of fear, and this drives to the root of the crucial role fear plays in sports. It doesn't matter what there is to be afraid of, whether it's death, or failure, or disgrace, or a double fault. The point is that there is something to cause fear in every avenue of sport, and whatever exists is sufficient. To the athlete, fear is a condition of the job.

Sometimes, after much research, a man announces that fighters or bull fighters or pitchers who have learned to beat the Yankees are the bravest men in sports. But no one knows the fear someone else feels, and so no one can prepare a valid yardstick of athletes' bravery. Only this much is sure: they are all afraid of different things in different ways at different times. It is never possible to conquer fear, but it can be subdued for a time. Watch the great athlete work at his craft, and you see someone who has known fear before and who will know fear again but who goes about his job fearlessly. This is the courage of an athlete and it is towering to behold.

Part 3

Changing Times

20

The Benching of a Legend

Sports Illustrated, September 12, 1960

Stan Musial has stopped hitting, and it falls to Cardinals manager Solly Hemus, himself no more than a journeyman ballplayer, to assign the great slugger to the bench.

Disturbing paradoxes surround an aging baseball player. He is old but not gray, tired but not short of breath, slow but not fat as he drives himself down the first-base line. Long after the games, when the old ballplayer thinks seriously, he realizes that he has become obsolete at an age when most men are still moving toward their prime in business and, in politics, are being criticized for their extreme youth. It is a melancholy thing, geriatrics for a forty-year-old.

To Joe DiMaggio, age meant more injuries and deeper silences. To Bob Feller it meant months of forced jokes, with nothing to pitch but batting practice. To more fine ballplayers than anyone has counted age has meant Scotch, bourbon, and rye. Athletes seldom bow out gracefully.

Amid the miscellaneous excitements of the current National League pennant race, the most popular ballplayer of his time is trying desperately to overcome this tradition. Stanley Frank Musial of the St. Louis Cardinals, now thirty-nine and slowing, intends to end his career with dignity and with base hits. Neither comes easily to a ballplayer several years past his peak, and so to Musial, a man accustomed to ease and to humility, this has been a summer of agony and pride.

Consider one quiet June evening in Milwaukee when Musial walked toward the batting cage to hit with the scrubs, dragging his average (.235) behind him. He had been riding the bench for two weeks.

"Hey, that's a funny-looking ballplayer," called Red Schoendienst of the Braves, who was Musial's roommate on the Cardinals for five years. Musial grinned widely. It was an old joke between old friends. Then he stood silently among anonymous second-liners, attempting to act as though he were used to the company.

"Stash," someone said, while George Crowe, a St. Louis pinch hitter, was swinging, "did you know that Preacher Roe was using a spitball when he pitched against you?"

The question snapped Musial to life. "Sure," he said enthusiastically. "We had a regular signal for it. One day Preacher goes into his motion, and Terry Moore, who's coaching at third, picks off the spitter and gives me the signal. Preacher knows I've got it, so he doesn't want to throw the spitter. But he's halfway through his windup, and all he can change to is a lollipop [nothing ball]. I hit it into the left-field seats, and I laughed all the way around the bases."

Musial laughed again at the memory, then stepped in to hit. He swung three times but never got the ball past the batting practice pitcher. A knot of Milwaukee fans jeered as Musial stepped out of the cage, and the sound, half boos, half yays, was harsh. Musial blushed and began talking very quickly about other games against Roe and the old Brooklyn Dodgers. "Yeah, I could really hit those guys," he said. It was strange and a little sad to see so great a figure tapping bouncers to the pitcher and answering boos with remembrances of past home runs.

Why was he doing it? one wondered. He was long since certain of election to the Baseball Hall of Fame. He was wealthy, independent of the game. (One friend estimates that Musial earns $200,000 a year, no more than $80,000 of it directly from the Cardinals.) He was a man who had always conducted himself sensibly. Now here was sensible old Stan Musial reduced to benchwarmer, as he waged a senseless war with time.

The answer, of course, is pride—more pride than most of us suspected Musial possessed, more pride than Musial ever displayed when he was Stan the Man, consistent .350 hitter, owner and proprietor of most National League pitching staffs.

The issues in the case of Stan Musial versus time have cleared considerably since his May benching and his dramatic July comeback. He was not through in June, though, as many suspected but, because Musial is well loved, few put in words. But neither was he the young Musial in July, as many said loudly but, I imagine, few really suspected. Both the benching and the comeback represent skirmishes in the continuing battle Musial joins each time he puts on a pair of spikes and heads out toward left field, trotting a shade more slowly than he once did.

After a career in which he had never batted lower than .310, Musial hit .255 in 1959. Since he was thirty-eight, the wise conclusion was that he was finished, and most baseball men assumed that he would retire. In fact, most hoped he would choose retirement instead of the awkward exit that seemed inevitable if he played this season. "No," Musial insisted during the winter, "I want to go out on a good year. I'm not quitting after a lousy year like that." Athletes, like chorus girls, are usually the last to admit that age has affected them, and Musial appeared to be following the familiar unhappy pattern. His timing seemed gone, changeups made him look foolish, and he appeared to be the only man who didn't know it.

During the winter Musial enrolled in a physical education program at St. Louis University. The exercises were orthodox push-ups and such but placed emphasis on tumbling.

He arrived in spring training splendidly conditioned and hit well, if not sensationally, during exhibition games. For the first three weeks of the regular season he played first base, batted about .300, and fielded poorly. Then his hitting dropped sharply for the next three weeks, and his average drifted toward .200. Finally, on May 27, Solly Hemus, the Cardinals' manager, benched Musial. The decision brought pain to Musial and pain to Hemus, too, since what the manager did, after all, was bench a legend.

"He'll be back," Hemus said vaguely to everyone who asked. When? Solly wasn't quite sure. "I'll play whenever they want me to," Musial said cheerlessly. But he didn't start another game for almost a month.

Hemus is a conscientious, combative man of thirty-six who joined the Cardinals in 1949 when Musial was already a star, a factor that complicated the usual manager-ballplayer relationship. "I'd never pulled much," Hemus recalls, "and when I first came up Stan gave me some tips. He told me to concentrate on hitting that right-field screen; it's close at Busch Stadium. I admired him, and I guess he liked me. It got so that when he'd come home, Janet, Stan's daughter, wouldn't start by asking if he got any hits. First she'd say: 'Did Solly get any hits?'"

Discussing the Musial benching troubles Hemus. He was buffeted somewhat in St. Louis sports pages for the move, and beyond that, it strained a friendship. But he talked about the benching at some length and with tremendous earnestness after one recent Cardinals night game.

"What's my obligation as manager?" Hemus said, staring darkly into a glass of light beer. "It's not to a friendship, no matter how much I like a guy. My obligation is to the organization that hired me and to twenty-five ballplayers. I have to win. Stan was hurting the club. He wasn't hitting, and balls were getting by him at first base. It wasn't something I wanted to do. I had to do it."

For all his attempts to show outward indifference, Musial hated the bench. He confided to a few friends that he wouldn't mind being traded to a club that would play him every day. A few hints appeared that he and Hemus were feuding. They weren't—they were just miserable about the situation—but Musial still says, in the closest he comes to a grumble: "Don't let anyone tell you they were resting me. I was benched."

On June 19, after Musial had spent three weeks in the dugout, Hemus said before a double-header: "Maybe I'll use you in the second game." The Cards won the first, and in the clubhouse afterward Hemus announced simply: "Same lineup."

Later Musial, deadly serious, approached him. "There's one thing you shouldn't ever try to do Solly," he said. "Don't ever try to kid me along."

Hemus said nothing. There wasn't anything to say.

"He caught me," the manager remarked over his beer. "He knows me well, and he'd caught me. I was wrong to kid him, but I did."

Hemus paused and gathered his thoughts. "I spent a lot of time, a lot of nights worrying about this thing," he said finally, "and I got to remember the coffin. What does he want to take with him to his coffin? Records. Something that people will remember. As many records as he can. Now what do I want to take to my coffin? Honesty. I always wanted to manage, and I want to know I managed honestly. I was right to bench him when I did, but I was wrong to kid him, and I know it makes me look bad to admit it, but I was wrong."

Hemus never evolved a plan to work Musial back into the lineup. While benched, Musial pinch-hit nine times but batted safely only once. There was no indication he was going to hit any better than he had.

On June 16 Bob Nieman, who had been hitting well, pulled a muscle, and suddenly Hemus needed a left fielder. He alternated Walt Moryn and rookie John Glenn, but neither hit at all. Then he turned to Musial, hoping for batting but not really confident that he would get it. . . .

On June 24 Musial started in left field against the Phils and got one hit in four times at bat. On June 25 he was hitless, but on June 26 he started again and that day took off on a devastating hitting tear (fifteen games, .500 batting average) that surprised everyone, except possibly himself.

What brought Musial back to batting form? "Well, one reason I didn't quit," he says, "is that they weren't throwing the fast one by me. Last year they were giving me changes, and I wasn't going good, so I kept swinging too hard. I figured that one out. Now I'm going to left real good on lots of the changeups."

Musial has also changed the unique stance that was his trademark. Remember the old crouch? Now Musial stands closer to the plate, a change that gives him better control of fastballs over the outside corner. He still crouches but less markedly. His stance remains unusual, but it is no longer radical.

He always concentrated when he hit, but Musial's concentration seems to have deepened further. It must make up for what age has taken from his reflexes, and he now plots his swings with great care.

Nobody around the league has an easy explanation of Musial's great hitting in July, because there is no easy way to explain great hitting by a washed-up thirty-nine-year-old ballplayer. "Hell," Musial himself says, "just use that old line of Slaughter's. Just say I never been away."

One night before the Cardinals played the Braves, Charley Dressen, a man who has more explanations than newspapermen have questions, agreed to study the revivified Musial and report on what he saw. Musial lined one of Bob Buhl's inside changeups high into the right-field bleachers for a home run.

"Ah," Dressen said later, "I know how to pitch to him."

"How?"

"Same as always," Dressen said. "Changeups."

"But he hit the home run off the change."

"Wrong kinda change," Dressen said, cutting off further conversation.

Fred Hutchinson, who manages Cincinnati and once managed the Cardinals, took up the Musial question several days later. "What can you say?" Hutchinson asked, shrugging. "He's hitting all kinds of pitches just like he used to."

On the field, during workouts, he tries to be as he once was, too, filled with small jokes and with laughter. "Do you know what sex is?" he may ask. "That's what Poles put potatoes into." Then, lest he offend: "You know I'm Polish."

Sometimes, while playing catch, he shows his pitches—he was a pitcher in the low minor leagues twenty-three years ago. "Fork ball," he'll say. "Me and [Elroy] Face. Next time I come back it's gonna be as a pitcher."

But once in a while pride, before now the unseen side of Musial, breaks through. He was chatting at a batting cage recently when Jim Toomey, the Cardinals' publicity man, approached and asked broadly if he was telling the story of his life.

"Yeah," someone said. "He's up to a Donors sandlot game in 1935."

"What did you do," Toomey asked, "get four hits?"

"I'll tell you this, buddy," Musial said, quite loudly. "You can bet I got two."

Since his July blaze, Musial has slipped somewhat. "One thing I know about him now," Hemus says, "is that when he gets real tired one day's rest isn't enough. If he needs it, he'll get a week off. If he goes real bad, he'll get plenty of time to get strong again."

The old 154-game-a-year Musial is vanished. The swift base runner, whose sloped shoulders suggested the contours of a greyhound, is slowed. The great batter, whose forte was consistency, now hits in spurts. Yet, in sum, this season makes for a graceful exit. Musial wanted to go out with a respectable year, and through concentrating on pitchers and conserving his own energies, he seems likely to achieve this.

But ahead lies one more trap, another season. Musial has not formally committed himself to 1961, but informally he drops hints that he may play again. He relishes his life in baseball, and when he hits well he seems to feel that he can go on hitting indefinitely. "Maybe my wheels are gone," he says, "but I'll be able to hit like hell for a long time."

Perhaps, but anyone who watched his prideful struggle this summer must wonder. Time presses. The benching can only get longer, the comebacks still more labored. He has been a fine and gracious man, Stan Musial. It would be nice to see him say farewell with a wave, a grin, and a double lined up the alley in right-center field.

21

Success and Ned Irish

Sports Illustrated, March 27, 1961

The boss of Madison Square Garden, arrogant Ned Irish, had a natural sports monopoly in the wealthiest American market, but his use of power and sour demeanor led to vast unpopularity.

Edward Simmons Irish, once the prophet of big-time basketball and now president of the worst team in the National Basketball Association, is a man virtually without casual acquaintances. Irish has enemies who suggest, "Cut the son of a gun and he won't bleed." He has friends who insist, "He's the finest buddy a man can have." But what are missing from the wide circle about the calculating, headstrong, occasionally brilliant New Yorker are the neutralists. No one is neutral about Ned Irish. No one says simply, "He's all right, I guess."

This vivid reflection of a promoter who has been a dominant figure in sports for twenty-seven years would seem to ally him with the strongest personalities of our time, from Cus D'Amato to Nikita Khrushchev. It is the strong and strident personalities who make neutralism an untenable policy. But Irish's personality, which mixes saber-rattling with intense shyness, does not fit into a familiar pattern. Like his success, it is something that is unique and puzzling, even to his friends.

Irish was farsighted enough to take basketball out of college gymnasiums and put it into Madison Square Garden. But he does not seem to know enough about the game to run a winning team. He was a diligent newspaperman who took delight in the craft of reporting. But his relations with reporters at large and with New York reporters in particular are a model of inept press relations. He was aware of the danger of fixed college games long before they were confirmed in court, but his reaction to the 1951 scandals was alternately naive and hysterical.

Last week his comment on the current scandal was more sober: "I would have thought the boys would have learned their lesson from 1951." But he still showed no awareness that the Garden atmosphere and the presence of gamblers there might contribute to the fixes.

Ned Irish is president of the Garden, a vast, aging arena on Manhattan's underdeveloped West Side that is famous nationally for bigtime sports and infamous locally for sullen ushers and 50 cent beers. On a fight night, when most of the floor is covered with removable benches, the Garden can hold almost nineteen thousand people, and for all the New York building boom, it remains what it was when Tex Rickard, using borrowed money, built it in 1925. The Garden is the only major indoor sports arena in the New York metropolitan area.

This is a rich and eager market, and Irish milks it mechanically and thoroughly, starting with the two teams the Garden owns. Through the Knickerbockers, for whose disastrous record he must be held responsible, he makes money. (The nearest rival team is in Philadelphia.) Through the Rangers, who have reached the National Hockey League playoffs only five times since World War II, he makes more. (The nearest rival team is in Boston.) In between these house promotions, Irish books college basketball double-headers, an ice show, professional wrestling, a horse show, track meets, a rodeo, a dog show, and, occasionally, a fight. The Garden is seldom dark and, however dull the attraction, seldom empty. It is the sort of natural monopoly to warm a poor man's dreams.

Irish was once a poor man, and unquestionably he dreamed, but his success has been a chilling, isolating thing. With few exceptions, sportswriters complain that he is arrogant and aloof. His current woes with the Knickerbockers have produced soft cries of delight throughout the NBA. It is easy to ascribe such unpopularity to a history of success, a phenomenon evidenced by the anti-Yankee bias of many New Yorkers. But Irish's unpopularity transcends resentment. One business associate calls him "the perfect mortgage forecloser."

At fifty-five, Irish is bald, sharp-featured, and thin-lipped. His voice is flat and colored by the accents of New York City. His manner is brusque and humorless; except with old and trusted friends, he creates the impression of a man preoccupied with people and things more important than the person or question he is facing at the moment. He guards his income figures fiercely, but sound estimates put his yearly take from all sources at something over $200,000, or almost a hundred times what it was when he left the newspaper business in mid-Depression.

The authorized account of Irish's emergence is probably most famous in the Bill Stern version, or Vulgate. Stern, whose fables were imposed on innocent radio listeners some twenty years ago, used to tell his audience: "The newspaperman sent to cover the game at the Manhattan College gymnasium found the gym so crowded that he had to crawl in through a window, and as he did, he ripped his best pair of pants. It was this that first led that newspaperman to dream of taking basketball out of the gyms, that prompted him to bring basketball into Madison Square Garden, to invent, yes, to *invent*, big-time basketball. And that man's name was [flourish of hautboys] Ned Irish."

For all its impact, this narration is weakened by several considerations, including fact. Irish did put basketball into the Garden on a regular basis, but the original idea was not his. He insists that he ripped his trousers, but Lou Black, now head of the Associated Press Sports Bureau in New Haven, Connecticut, covered the overcrowded Manhattan game with him and is not sure that anyone's clothing was torn, or that Irish's subsequent thoughts advanced beyond the usual newspaperman's complaint: "Something ought to be done about this mess."

Irish had worked as a student sports correspondent at Erasmus Hall High School in Brooklyn and at the University of Pennsylvania, where he was enrolled for a business course. Through a variety of promotions, which ranged from organizing a job-placement service to selling sheet music after musical comedy performances staged by The Masque and Wig, he earned as much as $100 a week while still an undergraduate at Penn, but sportswriting, rather than a business career, appealed to him. He wanted to be a good newspaperman, he said, and when he graduated he went to work for the *New York World-Telegram* at $60 a week, a sum he supplemented as publicity man for the New York football Giants.

For a few years Irish was just one of the brigade of sportswriters working in and around New York City. He was a good reporter, but at a time when W. O. McGeehan and Damon Runyon were gracing New York sports pages, no one noticed his writing style, which was adequate and undistinguished. Perhaps aware of this limitation, he began devoting more time to inside work—writing headlines, planning layouts, performing the important, anonymous jobs without which no newspaper can exist.

Basketball then was an unprofitable sport both for the colleges, with their small gyms, and for the promoters who matched pro teams in armories and in dance halls. Joe Lapchick, now head coach at St. John's and once the center of the Original Celtics, recalls, "The guys who played for the Celtics made a little money. The man who managed the team got free bus rides."

START OF THE BOOM

The first evidence of basketball's ultimate potential was provided by the late Mayor Jimmy Walker during dark Depression winters, when Walker, trying to raise funds for unemployment relief, organized a committee of sportswriters to promote basketball benefits in Madison Square Garden. On January 19, 1931, a college triple-header drew a capacity house; on February 22, 1933, a seven-game program that ran both afternoon and night attracted a total of twenty thousand. Big-time basketball had been born. Irish attended the birth as junior member of the sportswriters' committee.

Afterward, a number of people approached the late General John Reed Kilpatrick, president of the Garden, with schemes for promoting basketball regularly. "We were more interested in ability than in security," Kilpatrick said later. "We wanted someone with a concrete program."

When Irish approached Kilpatrick, he had both a plan of his own and backing, apparently from the late Tim Mara, owner of the football Giants. Irish proposed to run college basketball as a concession, which is how large arenas customarily run parking lots but is not how they customarily run permanent bookings. As concessionaire, Irish guaranteed the Garden $4,000, which was then the average cost of renting the arena for one night. He would handle scheduling, control tickets, and direct the necessary publicity. The Garden was to share in profits above the guarantee on a percentage basis. Kilpatrick agreed, and under terms of the contract Garden basketball was established as Irish's dominion, and it was to remain his dominion as long as he met the minimum of $4,000 a night.

On December 29, 1934, Irish matched NYU against Notre Dame, and this game, which began a rousing rivalry that ran for twenty-three years, attracted 16,188 fans. It brought the Garden something in excess of $4,000 and brought Irish roughly the equivalent of six months' pay at the paper. Suddenly, Irish's future was as big as basketball's.

ON IRISH'S TERMS

He could not quite believe what had happened. When the *Telegram* refused his request for a leave, he quit, but he clung to his job with the Giants as a hedge against the day when his promotions might end as abruptly as they had begun.

They did not end, because both fortune and opportunism were on his side. With strong squads from NYU, City College, Long Island University, and St. John's serving as Garden home teams, plus the freshness of a fine sport's first blossoming, the 1930s were exciting times for college basketball. Irish had bottled the excitement, and as a concessionaire, he was accountable to no one for his methods. Any athletically ambitious college—which is to say, most major colleges in the United States—that wanted the attention of a Garden showing had to play for Irish on Irish's terms and on the date he assigned it. A few athletic directors grumbled over the college's cut ($500 on sellout nights in some cases), but Irish was Congress, court, and executive of big-time basketball. "My terms," he reminded athletic directors, "or go back to your gyms." Yet for all the strength of his position, for all his seeming assurance, the emperor of basketball doubled as a football press agent and kept on doubling until 1940.

Irish's instant success created instant arrogance. Except for a few reporters (Tom Meany, then of the *Telegram*, Arthur Daley of the *Times*), Irish walled himself off from his old newspaper associates. Lou Black, who had moved to New Haven, found himself involved in a Garden ticket mix-up and wrote Irish a letter of explanation. "Ned's reaction," Black remembers, "was that he was no longer a newspaperman but now an executive who wanted to know from nothing, from nobody."

For fifteen years Irish's successes were continuous and unrelieved, and although he antagonized some college officials and newspapermen, the worst anyone could say about him was that he had a sneer of cold command. Strangely, when trouble found him, it seemed to concentrate on the weaknesses in his makeup.

The first basketball-fix scandal, which broke at the Garden in 1951, called for humility and genius at public relations. Irish possesses neither. The scandal, which struck in many places, like a soap opera, involved at least six colleges, four of them in New York City, and thirty-three players.

Twenty-one of the players pleaded guilty to "dumping"; ten others, beyond the jurisdiction of New York district attorney Frank Hogan, admitted their guilt. Some players and bribers were sentenced to prison, and the careers of several coaches were ruined. This whole affair killed big-time college basketball in New York for many years.

"Underlying the scandal," Hogan said in a formal report, "was the blatant commercialism which had permeated college basketball. What once had been a minor sport had been hippodromed into a big business."

But Irish, the chief hippodromer, refused to accept any responsibility, though the presence of gamblers at Garden games was as obvious in those days as Major League baseball scouts are at an NCAA tournament. (In the years since the scandals, any sophisticated fan has been able to spot gamblers at a Garden college or pro basketball game.) Irish went so far as to accuse Frank Hogan of timing his arrests during the scandals for publicity purposes.

The 1951 scandal scarred and shocked, but it passed. The New York Knickerbockers, while hardly as dramatic a problem as corruption, are a continuing headache. When the Basketball Association of America, ancestor of the NBA, was organized in 1946, the plan was to create a pro basketball big league. Irish, with the Garden in his pocket, was assured of admission, but he did have one competitor in Max Kase, a popular newspaperman who is sports editor of the *New York Journal-American*.

The dozen men attending the organizational meeting appointed Maurice Podoloff, now the NBA president, as temporary chairman, and Podoloff began with a short talk, loosely lifted from the ceremony of marriage. "I'm going to call on each prospective member in turn," he said, "and if anyone else has an objection, let him speak now or forever hold his peace."

IRISH GETS THE FRANCHISE

Podoloff then called representatives of cities about which there was no dispute—Cleveland, Philadelphia, and so on—until the unborn league was ten teams strong and only New York remained unsettled.

"I represent a corporation with more than $3.5 million in assets," Irish began his speech.

Kase later outlined a scheme for a team that would play in a Manhattan armory. "Three and a half million," Irish broke in from time to time. When the matter was put to a vote, Irish—or Madison Square Garden—won handily.

"But," recalls an owner, "Irish also won a lot of resentment with his patronizing big-money talk. We didn't need him to tell us about Madison Square Garden."

From this sour start, Irish proceeded to sour matters further. He immediately insisted that the home team keep all the receipts, an arrangement ideal for the Garden but brutal for owners stuck with small arenas who'd been hoping for paydays in New York.

When the BAA swallowed the old National Basketball League in 1949, the temporary result was a seventeen-team hodgepodge, including an entry representing Moline, Illinois; Rock Island, Illinois; and Davenport, Iowa, which was called Tri-Cities and was run by Ben Kerner, who now runs the St. Louis Hawks. Irish promptly told Kerner that he was not going to cheapen his marquee "by putting 'Tri-Cities' up there."

"Okay," Kerner said, "but when we play you at home, we're not gonna put New York on our marquee."

Consistently during this period, Irish announced that unless things went his way he was going to pull out of the league. "The way college basketball draws," he confided, "the Knicks are nothing but a tax write-off anyway."

Tax write-off or not, Irish wanted the Knicks to win, and he hired Joe Lapchick as coach. While Lapchick ran tactics and the bench, Irish ran power plays behind the scenes. After the season of 1948–49, Irish decided to bolster the Knicks with both Vince Boryla, an itinerant collegian, and Ernie Vandeweghe, probably the best basketball player ever to attend Colgate. Under the complicated draft rules of the NBA he probably could have landed one or the other, but not both. "If I don't get both, the Knicks will have to fold," he told the other owners. He got both.

When he heard bright reports on Harry Gallatin, a blond forward at Northeast Missouri State Teachers, Irish concluded that he had to have Gallatin, too. He signed him, although Gallatin had finished only two years of college and, supposedly, was not eligible to be signed.

When he saw Nat "Sweetwater" Clifton bull his way toward rebounds for the Harlem Globetrotters, Irish told Abe Saperstein, the proprietor of the Globetrotters, that he wanted to buy Clifton.

The Globetrotters' regular bookings at the Garden are not only profitable for Saperstein but give the team valuable big-city exposure. Saperstein didn't have to be told the facts of life.

"I'll be glad to let you have Clifton—and, by the way, how's the family?" Saperstein said, in effect.

Each of these maneuvers enraged Irish's NBA colleagues.

After nine years and seven first-division finishes, Lapchick, grown gaunt from too much travel, resigned and returned to his old coaching job at St. John's. With the wise, respected old pro gone, Irish assumed a more active part in both the planning and the running of the Knicks. His draft choices, since Lapchick's resignation, have been consistently wasted. He has traded carelessly, losing, among others, Gene Shue, who made the all-league team in 1960. He has fired two coaches, although one, Vince Boryla, now works for him out of Denver under the sententious title of "general manager player personnel."

The current Knickerbockers are the cumulative result of Irish's policies and actions and, as such, with the worst record in NBA history this year, are a source of great embarrassment to him. Since he can no longer bully other NBA owners, Irish was recently reduced to threatening to fold the team because "the Garden can't be in the position of supporting a failure." The Knicks make money, and the Garden is a corporation that feeds on profits. This was a caricature of a threat.

A HARD MAN TO INTERVIEW

For all of his bluster and braggadocio, Irish, as one meets him across a table, is not a blustering man. His answers are clipped and uninformative. He seems uncomfortable during interviews, as though he would prefer checking the books or going about his business to discussing what it is that makes his business exciting. He keeps his wife and two sons in the background, and he tries to dismiss public relations by insisting, "I don't care what they say about me as long as they buy tickets." He has never been able to go much further than that, or to explain a devotion to the Garden so intense that he has hidden in distant reaches, waiting to spring when he catches an usher moving a $2 customer to a $3 seat in exchange for a $50 tip.

"I think," says one old acquaintance, "that Ned is really a hell of a nice guy. The trouble is, he's afraid somebody might find out." On that score, as matters stand, he is in no danger.

But there is more than a wisecrack to this sad success story. Perhaps more conclusively than anything else now before us in sports, it demonstrates that success does not necessarily warm the spirit or automatically provide a glittering armor in which to stride through life. It can be a burden or even a disaster. After all these years, Ned Irish, who is more feared than admired, more accepted than liked, has become almost a walking advertisement for failure.

22

Baseball's Secret Weapon: Terror

Sports Illustrated, July 10, 1961

*Despite official denials, pitchers throw at batters—to knock them
down, to brush them back, sometimes to brain them.*

No one remembers the place or the names because it happened a long
time ago, but in that forgotten spring a rookie pitcher turned to the
manager of a big-league ballclub and asked: "What's the best pitch in
baseball? Is it a curve, a fastball, or what?"

"Kid," the manager answered, undisturbed, "the best pitch in baseball is a strike." He waited so that the rookie could grasp a point, put
to perfection. Then, very slowly, the manager added, "And the second-
best pitch is the knockdown."

One reason no one has carved this counsel into marble is that so
far no one has had to. The manager's words and sentiments endure,
by themselves. Only two weeks ago Jim Bunning, a long-armed Detroit
right-hander, knocked down Jim Piersall, a short-tempered Cleveland
outfielder, with predictable results. Piersall, hit on the right wrist, arose,
marched to the mound, and threw a left hook at Bunning. (Since Piersall hooks like a ballplayer, not a boxer, no one was hurt.) Earlier this
season Lou Burdette, Chuck Estrada, Pete Ramos, and Mike Fornieles
were all threatened by hitters rising from the dirt in fury.

Baseball propagandists, such as league presidents, say that the knockdown is overemphasized in the newspapers; this gives them a chance to
get back at the press, which calls them baseball propagandists. Then,
lately, there has been a curious tendency to mysticize and romanticize
pitching. A pitcher has written a book and mentioned Bartok. A writer
has pitched an inning and mentioned himself, along with Mantle and

Mays. Amateurism flourishes, and one tends to forget that no one hits a home run when he is afraid that the pitcher will throw at his head or at his ribs or at his groin. One tends to forget that, for all its art, Major League pitching is largely a business of terror.

Consider a familiar tableau. The batter stands poised, bat cocked, leaning slightly toward the plate, the better to hit the outside curveball he expects. As the pitcher throws, the batter strides forward. He wants all his weight behind his swing. Then, as he realizes that the ball is hurtling at him, that there will be no swing, the batter comes unhinged. He heaves his bat. His feet fly forward. His body twists down. He needs the ground the way an infantryman needs the ground. He wants to embrace it.

After the ball has passed overhead, the batter lingers in the dirt, breathing and relishing the privilege. When at last he gets up to hit again there is something he must regain, along with his bat and cap— his poise. One more barrier has been erected between the batter and a base hit.

The barrier is older than anyone really knows. Possibly it dates from 1867, the year in which Arthur "Candy" Cummings invented the curve and, presumably, quickly discovered that terror made his new pitch doubly effective. Through the decades the knockdown has gone by different names and, like any weapon, been used in various ways by various men. There are shadings, subtleties, and nuances, hypotheses, theories, and countertheories, but primarily, all one needs in preparing "A Practical Handbook for Terrifying Batters" is a working understanding of three terms.

The BEAN BALL is thrown to hit the batter in the bean, or cranium. It is employed for reasons ranging from dyspepsia to viciousness and is specifically outlawed by Baseball Rule 8.02 (c), which is not to say that it does not exist. Spitballs, as Preacher Roe once pointed out, have been outlawed, too. To throw the classic bean ball, one aims at a point shoulder high, about a foot behind the batter. As the batter strides he loses height. As he ducks he falls backward, exercising a conditioned reflex. The ball is below and behind the head; the batter falls down and back. Voila.

On August 16, 1920, Ray Chapman, a Cleveland shortstop, was struck near the temple by an underhand fastball thrown by Carl Mays, who won twenty-six games for the Yankees that year. People who were there say that Mays's pitch—a "submarine ball" in the post–World War I argot—was only slightly higher than the belt. Chapman dropped into its path. He died the next morning in a New York hospital. A committee of baseball officials later exonerated Mays of any intent to hit Chapman.

The BRUSHBACK is thrown to frighten the batter, to make him step back, with no intent to maim. It is employed routinely as part of a pitcher's assortment, frequently to set up a curve or, for that matter, any outside pitch. Ordinarily, one brushes a hitter by throwing at or close to the front part of his body, from the level of the uniform letters on up. Plate-crowders, such as Minnie Minoso, have some difficulty in dodging brushbacks, but the great majority of big leaguers avoid them simply by leaning back or spinning away from the plate.

Unfortunately, it is impossible to tell a brushback that slips—goes an extra foot inside—from a bean ball, and on this issue many baseball wars begin.

"Oops," remarks the pitcher.

"——!" replies the batter. Shouting follows, and sometimes blood.

The KNOCKDOWN describes any pitch that sends a hitter into the dirt, covering both the deliberate bean ball and the brushback that got away. It is almost, but not quite, a generic term. A pitch thrown at a batter's knees is an excellent messenger of fright but cannot be called a knockdown. Following semantics, the proper term would be "springback" or "shins aloft." The special importance of the word "knockdown" is that it covers the pitch that slips, the errant brushback that looks like a bean ball. Pitchers occasionally bounce pitches, missing their target by several feet. Fastballs sail and get behind the hitter, and sometimes a curve completely escapes control.

Don Zimmer, recently sentenced to serve as captain of the Chicago Cubs, was terribly injured in Columbus eight years ago when a high curve struck the side of his head. Two operations were required to save Zimmer's life, and afterward he had to learn to talk all over again. He had been struck near the speech center of the brain.

Whatever the name, the type, and the intent, a close pitch, particularly an unexpected close pitch, shocks a hitter to his ganglia as it approaches, after which a number of things may happen:

1) The hitter does not duck quickly enough, with results ranging from extremes of horror and suffering to minor nicks, as with careless shaving.

2) The hitter curses, spits tobacco juice, and hits the next pitch 480 feet. This demonstrates that the knockdown is the second-best pitch in baseball, not the best.

3) The hitter panics, swallowing the tobacco, and elects to swing at anything, just to escape the awful menace of the baseball.

4) The hitter rages and tries to ram the next pitch back at the mound. Such substitution of determination for poise is rarely successful. Lining a baseball off a pitcher is a fantastic feat of marksmanship.

5) The hitter, neither in rage nor in panic, loses confidence and, when he swings again, pulls away from the plate in an involuntary action. The hitter is not trembling, but he is rattled.

The furthest extreme, of course, was the Chapman case, the only occasion on which a Major League batter has been killed by a pitch. Occasions on which Major Leaguers have been seriously injured are more numerous—so numerous, in fact, that one can select an excellent All-Star team of beanees across the years. Mickey Cochrane (fractured skull) or Roy Campanella (fastball into left ear) is the catcher. Around the infield are Jackie Robinson (fractured batting helmet) at first base; Cass Michaels (fractured skull) at second; Pee Wee Reese (concussion) at short; Pete Reiser (concussion) at third. Joe Medwick (fractured skull), Hank Leiber (concussion, shortened career), and Carl Furillo (six beanings, various effects) make up the outfield. Picking a pitcher for this squad seems innately wrong and hence will be skipped. Robinson admittedly makes it on a pass, but 1) after Steve Ridzik hit him Robinson's helmet looked like a relic of Hiroshima and 2) I want him on my team. For purists, Joe Adcock (concussion) is offered as alternate first baseman.

Beyond this distinguished group of victims stands an army of walking wounded, ballplayers who have been hit on arms and elbows and as a result missed days or weeks of play. Dick Groat, the Pittsburgh shortstop, was sidelined for a month last season and almost missed the World Series after Lou Burdette fractured his wrist. Dodgers veteran Duke Snider reported trim and eager this spring and hit well until Bob Gibson's fastball fractured his elbow on April 17. To any batter, the inside fastball is a clear and present danger whether it comes dramatically as a bean ball or routinely as a brushback that flicks the letters at ninety miles an hour.

Before batting helmets were adopted, there was a distinct sound associated with beanings, a sound oddly and irrevocably wrong. It was deeper than the sound of a ball hitting a bat, softer than the sound of a ball striking the catcher's mitt, less crisp than the sound of a ball striking a concrete wall. It was always unfinished, a thump that died as it was born, died quickly, but not before one knew what lay ahead. This sound without echo meant—always—a solemn circle of men, busy trainers in white, and finally the stretcher, borne by the victim's teammates, on whom baseball uniforms suddenly looked out of place.

The batting helmet has changed the sound and substantially reduced the number of skulls fractured by baseballs. But there is no armor against fear. The helmet has not significantly changed hitters' attitudes, nor has it provided complete protection. It does not cover the ears.

Adcock suffered his concussion while wearing the helmet and afterward somberly displayed it in the clubhouse. Red marks had been blasted into the dark blue plastic by the stitches of the baseball. A few reporters told Adcock he was lucky to have been wearing the helmet, but except for that the dressing room was quiet.

Ballplayers are neither more nor less heroic than any other group of young men, but they necessarily have adopted general codes toward their occupational hazards. Most accept the brushback for what it is— an impersonal reminder that the ball is hard, that the pitcher disapproves of anyone leaning in.

"Ain't gonna hit me that way," Willie Mays says. "They can throw close all they want. I ain't gonna be there."

Mickey Mantle goes further. He endorses the brushback. "You got to throw at hitters up here," he says, "and if I was a pitcher I would. Otherwise, they'd wear you the hell out."

There is a good deal of pragmatism to this approach. Pitchers are going to continue brushing hitters in their impersonal, nonmalignant way as long as the ball remains hard, and the hitter who makes a fuss about brushbacks is obviously troubled. He thus becomes a candidate for impersonal, nonmalignant brushbacks every time he comes to bat.

But one suspects that many players who kid about the subject are not really so delighted to be brushed as they would like to appear. For public consumption they follow an old approach to unpleasantness: don't admit it's unpleasant, and maybe it will go away. A few hints of resentment slip through. Early Wynn once was batting against Allie Reynolds, the old New York Yankees right-hander, when Reynolds spun Wynn backward with a fastball. "Yogi," Wynn said to the embryo author behind the plate, "you better tell your pitcher to start pitching me outside, because if he doesn't, Yogi, I'm gonna start pitching you inside." Berra pirouetted to the mound, and Reynolds switched to the outside corner. Wynn, armed with his own considerable fastball, could afford to issue an ultimatum and make it stick. Other ballplayers, however—lacking Wynn's temperament, reputation, and position (pitcher)—cannot.

In the case of the bean ball, acceptance is neither required nor expected; it has been the Sumter of a hundred baseball battles. The batter, if he survives, may bunt toward the first baseman. This forces the pitcher to cover first, where he can be spiked or mauled. Maglie threw behind Jackie Robinson in 1955—he claims the pitch slipped— and Robinson saved himself by standing stock-still. Then he bunted toward first. Maglie, outweighed, refused to cover. A second baseman named Davey Williams, who had a history of back trouble, did, and Robinson banged into him so hard that Williams was never able to play regularly again.

Eschewing the bunt, the batter may rely on team loyalty, in the form of a retaliatory bean ball. Most managers recommend throwing retaliatory bean balls at big hitters on the opposing team, telling their pitchers, in effect, "You've got to protect our hitters." In one recent game a pitcher threw a bean ball, and half an inning later the other pitcher threw an equalizer. The plate umpire walked to the mound, summoned both managers, and announced: "Okay. You've each had your shot. Now the next time there's a bean ball the pitcher gets fined." Alvin Dark, the manager of the San Francisco Giants, recently announced an interesting variation on this. From now on, he said, the Giants would throw only at rival pitchers and catchers.

The ultimate counter to the bean ball is to start a riot, preferably on the pitcher's supine form. Don Drysdale threw behind Johnny Logan's neck when Logan played for Milwaukee, and Logan led a battalion of Braves in a short charge. Eddie Mathews worked on Drysdale's head, Logan handled the body punching, and after the tall pitcher had been felled, Carl Sawatski, a large-hipped catcher, sat on his chest. Drysdale escaped with contusions—which, considering the odds, was a tribute to his powers of self-preservation.

Joe Adcock, convinced that Ruben Gomez was throwing at him, once sprinted to the mound, whereupon Gomez sprinted to center field—a distance of seventy yards—in 7.2 or 7.3 seconds. (As always, officials' watches varied.) Other inciters include Billy Martin and Carl Furillo, the latter establishing a National League record for slow reaction time. After being hit on the wrist, Furillo trotted to first base, mused extensively on man's inhumanity, and finally bolted toward the Giants' dugout, where he was ultimately diverted from his intention to assault and batter Leo Durocher, the once and future manager. Furillo had decided that Durocher ordered the pitch.

Such considerations as these, rather than Rule 8.02 (c), make most pitchers somewhat reluctant to throw bean balls. The brushback is effective enough, and besides, there are other means of squaring personal grudges. "I like to hit a guy once in a while," one veteran concedes. "I don't want to murder anyone, but I want them to know that when I'm working they can get hurt." This pitcher has perfected a fastball at the rib cage. "Nobody gets killed that way, but when a guy takes my fastball in the ribs, he knows he's been hit." Jim Brosnan of Cincinnati is on record with a statement that he has tried to hit batters, and of course an enraged pitcher may try to bean a batter at any time.

It is difficult to determine whether more bean balls and brushbacks are thrown these days than formerly. Branch Rickey has said that pitchers throw at, or close to, hitters less; Andy High, a fine third baseman in the 1920s, feels that pitchers throw toward hitters more. A greater number of old-timers agree with Rickey, but many of them suffer from the Cobb syndrome: that is, baseball was better, rougher, and more American in the old days. The weighted results of a poll prove nothing.

Most of the truly great pitchers brushed back hitters, but only incidentally. "It would be an insult to the memory of Christy Mathewson to call him a knockdown pitcher," Rickey says. "Matty was a master of velocity and rotation. He could learn to throw any sort of breaking ball as soon as he saw it." Still, a hitter leaning in to hit one of Mathewson's breaking pitches courted Mathewson's fastball, high, tight, and hard.

Grover Cleveland Alexander, who pitched sixteen shutouts in 1916, possessed a quick curve and a fine sinker. "Alex didn't knock you back much," recalls Hans Lobert, who hit against him, or tried to. "But whenever he did wing you, it hurt like hell. He threw a heavy ball. It felt like a chunk of cement."

Walter Johnson, probably the fastest of all pitchers, was one of the few who was genuinely afraid of hitting anyone. Ty Cobb reportedly crowded the plate against Johnson, and the pitcher, considering his speed and his conscience, felt obliged to work the outside corner. It was a neat trick but never widely popular. Plate-crowding against Johnson demanded arrogance and a taste for self-destruction.

Although Mathewson, Alexander, and Johnson are a trio not easily matched, pitching generally has grown better and more sophisticated, as befits a semiscience, and there is not much question but that Sal Maglie carried knockdown research further than anyone had before. Reflecting in tranquillity now, as a coach with the Boston Red Sox, he points out: "It depends on the ball game when you use it. The pitch is no good for a two-strike, no-ball situation [which is when it was traditionally used—the son of a *Sports Illustrated* editor was beaned in a Little League game last week on a two-strike, no-ball count, showing that children are traditionalists after all]. There it's routine. It's expected. A good time is two and two." By using the knockdown when it was unexpected, Maglie made it the expected pitch every time he wound up.

Hitters' choices as the best knockdown pitchers practicing today are Drysdale, Larry Jackson of the Cardinals, Art Ditmar of the Athletics, Jim Coates of the Yankees, Jim Perry of the Indians, and Early Wynn. Drysdale, Jackson, and Perry, comparatively young, undoubtedly profit from the lessons Maglie learned. Wynn, a contemporary of Maglie's, has conducted his own independent research. His particular contribution to the art of the knockdown is a glare, devoid of expression and therefore devoid of humanitarianism, preceding each pitch. It has been known to intimidate not only the batter but the man in the on-deck circle.

How important, then, is the knockdown in winning games? By itself, it has no importance. Any muscular young man can throw at other people's heads, but few muscular young men can win in the Major Leagues. The knockdown is important only when a pitcher knows how to use it, working it into a combination of curves and fastballs and sliders. Then it changes the very nature of the game.

Ultimately, contemporary baseball has been created in the image of Babe Ruth. The home run, that utter negation of the pitcher's might, dominates. It is what fans come to see. It is why fences are close. It provides the climactic instant of modern baseball.

More than any other single act, the high, inside fastball alters that emphasis. Bean ball, brushback, knockdown—all these terms conjure up the image of a fallen man. Perhaps he is twitching. Perhaps he is lying still. Either way, the game is forgotten. When it is remembered and resumed, the fresh image lingers. The pitcher suddenly seems vicious. Each pitch becomes explosive with danger. For that time at least, in a hitters' game, the balance has shifted. For that time, the pitcher rules and the shade of Ruth lies still.

Once long ago I walked into the Dodgers' trainers' room, just after Carl Furillo had been felled. The ball had struck his hand and smashed into his nose, remodeling it. Furillo, a powerful, perfectly proportioned man, was lying on a table, ice packs covering his nose and his eyes so that he could not see. He was lying very still, very quiet.

"How do you feel?" I asked, offering my hand.

He clutched the hand hard, as one does in blindness. "That you?" he wanted to know, calling my name.

"Yes."

"Hey," Furillo said, "am I gonna be okay?"

Only a few days later I heard a baseball official say that knockdowns were not much of a factor in the game. They didn't bother ballplayers, he said. Only fans and newspapermen.

23

Pursuit of No. 60: The Ordeal of Roger Maris

Sports Illustrated, October 2, 1961

When he hit his fifty-ninth home run of the season in Baltimore's Memorial Stadium one night last week, Roger Maris stood one swing away from baseball's chubby household god, George Herman Ruth. For the entire previous month, as he pursued the magic mark of sixty, Maris lived under unrelenting pressure—pressure such as no ballplayer before, not even Ruth himself, had to endure. Throughout that month I was a constant observer of Maris's triumph and trials. Here is his story.

Someone has described Roger Maris as "the most typical ballplayer in the world." Like all capsulizations, the description is incomplete, but it is a starter. Beyond anything else, Maris is a professional baseball player. His speech, his mannerisms, his attitudes derive from the curious society that is a ballclub. But into this society he has brought an integrity that is entirely his own, a fierce, combative kind of integrity that is unusual in baseball as it would be unusual anywhere. It is the integrity, and his desperate effort to retain it, that has made the ordeal of Roger Maris a compelling and disturbing thing to behold.

Maris is handsome in an unconventional way. Perhaps the most arresting feature of his face is the mouth. The points of his upper lip curl toward his nose, creating the effect of a cupid's bow. He smiles easily, on cue. When one of the blur of photographers covering him orders, "Come on, a nice smile," the response is quick. Then as soon as the picture is taken, the smile vanishes. This knack—the forced unforced smile—is common enough among chorus girls but not among ballplayers who, after all, are not in the smiling business. It is the only public relations device that Maris has mastered completely.

When Maris is angry or annoyed or upset, the mouth changes into a grim slash in a hard face. His nose is somewhat pointed, his cheekbones rather high, and the face under the crew-cut brown hair can become menacing. Since Maris's speech is splattered with expletives common among ballplayers, some observers form an unfortunate first impression. They see a hard-looking, tough-talking man and assume that is all there is to see.

Maris's build bespeaks sports. He was an outstanding right halfback at Shanley High School in Fargo, North Dakota, and he might have played football at Oklahoma "except during the entrance exams I decided not to." He is a strong six-footer of 197 pounds, with muscles that flow, rather than bulge. He would be hard to stop on the 2-yard line.

At bat he is unobtrusive, until he hits the ball. He walks to the plate briskly, pumps his thirty-three-ounce bat once or twice, and is ready. He has none of the idiosyncrasies—Musial's hip wiggle, Colavito's shoulder shake—by which fans like to identify famous sluggers. Nor does he, like Ruth and Mantle, hit home runs of 500 feet. By his own estimate, "If I hit it just right, it goes about 450 feet, but they don't give you two homers for hitting one 800 feet, do they?" His swing is controlled and compact. He uppercuts the ball slightly, and his special talent is pulling the ball. Maris can pull any pitch in the strike zone. Only one of his homers has gone to the left of center field.

His personality is unfinished; it is easy to forget that he has just turned twenty-seven and only recently become a star. He may change now, as his life changes, as his world grows larger than a diamond, but at the moment he is impetuous, inclined to gripe harmlessly, and truthful to a fault.

Recently a reporter, preparing an article for high school students, asked, "Who's your favorite male singer?"

"Frank Sinatra," Maris said.

"Female singer?"

"I don't have a favorite female singer."

"Well," the reporter said, "would it be all right if I wrote Doris Day?"

"How could you write Doris Day when I tell you I don't have a favorite?" Maris said, mystified by the ways of some journalists.

In Detroit after Maris hit his fifty-seventh home run off the facade of the roof in right-center field, Al Kaline picked up the ball and threw it toward the Yankees' dugout.

"Wasn't that nice of Kaline?" a reporter asked.

"Anybody would have done it," Maris said. "It was nice of Kaline, but any ballplayer would have done it."

In Chicago someone asked if he really wanted to break Ruth's record. "Damn right," Maris said, neglecting to pay the customary fealty to the Babe.

"What I mean is," the reporter said, "Ruth was a great man."

"Maybe I'm not a great man," Maris said, "but I damn well want to break the record."

Later Rogers Hornsby suggested a pitching pattern to stop Maris. "Throw the first two inside and make him foul them," Hornsby said, "then come outside so he can't pull. It would be a shame if Ruth's record got broken by a .270 hitter."

"—— Hornsby," Maris said. "They been trying that on me all year, and you see how it works."

This is an era of image makers and small lies, and such candor is rare and apparently confusing. Newspapers have been crowded with headlines beginning "Maris Blasts"—which is a bad phrase. He doesn't blast; he answers questions. Fans, some rooting for Ruth's memory but others responding to the headlines, have booed Maris repeatedly. "Hey, Maris," someone shouted in Chicago, "the only thing you got in common with Ruth is a belly!" In Baltimore, fans called, "You'll choke up on your glove." It has been a difficult time for Maris and a bad time for truth.

Every day Maris has been surrounded before and after games by ten or fifteen newspapermen. Necessarily many questions are repeated endlessly. Inevitably some of Maris's answers are misinterpreted. Occasionally taste vanishes.

"Do you play around on the road?" a magazine writer asked.

"I'm a married man," Maris said.

"I'm married myself," the writer said, "but I play around on the road."

"That's your business," Maris said.

A reporter from Texas asked if Maris would rather bat .300 or hit sixty home runs, and a reporter in Detroit wanted to know if a right-hander's curve broke in on him. ("I would suppose so," Maris said with controlled sarcasm, "seeing that I bat left.") But aside from such extremes, most of the questions have not been either very good or very bad. What they have been is multitudinous.

HURT AND ANGRY

Under this pressure, which is both the same as and distinct from the actual pursuit of Ruth, Maris has made four mistakes. A wire service carried a story in late August quoting Maris as saying that he didn't care about the record, that all he wanted was the money sixty-one homers meant. "I don't think I said that," Maris says, "and I know I didn't say it like it came out." Then, in the space of ten September days, he criticized the fans at Yankee Stadium, the calls of umpire Hank Soar, and finally, hurt and angry, refused to meet the press after a double-header in Detroit.

"An unfortunate image," comments Hank Greenberg, who as Cleveland general manager signed Maris for a $15,000 bonus in 1952. "I know him, and he's just a boy. They get him talking, and he says things maybe you don't say to reporters. The year I hit fifty-eight [1938] the fans got pretty rough. Drunks called me Jew bastard and kike, and I'd come in and sound off about the fans. Then the next day I'd meet a kid, all popeyed to be shaking my hand, and I'd know I'd been wrong. But the writers protected me then. Why aren't the writers protecting Maris now?"

Even if they chose to, reporters could not "protect" Maris because Maris is being covered more intensely than any other figure in sports history. Not Ruth, or Dempsey, or Tilden, or Jones was ever subjected to such interviewing and shadowing for so sustained a period. No one can protect Maris; he must protect himself. But to do this, he would have to duck questions and tell half-truths, and both are contrary to his nature. Such is his dilemma. Obscurity is the only cure.

Roger Maris talks softly and clearly, but he is not a phrase maker. He is not profound. He is a physical man, trying to adjust to a complex psychological situation. This day he is wearing a tomato-colored polo shirt, and he is smoking one of the cigarettes he is paid to endorse.

He is asked what word he would use to describe all the attention he has received.

He thinks for a moment and says, "Irritating. I enjoy bull sessions with the guys [reporters]. But this is different, the questions day after day, the big story. I say a guy [Hank Soar] missed a few. I've always said it. Now it's in the papers, and it comes out like I'm asking for favors. I'm saying"—a touch of anger colors his voice—"call a strike a strike and call a ball a ball, but in the papers it appears like I'm looking for favors."

About the people he meets?

"Mostly they're inconsiderate. The fans, they really get on me. Rip me, my family, everything. I like to eat in the Stage [a Jewish delicatessen in New York], and it's got so bad I can't eat there. I can't get a mouthful of food down without someone bothering me. They even ask for autographs at mass."

Now he is talking more easily, going from topic to topic at the drop of a word. Like this:

Babe Ruth: "Why can't they understand? I don't want to be Babe Ruth. He was a great ballplayer. I'm not trying to replace him. The record is there and damn right I want to break it, but that isn't replacing Babe Ruth."

Old-timers, generally: "It gets me sore; they keep comparing me to Ruth, running me down, and I'm not trying to be Ruth. It gets me damn sore."

Money: "I want enough for me and my family, but I don't really care that much for money. I want security, but if I really cared about money I'd move to New York this winter, wouldn't I? That's where the real money is, isn't it? But I'm not moving to New York."

Frank Scott, the agent who declared that Maris could earn $500,000 by hitting sixty homers in 154 games: "It's a business relationship between Scott and me, that's all. He lines up something good, and I say okay."

Fame: "It's good and it's bad. It's good being famous, but I can't do the things I like any more. Like bulling with the writers. I like to go out in public and be recognized a little. Hell, I'm proud to be a ballplayer. But I don't like being busted in on all the time, and now, when I go out, I'm busted in on all the time."

Cheers: "I don't tip my cap. I'd be kind of embarrassed to. I figure the fans who cheer me know I appreciate it."

His current plight: "I'm on my own all the way, and I'm the same me I was, and Mickey is, too. Once in a while, maybe, it makes me go into a shell, but most of the time"—pride stirs in his voice—"I'm exactly the same as I was."

Pressure: "I don't feel a damn thing once the game starts. I honestly don't. But before the game, and afterward, the writers and the photographers and the questions. That's pressure. That's hard. In the game it's the same as always. I been taking my swings. I've had some good swings, but I've fouled some good pitches back. I'm not losing any sleep or anything like that, but I'm damn tired, and when the season ends, I'm going right home and rest."

HOUK ON MARIS

Ralph Houk, the manager of the Yankees, won a Silver Star and a Purple Heart in Europe during World War II and so is familiar with pressure. Of Maris he said, "I'd say it really got bad for him in Minneapolis. I'd say it began, you know, real bad, when we were out there." Houk paused. "Some funny things happen," he said. "Remember at the Stadium when the Indians knocked out Whitey Ford in the second inning? I was worried. His leg was bothering him, and Ford is a hell of a Series pitcher. So when the game was over I started figuring what I'd tell the writers when they asked me what was wrong with Ford. You know something? Nobody asked." Ford himself, a worldly young man, added, "It's the damnedest thing. All my life I've been trying to win twenty. This year I win twenty-four, and all anybody asks me about is home runs." Ford's tone was pleasant, a trifle puzzled but not angry.

When the Yankees arrived in Minneapolis on that trip late in August, Maris had fifty-one homers and Mantle forty-six. Both were comfortably ahead of Ruth's record pace, and both had to share uncomfortable amounts of attention.

A chartered bus appeared in front of the Hotel Radisson well in advance of each game to carry the Yankees to Memorial Stadium. The downtown area of Minneapolis is compact, and the bus served as a signal to hundreds of Minneapolitans. As soon as it appeared, they herded into the hotel lobby. "Seen Rog?" they asked. "Where's Mick?" Enterprising children posted a watch on the eighth floor, where many of the Yankees were quartered. When Maris or Mantle approached the elevator, a child scout would sprint down eight flights and shout to the lobby, "Here they come!" (Fortunately for the child scout, the elevators were unhurried relics of a more leisurely time.)

What followed in the lobby was the sort of surge one associates with lynchings. Maris and Mantle survived that first day because they are powerful men, but the next, tipped off by a friendly bellman, they began leaving the elevator on the second floor and taking a back stairway to the street.

Nothing much happened the first night in Minneapolis, except that Camilo Pascual of the Minnesota Twins became the father of a son and pitched a four-hit shutout. But a day later Mantle hit his forty-seventh, lifting a slow curve over the left-field fence.

Reporters gathered around him afterward, and Mantle handled them easily. "I tell you that was the most surprised I've been all season," he said. "If I'da missed it, I woulda been on first anyway. The catcher couldn'ta caught it." Later Mantle cut his cheek shaving, and Gus Mauch, the Yankees' trainer, had to be summoned to stop the bleeding.

"Gillette?" someone asked.

Mantle grinned.

On the third day, the mayor of Fargo appeared at the ballpark to present Maris with a "certificate of appreciation for your loyalty and devotion to your hometown of Fargo." (Maris was born in Hibbing, Minnesota, and lives in Raytown, a suburb of Kansas City, Missouri. But he did spend his boyhood in Fargo and played American Legion base-ball there.) Mantle hit No. 48 in the fourth inning. Maris did nothing.

The Yankees flew to New York, where they settled the pennant race by sweeping a three-game series from Detroit. They beat Don Mossi 1–0 in the first game on Bill Skowron's single in the ninth inning. Maris and Mantle were hitless, but still they attracted the largest crowds in the clubhouse.

"Mossi had good stuff," Mantle said of his own effort.

"When you're going lousy, you're lousy," Maris said of his.

The next day Maris hit two home runs, No. 52 and No. 53, but Mantle pulled a muscle checking a swing. "I'll take you out," Houk told Mantle on the bench. "I'll help," Mantle said. "I'll bunt. I'll field. I'll get on." Mantle stayed in the lineup, and a day later he hit two, his forty-ninth and his fiftieth. The Tigers never recovered and now—with the Yankees all but certain to win the pennant—fans, reporters, and photographers turned all their attention to Maris and Mantle. Newspapers started guessing games, with cash prizes for those who forecast how many homers the two would hit. A stripper, playing a minor burlesque circuit, adopted the name of Mickey Maris. A Japanese sports editor sent a list of eighteen questions to the Associated Press in New York, requesting that Maris and Mantle answer all of them.

After hearing five or six, Maris said to the AP reporter, "This is driving me nuts."

"That's my next question," the reporter shouted. "They want to know how you're reacting to all this."

During the next week at Yankee Stadium, Maris hit No. 54, a fierce liner to right-center off Tom Cheney of Washington; No. 55, a high drive into the bleachers off Dick Stigman of Cleveland; and No. 56, another drive into the bleachers, off Mudcat Grant, another Indian. Mantle also hit three, and this week, which ended on September 10, was the last in which Mantle fully shared the pre- and postgame pressures.

As a young ballplayer, Mantle had been almost mute in the presence of interviewers. "Yup" was a long answer; "maybe" was an oration. But over the years he has developed a noncommittal glibness and a fair touch with a light line. "When I hit forty-eight," he told a group one day, "I said to Rog, 'I got my man. The pressure's off me.'" (The year Ruth hit sixty, Lou Gehrig hit forty-seven.) Such comments kept Mantle's press relations reasonably relaxed, but Maris—three years younger than Mantle, ten years younger a star—had to labor. Maris insists that such laborings had no effect on his play, but others close to him are not so sure. "Those daily press conferences didn't do him any good," remarked one friend.

Two days before the Yankees' home stand ended, a reporter asked Maris about the fans behind him in right field. "Terrible," Maris said. "Maybe the worst in the league." He recounted a few unprintable remarks that had been shouted at him and, under consistent prodding, ran down the customers for ten or fifteen minutes. The next day after reading the papers he said to an acquaintance, "That's it. I been trying to be a good guy to the writers, but I quit. You heard me talking. Did I sound like the papers made it look?"

"No."

"Well, from now on I'll tell the writers what pitch I hit, but no more big spiels."

"Because one or two reporters roughed you, are you going to take it out on everybody?"

Maris looked uncomfortable. "Listen," he said, "I like a lot of the writers. But even so, they are No. 2. No. 1 is myself. I got to look out for myself. If it hurts someone else, damn it, I'm sorry, but I got to look out for myself more than I have."

A BAD PRESS

Maris hit no homers in the double-header that concluded the home stand and afterward committed the only truly graceless act of his ordeal. "Well?" a reporter said to Maris, whose locker adjoins Elston Howard's.

"He hit a homer, not me," Maris said, gesturing toward Howard. "Mr. Howard, tell these gentlemen how you did it."

"If I had fifty-five homers, I'd be glad to tell the gentlemen," Howard said, pleasantly.

"Fifty-six," Maris corrected. "What are you trying to do? Shortchange me?" Then he marched into the players' lounge to watch television.

A fringe of Hurricane Carla arrived in Chicago on Tuesday, the 12th, shortly after the Yankees. The game had to be called in the bottom of the sixth, when a downpour hit Comiskey Park. Maris had come to bat four times and gone homerless. Reporters asked him if he'd had good pitches to hit.

"I didn't get too many strikes," Maris said. "But they were called strikes. Soar had me swinging in self-defense."

The next day's newspapers headlined that casual, typical ballplayer's gripe. Maris was shocked and horrified. Until that moment he had not fully realized the impact his words now carried. Until that moment he had not fully realized the price one must pay for being a hero. He was disturbed, upset, withdrawn. Tortured would be too strong a word, but only slightly. He showed his hurt by saying little; his mouth appeared permanently set in its hard line. He hit no home runs in

Chicago, and when the Yankees moved on to Detroit he hit none in a twi-night double-header.

That was the night he declined to meet the press. His brother, Rudy, a mechanical engineer, had driven from his home in Cincinnati to see the games, and later Roger and Rudy sat in the trainer's room, from which reporters are barred. "Get him out," a reporter told Bob Fishel, the Yankees' publicity director.

Fishel talked briefly to Maris. "He says he's not coming out," Fishel announced. "He says he's been ripped in every city he's been in, and he's not coming out."

"Rog won't come out," a reporter told Houk.

"That's his business," Houk said.

"How come we can't go in and talk to him, and his brother can?"

"Are you trying to tell me how to run my clubhouse?" Houk said, flaring. "Is that what you're trying to do?"

"But his brother—"

"That's right, he's talking to his brother, and if he had 150 brothers they couldn't all come in, but he's only got one. If that isn't the funniest thing all year, you telling me a man has no right to talk to his brother."

When things calmed, someone said quietly to Houk, "The important thing is for him to make an appearance."

"I know that," Houk said, "and I know Maris, and now is not the time to talk to him. We'll all be more relaxed later on."

Eventually Maris reconsidered, relaxed, and emerged.

"Any complaints about the umpiring tonight?" a Detroit newspaperman asked.

"Nope," Maris said, "and you got me wrong. I don't complain about umpiring."

When the reporters left, Mantle walked over to Maris. "Mick, it's driving me nuts, I'm telling you," Maris said.

"And I'm telling you, you got to get used to it," Mantle said. Houk then joined Mantle, and the manager talked to Maris for a long time.

The next night Maris hit No. 57, the one Al Kaline retrieved, and a day later, after missing a home run by a foot when he tripled off the fence in right, he won the game for the Yankees in the twelfth inning with No. 58, a drive into the upper deck in right-center field.

As the ball carried high and far, the Yankees' dugout erupted in excitement. "Attaboy, Rog!" the most sophisticated players in the Major Leagues shouted, and "Yea," and "Attababy."

"It was one of the warmest things I've seen all year," said Bob Cerv, the outfielder. "We all know how tough it's been for Rog, and I guess we all decided right then, all at once, that we wanted him to know how much we were for him."

The team went to Baltimore by train. Maris had hit and lost a homer there on July 17, when rain stopped a game in the fifth inning before it was official. He had hit no other homers in the Orioles' large park. If he were going to catch Ruth in 154 games, he would have to hit two there in two days.

He hit none the first night, dragging through a double-header. Now, in addition to hoots from the stands, he was getting hoots by mail (two dozen letters) and wire (six telegrams). "A lot of people in this country must think it's a crime to have anyone break Ruth's record," he said.

The second night, in the Yankees' 154th game, Mantle, who had long since left center stage, vanished into the wings with a cold. Before the game his eyes were glazed, and he was coughing and spitting phlegm. He wasn't well enough to play, and game 154 was left to Maris alone.

No one who saw game 154, who beheld Maris's response to the challenge, is likely soon to forget it. His play was as brave and as moving and as thrilling as a baseball player's can be. There were more reporters and photographers around him now than ever before. Newsmen swelled the Yankees' party, which normally numbers forty-five, to seventy-one. And this was the town where Babe Ruth was born, and the crowd had not come to cheer Maris.

The first time up, Maris shot a line drive to Earl Robinson in right field. He had overpowered Milt Pappas's pitch, but he had not gotten under the ball quite enough. Perhaps an eighth of an inch on the bat was all that kept the drive from sailing higher and farther.

In the third inning Maris took a ball, a breaking pitch inside, swung and missed, took another ball, and then hit No. 59, a 390-foot line drive that all but broke a seat in the bleachers. Three more at bats and one home run to tie.

When he came up again, Dick Hall was pitching. Maris took two strikes and cracked a liner, deep but foul, to right. Then he struck out. When Maris came to bat again in the seventh inning the players in the Yankees' bullpen, behind the fence in right-center, rose and walked to the fence. "Come on, Roger, baby, hit it to me," shouted Jim Coates. "If I have to go fifteen rows into the stands, I'll catch that No. 60 for you."

"You know," said Whitey Ford, "I'm really nervous."

Maris took a strike, then whaled a tremendous drive to right field. Again he had overpowered the ball, and again he had hit a foul. Then he lifted a long fly to right-center, and there was that eighth of an inch again. An eighth of an inch lower on the bat and the long fly might have been a home run—*the* home run.

Hoyt Wilhelm was pitching in the ninth. He threw Maris a low knuckleball, and Maris, checking his swing, fouled it back. Wilhelm threw another knuckler, and Maris moved his body but not his bat. The knuckler, veering abruptly, hit the bat; the ball rolled back to Wilhelm, who tagged Maris near first base.

"I'm just sorry I didn't go out with a real good swing," Maris said. "But that Wilhelm." He shook his head. He had overpowered pitches in four of his five times at bat and had gotten only one home run. "Like they say," he said, "you got to be lucky."

Robert Reitz, an unemployed Baltimorean, retrieved No. 59 and announced that the ball was worth $2,500.

"I'd like to have it," said Maris, blunt to the end, "but I'm not looking to get rid of that kind of money for it."

The Yankees won the 154th game, 4–2, and with it clinched the American League pennant. Maris wore a gray sweater at the victory party, and someone remarked that in gray and with his crew-cut, he looked like a West Point football player. One remembered then how young he is, and how he believes in honesty as youth does.

"The big thing with you," a friend said to him, "is you tell the truth and don't go phony."

"That's all I know," Roger Maris said. "That's the only way I know how to be. That's the way I'm gonna stay."

Not notably eloquent, perhaps, but a wholly admirable credo.

24

Robert Frost: A Reminiscence

The Nation, February 9, 1963

An intimate remembrance, written shortly after Frost's death on January 29, 1963. (Once Frost wrote, "And I may return / If dissatisfied / With what I learn / From having died.")

This is a strange night, heavy with death, unrelieved by miracles. Robert Frost is dead, and my mortality and yours are thus more stark. Very soon I shall be telling young people that I knew him and what he said and how he smiled at my son, and the young people will look blank and tolerant, as though I were speaking of Sophocles. In death, an hour is as centuries.

Yet one rejects such truth. Grief work is what psychiatrists call it. They say that minds adjust in ordered patterns to the multitudinous facts of tragedy, and it is odd that one should think of this, for Robert Frost stood, perhaps above all other things, for the pristine privacy of the mind. . . .

"What does this poem mean?" some ask.

"It means what it says."

"I know what it means to me, but I don't know what it means to you."

"Maybe I don't want you to."

Frost wrote many kinds of poems about many kinds of things, and he resented all attempts to explain or to restate what he had labored to produce. Once, when someone plagued him to please explain that poem, he remarked, "Do you want me to say it in worse English?"

I knew Robert Frost, and we talked of writing and baseball and politics and religion and love and lust and loneliness. And even death. He didn't want to die. He said he was too curious about unfinished business. Us and Russia. How will that come out?

I think I knew him well enough to disqualify myself as a critic, which is fortunate. A fine immediate criticism was written in London forty-nine years ago by a man who was killed in the First World War. "These poems," Edward Thomas commented of *North of Boston*, "are revolutionary because they lack the exaggeration of rhetoric." Final criticism is premature in 1963. Was Frost, as he himself liked to suggest, a culmination of New England culture, an end product of Longfellow, Emerson, and a hostile soil? Or was he a precursor? Or was he both? As I say, answers are premature. Many still argue whether Mozart crowned Haydn or created Beethoven.

Many were confused by Robert Frost. They saw him as a gentle New Englander, which he was not. They saw him as a simple farmer who wrote simple poems, which he did seldom. They saw him as a placed figure, forgetting, because he did not remind them, that his art, like his life, was wrought of restlessness and torture, as well as moments of controlled delight.

"You can quote me on anything," he once said, "except writers and writing."

"Why?" I asked.

"Because," he said triumphantly, "I'm not a critic."

That was his pride, a pride almost ferocious.

I think it is fair now to report some of our talk about writers and writing—fair and important because his words should be preserved. This was not idle talk. It built toward a philosophy.

"I was always afraid of rejection slips," he said. "I had to guard my pride. But when I went to England [in 1912, when he was thirty-six] I took a bunch of verses down to a little publisher in London—not a vanity press, mind you—and he liked them and he printed them. I'm not a literary man, but after that they wanted me to join the literary life and asked me to a group that Pound ran.

"Economy. That was what Pound wanted. I write a poem and give it to you; you write it in fewer words. Six people sitting around a room, writing poems in fewer words. Pound said, 'Got a poem on you, Frost?' I pointed to my head: 'Up here.'

"I wrote it out. . . .

Sea waves are green and wet
But up from where they die
Rise others vaster yet
And these are brown and dry.
They are the sea made land
To come at the fisher town
And bury in solid sand
The men she could not drown.

"Pound came back in a little while. 'Don't have too much on you, Frost. Took you forty-five words. Best I could do was forty-two.'

"'Yes,' I told him, 'and destroyed my rhyme and destroyed my meter and probably destroyed my sense.'" . . .

Frost jabbed an elbow into my ribs. "That settled Pound's hash," he said. "He never tried to tell me how to write poetry again."

So he was fiercely proud of his art long before presidents and college professors knew that the art existed, and he kept this pride, very much as it was, through all his years. "I don't change," he said. "I don't get over things. I don't even grow. They're a lot of fools, the people who say that you get over things, a love or a poem."

He rejected Pound's advice and Pound's way, but because Frost was for poetry, he never rejected Pound. He visited Pound at St. Elizabeth's Hospital in Washington. Afterward, he summoned Sherman Adams and said that Pound ought to be freed.

"It is wrong to imprison poets," Frost said, explaining later, "but since he's been freed Pound has been writing me unpleasant letters. Scatological. He keeps using the word 'shit.'"

From Frost, the word shocked. . . .

"But that's not the worst thing," Frost said. "The worst is what he's doing to Eliot. He writes Eliot and says, 'I was wrong about you. You're not a good poet.'"

Frost . . . believed, as did Shakespeare, in the sound of words, in the immediacy of the phrase, in the transcendent fact of rhythm. "Could you ever teach rhythm?" I asked him once, as we stood on the hill near sunset.

"No," he said, touching his ear. "It's either there or not."

"That cheers me," I said, "because my son is three and listens to Elizabethan lyrics and doesn't understand the words."

"Three years old and responds to rhythm, you say?"

"Yes."

"Of course," Frost said, "because his heart beats and he's seen the waves."

So he was—and nothing else is as important—a lyric man who loved beauty and who moved with beauty and who spoke with beauty, wholly original and unique.

I brought my son to see him a year later, on a day when Frost wanted to talk politics. I listened, disappointed—I wanted to talk writing. The child ran out into a cornfield and played. Then it was time to go, and I gathered the child, hiked him onto my shoulder, and started down the steep hill. Frost ran to the porch, calling, "The boy, the boy. I have to say good-bye to the boy." I turned and then the boy stared at Frost, who was eighty-seven, all wonder, and Frost looked back again. . . .

Down the hill, I heard Robert Frost cry after me, "Come back again, if you'd care to." Because trivialities crowded my time, I never did.

25

The Time of the Hustler

Show Magazine, October 1963

Advertisers, lawyers, agents, deal makers of all stripes so crowd the World Series that the baseball itself becomes almost an afterthought.

The World Series was conceived in commerce and dedicated to the proposition that a few thousand extra dollars never hurt anyone who owned a baseball team. That is how it was in 1903, when the Series began, and that is how it is in 1962, except that the few thousand has become a few million, partly because of inflation, partly because of bigger ballparks, and largely because the National Broadcasting Company is willing to televise the Series at the rate of $3,750 per pitch.

It would be nice to believe that the Series is what it pretends to be, a beery kind of Hellenic ideal, an Olympic for the populace. It would even be nice to think of it as a monster but innocent. The World Series is neither Hellenic nor innocent. It is a quick, incredibly successful grab for money and attention. It is a monument to the fast buck. It has become the time of the hustler.

Ride a taxi after dark in a World Series city, and you find yourself trapped in a seemingly innocent opening: "See the game, Mac?"

"Yes, I did."

"Here for the Series, huh?"

"That's right."

"Listen, Mac, I know this town, and you don't wanna go where you're goin'. I'll take you to this joint; they got these three girls and . . ."

Talk to a ballplayer and the conversation is equally unpleasant:

"Hello, Berwyn. Nice hitting out there today."

"I can't tell ya about it."

"Why not?"

"The *Saturday Evening Post* and *Life* and *Look* are bidding for my story. They want me to write this here excloosive article."

Talk to no one, stand in a saloon by yourself, and someone knees you in the coccyx, then roars, "Howrrya. I'm Wendell Lethune from Mason City, Iowa, and I sell air conditioners. Wha's your line, ol' buddy?"

Stay in your hotel room, flick on the television, and a hearty stranger shouts: "Hi there, folks. Al Mellon here. It's a great pleasure to be bringing you this great 1962 World Series on behalf of the makers of Gasho, the razor with the bandage in the package, and Agon, the Purple Heart cigarette."

The World Series is when the Pennsylvania Railroad charges extra for soda (as in Scotch and soda) on its Baseball Special. It's when room clerks ask, "What the hell do you mean, you can't find the closet in 2137? You're in it, feller; who's next?"

It is when a short, dark, fast-talking man named Frank Scott, the MCA of baseball, peddles the off-field services of ballplayers who are willing to address civic groups, lend their names to spurious juvenile fiction, eat in certain restaurants, and endorse certain underarm deodorants. It is also the time when some good baseball games are played. Al Mellon and the other six hundred reporters assigned to cover each Series may well tell you more than you want to know.

The operative word is excess. Baseball is a crass, vulgar side to show business and, to those of us who like it, magnificent entertainment, sometimes art. The business of baseball is at its worst during the World Series. The game of baseball is sometimes at its best.

The Series brings together the pennant-winning teams from the National and American Leagues, big league in the argot of sports, Senior Circuit and Junior Loop in the cliché. The teams then play until one of them has won four times, creating a series that lasts from four to seven games and that operates as a super-shuttle. The first two games are played in the home city of one team. The scene shifts, and the next three are played in the other's town. Finally, the sixth and seventh games, if necessary, are played where everything began. An Aristotelian unity of locus, as Giants outfielder Willie Mays puts it. . . .

Technically, it isn't a world series at all, since teams from, say, Japan or Mexico are not represented. But only technically. American Major League baseball is the best baseball played anywhere, and the only man I ever heard challenge that was a Russian journalist who worked for *Trud*. "Is like our game lapta," the man said, "except lapta more exciting and lapta players better. Lapta championships in Voronezh real World Series."

"Mickey Mantle's grandchildren will bury your lapta players," I said, after which the conversation got out of hand.

What one can challenge, without dialect, is whether Series entertainments settle anything but which team is better counting or not counting the breaks during a single week of autumn.

The regular baseball season, which is to say games between spring training and the Series, runs almost six months, and as baseball people mouth at the drop of a question, "Over the season, the breaks even out." Probably they do, but over any single week of baseball games, luck is an immense consideration. A Series player, or observer, does well to remember the philosophy of a star performer, Vernon Gomez, who once remarked, "I'd rather be lucky than good." (As it happened, in the Series, Lefty Gomez was both.)

The Yankees lost the 1960 World Series to the Pirates because a ground ball bounded erratically off the anthracite infield of Forbes Field in Pittsburgh and struck Tony Kubek, a Yankees shortstop, in the throat. "Urrgh," Kubek said. He then failed to make a play, and a winning rally began. The Brooklyn Dodgers lost the 1952 World Series to the Yankees because a pitcher named Billy Loes lost a ground ball in the sun. It was late afternoon, and the sun sat amid naked girders in back of the lower deck at Ebbets Field. Gene Woodling of the Yankees tapped a ball toward Loes, and it flashed before the sun on its first bounce and glanced off Loes's knee on its second. A dozen World Series have been decided by similar whims of Atropos.

Beyond fate, the Series places a disproportionate premium on the endurance of star pitchers. Ordinarily, star pitchers husband their energies, working one day out of five or six, drinking beer in between and musing about the delicacy of the full-muscled masculine arm. Since the difference between winning and losing a Series is roughly

$3,000 per player, including star pitchers, this is no time for either musing or delicacy.

"How come all of a sudden you can pitch three games in seven days?" I once asked a star pitcher named Lew Burdette, who had not only pitched against but beaten the Yanks three times.

"Cuz I got all winter to rest up," Burdette said, "but don't use that; I got an offer from the *American Weekly*."

The *Weekly* piece has long since been ghosted, leaving me free to quote Burdette and also to point out that money, not Anacin, best relieves tension and palliates nagging pains, even in the pitching arm.

Transcending everything else is the element of momentum. Baseball has been subjected to analysis by everyone from Heywood Broun to Casey Stengel, and no one has yet explained why a ballplayer performs superbly for one fortnight and abysmally for the next. There are terms—hot streak, slump—but they are not explanations.

Using a round bat, one must connect with a round ball, traveling at ninety miles an hour, hooking, dipping, or sliding out of its natural path. A batter has roughly a fifth of a second in which to decide whether to swing, perhaps a tenth of a second in which to whip his bat. The timing of batters—all batters from Ty Cobb to this year's nine-year-olds—comes and vanishes in mysterious ways. What makes Mickey Mantle, Willie Mays, or Stan Musial slump? What makes an obscure ballplayer a slugger pro tem? Why isn't hitting as predictable as acting or dancing or fiddling, even among its very best practitioners? "Timing," say baseball men, describing a symptom, not a cause.

Unfortunately, the causes of bad individual timing and team inertia are no more treatable than understandable. A good team, last year's Cincinnati Reds, went into a Series without momentum and prompted Jimmy Cannon to write, "Imposters. They should have paid their way into the park." A team no better, the 1959 Los Angeles Dodgers, went in hot, won the Series, and was acclaimed by politicians and adulated by the sports staffs of Henry Luce publications.

Not wives nor mistresses nor managers can generate momentum, although managers invariably try, by such means as orations, fines, and suggestions. "Everybody go out and get drunk so we'll all be loosey-goosey tomorrow." The team goes out and drinks and a day later is not only beaten but hung over. The truth is that players are loose or not in response to complicated eye-to-hand coordination. All anyone knows is that no one knows much about it.

World Series baseball is different from regular season baseball. In a sense, it is instant baseball. Mix two teams, stir briskly, and what is supposed to come out on top is the finest ballclub in the cosmos. Perhaps. But what invariably surface are the wheelers and dealers, the pitchmen and gimmick guys. Like an outstanding Broadway hit or an important movie premiere, baseball's big show attracts hordes of first-nighters who, the scalpers know, will pay anything not to see the game but be seen at it. The Series on and off the field becomes a celebrity circus. There are a number of reasons for limiting the Series to the first week in October, among them the north wind. But brevity is the soul of promotion.

"Look," goes the spiel. "Here. Now. Quick. This is the best thing in baseball. Pay attention!"

"But it's really a kind of publicity baseball, isn't it, sir?"

"Hurry, hurry. Pay attention."

Almost everyone does. NBC estimates that this year's Sunday Series game will flicker on 60 million television sets, a statistic so large as to be almost meaningless, except in terms of money.

NBC's complex contract with the Major Leagues provides a basic annual Series pot of about $3.75 million. Ticket sales, at $10 for boxes and $8 for most other seats, sometimes add another $3 million. Sales of hot dogs, peanuts, programs, pennants, plastic baseballs, and busts of Commissioner Ford Christopher Frick approach $250,000. The magic number is $7 million, so that for a seven-game Series, the longest, the corporate take holds at $1 million a day.

Wherever there is that much money, there are operators. Around any million-dollar-a-day business, operators materialize as spontaneously as maggots on the *Potemkin*. Some should not be trusted in a room with one baby and one bar of candy.

So there are angles, and the anglers talk to the ballplayers and the ballplayers start angling and the anglers talk to sportswriters and television folk, and these start angling, and somewhere the idea of the whole affair to hit a round ball with a round bat is forgotten. Each winning player earns about $9,000 for a week's work, and each losing player earns about $6,000. The Series atmosphere, reeking with millions, gets too heady for most integrities.

There is no validity in arguing that a ballplayer earning $9,000 a week is overpaid any more than a big movie or television draw, because there is no validity in arguing against a free economy. British soccer players, good and ordinary, are union workers on scale. Soviet hockey players are army men who rise at the rate of two and a half ranks for every three victories over decadent capitalists. Our system may be more ridiculous than that of the Limeys or the Ivans, but at least it seems better to us. Where we get excessive is in trying to transform instant baseball into instant fortunes.

To these ends, the baseball commissioner's office subsidizes the establishment of two angling rooms. The euphemism is hospitality room, "hospitality" referring to free food and drink. Each Series club owner rents a hotel ballroom, customarily used for the wedding receptions of surgeons' daughters, and throws the doors open to the initiate for two meals and a Niagara of drink a day. Among the initiate are sportswriters, baseball officials, hangers-on, agents, railroad and airline employees, managers and coaches, but never players or women. The club owners don't quite trust ballplayers exposed to free booze and don't trust themselves exposed to booze and women simultaneously. Nevertheless, the angling room is the real backstage of the Series.

It was in one of these rooms that a magazine editor approached Frank Scott, the agent, and said, "I'd like to buy Lew Burdette's byline."

"So would a lotta guys," Scott replied.

"Yeah, but the thing is I want him to say that he wins because he throws the spitball."

Since the spitball had been outlawed, Scott said, "How much?"

Editor: "Five thousand."

Burdette and Scott made their decision. "For five thou, we won't say he does throw the spitter," Scott reported, "but we also won't say he don't throw it. No deal."

At another Series, another pitcher, who had previously agreed to sell his byline for $1,250, approached a journalist I know and said, "Hey, now that I'm really in the Series, can't you get 'em to give me a little more, maybe fifteen hundred?" The writer repaired to the angling room and bearded the editor over martinis. "He wants a little more," the ghost said.

"Will thirty-two hundred keep him happy?" asked the editor.

"Deal."

The pitcher has been buying his writer drinks ever since.

Scott is incontestably the boldest of dealers because he represents nearly every Major League baseball player, a position won by shrewdness and default. In the early 1950s Scott was traveling secretary of the Yankees, a job requiring him to see that players did not miss trains and that hotels had rooms ready for twenty-five athletes. The Yankees later asked him to assume an additional assignment. Would he report on the alcoholic and sexual exploits of his charges? Scott said he would not. He was fired.

"I looked around," Scott says, "and figured what could I do. I mean, I love baseball, and you know a lot of players had been always asking me for advice on endorsements and stuff like that, which I gave 'em free when I was road secretary. So I figured I might as well go into business. There weren't any active agents around, and I started with the Yankees. Yogi Berra. And I got Mantle out of a bad deal. Now I got just about everybody. Anybody who wants a ballplayer for something oughta see me."

Scott, a small, sharp-featured man, evaluates World Series performances pragmatically. "Now you give me a guy they don't know much, not a Mantle," he says, "and give him a helluva Series, and I'll make him fifteen, twenty-five thousand over the winter. Everybody follows the Series. You want an overnight hero? Just tell him to be great in the Series."

The astronauts have agents, Liz Taylor has agents, and there is no reason why professional ballplayers should not have agents. Before long, successful agents will have agents. But Scott's power during the Series is unnerving. Sportswriters seek him out and ask, "If you sell a Whitey Ford story, can I write it?" Editors try to pin him down with early bids for stars. TV producers corner him for personal appearances of his charges. Press agents wheedle him with pleas and cash to have players show up in stores, theaters, and restaurants. In the hour of the

Series angle, the star player is hot, the sharpest agent is king. Scott does considerably better than most theatrical flesh peddlers.

During the 1960 World Series, he established bidding for the recollections, but not confessions, of Casey Stengel. *Look* dropped out quickly, at $60,000 or so, and *Life* at $150,000. The *Post* won by paying Stengel $155,000 for five articles, which could be called incredible, except that I write and I hesitate to criticize high rates.

Still, one can wonder. What makes our World Series and its heroes so commercial? What joins editor, writer, bubblegum salesman, TV man, cereal packager, and scalper in a common plea for a piece of the action? Why has the World Series become less of an entertainment classic than a gigantic carnival dedicated to aweing and shaking down the rubes?

An enduring fault must be laid to newspapers. The *New York Times* automatically assigns five men to cover the World Series, which already is (a) televised, (b) broadcast, and (c) covered by ten to fifteen men from the Associated Press. Last fall it was possible to read the front pages of the *Cincinnati Enquirer* and *Post* and *Times-Star* during the Series week without encountering either the word "megaton" or the name Khrushchev (although that week Kennedy and Gromyko conferred at the White House on the Berlin crisis and Laos; the Russians beefed up the strength of their East German garrisons; and the United Nations General Assembly was orating in New York). The Series sells papers, say circulation men, and so it does, but there comes a point when a paper's editors might remember that a free press should be responsible and maintain a sense of proportion. When one Series reporter writes a lead story, another writes a column, a third writes of the winning clubhouse, a fourth writes of the losing clubhouse, a fifth describes miscellany, I'd say that point has been passed.

Similarly, magazines cover the Series hysterically. The standard approach is to blurb on the cover, "How I Beat the Yankees, by Pitcher Sol Strumpf." Inside, one learns that Strumpf comes from West Virginia, that he prefers ball fields to slag heaps, and that his daughter, Athena, gave him a lucky penny just before the big game, which is what did it. One does not learn how Strumpf beat the Yankees. Strumpf is no man's maniac. He will have to pitch against the Yankees next year. He won't tell how he defeated them to his parish priest, much less the world at large. By keeping his pitching secrets to himself, he may defeat them once more, after which he can sell to another magazine, "How I Beat the Yankees Again, Exclusive!"

As might be expected, television outdoes both newspapers and magazines in blind exuberance. Baseball officials retain a veto right in the existing TV contract, and any announcer who yawns or hints that an 11–2 game is one-sided can be dismissed. Awe is a job requirement for television reporting; an orbital flight, an inauguration, the opening of a supermarket, a World Series are all thrilling, deeply moving, an honor to be here to see.

The public buys. People purchase more newspapers during the World Series. A catchy cover line sells extra magazines. Millions sit before television sets. Salesmen struggle to find Series seats for customers. Corporations purchase blocks of tickets. Americans respond when a Series hero says to buy hair tonic or undershorts or bread. The nation is not raped by the World Series. It lies down willingly, voluptuously.

The danger is in confusing love with commerce. We have this marvelous game, which wasn't invented but which evolved slowly from old English games of bat and ball, which grew here in town and field even as the towns grew, which fathers teach to sons and which sons discuss with fathers before they can discuss much else beyond the heart. We have this game, which is our own, which prompts novels and verse and even poetry and stirred the genius of Ring Lardner. We've taken this game and turned its denouement into a parody of Dionysia, complete with sales conference attached.

Next month, two teams will again try to carve each other down to size. The playing may be good, possibly great, but you will have to be a knowledgeable and canny fan to distinguish between the main performance and the sideshow. When the operators take over, they spotlight the spectacle and dim the sport. As baseball, the Series is declining. As a hoax on the folks, it's on the way up.

Around any million-dollar-a-day business, operators materialize as spontaneously as maggots on the *Potemkin*. Lardner was writing in 1925, a comparatively quiet time.

Part 4

Getting Closer

26

Writing Sports

Esquire, August 1970

A look at the craft as the press gives way to the media.

During the mauve years of Richard Nixon's vice presidency, I served the hierarchy of a major magazine as sports editor. This was preferable to evisceration, although the distinction was not always clear.

My immediate superior had written sports in Bridgeport. There he learned to mistrust dialogue. "It makes for short sentences," he complained, "and wastes space." His superior had published a sports magazine that failed. He knew a number of anecdotes that he habitually excised as stale, and did not know a number of others that he excised as obscure. The executive editor was big, square, Yale, and doggedly elitist. Finally, the editor himself indulged certain prejudices.

"Writing about niggers again, Kahn?" he said once.

"Look," I said. "It's my sports section."

"Yes," the editor said, "and it's my magazine."

As with cigarettes, the deleterious effects proceeded subtly, but when I left the magazine after four years, I found myself in agreement with an old *New York Times* sportswriter who liked to say, "Very little matters, and nothing matters much."

I contracted to rewrite a doctor's diet book; the chore consumed three weeks and produced a bestseller. For no reason beyond vague curiosity about Hollywood, I ghosted Mickey Rooney's autobiography. We reaped large sums from editors who burned to know how the first Mrs. Rooney, Ava Gardner, behaved in bed.

Through these affluent, obscene, dissolute days, sports shone, a beacon to my conscience, and when Ingemar Johannson, the Goteborg Juggernaut, agreed to face Floyd Patterson for the third time, I got word to Stanley Woodward of the *Herald Tribune* that I would like to cover the fight and could work cheap. Woodward, an earth force disguised as a sports editor, said, "If you file a thousand words of notes and cover a dressing room, I'll pay you ten dollars."

In Miami Beach before the fight, Max Schmeling strolled Collins Avenue to modest applause. Since Schmeling had represented Adolf Hitler as a paratrooper, the scene was troubling. "Of course Schmeling was not a Nazi," I explained. "As I get the picture, there were never more than six or seven Nazis in Germany. But they worked very hard." Then the sour memory of the mangling magazine editors charged to mind. Lufthansa, Volkswagen, and the Argentine Tourist Bureau were advertisers. I placed the comment near the end of the notes.

After printing the entire story, Woodward sent a message saying that he had liked the stuff enough to pay five times the agreed-upon price. With his $50 came an invitation for another drink.

I strutted into the Artist and Writers Restaurant. "Hello, Coach. Glad you liked the piece."

"Why did you bury the lead note?" Woodward growled.

"The Schmeling thing? I thought if you saw it you might kill it."

"You are a stupid son of a bitch," Woodward said, turning and showing a back that was broad as Asia. He would not speak to me for twenty minutes, and I had to pay for my own Scotch. It struck me then that I had been found out, and through sports. . . . I have not since ghosted a book or consciously buried a lead.

From a distance, sports appears to be the shallow end of the American sea: puerile speeches at the letter club banquet, the hustling of transparent con men, simple adults pursuing childhood activities, amiable anecdotes repeated on old-timers' day. The same man who demands harsh film criticism and likes his political reporting merciless accepts a pabulum view of sport. He may find it sheer relief to turn to the sports page as a kind of toy department. He may have suffered from myopia at seven; in that case he enjoys putting down great hitters by pointing out that baseball is only a game.

Well, professional football is only a game. Its heroes drive forearms into throats at 4:15 p.m. They then kneel in group prayer at 4:20. No one who knows that should have been surprised when the administration ordered Cambodia invaded on Thursday and proclaimed for Sunday, "Let us pray." Without confusing football with holocaust, this department will take sports seriously. Sports tells anyone who watches intelligently about the times in which we live: about managed news and corporate politics, about race and terror and what the process of aging does to strong men. If that sounds grim, there is courage and high humor, too. In a sort of converse to the Woodward experience, I find sport a better area than most to look for truth. A great hockey goalie, Glenn Hall, describing his life on ice, once said, "That puck comes so hard, it could take an eye. I've had 250 stitches, and I don't like pain. I get so nervous before every game, I lose my lunch."

"Some football players," I said to the goalie, "say that when they're badly scared they pray."

Hall looked disgusted. "If there is a God," he said, "let's hope he's doing something more important than watching hockey games." Offhand I can't recall a better sermon.

Without question we stand in the middle of a national sports boom. More teams. Greater attendance. Better athletes. Precisely where we stand in national sports journalism is less apparent.

The craft begins, I suppose, with Heywood Broun and Ring Lardner. What went before was primitive and irrelevant. Broun is renowned for getting himself fired from the *New York World* when he would not stop defending the rights and subsequently the memories of Sacco and Vanzetti. He was happier playing right field in a Connecticut meadow.

Broun relished sport, and he took football, baseball, and boxing as frames on which to mount personal essays. A fight between a wild swinger called Rocky Kansas and the ultra-smooth Benny Leonard became a contest between Dada and tradition. At one point, Broun wrote, "Rocky Kansas partisans in the gallery began to split infinitives to show their contempt for Leonard and all stylists." I envy him a particular mix of metaphors: "The underdog can and will lick his weight in the wildcats of the world."

Lardner was cursed/blessed with genius. . . . *You Know Me Al* and its obscure sequel, *Lose with a Smile,* may be the only works of art built around American sport. "And," John Lardner said proudly, "in both books what my father called a sun field really was a sun field, and second base was always right where it belonged."

By contrast, Lardner's nonfiction suffers, but sometimes the shocking wit bursts through. He kept trying to see Georges Carpentier, a stylish Frenchman who was training to fight the mighty Dempsey, and was put off three times with, "M. Carpentier is sleeping." He then wrote, "Carpentier is practicing ten-second naps."

Like the present, the 1930s writhed with excess and sorrow. Grantland Rice, the reigning sportswriter, was a lovely man who followed a flowery muse. His most famous story begins: "Outlined against a blue, gray . . . sky, the Four Horsemen rode again. In dramatic lore, they are known as Famine, Pestilence, Destruction, and Death. These are only aliases. Their real names are Stuhldreher, Miller, Crowley, and Layden." Rice was describing a fine Notre Dame backfield. Although the paragraph is a remarkable bit of work against a deadline, it is composed of a dangerous mix: fancy and overstatement. A Rice disciple, covering a football game at Annapolis in 1933, had poorer luck:

"Navy's ship of success foundered on the banks of the Severn today, wrecked by the rugged rocks of Pittsburgh. After a safe passage past Columbia, Penn State, and Notre Dame abroad, the gallant craft came to grief at its home port, sunk by the waves of Pittsburgh's power."

Just about everything is wrong with that opening. It does not mention the sport, the crowd, the game, or the score, and the conceit is atrocious. For years this sort of prose raged on sports pages everywhere. Miasma, Woodward called it.

Somehow, perhaps through the solemnity of World War II, sportswriting and the English language were reunited in the 1940s. Immediately, the craft flowered. Jimmy Cannon developed his powerful, imagistic style. W. C. Heinz and later Ed Linn created a series of remarkable verismo magazine articles. A renegade English instructor, Joe H. Palmer, wrote marvelously about racing and its spas. Once he defined a horse lover as a horse that loves another horse. It is difficult to snatch epigrams from Red Smith's columns; the best are nearly seamless. Writing eight hundred words a day six times a week—"my daily spelling lesson," he said—Smith captured the fun of sport with endearing irreverence.

"Do you have any superstitions?" I asked him once.

"Only the Roman Catholic Church," Smith said. And, to reverse Maugham's mot, the man was the style.

Ultimately, tall, silent, bespectacled John Lardner guarded his family name and pride by writing a column for *Newsweek* once a week. "I couldn't make it right every day," he said. Listen to Lardner in 1957, discussing the dramatic one-punch knockout of Gene Fullmer by Sugar Ray Robinson in Chicago:

> An oddly shocking and confusing thing—neither good nor very bad, neither just nor very cruel—happened to Gene Fullmer, the young Mormon prizefighter, in the boxing hall here the other night. When he went into the ring, his life was at its peak. He was famous, newly rich, powerful, confident, rising. A few minutes later he fell from power and glory to frustration and relative nothingness. And he cannot tell you from his own knowledge what happened. Not only power and glory are gone—the facts are missing, too. Thirty seconds of time, at the climax of his existence, are lost to him.
>
> To know what went on he has to be told. To believe it he has to look at a set of pictures. And this will be true for the rest of his life. It will be a strange, unsettling way to live.

For the right reader at the right time, these lines transcend sport. They ask how many of us have been unconscious, or at least unaware, as the most important event in our life passed quickly by.

"Why in hell didn't he get bigger obits? Why didn't they make more fuss? A guy like that kickin' off?" The outraged speaker was Jimmy Breslin . . . after John Lardner had perished of general woe.

"I guess, Jim, because he wasn't much at sociability or self-promotion."

"Well, Christ, it ain't right," Breslin said and stormed out of Pete's Tavern to begin a campaign of self-promotion without rival. Successful campaigns attract cults, and when Breslin began making noise and money, the cultists prattled about a new sports journalism blending fiction and nonfiction.

I am mystified by what the cultists mean. One attacked Jimmy Cannon in 1959 for "making up details. Like how does he know the cigar the fight manager lights really is an Antonio y Cleopatra? He's faking."

The same man praises new journalists for not getting "hung by facts or bogged by details." I suspect the new journalism of sport is illusory. What exists in plethora is new flap copy.

Al Silverman, who as editor of *Sport* has to purchase a dozen articles every month, suggests that we are in the age of the chipmunk. A chipmunk is a hardworking reporter who asks impertinent questions, is not obsessed with protecting his sources, and scurries about for stories like a, well, chipmunk. "The Selma of the chipmunk movement," Silverman says, "was the World Series of 1962. Our magazine gave Ralph Terry a car for beating the Giants twice. His wife called him in the Yankees' dressing room to congratulate him and say the new baby was coming along fine.

"'Where's your wife?' a reporter asked.

"'Feeding the baby,' Terry said.

"'Breast or bottle?' asked the reporter.

"Terry answered the question, and that epitomizes the chipmunk approach and the interesting climate it creates."

Silverman's cheer at chipmunks, while remembering lions, is an emotion previously described:

Though the great song return no more
There's keen delight in what we have:
The rattle of pebbles on the shore
Under the receding wave.

I don't suggest that sportswriting in the 1950s was uniformly good. Much was dreadful. Nor do I demean chipmunks and other craftsmen: Maury Allen, Stan Isaacs, Neil Offen, Vic Ziegal, to name four chipmunks; Dick Young of the *Daily News*, a phenomenal reporter; Jim Murray of Los Angeles, Jack Murphy of San Diego, Wells Twombly of Detroit, and Arthur Daley, whose column in the *New York Times* glows with the amiability of the man. We have, however, been considering giants. Now there are none.

Woodward and Lardner have died. Heinz and Linn write novels. Living in Manhattan, I can no longer buy a newspaper that carries Cannon or Smith. And that leads to another dark side of the present.

We have lost not only remarkable men but institutions that supported remarkable men. The old *Collier's* and new *Saturday Evening Post* are gone. Thirty or forty newspapers have folded since the fifties. From my own loft, I share with Marcuse and Agnew a horror at monopoly journalism.

When nine men covered Ted Williams, it was impossible to conceal the fact that Williams, while an astonishing batsman, was a pill. If one writer courted the Thumper by refusing to report a tantrum, another inevitably seized the tantrum as news. Williams would then speak to neither, until he needed a favor. Regardless of each reporter's skill, an essential, imperfect system of checks and balances worked. If you cared enough about Williams, and I did, you could find a portrait that was honest by consensus.

Now two newspapers survive in Los Angeles, and only three sports sections are published every day in New York City. *Sports Illustrated's* reportage is excellent, but it is asking too much for one magazine to replace something like 120,000 columns of lost newspaper sportswriting a week. Competition has ebbed, and we lie at the mercy of other people's self-discipline.

Publishers celebrated the world championship of the New York Mets by commissioning a basket of books. Three contracts fell on reporters employed by the *New York Times,* and one day last spring a reviewer employed by the *Times* announced that he was evaluating the results.

According to John Leonard, *Amazing* by Joseph Durso of the *Times* and *Joy in Mudville* by George Vecsey of the *Times* offer livid detail and complement each other perfectly. *The New York Mets* by Leonard Koppett of the *Times* may be the best of the batch. But *Once Upon the Polo Grounds* by Leonard Schecter of *Look* is lightweight and was funnier in a shorter version that appeared in, of all places, the *New York Times Magazine.* John Leonard dismisses *Last to First* by Larry Fox, who works for the *Daily News,* and jumps heavily on *The Perfect Game* by Tom Seaver and Dick Schaap, a busy freelance. I suppose the Durso book is truly excellent, but how can one trust a *Times* box score that reads: *Times*-men, three good books out of three; everybody else, hitless?

As the media men say, TV makes every living room an arena. If that's what you want for your living room, televised sport can be thrilling. A good director shows aspects you cannot see on scene: lips moving in profanity, a loser's tears. But TV confuses people by forever mixing the true with the false. "Watch this on instant replay; see how the pitcher winces." And a moment later the same voice: "Glooble Beer will help you lose weight. And say, girls, it's also an excellent depilatory."

"Trivia," the estimable Otto Friedrich sniffs at sport in *Decline and Fall*, but clearly sport is significant. It is big business and that matters, and it is a theater of truth, and it holds up a mirror to society and humanity.

Willis Reed, a gigantic black of Bernice, Louisiana, and New York, is not only captain of the Knickerbockers but the team leader and protector. When someone turned on Bill Bradley, Reed informed the aggressor: "I'm king here. If any asses get kicked in, I do the kicking." Bradley, WASP, Princeton, Rhodes Scholar, is a happy member of King Willis's court. Under black leadership, Bradley feels proud rather than demeaned.

Two members of the St. Louis football Cardinals confessed last autumn they had joined the SDS. One described professional football in terms of society. "The structure is reactionary. We live in a goddamn military camp. The shit comes down from above."

The old Dallas quarterback Don Meredith has cried out against the duality of life. "I can't be somber," he told Gary Cartwright, "but some players don't understand this. They thought I was unconcerned. I had to pull away. I'm naturally gregarious, but ensign, it's a lonely life here on the bridge."

Sports is about people who are inner-directed, outer-directed, non-directed, and omni-directed. Frank Ryan, topologist, PhD, assistant professor of mathematics at Case Western Reserve, has signed on at thirty-four for another year as substitute quarterback in Washington. A black outfielder, Curt Flood, is risking income and a career by challenging the legality of baseball's standard player contract. In a basketball dressing room, on a night when fans have jeered Lew Alcindor, Alcindor's father considers a deeper cruelty. After four years at Juilliard, Alcindor père, a trombonist, was barred from orchestras because he is black. "I get more work now," he says, "but it is too late to make a living at it. Berlioz is my favorite." . . .

All around, basketball players discuss pickoff plays. Mr. Alcindor continues to discourse on trombones in Berlioz. The sports scene is forever surprising, forever fresh, forever forcing a kind of honesty. . . .

After quitting the magazine job, I ran with Vic Obeck, a genial man who had been a professional football player. We were leaving the dining room of Toots Shor's restaurant one night when Richard Nixon waved from a corner. He was out of office then and waving at everyone.

"Let me handle this," I said. I strode to Nixon's table and with the fierce courage of whisky introduced myself . . . and sat down. Nixon smiled greenly. Several lawyers in his party glared.

"I wonder if you'd say hello to an admirer of yours who is athletic director up at NYU?"

"Of course," Nixon said through the green smile.

"Hey, Vic!" I shouted, rising. "Come on over and meet my friend Dick Nixon."

"What else should I know about him?" Nixon said urgently.

"Guard. Football Dodgers. 1946. Good blocker."

Nixon's head jerked in a nod. "Vic," he began, "I'm really pleased to shake your hand, and we were just wondering here why the city doesn't do more for NYU sports. They ought to build a new basketball arena."

Obeck beamed.

"I remember you with the old Brooklyn football Dodgers," Nixon said.

"Really?" Obeck's . . . eyes became so bright that I was afraid he might weep.

"Yes, sir," Nixon said. "You were a great blocker. I'll never forget the way you blocked for Ace Parker."

The bright eyes glazed. Ace Parker played in the 1930s. . . . In sport, as in Southeast Asia, the blunderer gives himself away.

27

The Life and Hard Times of Jim Bouton

Esquire, December 1970

Everyone in the popular, randy book Ball Four *fairly explodes with lust, except the author, straight-shootin' Jim Bouton, the only virgin in the Major Leagues.*

At about the time petrifaction laid an icy hand on his pitching arm, James Alan Bouton appeared at the Methodist Office of the United Nations as the short reliever in a sorrowful little game. In front of an audience of one hundred, a black soccer player from South Africa was proposing that the United States boycott the 1968 Olympics unless the Boers were expelled, in protest against the apartheid and in the name of morality. . . .

The meeting's sponsors had recruited a black basketball player from Columbia, who sat silently at the South African's right. To his left sat Bouton, white, then a Yankee. . . .

"I have a question for Jim Bouton," called Howard Cosell, the Torquemada of the American Broadcasting Company. . . . "If South Africa is banned, what would you say to black American athletes who want to boycott the Olympics anyway because of alleged American racism?"

Bouton rose, looked evenly at Cosell, and said, "Howard, in view of what has happened in America, I can't condemn any protest black people make, as long as it isn't violent."

Bouton's mind was quicker than his slider. That June the Yankees had to send him to the minor leagues, because he could no longer throw hard.

Like almost every athlete, Bouton rejected the verdict of fate and time. He decided to master the knuckleball, a complicated pitch that enables one man per generation to reach his middle forties as a successful Major Leaguer. The knuckler is held with the fingertips and thrown with a locked wrist so that the ball sails almost without rotation. For reasons of aerodynamics, a good knuckleball celebrates its arrival at home plate with a giddy, unpredictable lunge: up, down, sideways, or at any of the intervening angles. It is difficult for hitters, humiliating for catchers, and almost impossible to control. Anyone with a fair arm can experiment with a knuckler. It is a rare man who finds the combination of touch, velocity, assurance, and control that makes it a viable pitching weapon. Among those whose fingertips missed the combination was Jim Bouton.

This predictable and ordinary failure provides the platform for *Ball Four*, a four-hundred-page diary that is described in the subtitle as *My Life and Hard Times Throwing the Knuckleball in the Big Leagues*. Bouton, the diarist, chips at tradition, ridicules stupidity, and makes jokes. When he learns that a teammate starred at Black Earth, Wisconsin, he composes a mock school song: "Black Earth, we love you. Hurrah for the rocks and the dirt." When he spots Bob Smith of the old *Howdy Doody Show* in a drugstore, he sings the complete *Howdy Doody* theme aloud. He laughs harshly at greenies—green amphetamine pills—on which some ballplayers depend. A quiet infielder named John Kennedy suddenly shrieks at an umpire and explains in the dugout, according to Bouton, "I guess my greenie kicked in."

In addition, Bouton is conventionally and comfortably liberal, in contrast to the conventional, comfortable conservatism of his teammates. He dislikes bigotry and cruelty to children. He also has little use for discretion, and there is the arrowhead of controversy. Bouton feels free to describe and laugh at the sexual habits of others, whom he names. . . . To Dick Young, the best of newspaper baseball reporters, such tattling makes Bouton a social leper. As Christmas approaches, the controversy endures, and sales of *Ball Four* climb over the magic number of two hundred thousand.

The genus of books by American athletes dates from at least 1912, when Grosset & Dunlap published Christy Mathewson's *Pitching in a Pinch*. Mathewson, a Bucknell graduate before the baccalaureate pandemic, worked with a ghost named John N. Wheeler, and the resulting book is remarkably funny.

A friend [wrote Mathewson cum ghost in 1912] who took a different fork when we left college was walking down Broadway in New York with me one morning after I had joined the Giants, and we passed a cross-eyed man. I grabbed off my hat and spat in it. It was a new hat, too. "What's the matter with you, Matty?" he asked, surprised.

"Spit in your hat quick and kill that jinx," I answered, not thinking for the minute, and he followed my example. I forgot to mention, when I said he took another fork, that he had become a pitcher, too, but of a different kind. He was a minister, and as luck would have it, he was wearing a silk hat.

"What's the idea?" he asked.

"Worst jinx in the world to see a cross-eyed man," I replied. "But I hope I didn't hurt your silk hat."

"Not at all. But how about these ballplayers who masticate the weed? Do they kill jinxes, too?" I had to admit that they were the main exterminators of the jinx.

"Then," the minister went on, "I'm glad the percentage of wearers of cross-eyes is small."

The style is addictive. Once you adjust, you admire Mathewson-Wheeler for their mixture of irreverence and dignity, and if you come to the book with the right spirit, the past and Great Matty's Ghost embrace you, and McGraw and Cobb and Wagner live by your side. . . .

Mathewson in real life appears to have been so fiercely competitive and so caustic that gentle people are said to have fled his company. If verity were all, his book could be forgotten, but it is a perfect period piece and the original of an entire genre. And so a landmark.

After *Pitching in a Pinch*, the star's byline above the handiwork of a ghost became an institution. Editors consistently promised the public inside tips from the secret life of Babe Ruth, Dizzy Dean, and Warren Spahn. This was (and is) a questionable business. Ballplayers are unlikely to tell on themselves, even for cash advances, and ghosting does not always bring out the artist in a collaborator. The result is a chrestomathy with climactic paragraphs that always seem to read about like this:

The bases were loaded now, and there I was, facing the best hitter in the business. With the count three and two, the manager came out and wanted to know if I was tired. Sure I was. I'm human. But this was no time to be thinking of myself. I thought of Luella and our lovely clapboard house six miles east of Bradford, Pee Aye, and our three daughters who go to Sunday school and how the whole team was counting on me. I told the skipper I could do the job.

He looked at me and must have thought of all our years together. It kind of looked like mist got in his eyes. I maybe prayed a little, and the Big Guy Upstairs must have heard me because I threw a curve that broke three feet. That was it. I had my strikeout. We had the Series. I want publicly to thank the Big Guy for giving me the strength to throw that curve and to add that those stories about me throwing an illegal spitball are being spread by agents of the devil.

The principle preserver of this form was the *Saturday Evening Post* during the disastrous late years of its old regime. At almost every World Series during the 1950s, a different *Post* editor appeared and signed a star to compose exclusive memoirs with a writer of the star's choice. Catastrophe came when Casey Stengel offered his reminiscences for sale. Stengel . . . was a free spirit, and the idea of a blunt book—sweeping from Dutch Stengel, Kansas City roughneck, to Charles Dillon Stengel, California bank executive and national shrine—had true appeal. In a sense, Casey and the United States had run certain parallel courses. As the agent who handled the bidding recalls, "*Look* quit early, at about $60,000 or so. But I had the *Post* going against *Life*, with book publishers as backup, and it wasn't until we hit $125,000 that I got a little scared. These things can blow up. So I said one more bid each. *Life* offered $150,000. The *Post* won with $155,000."

The judgment of years is that only the agent won. Stengel's memoirs were pale as beer foam and just about as substantial. The old man appreciated the money, but he was damned if he was going to tell about drink, cash, and the other hard elements in his epochal life. He settled for tedium, which helped kill the *Post* and which I keep close to the bed in book form because it is safer than Seconal and just as effective.

One clean blow for literacy was stuck in 1960 by Jim Brosnan, a tall, thorny, bespectacled intellectual who made a living by throwing sliders for the Cincinnati Reds. Brosnan recorded the year 1959, when the Cardinals traded him to Cincinnati, in a diary called *The Long Season*. It is candid, sometimes moving, and unpretentious. Brosnan . . . recounts the end of the great Sal Maglie with chilling economy. He makes a deal with a rival to throw fastballs to one another, is betrayed, and describes the other pitcher with a racial epithet. He misses his wife, who calls him Meat. He is given to grouches. He gets drunk. He relishes the smile of his manager. He wishes he were a better pitcher.

The diary form eliminated problems of organization and enabled Brosnan to concentrate on content rather than on form. His writing has little slickness and not much lyricism but carries an irresistible sense of truth.

> The last day of the season comes. The last time to pack the duffel bag with gloves and shoes, jock straps and jackets, souvenirs and clippings.
>
> The last hours of a team.
>
> The last moment to say good-bye . . . to say good luck.
>
> But it's also time to say, "See you in the spring, buddy." Every ballplayer thinks he can come back again. On that last day, baseball is a game professionals really do play; it no longer seems like work.
>
> I stuffed my glove into a duffel bag and picked up the last shirt from my locker. The empty locker symbolizes the cold blue sadness of the last day.

Sweeping afterward, the 1960s provided a kind of graft, combining the hand of the ghost, as in Mathewson, with the form of the diary, as in Brosnan. It is no longer possible to define obscenity, which is probably a good thing, but in lieu of definition, I can present an example. A two-man diary is obscene. A genuine diary, like Brosnan's, is an individual personal record. By the late 1960s sport was infested with gabby athletes and hungry ghosts, holding hands and microphones into which they murmured in infinite intimacy, "Dear Diary and others." This form of collaboration produces readability and sometimes sales, but it is built on a gimmick, and that is a dangerous way to start a book. . . .

Among forceful critics of pseudo-diaries was Leonard Shecter, who complained that they did not really tell as much as they pretended. Now Shecter appears as Bouton's partner in *Ball Four*, but, he indicated in the foreword, he is a shade of difference. The basic conceit of pseudo-diaries is that they are really the work of the athletes and that the hungry ghosts have helped with only commas, spelling, and typing. Describing *Ball Four*, Shecter concedes that he and Bouton had disagreements and suffered frayed nerves as they labored together. Score one point for Len Shecter and reality.

Like Bouton, Shecter is a man of unusual gifts. He appeared during the 1950s on a train bearing the Brooklyn Dodgers, saying, "They don't want me to write about the games." He meant that Ike Gellis or Paul Sann, his bosses at the *New York Post,* had told him to write about people, which he did, extremely well. He moved from the Dodgers to the Yankees, a journalist of intelligence and drive, and in time he tried a general column. When the project soured, he quit the *Post* to freelance. Four years ago, he called to ask if I'd write for a new weekly. "Pete Hamill and I are starting it. It'll be like a *Village Voice*, only well-written." I said that as an unsuccessful reader of Nat Hentoff I would be pleased to do what I could. But this plan died, too, for lack of funds.

In this role inflicted on him—freelance sportswriter—Shecter developed an interesting skeptical style. "A professional curmudgeon-in-residence," Bob Lipsyte has written earnestly in the *New York Times.* One did not have to accept Shecter's view of Vince Lombardi as a native fascist any more than one had to accept Bart Starr's sense of Lombardi as the Second Coming.

But sportswriting badly needs skeptics. The world is wide, and there is room in it for both Shecter and Starr to be wrong.

When *Ball Four* is at its very best, as in a description of Ted William's batting, an echo of Shecter's cold realism resounds.

He'd swing and hit a line drive.
"Jesus H. Christ Himself couldn't get me out."
And he'd hit another.

Then he'd say, "Here comes Jim Banning, Jim f—— Banning, and that little shit slider of his."

Wham!

"He doesn't really think he's gonna get me out with that shit."

Blam!

"I'm, Ted f—— Williams."

Sock!

That's it. That's Williams exactly. Shocking. Loud. And all those astonishing line drives. Where Bouton's notes feed Shecter's skill, one forgets that *Ball Four* is a pseudo-diary. One is simply swept along. But *Ball Four* is a pseudo-diary, and ultimately shallowness and artificiality are its undoing.

Throughout the book, Bouton-Shecter want to tell us about the lonely chaos of the road. That is an excellent goal, but instead of approaching the silver of, say, Willy Loman's fall, they adopt a superior and almost leering viewpoint. Quite literally, they laugh at other men's erections, as though immune.

One infielder announces on a team bus, "Boys, I had all the ingredients of a great piece of ass last night—plenty of time and a hard-on. All I lacked was the broad." Taste is subjective. What troubles me is that Bouton-Shecter elect to name the infielder and a dozen other people who make similar observations. The issue here is not Puritanism, Women's Liberation, or The *Playboy* Philosophy. Rather, it is intrusion from an outsider on tenuous human relationships. Ballplayers, and even their wives, are people; prick them and they bleed. Men ought to think extremely carefully before capitalizing on the gaucherie of someone else.

In the absence of rules, and there are none, the best test is to reverse roles. How would Bouton-Shecter like to read a smug account of their own wild road evenings, if any? "But I'm as rough on myself as on anyone," Bouton has protested. "Don't I put myself in a Hollywood pool, stripped to undershorts, treading water and holding a martini in each hand?" He does, and that is irrelevant. A Hollywood pool is not on the road. It's the American dream. I haven't been 100 percent faithful to the little woman myself. I've slipped at least three times. Let's see, there was Marilyn and Jackie and Liz. The road, and Bouton-Shecter know it better than I, is a dirty coffee shop at 2:20 a.m. with a brassy, buck-toothed waitress as the only game in town and, to your own horror, a certain rising interest.

The puritanism of sport is dangerous nonsense. Whole generations of Americans reach biological maturity still equating chastity with victory and virginity with no-hitters, after which they develop problems. Down with all scarlet letters. But Bouton-Shecter, by calculated, commercial finger pointing in *Ball Four*, give anti-puritanism a bad name.

My other reservations are more abstract. In *Ball Four*, Bouton is too often the unobserved observer, supplying facts (his salary), opinion (he likes Father Groppi), and nice incidentals (he is excellent at the game of trivia). But in serious books, the central figure begins as one person, clearly drawn. He then batters the walls of time. At the end, he and ideally the reader are forever changed. Unlike Brosnan, Bouton in the diary is shadowy, really a shadowy comic. Reading *Ball Four*, I sometimes felt I had stumbled into an interminable, gamy Leonard Lyons column. Sometimes I remembered an e. e. cummings dialogue with himself. "What happens to most people? What becomes of them?" cummings asks. And he answers, "Nothing happens to most people. They don't become." Jim Bouton does not become in *Ball Four*.

Finally one reaches the most serious deception, a reality that Bouton-Shecter have either missed or have chosen not to see. The Bouton of *Ball Four* is a lame-armed thirty-one-year-old pitcher who moves from an inept Major League team to the minors to a second big-league team that is mediocre. For a sensitive man, the experience is terrifying. "I can't pitch anymore. My arm is dead. We're going to starve. What will I do? I've started to die!" In *Ball Four* Bouton blames everybody else. The manager of Seattle was a clown. The general manager was fatuous. Perhaps. I know neither. But the pitching coach is a second-guessing simpleton, and here Bouton-Shecter give themselves away. The coach is Sal Maglie, whom we met in Brosnan's book, a ruined master of the pitching trade. As an informed reader, one has to say, if Bouton could not get along with Maglie or learn from Maglie or relate to Maglie, isn't some of the fault with Bouton? That is a question that Shecter the skeptical reporter would certainly ask. But Shecter the pseudo-diarist remains mute.

The essential absurdity of *Ball Four* is Bouton-Shecter's fatuous insistence that the hero is a good pitcher. For the season described, Bouton's earned-run average was about 4.00, which is dreadful for a reliever. During the following season, he was again sent to the minor leagues, whereupon he packed his royalties and quit.

Judging *Ball Four* against other pseudo-diaries, one finds remarkable merits. The same holds if one judges it against *A Boy's Life of Theodore Roosevelt.* But as Robert Graves suggested recently, anyone presuming to write seriously about sport had better recognize the existence of "To an Athlete Dying Young."

I had a friend once, an infielder of thirty-five years, whose right knee was going arthritic. He called before his team came to Yankee Stadium for an important series and suggested we go out after a day game. "Get me Jody," the infielder asked, mentioning the real name of the one famous sex symbol whom I knew.

Jody and I met at seven in a Second Avenue bar where framed Gibson girls hung from every wall. As a sex symbol, Jody found men forever leaping at her across the first drink, and she had adopted a hysterical defense. Whenever anyone leaped, she began to cry. Her point was that "sex symbol" and "tramp" were not synonymous. If, however, one let Jody set the tempo, a first date might very well end with body contact. She had healthy lusts and a remarkable build.

The infielder arrived ten minutes late, sat down, considered Jody, gasped in delight, and told a raunchy joke.

"Please," cried Jody, and the evening was done, although the ballplayer insisted on waiting until midnight to find out. Then, fairly drunk, he decided to call a Pan-American stewardess. She was in Rome. "The dice are cold," I said. "Let's go to sleep."

"The hell with that," said the ballplayer. We went to the Village, and in the cab he mentioned that he had cost his team the game that afternoon when his arthritic knee tightened and he missed a grounder hit to his right. We then sat in a cavernous Village club, drinking martinis that tasted faintly of prune juice.

"I'm gonna get that girl," the ballplayer announced, pointing toward a black-haired teenager with acne.

"Look," I said, "it's a bad day all around. Besides, the ugly ones can be as bitchy as the beauties."

"I want her," the ballplayer said. He composed a sequence of notes. Presently the ugly girl fled in terror.

The ballplayer turned and described the ground ball he had missed. More pruny martinis came. He had seen every bounce, and in his mind, he scooped the ball backhand and threw it hard. His arm was still fine. But on the field, pain had immobilized him. He made hopping limps toward the grounder, which carried by him. "That cuts you," he said. "To see the play and not be able to do it."

"You knew this was going to happen," I said.

"But it's happening." And this man, who was very brave and had a chest of oak, began to cry.

It is something to cry about, being an athlete who does not die young, and a hero's tears are the profound unbridgeable current between the bestseller *Ball Four* and a major, or even serious, book.

28

The Mick

Esquire, May 1971

Drinking, golfing, and cavorting in Texas with Mickey Mantle,
as he tries to adjust to his retirement from baseball.

It all passed so swiftly for Mickey Mantle—the vaulting home runs, cheers like thunder, and the dark, devil's wine of fame—that he cannot believe it is done. But it will not come again, except in dreams. "At night," he says, "my knee can hurt so bad, it wakes me up. But first I dream. I'm playing in the Stadium, and I can't make it. My leg is gone. I'm in to hit, and I can't take my good swing. I strike out, and that's when it wakes me. Then I know it's really over."

He is thirty-nine and so enormously powerful that he can drive a golf ball four hundred yards. But baseball begins with a man's legs, and Mickey Mantle's right knee is grotesque. Four injuries and two operations have left the joint without supportive structure. It flexes outward as well as in, bone grinding on bone, and there is nothing more that surgery can do. "A flail knee," doctors say and make analogies to a floppy rag doll. So, still sandy-haired, still young, but no longer able to play ball, Mantle sits in Dallas, living hard the way he always has, dabbling at business, working at golf, cheerful, to be sure, but missing Major League baseball more than he ever thought he would.

"I loved it," he says, his voice throbbing with intensity. "Nobody could have loved playing ball as much as me when I wasn't hurt. I must have fifty scrapbooks. People sent 'em to me. Sometimes after breakfast when the boys get off to school, I sit by myself and take a scrapbook and just turn the pages. The hair comes up on the back of my neck. I get goose bumps. And I remember how it was and how I used to think that it would always be that way."

For two decades, Mickey Charles Mantle of Commerce, Oklahoma, Yankee Stadium, New York, and Dallas, Texas, bestrode the world of baseball, a colossus. He could throw and he could run down fly balls. Someone with a stopwatch timed him from the batter's box to first base in 3.1 seconds. No ballplayer has yet matched that speed. He drove home runs for shattering distances: 450 feet, 500, 565. With any swing, he could make a ballpark seem too small. Sometimes when Mantle connected, the big number 7 stirring as he whipped around, it seemed that a grown man was playing in a park designed for Little Leaguers.

Center field at Yankee Stadium stretches toward monuments and flagpoles and a high bleacher wall, 461 feet from home plate. People talk about prodigious outs stroked there by Hank Greenberg and Joe DiMaggio. But one summer night not so very long ago, Mantle stepped up and swung there, and everyone watching knew this drive would not be caught. It climbed farther and higher than seemed possible, carrying over the center fielder, soaring over the flagpoles, finally crashing into a bench halfway up the bleachers. Briefly the crowd sat silent. You couldn't hit a baseball that far. Then came a swelling roar. "Make it an even five hundred feet," called a newspaperman, one hand to his face in amazement, "give or take a couple of miles."

I don't remember whether Mantle hit that home run batting right-handed or left-handed. From either side he had Herculean power. He hit the 565-footer batting right-handed in Washington. Batting left-handed he hit a line drive that was still rising when it hit the roof of the third tier, 108 feet high in deep right field at the Stadium. "The guys I played with," he says, "figure that was my best shot."

Mantle is not very big—about five feet eleven and 185 pounds at his playing prime—but there is no mystery to all that power. His frame was fashioned of thick, supple muscle. For all his strength, there is no stiffness, no weight lifter's rigidity. "The body of a god," said Gerry Coleman, a teammate. "Only Mantle's legs are mortal."

He played with a ferocity that approached destructiveness. He ran as if pursued. He cocked each swing for distance, and when he missed, the exertion drew a grunt. Watching him one could see a man driving himself harder than human sinew could endure until at last, too soon, the body yielded. Mantle disagrees with that view. He traces his physical problems to a single injury suffered in 1951. . . .

Even when relaxed, he tends to limit himself to short comments and dry one-liners. Interviews discomfit him, and in time he developed a special response to questions he did not want to answer. It was a baleful, withering look, scorn all the more startling on that open, country face. As he saw it, his job began and ended on the field. . . . Answering all those reporters—What did you hit, Mick? Where was the pitch?—was bullshit. . . .

Elvin "Mutt" Mantle, an Oklahoma lead miner, trained his oldest son to be a ballplayer. As Mickey remembers it, he began learning baseball in 1937 when he was five years old. Joe DiMaggio was a Yankees sophomore. Sandy Koufax was one year old. It was a familiar American scene, the father pitching relentlessly in the hope that the son might someday hit well enough to make the Major Leagues and carry the family out of a depleting existence. Not one boy in ten thousand is signed to a professional contract; no more than one professional in twenty-five is good enough to play in the Major Leagues. "But I got an idea," Mutt Mantle said. "A time is coming when ballplayers will be platooned. A boy who can switch-hit will have a real advantage."

When a right-handed batter faces a right-handed pitcher, the ball seems to be coming toward his ear. Then, as the batter fights a reflex to duck, the curve breaks down and across the plate. The batter sets himself and digs his heel spikes into the ground. Now the pitcher throws a fastball at the chin. In this frightening game, the pitcher holds the wild cards. But when a left-handed batter stands in against the right-hander, the balance turns. The ball seems to be coming from the outside. "You see it real good out there," hitters say. A curve breaking inward can be a fine pitch, but the illusion of impending concussion is lost. Everybody hits better from the opposite side, left against right and vice versa. The switch-hitter always bats that way.

Against both percentages and logic, Mutt Mantle's ambitious dream came true. The Yankees signed Mickey at seventeen. Two years later, when Mickey became a Major Leaguer, Casey Stengel was introducing platoons in Yankee Stadium, just as Mutt had foretold in Oklahoma fourteen years earlier.

Cancer invaded the Mantles' happiness. The Yankees won the pennant in Mickey's rookie season, but by World Series time, October 1951, Mutt lay in a New York hospital, slowly dying at thirty-nine. In the fifth inning of the second Series game, Willie Mays lifted a looping fly to right-center field. Mickey sprinted toward the ball; he had a chance to make a backhand catch. "I got it," called Joe DiMaggio from center. Mantle braked. His right spikes cut through turf and slammed against a hard rubber tube, part of the sprinkler system. His leg jammed, and he fell heavily. As the ball was dropping out of DiMaggio's reach, Mantle lay in motionless agony, knee ligaments terribly torn.

He was bedridden now, like Mutt, and by the time the father died, a somber identification had occurred. Mantle believed that an early cancer awaited him. When players discussed pensions at a clubhouse meeting once, he said, "That's for you guys to worry about. I won't be around." When someone made a remark that cancer was not purely hereditary, Mantle said, "Sure. And it killed my uncle, too."

His career mixed glory and pain. He was the hinge on which the Yankees wheeled to eight pennants in a decade. In 1956 he led the league in batting, runs batted in, and home runs. In 1957 he batted .365. In 1961 he hit fifty-four home runs. Through all these seasons injuries nagged him. With the bad right knee, he was forever straining muscles. As he was running to first base in 1962, a right hamstring tore. He pitched forward and crashed heavily on the left knee, the good knee. It was not a good knee after that. A year later he broke a foot. Throwing hard, he chipped a bone fragment in his shoulder. He kept playing, but the bone sliver worked its way into sinew, giving him a chronic sore arm. By 1965 Mantle, then thirty-three, could not play every day or hit .300. The Yankees have not since won a pennant.

He liked good living, but off the field he shied away from crowds. The New York pace excited him. But country stayed strong in Mantle. "I don't want no fuss," he said, "no big deals." If Babe Ruth's image shows an ultimate libertine and Leo Durocher is the corner crapshooter, Mantle by contrast has been a shadowy bucolic.

Last summer, Jim Bouton's unfortunate *Ball Four* pried into the Mantle mystique. Bouton drew Mantle as a voyeur who would not turn his eyes from an airline stewardess standing naked at a window; as a grouch who disliked autographing baseballs; as a hedonist whose training habits were less Spartan than, say, Jim Bouton's.

With his mustachioed ghost, Leonard Shecter, Bouton wrote: "I ached with Mantle when he had one of his numerous and extremely painful injuries." And to show the full measure of their hurt, Bouton-Shecter added, "I often wondered, though, if he might have healed quicker if he'd been sleeping more and loosening up with the boys at the bar less." . . .

Dallas was warm and windy, and Mantle said he was going to play some golf and make a talk and why didn't he start by showing me where he lived. He wore blue slacks and a blue shirt when he picked me up at a motel, slightly heavier than when he played but still boyish. He hadn't read Bouton's book, he said, just a chunk in some magazine. "Anybody," he said, "who's been on the road can write a book with sex in it. You could. I could. But I wouldn't do it. Why do you suppose the sons of bitches picked on me?"

"It was a commercial effort," I said, "and you're box office."

"Roger Maris hated Bouton. He always wanted to belt the bastard. Is the book rough on Maris?"

"He's hardly in it."

"The other guy, Shecter, was an agitator. I didn't speak to him for the last four years at the Stadium. I'd just give him the stare. Do you think maybe the book ought to read: by Shecter, edited by Bouton?"

"For lots of it, sure."

"Only thing that really bothered me was the stuff about autographs. New York was my town, but for all those years, I couldn't walk a block without getting stopped. I wouldn't sign? Hell. I've signed maybe a million." Mantle shook his head. "Well, come in and have a cup of coffee."

Mantle lives in a rambling buff ranch house, set on a cul-de-sac on the north side of Dallas. His wife, Merlyn, has decorated the den into a kind of private shrine. One wall shows twelve framed magazine covers of Mantle batting, running, smiling, glaring. Another is crowded with pictures of the Mantles and famous men, Babe Ruth and Bobby

Kennedy. Locked behind glass are the jewels of a great career: the silver bat he won as batting champion; his last glove, bronzed like baby shoes; three plaques celebrating the seasons in which he was most valuable player in the American League; a baseball signed by Mays, Mantle, Ed Matthews, Henry Aaron, and Ted Williams, an aristocracy in which everyone has hit five hundred home runs. Mantle stood in the den, shifting his weight from side to side. "All right?" he said. "Come on out back. I've got something to show you there."

Slingin' Sam is an electric batting machine. A spinning arm whirls a ball tethered to string in a sweeping arc. Dials control the direction of flight and speed, which can run to two hundred miles an hour. "The idea," Mantle said, "is to start at sixty-five and then work up. I can hit it at a hundred. Little Mickey, he's seventeen and about six feet, hits it harder than I." He demonstrated, batting right-handed and slashing into the rotating ball, the huge swing precise. "Run it the other way, I could bat left-handed, 'cept for my knee. Little Mickey's been working on this for four months, and he's started switch-hitting. He's probably going to make it in a rookie league this summer."

"You selling these things?"

"We hope to." Then, deadpan, "If I'd had a Slingin' Sam when I was a boy, I'da hit nine hundred home runs." Mantle grinned. "It's not the same as hitting against pitching. You know the ball won't hit you in the head. But switching is bat control, and that's what this can teach." He put his bat down. "What do you say we go on out to the club?"

Preston Trail Golf Club, limited to 250 members, no pool, no tennis, spreads over rolling acreage twenty miles north of Dallas. Under the clear wide sky, city towers shape a fringe of horizon. "Good weather here," Mantle said, "but sometimes it turns. It's warm, and then the wind shifts—a norther, they call it—and the sky gets blue as a marble, and you have to hurry to the clubhouse. It gets cold." He walked out to practice putting, and Gene Shields, the house professional, described Mantle's game. "Swing is a little flat, like all ballplayers, but he's the longest hitter around. Our tenth hole runs 495 yards, and last October, with a little wind, he drove to within 70 yards of the green." . . .

Mantle played in a fivesome of serious, laconic Texas golfers, who bet as they rode along in golf carts. Mantle's cart made the best time.

He whipped up knolls and spun around turns, the first to reach each tee. "You know the old rule," he said. "He who have fastest cart never have to play bad lie."

The wind gusted, eased, and gusted, disturbing the precision of everyone's game. Mantle smacked enormous, low drives, and his chatter was easy and professional. Landing behind a tree, he said, "Well, I can make a fine golf shot from here." On the eighth hole, hitting into a quartering wind, he drove an astounding three hundred yards. He waited impatiently for the others to make their second shots. . . .

As he roared toward the clubhouse in the cart, someone drove up, bellowing, "Mantle, Mantle! God damn it. Gimme your spare putter."

Mantle obliged with a small grin. "I got some clubs in the water myself."

The wind hoisted scores, and Mantle's 82 was good enough to win his bets. "Double J.D. and Seven-Up," he ordered in the locker room and insisted on taking the check. His limp was noticeably worse. "With the cart, it's not as bad," he said, "but without it, I can just about make eighteen holes. That's all the leg has left."

He spoke at a banquet in Fort Worth that night. "They say I was a hitter," he began, "but I struck out around seventeen hundred times. Then I walked around eighteen hundred. Figure that out, and it comes to five years I came up to the plate and never hit the ball." He made a modest pitch for Slingin' Sam—"My four boys and their friends keep the one in our backyard running all the time"—and plugged a clinic where he would be coaching. Three other Major Leaguers sat on the dais. Mantle was the star. Afterward he had to sign programs and base-balls for forty minutes.

We went to a Dallas club for a nightcap. . . . "You want to manage?" I asked when it was quiet.

"If they got a Major League team in Dallas. I had good managers. Casey gave me my chance. Ralph Houk kept saying, 'As Mantle goes, so go the Yankees. He's the leader.' Like that. It gave me confidence. I wouldn't want to manage outside of Dallas. I wouldn't want all that time on the road."

"What's tomorrow?"

"More golf. Talk with my lawyer, Roy True. We got things going. The employment agency with Namath. Some other things. I stay in touch."

"You bored?"

"Hell, no. I enjoy what I'm doing. I miss baseball, but I like to play golf. There's nothing bored about me, nothing sad. My health's good, 'cept for the knee. I'm not worried any more than anybody else."

He grabbed for the tab and said, "You got enough to write?" When I nodded he started out of the club toward his car, still looking like a kid from Oklahoma but limping from the agony that baseball has left him, along with scrapbooks and memories that give him chills.

29

Roy Emerson

Esquire, June 1971

Harold Hayes, for many years the editor of Esquire, was a weekend tennis addict. He suggested that I book a match with a world-ranked player, then write a column communicating to Hayes and readers what I had learned. Here mostly is what I learned: Roy Emerson, then ranked No. 4 in the world, played a better game than I.

It is not always a bad thing to lose innocence, I was musing the other day, when I found myself walking onto a tennis court to play a set with Roy Emerson, the great Australian. "Best of five?" he said, unsmiling. "Care to open up your pores? Loosen up, now. Might learn some things to beat your boss. You'd be the boss, then, eh, or fired."

"Fair dinkum, Emmo." I speak a clear, bell-like Aussie patois. Whomp, here came a ruddy top spin by my ruddy backhand.

"Good one, Roy," I called. "Nice shot." But we were talking, you and I, about innocence.

In the green years between Korea and Vietnam, I harbored the pathetic fallacy that, given sufficient court time and proper levels of competition, I would develop a triumphant game. A backhand cross court, Brooklyn 1953; a stretch of smashing forehands, Nassau 1955; a month somewhere when the first serves hit often and all the slicing serves drove deep, combined to fantasy. All I had to do was put the best shots of a decade into a single set, develop that set into my norm, and—madness.

Sanity struck in the form of a woman, one Gertrude Augusta Moran, who won admiration in late girlhood by wearing an exceptionally short tennis dress at Wimbledon and showing lace underpants when she stooped to half volley. We met and rallied and sipped aquavit martinis, and Gussie told me that it must be marvelous to be a writer. "I mean," she said, "you can just sit there and make anything you want come out of the typewriter."

"It wasn't that way, at least for me," I said, "and what was a nice girl doing in visible underpants?"

"Teddy Tinling of London designed my clothes that season," Gussie said. "If his skirts came up a bit short, usually it didn't matter. The English girls were wearing cotton underwear. But I was wearing nylon underwear, and I'm brunette. So we had to design extra pants to cover the nylon, and I put the lace on so they wouldn't be drab. Quite modest really."

I called for more aquavit and suggested we rally again the next day. Gussie smiled gently and asked if I thought Housman wrote well.

"Mixed doubles would be a good thing," I persisted. We were through *A Shropshire Lad* four times before Gussie acknowledged my request. "I have a court at three o'clock," she said by telephone one noon.

"Who we playing?"

"Don and Dee, and Don's strokes are really sharp." Don was Budge, Donald Budge, the California Comet, possessor of an enormous game, a matchless backhand, and an inclination toward surliness. He would not only beat you; he might stab you with humiliation.

"Tough to get away," I said.

"I thought it might be," said Gussie, "but when it gets warmer let's split an ale on Bredon Hill." . . .

No one really wants to bat against Bob Gibson or to play chicken with Evel Knievel, the elements of terror being as obvious as pain. But tennis is different, gentler. There the pathetic fallacy persists, like astrology and *The Merry Widow*, and the best one can truly hope for is to banish madness. You, myself, your club professional, Gussie Moran have no chance at all against Roy Emerson on your best day and his worst.

He is a rangy, gracious man who seemed relaxed during an eventful week. As we sat in the Vanderbilt International Racquet Club, an oasis sequestered within Grand Central Station, he talked about playing every day on a dairy farm in Blackbutt, ninety miles northwest of Brisbane. I could mention Blackbutt despite today's racial climate, he suggested, because it's one word, not two.

Emerson's parents were dairy farmers who loved to play tennis and had built a court. Roy worked hard developing inherent talent and won Australian youth tournaments season after season. He made the Davis Cup squad at nineteen and won two amateur championships at Forest Hills, two at Wimbledon, and six at the Australian nationals. He had dreamed of becoming a world-class player, without considering economics, and he is grateful to Philip Morris International for hiring him as a public-relations man during his amateur days. Lately, he has left Australia for Newport Beach, south of Los Angeles, where he plays at a club but has no private court. . . .

Last year, the Tennis Champions Classic began with purses of $200,000. Pancho Gonzales, charging toward money, upset Rod Laver with lobs and overpowered John Newcombe. Then Gonzales ran into Emerson at top form and lost straight sets. Months later Ken Rosewall came from behind and eliminated Emerson in the fifth set of a semifinal. Roy is said to have earned more than $100,000 playing tennis last year. Now in another season, again preparing for a semifinal, he said, "Tune me for Tom Okker, if you would."

We began with a drill, Emerson standing at net, and the two of us agreed to use half the width of the court. I hit ground strokes from the base line, tentatively at first, then harder. Emerson matched the pace, accelerating slightly. "This is a Harry Hopman exercise," he said.

Forehand smash. Back it comes. Forehand smash. Volleyed harder. Forehand smash. Volleyed to backhand. "Good one, Roy."

Backhand top spin. Volleyed to backhand. Backhand top spin volleyed to backhand, but a step farther away. Back slice volleyed to forehand. "That's a winner, Emmo."

Forehand smash volleyed to forehand. Forehand smash volleyed to forehand two steps away. No comment. Conserve wind.

"Not warmed up, eh?"

"Guess not, Emmo." It was exciting, thrilling really. Emerson volleyed hard shots and cripples with equal precision; his presence was exhilarating, and I was running, stroking, turning, stroking, stroking. Someone said that to sustain the tempo I had to hit twenty shots a minute. Five minutes, one hundred hard strokes without pause. . . .

"Towel?" Emerson called. "Dry off a bit. I'd like to hit ground strokes myself. Hit through. There's the idea. Hit through." I was drying my forehead at net. As Emerson spoke he moved his racket, a metal alloy made by Chemoid. "Quicker than wood. Less wind resistance. Helps an older fellow compensate. I'm thirty-four." He stroked through. The racket made a swishing sound.

Unspoken rules governed our set. He would not crowd my backhand with flat serves smitten at one hundred miles an hour. He did not put the ball away each chance he had. He was a gentleman professional, confronting an amateur, and he tried to keep the ball in play.

Deep slicing serves brought him the first game quickly. I served straight at him. "Good one," he said, picking off the ball without losing conversational tone. I had entered no man's land on the way to net, and a high lob sailed above, very deep. Too long, I thought. The ball bounced a yard within the base line. He had applied tremendous top spin, creating an effect like an overhand curveball, or drop. I served again. He lobbed again. I stopped rushing. He won the next two points with drop shots. "One bounce," he called. "This is a one-bounce game."

Normal tennis is dialogue. You serve toward backhand, forehand, navel as you probe. You run your opponent, power him, chatter, and he does the same to you. In ten minutes, assuming a rudimentary IQ, you each understand how to defeat the other. The set then is a question of execution, nerve, and stamina.

On court with Emerson the dialogue was a flute piping against a Mahler orchestra. In game 3, I guessed right and slammed a sliced serve deep into the backhand corner, a passing shot, low, accurate, and hard. Emerson did not merely reach the ball. He overwhelmed it. He drove a blinding winner down a line. My horizon lowered. I would settle to win one point.

In game 4 he put away two serves. Then running full out, I reached a drop shot, looked cross court, and hit the ball the other way. Emerson had moved with the look. He watched my shot find a corner, then dropped the racket between his elbows and clapped. I have had worse moments than that one, standing near net, sweat running down my neck, watching Roy Emerson applaud a shot.

He missed a backhand then, slicing the ball into an alley. The game stood 30 all. I served. His backhand smash could have crushed toes, but I was able to deflect it sideways: 30–40. I needed deuce. I'd won my point. It would be a fine thing now to win a game. I served a slow slice. Fake run to net. Even within unspoken rules, one could use tactics. Watch for the lob. Goddamn. He's dropping this lob into my backhand corner. I reached the ball. I had been working for thirty minutes against a world player. My arm was granite. The shot went wild. It was my turn to applaud the gorgeous lob. I had to breathe, first. "Towel again?" Emerson said. "Need a blow? Let's hear you whistle." I won two more points before losing, 6–0.

"Good enough," Emerson said at net.

He took my racket—wood, Cragin Simplex—and gazed. "So this is the weapon."

"Yes, sir." I possessed two syllables of breath.

"Thanks for the work. I have to hit now with Lod Raver."

"Lod Raver?" Three syllables. I might see another dawn.

"That's what they call him in Japan. Say, you ran about a bit. You know, you ought to play more often."

At Madison Square Garden the next night, Laver demolished Dennis Ralston, and Emerson faced Tom Okker, a swift, thin Netherlander. . . . Okker took a set, 6–4. Emerson won two, 6–2, 6–4. A final of Emerson vs. Laver seemed likely. Then in set 4 Roy's serves began to carry long. "Oh, come on," he told himself. "Unbelievable," he said. Okker won, 6–3. Now at 11:35 Emerson was going out to play a single set against a man seven years younger. A flat $25,000 rode on the outcome.

The serve would not come back. Okker broke Emerson, who then rallied and broke back. 1–1, 2–2. Ahead 3–2, Okker served hard and smashed for the first point. Emerson hit a glorious winning forehand into a corner. But on successive points he lobbed short and lobbed long, simply an error. Okker led, 40–15. Emerson caught the next service and put it away with a down-the-line backhand. Okker breathed deeply. He put a serve into a corner. Emerson reached it and hit it hard. Okker stroked a small, deft drop shot. He led, four games to two. He would win the $25,000 set, 6–4. This was not club tennis but another game.

"Most times when you serve badly you play badly," Emerson said the next night in a dressing room. Outside, Okker, perhaps tired from the exhausting match, wilted before Laver in the Tennis Champions Classic final. Emerson, sipping beer, had walked through a doubles exhibition. "When you serve well, usually you play well. My service is nothing to write home about, but I work at it continually. I should think a hacker ought to do the same." He grinned.

"A hacker's practice often lacks purpose. You want to organize; no need to run around Central Park Lake. You aren't practicing for a marathon. There is a way to do everything, build stamina, legs, arm, and practice hitting under pressure. That was the drill we worked at, half court. You can play that way against any decent volleyer, and ten minutes does as much for stamina as an hour's jog. You can do everything on half a court—strengthen your arm and legs, hit under pressure, all at once.

"The discipline is to remember position. Have your feet positioned properly. Get the racket back. If you're in position and ready, you'll hardly ever hit a bad shot. Work out every day. If there's no one to work with, find a wall. But every day."

"About service."

"Hackers put too much stress on first serves. The second is the one you must control. Keep it deep. Watch John Newcombe for a second serve.

"Now, if you're positioned and serving, you come to judgment. Where to hit when. Where to move. For movement watch Laver. Notice his balance. He can go any way for any shot."

Emerson fetched more beer. and we began to talk about the hacker who finds himself suddenly and terribly overmatched. "When that happens," Emerson said, "you need two things. Legs and guts. You have to be willing to chase and chase and keep hitting your best strokes. After a while you can frustrate the other fellow and perhaps win points you have no right to win. The drill will build your legs and get you used to pressure."

"Suppose I find a wall and work and come against you in June?"

Emerson's face lit. "Have a go again, would you?"

"Yes, if you're up to it."

"Ah, but you see there is no way, no way at all, for an ordinary player to give a good player a hard game, except with handicaps."

"Such as?"

"Next time, we might play a thirty-one-point set. I'm allowed only one service, a single fault costs me, and you start with twenty-seven points, 27–love, against me. I can only afford four errors. That might concern me. And, of course, you'd be adding to the pressure."

"No, Roy. I don't think I would."

He nodded. I had listened carefully. I had watched him in breathtaking competition and felt his power to the limits of my wind. On a tennis court I did not have the means to make him sweat.

Except if I put aside my work and labored against a wall, concentrating on position. That would occupy afternoons. Mornings would go to the second service. Ninety messianic days, marching toward tennis. Then I'd reach those lobs with a strong arm and lob myself. And in a single set I'd hit the forehand, Dearborn 1966; the Bermuda backhand of '68; the serve that grazed a pompous author's belly in Queens, 1969. The best shots of a second decade in a single set.

Nonsense. Farewell, surrealism. Pay the grocer.

"Another beer?" Emerson said in the catacombs beneath the Garden. "I've some matches in Chicago, but there's time to work off a few."

We lifted fresh bottles. Emerson agreed that tennis madness was benign. "Play you again," he said, "any time we're in the same town. You work hard till then. I enjoyed it." It isn't every month or year that a man writing a sports column gets to meet a sportsman.

30

Bob Gibson

Esquire, July 1971

The great St. Louis right-hander loses a tight Opening Day game to
Ferguson Jenkins. Then he uncorks a bottle of Bordeaux and opens up.

Before agents of the Internal Revenue Service captured Toots Shor's
restaurant in what is claimed to be the greatest victory for federal forces
since the zapping of My Lai, I sat near the old round bar and watched
the old round proprietor bungle into conversational conflict with the
premiere pitcher of our day.

"You're some wunnerful ballplayer," Shor said to my companion,
Bob Gibson. "Seen ya many times. Credit to the game."

"Can you suggest a good Bordeaux?" Gibson said.

"Get this man fine wine," Shor ordered. Then, to Gibson, "Isn't it
great about the Hall of Fame opening a special place for the best fellers from the old colored leagues?"

"I don't like the separatism," Gibson said.

"Well, sure you should be together eventually, but you got to start
somewhere. Even Jackie Robinson had to compromise."

"That was twenty years back," Gibson said. "We don't want compromise anymore."

Shor blinked several times. A learning process took hold. Then on
Opening Day of the baseball season, by which time his bar was pad-
locked, he sent Gibson a telegram of good luck, prepaid. . . .

Gibson earns more than $100,000 a year to pitch for the St. Louis
Cardinals, and this success, reaching beyond what he once knew how
to dream, has wrought a passionate faith in capitalism. "The answer
for the ghettos now," Gibson says, "is not black power but green power.

I'm talking about economic stability." Gibson has spread his own wealth through a variety of investments. . . . He is perhaps proudest of Station KOWH in his native Omaha. "We play soul stuff," he says. "After I bought it, I went through the black community selling shares. It doesn't make a fortune, but it shows a beginning of black capitalism." . . .

He has heard all the bad words of bigotry, and they have wounded him, but he has stayed above the fray without yielding a flicker of competitive fire. On July 15, 1967, a line drive rocketed into his right shin. Gibson fell, arose, said he was all right, and resumed pitching until he fell again. The line drive had fractured his tibia. Gibson pitched to two Major League batters with an unset broken leg.

"When you beat him," says Leo Durocher, the great pragmatist, "you haven't done a day's work, you done a goddam month's. What a pitcher. Quick. Thinking. I mean, he can't only throw through a stone wall—and buddy, he can do that—every pitch has got an idea behind it."

He stands on the mound, slim, steely, six feet one, very dark in Cardinals red, staring at his catcher. "What an education," says Ted Simmons, a bright, square-chinned twenty-three-year-old. "I mean two years ago I caught for Western Michigan. Now Gibby. Have I learned!"

Currents run as Gibson stands. Who is the batter? What did he hit this day, this week, this month, or on July 15, 1967? How does his own arm feel? What stuff is working best? Thoughts sort themselves as swiftly as a blink. Then Gibson decides which of his four pitches he wants to throw where. . . .

A fine way to understand what Gibson does professionally is to start with a table-tennis ball. After loosening your arm—twelve-year-old Scotch is splendid here—throw as hard as you can three-quarters overhand. That is, throw in the normal way, the arm slanting across the chest. Assuming you are right-handed and have not become too loose, the ball will drive up and in to a right-handed batter. Now throw the same way, and at the moment of release roll the fingertips slightly inward. Delivered low, this fastball sinks. Discussing his slider, Gibson speaks of cutting three-quarters through the ball. The curve, not only Gibson's but the curve generic, can be the subject of ten years of seminars.

As you and I—people who by Gibson's standards have not played the game—can dazzle urchins with a Ping-Pong ball, Bob Gibson throws the real thing. He won twenty games in 1965 and except for the year of the broken leg has won at least twenty every year since. Once he prevailed through a full season without being knocked out—technically taken out in the middle of an inning. That year, 1968, his earned average was 1.12, which wiped out fifty-year-old records set by Grover Cleveland Alexander, an epileptic who somehow never suffered a seizure while pitching, and Walter Johnson. . . .

"Questions," Gibson was saying across a breakfast table in Chicago. . . . "I have a reputation for being difficult to interview, but all I dislike are questions that are asinine. How do I feel about being thirty-five? That's this year's favorite. What do they want? Terrible? Frightened? Nothing? How does any athlete feel about being thirty-five?"

"Ten years worse than being twenty-five."

"And it's always, 'What pitch did the guy hit?' Can't they see?"

"A lot of times you can't tell a fastball from a slider. Sometimes you look for confirmation. That's not asinine. Good reporting builds on details."

"I guess I object to how it's used. The papers always have the big hit off the high curve or the belt-high fastball. Read the papers and you never find out a hell of a lot of hits come off good pitches."

"And bad pitches get popped up."

"Pitching is inexact," Gibson said. "It begins as a craft, working with your hands, but the longer you can go, if you know how to think, the more it becomes art.

"You have variables. The catcher calls a pitch. I can go along or shake no. The hitter's guessing. Now suppose in one spot I throw five straight fastballs. Simple, except two or three times the hitter will guess curve. So it isn't simple, and maybe he's struck out.

"To protect our own men, I've thrown at hitters. Baseball has a rule against that, which everyone ignores and works out stupidly. Come close to a hitter's head and you're fined. Plunk him good and nothing happens. You're penalized for good aim. I throw at hitters less than I used to. With years you get more passive, and as the art develops, you understand. Some of them are afraid of my fastball whether I throw close to them or not."

At coffee, a well-dressed man extended a hand and said, "I want to shake with a great pitcher."

Relaxed, Gibson's face assumed a distant expression. You see that in the eyes of men near death or those so full of life that they live on multitudinous levels all at once. Gibson stared hard but did as he was asked.

"That's all," the man said. "I just wanted to shake."

Gibson thanked him, then said, "After a while you get suspicious. Usually people come over for one question, and then it turns out they don't want to listen but talk at you, and there goes breakfast, but this was very straight, very nice."

"Whites and blacks come at you differently?"

"Not as much as some would like to think. Maybe ten years ago *Sports Illustrated* had a story on blacks in sport that was really separatist. And to show separatism they ran a picture of me and George Crowe, the first baseman, sitting together in the clubhouse. I don't know photo techniques and lab stuff, but when the guy took it we were sitting with some whites, and when they printed it all the whites were gone. We were two segregated cats. I've made it a point never to look at *Sports Illustrated* since."

This was the first morning of Bob Gibson's thirteenth Major League season, and he was, to be sure, the Cardinals' pitcher. It was a chilly, gusty day, and outside Executive House he wore a light-gray sealskin jacket. "A gift from my wife," he said. "We bought each other coats. I'd be disappointed if Charlene hadn't got the better of that deal."

Bob Gibson began life in a shack on the north side of Omaha, part of a family of seven pressed into four rooms. . . . He remembers the house without affection. It was there that a rat bit one of his ears.

His mother worked in a laundry; the older children looked after the younger ones; his father died three months before he was born, and he never even saw a photograph of the man. It is a familiar, heartbreaking story of black boyhood. Not until high school did the athlete's body develop. Bob entered Omaha Tech at four feet ten inches. By his senior year he had grown to six feet. He could high jump six feet one and broad jump twenty-two feet and run or hurdle with any-one, except he did not like footraces. Baseball and basketball were his sports, and he remembers setting his dreams on a grand career at the University of Indiana. He also remembers a letter from Bloomington: "Your request for an athletic scholarship has been denied because we have already filled our quota of Negroes." He settled for Creighton, and the picture of Gibson's 1954 basketball team remains oddly shocking. Thirteen players are arrayed conventionally against a gymnasium wall. Basketball is a ghetto game, but Gibson is the only black.

When he graduated, he signed with both the Harlem Globetrotters and the Cardinals' farm team in Omaha. He was newly married, and by playing professional sports for twelve months, he could gross $8,000, which seemed a fortune. Presently the Cardinals recognized what they had and talked him away from basketball. In the midsixties, just as the strains of pitching were driving Sandy Koufax into retirement at thirty-one, Gibson emerged as the greatest pitcher on Earth.

The wind slanted off Lake Michigan through the high-rises on Marine Drive and the squat homes near Clark Street. It cut across Wrigley Field, and despite clear skies, the day seemed colder than its 35 degrees. The gusts would hold up some long drives but increase the stresses on a pitcher's arm. "You don't worry too much about Gibby," Stan Musial said in the press box. "He's not only a great athlete, but he can pace himself fine." Then we settled back to behold a performance.

Gibson was fast and commanding, but so was Chicago's Ferguson Jenkins, and you could tell very soon that runs would come hard. In the fourth inning two Cubs reached base, and Gibson concentrated on John Callison, a left-handed batter with a smooth, compact swing. He threw a fastball up and in, and Callison hit it with the handle of his bat, the ball fluttering toward short right, a sick pigeon beyond everybody's reach. Chicago, 1–0. Joe Torre's homer tied the score in the sixth, but Gibson found trouble in the eighth, two on, two out, and a rookie named José Luis Ortiz batting. The pitch Callison hit had been a fine one. Now Gibson threw a curve perhaps four inches higher than he intended. Ortiz flied out. Musial, who works for the Cardinals, gazed expressionless. I jabbed his arm. "We got away with one," he said, very softly.

The tie held through nine innings. Then Barney Schultz, the Cardinals' pitching coach, suggested some relief, but Gibson said he thought he'd pitch one more inning. Shadows falling across the park left home plate in darkness. Still, the mound was bright. "Change speeds now," Stan Musial said. "Batters can't pick up the ball."

With one out in the tenth, Gibson threw a fast strike past Billy Williams, a lithe left-handed batter out of Whistler, Alabama. A slow-breaking ball stayed wide. Gibson returned to the fastball and threw it low, an excellent pitch in the bad light, and Williams slammed a tremendous home run into the wind. Chicago, 2; St. Louis, 1. A cold day's labor come to nothing. Gibson turned to watch the ball. . . . "Oh, fuck," he told himself. "Oh, fuck." And he squared his shoulders and walked off the field.

"I wondered," a reporter said afterward in the dressing room, "if you felt tired."

"No," said Gibson. "I never get tired pitching ten innings in 35-degree weather."

The aches would come slowly, he knew, through arm and knees and back. For such things medicine has nostrums, which are more dangerous than anyone yet knows. The best cure makes the body heal itself. Next afternoon, when he would have preferred soaking in a hot tub, I found Gibson playing third base during Cardinals infield drills. He made quick, brilliant stabs. Then, getting ready for his next start, which he would win in San Francisco, he threw accurate underhand tosses to first.

"You've got the glove to make it at third," I suggested in the clubhouse. "The only question would be your arm."

"See me throw in a couple days," Gibson said, deadpan. Then, grinning, "How did you like yesterday? Good pitches get hit. Asinine question. Just what I told you."

"Why did you go and make yourself pitch the tenth?"

"I had a chance to win. You don't ever want to come out when you have a chance to win." He looked distant, then directly at my eyes with sudden, surprising, touching intimacy. "I love the competition," he said. "Me with the ball. The hitter with the bat. I love that. And all the rest is horseshit. Except I like the money."

A quarter century ago the St. Louis Cardinals discussed a strike against Jackie Robinson. That is, in Bob Gibson's baseball town, ten or fifteen white jocks did not want to step on grass available to a black genius. . . . Now twenty-five years later baseball is admitting the greatest of the pre-Robinson blacks to its so-called Hall of Fame in a segregated alcove where their busts will not be close to the bust of anybody's sister.

"Hope," Gibson said. "I feel a lot of hope, except it's kind of hard to explain."

For myself as much as for him, but some of my own hope grows from the complex fact that out of this rent, beloved country comes Bob Gibson.

31

Scuba Diving

Esquire, January 1974

As his marriage breaks up, the author, who likes to live dangerously, takes up scuba diving. He survives both the divorce and a free ascent (no breathing tube) from one hundred feet beneath the Caribbean.

There was a lady once, not the right lady to be sure. But she led me down to the sea. She was small-busted and somewhat mousy in the north, but the tropics made her bloom, and there she stood on the seacoast of Barbados, holding snorkel, flippers, and a mask and beckoning. Pastel flowers brightened her bikini. I swam for a long time behind the flowers and a glory of thighs.

When at length I turned, sea fright seized me. The shore must have been a mile away. But a snorkel tube is a dependable friend, and I banished the fear and lived a week beyond forgetting. The warm Caribbean. Icy pink gins. A girl offering what I misread as love.

She was passionate in her fashion but faulted. She never dared or cared to dive beneath the surface, either in life or in that sensual sea.

Now, in another decade, it has come time to challenge depths. "We'll get you to 130 feet in a few days," says Gardner Young of Nassau, as casually as though diving certain fathoms deep were an elevator ride.

"What will be down there, Gardner?" I say, thinking: These are pearls that were his eyes.

"Nothing to be afraid of, except yourself."

Gardner Young, forty-three, out of Boston and a Marine Corps close-combat unit, would have entranced both Hemingway and Maugham. He is clear-eyed, agile, powerful, running about 220 solid pounds, and he has strong, confident tastes in people, lifestyle, and poetry. "I want poems to tell a story," Young says, and when the Heineken flows fast, he quotes substantial chunks of "The Cremation of Sam McGee," or "Boots," or Alfred Noyes's hypnotizing "The Highwayman."

Young runs a number of sea businesses in Nassau from a little office on East Bay Street and under a salty saloon called the Cove. Through Underwater Tours he takes sport divers, novice and veteran, down to reefs that glow with parrot fish, royal gramas, groupers, and grunts. Through Underwater Engineering he undertakes variously hazardous professional work.

After Hurricane Betsy assaulted Nassau in 1965, a colony of underwater pipes ruptured. Sealing off oil was bad enough, Young reports, but tolerable. The worst was a twelve-inch pipe owned by the Baccardi Company that pumped molasses under high pressure. "Can you imagine trying to plug a line gushing and gushing molasses? Every part of my body got covered and caked. But I plugged it, and then there wasn't much to do but lie on a beach and wait till the molasses changed to rum."

Movie executives, re-creating Nemo stories, are always summoning Young for technical advice. He helped with *Thunderball* and some forgettable films and with one *Flipper* sequence in which the dolphin was supposed to save a small boy by butting a shark. "The shark is monarch," Young says. "He knows it, and so does everything else. We set up a cage, and as soon as the dolphin realized he was near a shark, he blew the script, forgot the kid, and tried like hell to get out. The shark Flipper finally butted was a dead one."

Young is a splendid teacher of the sea. He does not minimize the dangers. He is encouraging, without recklessness. After a week with him a man recognizes the splendors of sport diving and an important truth. Provided you have good teaching and know how to beat back fear, sport diving is exciting as anything a man could ask, without being perilous.

The dangers, aside from yourself, are mostly passive. . . . Fire coral inflicts a nasty sting. Touching it is as sensible as touching poison sumac. The Portuguese man-of-war, a kind of jellyfish, is actually a floating colony of polyps. Stinging cells line the man-of-war's tentacles, but the creature is a drifter borne by currents, and to meet one you have to swim into it, like hitting a mine. Moray eels hide in coral crannies. Blindly inserting a hand invites a bite. The great barracuda, ten feet long, looks like a nightmare of teeth. "But man is too big a prey for barracuda," Young says. "You're in more danger in a lawyer's office."

A good perspective on Young's monarch, the shark, appears in Joe Strykowski's book *Diving for Fun*. "When so much hatred and fear have been generated by fable," Strykowski writes, "it is difficult to view the shark objectively. There are 250 species, of which only a handful can be listed as so-called man-eaters. Yet the sight of a dorsal fin cleaving the water will throw most people into absolute panic. The fact of the matter is that the chances of being struck by lightning, approximately one million to one, are far greater than being attacked by a shark." It makes more sense to abandon golf for fear of thunderstorms than to eschew diving for fear of shark.

We began at a pool, Young helping me into my gear and offering a calm flow of instruction and direction. "You had some beer last night?"

"Stronger stuff."

"Well, if a man can't drink all night and dive all day, get out of the business."

I stepped into blue flippers. Young helped me strap on a tank that was full of air under 2,200 pounds of pressure. You inhale through a mouthpiece, breathing, as Young says, with all your lungs, not just the tops. Regulators do the rest. Inhale normally at depths, and the tank provides precisely the air the body requires to compensate for the pressure of the sea.

Then there was a belt of weights and a life jacket. "Never hurry under water," Young said. "Walk, don't run. If you're tired, don't rush to the surface. Sit on the bottom. It's hospitable down there."

"And if I run out of air?"

"This is a pool. We worry about that another day."

The bottom of the pool was white cement. I could feel ten feet of water on my ears. I cleared my Eustachian tubes, pressing my nostrils shut through the mask and exhaling hard. Then the only sound was the soft bubbling of breath. It was comfortable down there, no telephones, no bills. Ten feet below one feels stirrings of superiority. Ah, the pallid mortal limbs and bellies above.

"What are you going to do if your mask fills with water?" Young asked when I had surfaced. Then he explained. You roll your head backward, press the top of the mask to your brow, and blow through your nose like hell. The rules of physics are mysterious but immutable. Air pressure expels the water. The mask is clear.

"Now throw your mask away, go down to the bottom, get it, and clear it," Young directed. That proved easy, made more so by a faint sense of accomplishment. Now it was noon and time to repair to a Nassau bar, where one can sit on a stool and meditate or stand in four feet of water, sipping, wading, tasting the sun. . . .

The next morning twenty of us sailed out from Nassau toward Rose Island and a reef that ran twenty-five feet deep. Joey Lewless, the dive master, and Emerson Roberts, the captain, divided the passengers between divers and snorkelers and set up a buddy system. One does not dive alone, and on a Young boat a professional safety man is assigned to monitor every two or three divers.

The crowd was varied and bubbly: A leggy redhead from Toronto. Some intense people from the dry wastes of Texas. Couples from Long Island and Montreal. One man had packed a wet suit and chisels to chip coral. "We use a code," Young said quietly. "wc means watch closely. wvc means very closely. When we see someone like that, with all kinds of equipment and a wet suit to go down twenty-five feet in 85-degree water, we mark him wvvvvvvvc. All the *V*s stand for very. . . .

"We've lost only one person ever," Young said later, "a man in his late thirties who had a coronary while snorkeling. No thrashing. Just suddenly he lay still. We had an autopsy. He'd been crash dieting, with lots of pills. That killed him, not the water. . . .

"All right," Young said, back at the Cove. "Up to now equipment has worked for you. Suppose some idiot underfills your tank, or you're the idiot and hook your tank under coral. How do you get to the surface?"

"Jettison the tank and come up fast."

Young ran a thick hand over his black hair. "Slowly, slowly," he said, presaging the penultimate adventure.

Young's real boat, a twenty-footer called *Super Hooker* for some for-gotten lady, makes fifty-four miles an hour in open sea. We boarded and beat across three-foot swells, the Fiberglas bottom slamming with startling impact. . . .

"We're going to seventy-five feet. Once you clear your ears at ten feet and at about forty, they'll probably take care of themselves. Then you'll remove the regulator from your mouth and make a free ascent. That means that no machine is compensating. You are. Put your head back and exhale gently. As long as you rise more slowly than your bubbles, you'll be fine. No bends. No embolism. You'll be fine."

"And if I don't?"

"I'll grab a flipper and you go back to breathing through the regulator."

The sense of sea at seventy-five feet is glory. Sun illuminates green water. Blue groupers swim about. And the reef overhung us, an irregular funnel casting magic shadows. I was exploring when Young motioned for me to withdraw the regulator from my mouth.

I cleared the mask and held my head back. I removed the regulator. With it went air, breathing, life. As I ascended the sun approached. . . . Pain attacked me. I wanted to inhale, first a little and then very much. Without the regulator there was nothing to breath but sea.

Ten feet below the surface, I grasped the regulator. On top again, Young shook his head. "You had more air in your lungs. You could have made it."

"I didn't think so."

"Take it easy. Take it easy. Try again."

We dove, and then from the depths I slowly followed bubbles I was making. This time I knew. Somewhere I did have the air. Head thrown back I watched bubbles. The green sea grew more light. I followed bubbles toward the green-white sun. Bursting the surface, I held both fists aloft like a hockey player who has scored the winning goal. Fear? The hell with that. Shark? Barracuda? They were my friends. Jubilantly, I drew a great open-mouthed breath. It was a minute before I had coughed out all the water.

Ground swells spoiled the plan to seek 130 feet. Instead, on a clear morning, Young piloted *Super Hooker* toward Highbourne Cay, an island of three houses and a single road with the green Caribbean lying to one side and blue Exuma Sound rolling to the east. Some others arrived by boat, and we roasted a pig named Bobby (for Riggs) and sat under slow-turning fans sipping champagne and whiskey.

A recollection of the girl in the flowered bikini charged to mind. "Forget her," Young said, rather like Bogart. "The world is full of nice bottoms in flowered bikinis." We talked about a truer mistress, poetry. . . .

He began reciting with one of the rhythms that rule our tongue. It was a poem about the sea and divers.

For the ocean's a whore
And she'll spread her waves with a smile.
She'll beckon you in, like original sin.
She'll coax and cajole and beguile.

He writes such stuff on paper napkins in the bars of Nassau. Then Gardner Young throws the napkins away.

32

A Shrine in Brooklyn

Sports Illustrated, August 5, 1974

It was too small. The public urinals were fetid troughs. Its architecture suggested a mail-order tool shed, and every August the grass began to die. Then work crews had to spray the outfield with green paint. There weren't enough seats and the parking was impossible and worst of all it had been designed in days when a baseball possessed the resiliency of a rolled sock. Later the ball would leap from bats, and pitchers working there developed sore arms, Jell-O hearts, shell shock. Ebbets Field, 1913–57. RIP.

Now, having made this obeisance to truth, we may, perhaps, begin? It was a ballpark. Not a stadium or a superdome or a multisport arena. A ballpark, bad for football, unsuitable for concerts, unthinkable for track. You scrambled to get there, riding a subway or a trolley car, and you fought for a ticket and you walked steep runways with a loping gait. Two runways and a quick, sharp turn, and there the diamond lay, so close you felt that you could reach it in ten strides. There were the Dodgers, gabbling through infield drill, wearing white and blue, standing so near that you could almost hear their chatter.

In 1951, the year of Bobby Thomson, a stately English literary critic asked me to take him to Ebbets Field. We rode the BMT to Prospect Park, the critic bristling with concern that he might show enthusiasm. "Promised some people a book," he said. "American mores. Need to see baseball. Ebbets Field. Waste of time."

We climbed from the subway, and Ebbets Field loomed, gray and sooty. The critic seemed to shudder. We found our tickets, walked the runways, and we turned. There was the painted outfield and the diamond, Pee Wee Reese and Jackie Robinson and Gil Hodges wearing white and blue.

The Englishman stopped stock still, and he fell speechless. Somebody bumped him. "Beautiful," the stately Englishman said. Although I had been journeying to Ebbets Field almost from the beginnings of memory, I would not have thought to call it so.

In time, it became a divine prison. I had this job, covering the Dodgers for the *New York Herald Tribune*, $72.50 a week plus the champagne of a daily byline, and Ebbets Field was where I worked. Most days, across the brightness of mild seasons, I drove a honeydew Chevrolet convertible—honeydew, the salesman said, is the color of the Chevy *Dinah* drives—to an alley where a man called Frank barked, "Move it. Move it closer. Hell, you reporters can't drive worth a damn." Park the car and once a month slip Frank $2. That made sure no one, certainly not Frank himself, slashed the car's black canvas top. (Honeydew and black, the salesman said, is a *terrific* combination.)

Climb out onto McKeever Place and pass the rotunda, where tiles were worked into designs of ball and bat. Walk toward the creaking sign marked PRESS GATE. You could not help but swagger. If you covered the Dodgers regularly, you didn't have to show a press card. "Hiya," the gatekeeper said, and you answered with a magisterial nod. Press through the groin-high turnstile. Behind, laity milled about and swarmed for tickets.

But once inside you had to go to work. Check the pitchers. "Yeah, my arm hurts," Billy Loes said. "It always hurts. A pitcher's arm hurts all the time. Write that." Read the team. How was it with the Duke of Snider? "Damn you guys. I'm hitting .280, and you keep writing I should hit .320. What the hell's wrong with .280? And why are you always comparing me with Mantle and Mays? We're different guys." Snider and Mantle and Mays. What a beneficence of center fielders. Sure, Duke. Easy, Duke. Hit two tonight, and you'll be up at six to buy the morning papers.

Try the other clubhouse. Warren Spahn skipping a turn? "Yep. Spahnie's having some trouble with his back." Actually, Spahnie had been having ten years of trouble with right-handed power hitters in Ebbets Field. His back would heal on the plane back to Milwaukee.

Ride the press elevator, small as a coffin, and ask the operator if the general had come. Douglas MacArthur was an Ebbets Field addict.

Climb to the press box, hanging from the roof. Reach for the yellow Western Union paper and begin:

"Carl Erskine was on the mound seeking his fourteenth victory last night as the Dodgers faced the Milwaukee Braves before an estimated twenty-eight thousand at Ebbets Field. The Braves, nine games behind the Dodgers, countered with Gene Conley, a right-hander, who is very tall for a pitcher."

Editions closed till midnight, and keeping up with them you typed constantly, trying to remember (or forget) that someone had defined journalism as literature under pressure. After the game, Dick Young of the *Daily News* would say, "I got a lead for you."

"What's that?"

"Under leaden skies."

"Good, Young, but I won't plagiarize your stuff. Now hold it. I have to write eight hundred words in twenty minutes."

"Under cloudless skies?" Young said, smiling an evil smile.

I have been trying to find a single memory so vivid and so real that one can understand, with the shock of recognition, what the place called Ebbets Field once meant. It was my ballpark, and before that it was my father's ballpark. It served for ghastly Brooklyn teams and for the Jackie Robinson Dodgers. It was the Elysium of boyhood, the one place above others, where one was safe from algebra and other casual woes. It was secure. Then, so quickly there was not time to sort this change of circumstance, it became the building where I went to earn a living.

Furillo and the wall. Were ever man and magic better fused in baseball? A line drive crashed into that wall, the screen rising above, the scoreboard jutting onto the field. Carl Furillo calculated the carom. He gloved the ball and exploded a throw. How had he figured that carom? How could anyone throw a ball that hard? "This man," said the ancient reporter from the *New York Times*, "is armed."

Robinson in a rundown. One black man, dodging among whites, in those embattled times when baseball people said you couldn't hire a Negro. Robinson, the great gate attraction of his era, sprinted and stopped, feinted and skidded, sprinted and broke free. Above all ballplayers, Jackie Robinson would not be penned.

Alan Paton of South Africa arriving in the press box. I like to pretend that I met Paton, shook his hand, and thanked him quietly for *Cry, the Beloved Country* and *Too Late the Phalarope*. But that night I was off. "Mr. Paton," said Dick Young, in the strident accent of New York, "what's a phalarope?" Paton answered solemnly, "It's a boid."

The wrecker's ball, crashing against Furillo's wall, destroying mortar, laying waste a monument. Steam shovels assaulting soil that had felt the spikes of Reese and Robinson. We thought, we had always thought, that Ebbets Field would stand for centuries. As Red Smith says, the oldest building in Rome is the Colosseum.

The borough of Brooklyn, extending eight miles from the East River to the Atlantic Ocean, was once a vital collection of communities, with names like Greenpoint, Bay Ridge, Sheepshead Bay. Brooklyn was rich in middle-class high schools, thick with churches, and populated by about three million souls. In one neighborhood called Brownsville, Jewish children who would grow up to teach philosophy lived beside incipient terrorists who became loan sharks, basketball fixers, even killers. Park Slope was heavily Italian, mixing longshoremen, musicians, and goons. On Sundays the Irish of St. Theresa's Parish worshiped a gentle Christ. Other days some of them distributed the fascist newspaper *Social Justice*, which warned of a revolution being organized by Jews. In bleak pockets near Atlantic Avenue a small, profoundly depressed black seedbed endured.

Brooklyn was troubled—it is a dangerous fiction that urban troubles are new—and contentious and disparate and joined. What joined all Brooklyn was a sense, when we were young, that everyone outside was laughing at us. If you listened to a radio quiz program and a contestant said he came from Brooklyn, you next heard a clamor of laughter from the studio audience. If you went to a set-piece war movie, there was one soldier out of Brooklyn. He might be heroic, but Gary Cooper never played him. The best we got was William Bendix throwing grenades and bawling, "Dis is for da folks on Flatbush Avenyuh." Sometimes the Nazis cut him down, but Brooklyn Bill Bendix never died like Hamlet. Nobility was reserved for taller figures from the prairie.

One's father's memories seem grander than one's own, which may be how gods were first invented. My father, a courtly, private, thickwristed man, lighted my childhood with stories of ballplayers I had never seen. He had been rooting for the Dodgers since the first decade of the century. "They weren't called the Dodgers then. They were the Superbas, and there wasn't any Ebbets Field. The Superbas played in Washington Park."

"What was it like?"

"There was a hill behind the outfield. More people sat on the hill than bought tickets. That's why we had to build Ebbets Field."

He had admired a first baseman named Jake Daubert, who batted .350 in 1913, and a splendid outfielder, Zack Wheat, and he recalled, as an old general recalls his soldiers' victories, how Brooklyn had won pennants in 1916 and 1920. "We had a spitball pitcher named Clarence Mitchell, who was also a pretty fair hitter. But in the '20 Series, Mitchell hit into a double play and a triple play in consecutive turns at bat. Two swings. Five outs. Efficiency." By this time, the 1930s, my father had developed protective, defensive techniques of rooting. The Dodgers were a dreary club, with no visible tomorrows, and a grown man learns to hide his disappointments.

We first voyaged to Ebbets Field in 1935, traveling by trolley and on foot. We were to see Babe Ruth, who was drinking through a drab finale with the Boston Braves. Ruth didn't play that day. We went next to see an exhibition between the Dodgers and the Yankees. Lou Gehrig, the Iron Horse, passed up the game. A thumb was aching. We went afterward, four times a year, enough so that memories developed and not so often that the trip became routine.

Because the park was compact, you caught interplays between the players and the fans. "Hey, Schnozz," someone shouted at Ernie Lombardi of the Cincinnati Reds, "pick up your cap so we can see your big nose." Lombardi grinned and raised the bill of the cap. That nose could well have startled Cyrano.

"Hey, genius," someone bellowed at the Dodgers' shortstop, Lonny Frey, who made fifty-one errors in 1936. "What ya got the glove for? A decoration?" From the $1.10 seats you could see Frey redden.

Bright moments came seldom to the Dodgers of the mid-1930s, and people said they ought to hire Alf Landon to manage. "I mean you need a man who's had experience getting beat." But once an old

pitcher named Freddie Frankhouse held off the Cardinals with breaking stuff. "A roundhouse curve," my father said with great authority.
"Very few can get away with that in the Major Leagues." A brilliant center fielder, Johnny Cooney, dived and somersaulted and stole a double
from the grass. Van Lingle Mungo, fierce and black-haired, fired fastballs behind a mighty kick. "Whatever you hear about this team," my
father said, "remember this. They're Major Leaguers. Nobody playing
in Ebbets Field is a bum."

When you reached ten, you began to explore the ballpark by yourself. It was curiously shaped, as most old ballparks were, lending variety to the game of baseball. It had been built of brick and mortar
with repeating arches framing little windows, the kind that are always
broken in old factories. Two tiers of pillared grandstand ran from the
right-field corner toward home plate, then out toward left and behind
the center fielder. There the stands ended.

The right-field wall sloped upward for perhaps eight feet and rose
straight for another seven. Above the wall a stiff mesh screen extended
forty feet into the air. A black scoreboard jutted out in right-center,
describing angles that Furillo would master. The playing field was a
narrow cockpit: 297 to right, 348 to left, and 393 to straightaway center. Batting left-handed, Mickey Mantle hit a screwball into the upper
left-field stands during the 1953 World Series. A good power hitter
could drive a ball out of Ebbets Field at any point.

But long ago it seemed a fortress, and like all fortresses it had to be
attacked. A seat in the bleachers, actually the covered upper deck in
center, cost 55 cents. Lacking that, there were other means to violate
the place. Across Bedford Avenue, which ran behind right field, there
lived a popular boy named Herbie Friedman. Herbie was popular
because his bedroom overlooked the screen. Standing at his window,
you could see the infield, some of center, none of right. Every weekend, Herbie, who did not like baseball, had to suffer sunshine friends.

In right-center, where stands and wall met, two heavy iron doors
formed the Exit Gate. The doors did not quite reach the pavement, and
by lying on the ground you could peer through a crack twice as wide as
an eyeball and see a game. Or part of a game. Eventually, a policeman
tapped a billy on the soles of your shoes and said, "Get going, buster."

"What's the matter?" you said to the policeman. "Weren't you ever a kid yourself, sir?"

It was a community ballpark, set among apartment houses, frame buildings, and garages. The same cops worked there every day, and the same children loitered around the green in the middle of a city that was not a city but a borough. Early I rooted for good journeymen, Jersey Joe Stripp and Pete Coscarart, watching the way Stripp backhanded a shot toward third and how Coscarart sped behind second and set his foot and threw to first. Through the eyes of youth, a bad team in a tiny ballpark looked glorious.

When boredom might have entered, a winning club was born. Larry MacPhail, trumpeted into town by Brooklyn bankers, assumed the leadership of the Dodgers in 1938. He set lights on the roof, and for the first night game—the first game *under arcs* the papers said—Johnny Vander Meer pitched a no-hitter. We were still losing but now with style.

MacPhail bought the team satin uniforms that shone under the lights, and in a way no longer possible, with current baseball talent stretched to transparency, he began dealing for box office and strength. Babe Ruth came out of retirement to coach first base. According to Leo Durocher, Ruth never learned the Dodgers' signs. Still, we went to see the big man clap hands and shout, "C'mon. Get holda one, kid." Durocher arrived from St. Louis, intense and loud and damned if he would lose. MacPhail rescued Whitlow Wyatt from the minors and snookered Kirby Higbe from the Phillies. He dealt for Dixie Walker, purchased Pee Wee Reese, and signed a young free agent named Pete Reiser. Dolf Camilli came to play first base—almost as gracefully as Jake Daubert, my father conceded—and Billy Herman, master of the hit to right, took over second.

Suddenly—the year was 1941—the Dodgers were no longer funny. In a magnificent race with the St. Louis Cardinals, they won a pennant. Although the Yankees outmatched them in the Series, that pennant reinforced our sense of who we were, or would like to be. "So Brooklyn's a joke? Well, try a Wyatt fastball at your chin and see who laughs." The place where we climbed out of clown suits was dun-colored Ebbets Field, the ballpark. That made the autumn of 1941 glorious in Brooklyn, although Hitler raged and Japanese admirals were preparing the devastation of Pearl Harbor.

Red Barber, the Dodgers' broadcaster, made splendid phrases. Durocher, ranting at an umpire, was "tearin' up the ol' pea patch." Fred Fitzsimmons, ahead 7–0, was "sittin' in the catbird seat." The public address announcer, gravel-voiced, porky Tex Rickard, had his own encounters with the mother tongue. Once he announced, "Attention, please, a child has been found lost." One Sunday he offered, "Will the fans with their coats on the outfield railing please remove their clothes."

MacPhail himself had spirited moments. "What's the score?" he asked Bill Boylan, who tended bar in the cramped press room.

"We're losing, 6–2," Boylan said.

"You're fired," said MacPhail.

Everything happened in Ebbets Field. Red Barber announced, day after day, and then war came. MacPhail enlisted. Branch Rickey succeeded him, but the Dodgers, ravaged by the draft, fell to seventh place. "Lose 'em all," wrote Roscoe McGowen of the *New York Times*. "The long and the short and the tall." . . .

There was one moment, and one only, when baseball truly led the country. That was in 1947, when Rickey brought Jackie Robinson to Ebbets Field. It is difficult these days to imagine the climate of a quarter century ago, how the right of one lone black to play infield rent America. But after Robinson was signed, the man who ran the minor leagues declared, with leaden sarcasm, that a temple to Rickey would soon be built in Harlem. Major League owners sought a way to drum Rickey from the game. The Cardinals tried to organize a strike.

At the ballpark in Brooklyn, people cracked small, uncertain jokes. "You can tell which one is Robinson. He's wearing number 42." You recognized Robinson by his color: imperial ebony. Watching the big, pigeon-toed, solitary man, you had to face what you had long repressed. Baseball everywhere, even in Brooklyn, had been a cruelly racist game.

In that small park, the electricity that was Robinson, the bar of music that was the man, leaped from field to grandstand. In the boxes close to first and just as surely in the poorer seats, you felt his vibrance. The crowds were bigger now, bigger than we had known them. In that bandbox, the Dodgers drew 1.8 million, a record for the National League.

You couldn't hear the chatter any more. Too many people. Too much noise. But you could see a struggle waged in pantomime. The infield went: Spider Jorgensen, Pee Wee Reese, Eddie Stanky, with Robinson at first, a new position for him. They all wore white, the home team, with DODGERS written in blue script on their jerseys.

Some Dodgers were themselves racist. Later Robinson said that whenever he was on base and Dixie Walker hit a home run, he ran straight to the dugout, forgoing the handshake at home plate. "I didn't think he'd take my hand, if I offered it," Robinson said, "and I didn't want an incident." But most of the Dodgers, including Reese and Ralph Branca, stood with Robinson. Waves of hate came from the other side.

Ben Chapman led the Phillies in cacophony. "Alligator bait," was his preamble. Enos Slaughter, running out a ground ball, tried to plant his spikes in Robinson's Achilles tendon. And many a pitcher sought to drive fastballs into Robinson's skull. The assault was savage and ceaseless.

Here was a borough that had been torn by gibes. Hadn't Brooklyn always been something to laugh at? Here was a ballpark where you sat so tightly that the field embraced you. The fans—Irish, Jewish, and Italian—pulled for Robinson, self-conscious, to be sure, but not for long. In the 1930s, we had developed a simple New Deal view of life: pull for the underdogs (provided they were not the dogs next door). In 1947, the team looked really good. Now if this colored guy on first can make it big, we've got a chance. He made it.

After that came my newspaper job, and the magic fled. I came to know the Dodgers and to relish their company, as I still do, but Ebbets Field was at length a place of work. Watch a ball game every day, and sensibilities begin to dull. You could analyze the way the Dodgers' pitchers contended with Stan Musial. (Nervously and not well; part of Furillo's wall belonged to Stash.) You could find nuance and glory in watching Billy Cox play third. But as a professional, you came to recognize a formula of baseball. In an average week, two games will be good and two will be fair. Three will be exercises in tedium.

Nor did everything happen in Ebbets Field. When finally, unbelievably, the Dodgers won a World Series from the Yankees, the seventh game was played at Yankee Stadium. Ebbets Field lay empty on that October day, and later I remember drinking with Pee Wee Reese and wishing that my father were alive.

When the wreckers came in 1957, I felt no pangs. Walter O'Malley was a money man. The place was too damn small. Let it go, let it go, like the past.

Now through the years it haunts me, like the fresh-faced, ardent girl you never married. I can see again a child's forgotten afternoon, when he walked with his father through arcs of sunlight and saw the bright flags, blue and green and white and red, the flapping flags that meant Ball Game Today. I wonder if a child can feel such stirrings walking toward the modular stadiums of the present. I wonder if children lack for having no neighborhood ballpark; no preposterous right-field wall, or any Carl Furillo; no sense that this park represents their town, which is itself unique, as cities were before the planners came with steel and glass skyscrapers.

One scene endures. Jackie Robinson is leading off third. The pitcher fidgets. Robinson glares at him, saying nothing. The pitcher winds up. Robinson breaks. "He's going," cry thirty thousand voices. The big man slides, hurling his body at the catcher, intimidating him. Then, at the last instant, Robinson hooks his frame toward first and sweeps the plate with the tip of one spiked shoe.

Safe.

Jackie Robinson arises, smiling that inward, private smile of his. Everyone stands and cheers, and some men's eyes glisten. In Ebbets Field they have rooted for a ballplayer, some ignoring another person's color for the first time.

Well, Ebbets Field is gone, but perhaps we can preserve the brilliant bunting and the clear prism of that memory.

33

Cheer, Cheer for Old Ezra Pound

Esquire, November 1974

How eminent humanities professors feel about working on a campus where, at least as the world perceives it, football is king.

"Slough of unamiable liars, bog of stupidities," runs a passage from Pound's "Canto XIV." . . . Professor Joseph M. Duffy of the Notre Dame English department employed the passage as a theme of an essay on Nixon and Nixon's accomplices. He published the essay during the 1972 campaign, before the Watergate slime had surfaced.

"There was some displeasure," Professor Duffy said, in his office at Memorial Library, "but I wasn't muzzled, and I didn't lose my job."

"What about football?" I said.

"What about football?" Duffy said. He is a tall, graying, soft-voiced man in his midforties. "Football is simply irrelevant to my life at Notre Dame. I don't own a television. I simply leave the campus on Fridays and come back on Mondays. I've seen one game in twenty years. I'm not sure who won. I remember being awfully cold."

The tradition of powerhouse football at Notre Dame traces at least to 1905, when the Irish eased past American Medical College, 142–0. Although the effort was good, it lacked perfection. Notre Dame scored twenty-seven touchdowns but missed twenty extra points. Knute Rockne became head coach in 1918, and during his thirteen seasons Notre Dame, playing the roughest competition, won 105 games and lost 12. More than that, the university, like Rockne himself, became the stuff of legend.

Breathes there a fan with soul so dead that he has never heard of "Win one for the Gipper"? George Gipp, a magnificent halfback, died of a strep throat at the age of twenty-five, and on his deathbed, so Knute Rockne claimed, Gipp made a stirring plea: "Someday, when the going is tough and a big game is hanging in the balance, ask the team to win one for the Gipper." . . .

In 1924, Rockne . . . told the Gipp story to an undermanned team that was meeting Army in New York. When Rockne finished, there were only two dry eyes in the dressing room. These were Rockne's. The old man was a pragmatist. Notre Dame's football players then choked down their sobs and defeated Army 13–7.

This is the kind of romanticism that ran through sports in the 1920s, and specifically it is the kind of thing that transformed Notre Dame from a relatively obscure institution to the most famous Catholic college in the country. Football, along with daily mass ("We pray that nobody gets hurt"), lay at the core of Notre Dame then. It was the tool ambitious educators used to attract endowments, to make money, and to grow.

Today Notre Dame is fully grown. A huge mosaic on the library tower depicts Christ with both arms in the air. Touchdown Jesus, the students call it. A statue of Moses points toward an opening in the Red Sea. The students call that We're-Number-One Moses. Most faculty and trustees are laymen now. The nuns one sees on the campus wear short habits, showing calves. Women are admitted as undergraduates. Considering liberal Notre Dame today, Knute Rockne would have blanched. George Gipp, who lived hard, would have blinked.

But football remains a big part of the place, and I think it is fair to wonder why a university as vital as Notre Dame stays in the football business. It is equally fair to wonder the same thing of Harvard, Princeton, and Southern California, but Notre Dame, at the top, is a good place to start.

The Notre Dame athletic program provides for about thirty football scholarships a year, giving coach Ara Parseghian 120 candidates for his squad. A football player at Notre Dame is not treated like everyone else. An engineering professor named Mike DeCicco supervises the tutoring of athletes. DeCicco is a broad, powerful, forceful man who reminds you somewhat of Vince Lombardi. He works closely with Parseghian in a steady struggle to keep the athletes' grades satisfactory.

Certain professors resent what they read as the athletic department's intervention in classwork. "I am regularly requested to keep certain people informed on the marks of every athlete I teach," one told me. "I refuse. If I report that an athlete is doing poorly, platoons of tutors will descend on him like locusts, tutors I have not selected myself. If anyone in my class is having trouble, I'm more than happy to tutor him myself, but I insist that all my students be treated equally. That's what I do."

Aside from such intramural tensions, larger football questions arise. More and more, American sport tends toward professionalism. Sport is entertainment. Is it rational for Notre Dame or Harvard to compete for entertainment dollars against the Cleveland Browns or the New England Patriots? Beyond that, universities like to describe themselves as places of rational discourse, education, research. What are places such as these doing in the sports business anyway?

"You may have heard talk that football molds character," associate professor Les Martin of the Notre Dame English department remarked in his office at the library. He is a dark-haired man who specializes in eighteenth-century drama. "I don't think that position can be defended. Once I gave a particularly strong orientation lecture for a survey course, suggesting that everyone would have to learn some Middle English. The three football players in attendance dropped out right then. Once I flunked two football players. I didn't see another athlete in my class for years. . . .

"Football put this place on the map. Then there came a time in the late 1950s when we ceased to need it. It might have been prudent then to de-emphasize. Now one wonders if we could afford to de-emphasize if the powers that be wanted to."

"Do you find football disruptive to your teaching?" I said.

"I try not to let it be," Martin said, "but before a football Saturday there is a cicada-like nuance in my classroom. The air begins to vibrate. It is disruptive, yes. I try to combat that with humor of a sort. I suggest that football is a prolongation of a pubic rite, a sort of fertility rite really. The opposing team's end zone is the sacred grove where, in this rite, one attempts to bury the head of the god."

Martin paused. "Look," he said, "football can be justified as a business enterprise. This university has a number of business enterprises, including a television station and a football team. Football gives plea-sure, and it can be justified on that basis, too. But as for character building . . . well, one of the rituals of football here is drinking, and on Sunday morning after a big game the campus is stained with the residue of retching.

"It gives me a certain pleasure to announce when the season is over, 'Football has ended. It's Chaucer time again.'"

"Would you like football abolished here?" I said. . . .

"It's complicated. One has a difficult time arguing for the abolition of a goose that has laid a pretty valuable egg. My argument really is to see football viewed realistically and stop the prattle about its molding men."

The old Irish guard was shocked, or at least surprised, when Notre Dame announced last summer that six football players, including four starters, were being suspended for a breach of university rules. Indeed, the breach was wide. All six were alleged to have had intercourse—sequentially—with the same eighteen-year-old woman in a . . . cam-pus dormitory.

Here the story clouds somewhat. The young woman claimed that she was raped. The football players insisted that the woman was having the time of her life. "How can it be rape," one player said, in effect, "when a woman keeps crying, 'More, more'?"

Whatever, the six are out for this season, and the *New York Daily News* was able to run the joyous headline: "Sex Scandal Ousts Six Notre Dame Gridders."

"This," suggested Father Ed Joyce, "is the worst thing that has hap-pened in my twenty-three years at Notre Dame."

"If what the men say is true," I said, "it's pretty much what happens on campuses all over."

Joyce's face showed pain. "But not here," he said.

The Reverend Edmund P. Joyce, executive vice president of Notre Dame, is a handsome, graying man, conservative by his own account, who is the chief financial officer of the university. His office is in the Administration Building, a landmark topped by a golden dome that towers above the campus and sparkles in sunlight.

"Why football?" Father Joyce said. "Well, it was significant in my coming here in the first place. I grew up in South Carolina, and there aren't too many Catholics in South Carolina. As a boy I heard Notre Dame games on the radio and wanted to come here. Otherwise?" He shrugs expressively. "I might have gone to West Point."

"How much does football earn for Notre Dame?"

"Football covers the cost of our entire athletic program. . . . It nets us between two and three hundred thousand dollars a year."

"Can you measure," I said, "how much football brings you in endowments?"

"That's difficult," Father Joyce said. "In the bad years, when we had losing teams before Ara came, there was no falloff in gifts. But certainly football plays a role. We've had a rather happy instance where a benefactor named I. A. O'Shaughnessy, who was first attracted by our football, ended up giving millions for our library. Our endowment is now about ninety million dollars. That's several times the endowment of any other Catholic college." . . .

"Do you still need football?" I said.

"I think it's useful," Joyce said. "Most of the students love it. The fall hysteria's a good way for everyone to let off steam. And the point is that we keep the football program controlled.

"Right now the question of football ties into a larger one. Our costs continue to rise and rise. We've had to increase tuition again this year, and I wonder how much longer we can keep doing that, how long it will be before the middle class, or the upper-middle class, which is our constituency, simply can't afford us any more and has to send the young people to state schools.

"That's my largest concern. Will any private education continue to exist in America in ten or fifteen years?"

Notre Dame State? A constitutional question exists there, just as it does with Joe Duffy's slough of unamiable liars. Meanwhile, you can cheer, cheer for Ara Parseghian's warriors, while your operative, who prefers pro football anyway, will reserve his highest Notre Dame enthusiasm for English professors who risked distinguished careers to say things that had to be said about Richard Nixon.

34

The Good and Bad Times of Don King

Esquire, November 1975

The fight promoter and former prison inmate talks from his football-field-sized office on the top floor of Rockefeller Center about violence, Shakespeare, racism, and even a little boxing.

From Don King's penthouse suite, above the Rainbow Grill in Rockefeller Center, you look from horizon to horizon and see low hills sprawling in Westchester County and fat tankers nosing through the Narrows into New York Harbor and all the troubled city in between. But from sixty-seven stories up, the city does not look troubled. No rat's alley, no ruin of highway shows. You see masonry, steel, glass, towers fixed in the neighboring sky, and Abe Beame's best New York seems secure.

"My man, my man," says Don King, smiling. "How does all this strike you?" A portrait of Muhammad Ali hangs behind King's desk. The painter is LeRoy Neiman, a coloratura artist—more tone than substance usually, but this time Neiman has caught something distinct. Ali's arms are raised in victory. He has won his fight. Somehow Neiman makes the victory posture suggest crucifixion.

The penthouse ceilings are fifteen feet high. The rent is $85,000 a year. The elegance is anachronistic, and I expect Ginger Rogers to come dancing in . . . and offer me a sloe-gin fizz. "It's high living," Don King says, "and I don't know how long I'll stay on top, but at least I've gotten here. If a time comes when I have to leave, I'm taking the elevator down. I'm not stepping off the terrace." A second smile—a serious smile—and King follows with a rush of words, from Voltaire, Shakespeare, Machiavelli, Frantz Fanon, and the Cleveland ghetto.

Don King is the most successful fight promoter now practicing. That is, he has beaten a clutch of driving lawyers, a gaggle of Hollywood hustlers, and he has all by himself promoted $30 million worth of boxing during the last two years. Before that he booked numbers in the Cleveland slums, and from 1967 to 1971 Don King was inmate No. 125784 at the Marion Correctional Institution in Ohio. The charge was manslaughter, and King concedes that he is guilty of killing, without endorsing the severity of his punishment. "I had him down," he says, "and then I kicked him in the head.

"In there," he says of prison, "you find Barbaria. The jailers are like the white straw bosses on the plantations. The straw boss rode the horse, but he resented how the big boss lived in the big, white plantation manor. He took his resentment out on the slaves. Your prison guard's education is nil, but his resentment runs high. Your hard-core prisoners want to penetrate young men. A young man resists; you get a murder. Your prison officials worry about boards of inquiry. Here comes a board. Boom. The menu switches. No more hot-dog soup. A rib-eye steak instead. But these murders keep happening and you get no conjugal visits and do we want to turn our men prisoners into women? It's all worse than the horror of Dickens, man. In a prison we can recycle people, or we can burn them up. Our prisons are just crime factories. I worked days hauling hog manure. Nights, I read."

King, who is forty-four, stands six feet two inches, with a chest as stout as a youthful oak and an Afro that springs from his brow to stiff attention. His vocabulary has grown so rapidly that it has outrun his pronouncing skills. King calls the German philosophers "Hee-gel" and "Neetsh" but also has read Hegel and Nietzsche.

In the penthouse suite, he races across literature and philosophy nonstop, offering a breathless, booming lecture on the humanities. "I got no real degree," King says. "I'm a PhD from the ghetto. I read everything in the prison library. I took extension courses. Still lots of people figure I'm just a nigger.

"But now I'm setting up the Ali-Frazier fight, and President Marcos of the Philippines is very proud of his wife's looks. And I say, 'Mrs. Marcos, age cannot wither you, nor custom stale your infinite variety.'

The president blinks. That's from *Anthony and Cleopatra.* They didn't expect to hear a Cleveland nigger spouting lines like that.

"I read in prison every night. I took every extension course I could take. Oh, the sweetness of adversity. I took the jewel out of the brow of adversity. Shakespeare. I read Voltaire. How to vilify but be accepted. Machiavelli. The strength of the lion and the cunning of the fox. It is better to be feared than to be loved. Frantz Fanon. You are either the victim or the victimizer. Demosthenes. He described a bribe as a promoter of friendship, but he also said a statesman was one who sees and foresees. The black condition. They promised us forty acres and a mule. They gave us neither." King blew air through his cheeks and studied a Telex from the Shah of Iran.

"When I got out of that fucking prison in 1971, I was a dangerous character. I was armed with knowledge."

The ghetto is frightening, most of all to the people who live there and who die there, but it is vital and throbbing and heterogeneous and dynamic. Each ghetto is a graveyard of stunted lives, but now comes someone like King, and you remember that ghettos always seem strange to outsiders and that side by side with vitality lives terror.

The movies fooled us. They told us that ghetto people were Irving Berlin and George Gershwin and that a ghetto crisis was finding money to pay the music teacher. The movies left out tuberculosis, bookmaking, pimps, Murder Inc., Meyer Lansky.

Don King, whom *Time* describes as "one of the most successful black businessmen in America," lived among pimps and racketeers before he killed the man he now refers to only as Sam. King was famous in the ghetto and wealthy in the ghetto long before he crashed the boundary into the white world.

"We weren't poor," he said in the penthouse. . . . "For black people, we were middle class. My father worked as a laborer at Jones and Laughlin, pulling the plug from a steel smelter. One day, easy to remember, December 7, 1941, the plug stuck. The smelter blew and killed my father. There was a settlement. In the ghetto we call that 'tragedy money.' My mother took the money she got for the flesh of my father, Clarence King, and there were seven kids and she went and bought a house. I was ten years old."

King liked boxing, dabbled at high school, and drank the life around him in leviathan gulps. He considered ghetto religions. "They program black people for death. You get a band in spats for the funeral. Pie in the sky when you die. But when you're around, there's nothing sound on the ground." He learned street lore, the look of whores, the flesh of pimps, as suburban children learn the steering characteristics of a Mercedes.

Contemplating careers, King thought of law, but that was remote, a world away, white man's stuff. Then he decided to work the numbers racket. "Doesn't hurt anybody much," King says. "Gets some people nigger rich. You know, like bingo in the white community."

To play numbers you buy a slip for a dollar or two or five, and you pick three numbers, say 6-8-5. If you hit, you are paid off at about six hundred to one, although the actual odds are almost nine hundred to one. Each day's winning combination—this varies with the ghetto—may be the last three digits of the U.S. Treasury statement. A well-run numbers game is probably as fair as a state lottery, but being illegal and black, it is more exotic.

Dream books flourish in the ghettos. They explain what a specific dream foretells in numbers. Did you dream of death? One book says play 9-6-2. Did you dream of kissing? Try for 3-4-7. Keep buying. Keep trying. Keep dreaming. Someday you'll hit.

In each community, numbers operators work in a loose federation. If one man comes up with more action on a certain number than he feels he can handle, he makes a lay-off. He replays some of his action with a bigger operator. "The numbers people have to work with each other to stay alive," King says. "You need a rhapsody in black."

King ran his own numbers games flamboyantly and soon bankrolled other operators. It always paid off in public and in full. "There's a psychology to paying off. I'd have the winners meet me in a bar. I'd be a few minutes late. Let the tension grow. Then I'd park my Caddy and come in and pay them off with small bills, looked like a fortune, and there'd be lots of people around. I'd say, 'When you win with Don King, you're guaranteed to get paid.' I'd say, 'Don King is as sound as the Federal Reserve.'"

Sam, the man Don King would kill, was an ex-convict whom King had set up in the numbers business. King himself placed a bet with Sam on 3-4-7, the kissing number, and 3-4-7 hit. Sam never paid. "You've got to take care of this," King told Sam in a bar. "I've got to keep my reputation."

"I will take care of it," Sam said. "It's an overlook."

"You better take care of it," King said, "if you ever want to work with me again."

Voices rose. King walked out into the street. Sam followed him shouting. The men began to fight. King knocked Sam down and kicked him. Sam's head hit a concrete curb. Seven days later, he died.

According to King, the first charge against him was aggravated assault. "What the hell was it to white cops," he says, "two blacks fighting and one dies?" But King was famous in certain quarters of the Cleveland Police Department. "Numbers Overlord was my title of damnation, and when they found out that I was that Don King, the charge escalated to murder two, second-degree homicide. I felt despair. How can you beat a charge like that? The judge reduced it to manslaughter, but at the trial I had no chance of getting another reduction or going free. I might have if ghetto people judged me, but I didn't have a jury of my peers. I was tried before a jury of middle-class whites shortly after the riots of the 1960s. When I was arrested, I was driving a new Caddy, and I was carrying eighteen hundred dollars cash. That jury seethed when they looked at me. They thought, 'Jail him and we jail our own miseries.' They heard what happened, but they weren't listening. I got one to twenty years."

While King writhed and read in prison, his wife, Henrietta, maintained the rolling suburban farm he had bought, and the family remained solvent. Six months after his release, stirred by guilt and a new sense of mission, King organized a promotion for Forest City Hospital in Cleveland. Wilson Pickett sang. Lou Rawls told jokes. Muhammad Ali fought four different men in ten rounds of sparring. The promotion was a smash. King raised his sights from numbers to boxing.

"It's the damnedest thing about fight promoters," says Harold Conrad, who has worked for many. "The straightest guys get a license to steal." Conrad mentioned some names. "Of course, we don't always get the straightest guys. Something King has going for him is that he delivers what he promises, and on time."

Something else is his ability to see and foresee. Booking a fight now, with Ali et al. demanding $10 million in guarantees, exceeds the resources of any arena and indeed most cities. King does not look for cities; he looks for countries. Through heads of state, he has booked Ali into Zaire, Malaysia, and the Philippines, and while we talked that wire from the Shah sat on his desk. "Saudi Arabia," I said. "You ought to book a fight there and bring home petrodollars."

"As a matter of fact, I have to meet an Arabian representative at the UN next week. I can talk to them at the UN, but I can still talk to young fighters, give them that jive talk, too."

Some month I may go through a fight promotion at the side of King, hear the jive talk, see him rage and sweat and hustle. But now I have met him and seen Horatio Alger, rewoven into black on black. If you want to argue the morality of numbers, you'll have to do that with an honest ghetto cop, if you can find one. Not here. "Hell," Don King says, selling his former business, "for years numbers was the only insurance a black person could buy. Not guaranteed, but the best around. That's why they call the numbers 'policy.'

"I want to serve," Don King thunders above the Rainbow Grill, selling his new business. "What Muhammad and I and the rest of us make every fight, half of that goes to the government. We help the balance of trade. We show them a rugged image of America. I'm making money, $200,000 some days, but I'm serving too. I've made it because I'm straight. Being black helps me with Ali, but so does the fact that I work eighteen hours a day. I'm straight, and I don't hesitate."

He smiled and asked if I'd like to visit his farm near Cleveland and meet his wife and his children and his pet elephant. "I told you straight about the numbers, about the killing," he said. "I hope you write it straight."

I said I'd try, but I was thinking about the pet elephant.

35

George Foreman Is Down but Not Out

Esquire, May 1976

After a tough loss to Muhammad Ali in Zaire (the Rumble in the Jungle), genial George sets about gathering himself and rebuilding his career and his life.

Among the performers and hustlers, pinboys and robber barons who compose the dramatis personae of sport, one unifying strain endures. Within each sturdy athletic torso, a critic slouches waiting to be born.

This is not to bracket every jock with Ruskin or even Jonathan Yardley, but sports people early develop an unshakable sense of the written word. They are convinced the press exists to praise. A good reporter, to them, writes that the loser played well, that the winner played better, and that the men who own franchises are all Galahads in the rough. The reporter who suggests that games are dull or that the proprietors of teams are princes of avarice wins no praise for integrity within sport. In terms originally applied elsewhere, he is no writer. He is a moronic malcontent. . . .

In a rambling suite at the Beverly Wilshire Hotel . . . George Foreman, a huge, sensitive, complex fighter, sat restlessly taking his ease. He had been heavyweight champion, and he had put $1 million in the bank, and he had driven back to the wretched Fifth Ward in Houston in a $56,000 Rolls-Royce; now he was preparing to act with Redd Fox in a sequence of *Sanford and Son*. He had been reading poetry, a volume by Nikki Giovanni, learning and growing and traveling, but something had gone wrong. He was not heavyweight champion anymore.

Foreman won the championship in 1973, when he was twenty-four, by devastating Joe Frazier within two rounds at Kingston, Jamaica. Nobody has devastated Frazier before or since. Once, saying good-bye to Joe, I clutched his left forearm and felt I was clutching vanadium steel. But Foreman destroyed this splendid heavyweight, then went on and knocked out José Roman of Puerto Rico in one and Ken Norton, the man who broke Muhammad Ali's jaw, in two.

Through the mythology that springs up about strong heavyweights, George Foreman became both an immovable object and an irresistible force. Before fighting Muhammad Ali in Zaire in the autumn of 1974, he had won all forty-nine of his professional fights, thirty-seven by knockouts. Just before the African encounter, certain people close to Ali feared that Foreman might kill him in the ring. Alone, Ali is not the blustery braggart one sees at press conferences. Now he fell to his knees and prayed. At length rising, he said, "It's in the hands of Allah."

God, Napoleon reminded us, is on the side of the army with the most cannon. Ali slipped, moved, cowered up against the ropes until finally George Foreman, the indestructible, had punched himself weary. Foreman's artillery was silenced, and Ali knocked him out in round 8.

To this day, Foreman believes that Ali did not defeat him. "I beat myself," he said. "I believed in my own indestructibility. Same thing happened to Sonny Liston."

Foreman's Zaire purse was $5.5 million, but with the millions came hard times. In a single encounter, his proud and hard-bought sense of what he was had been ripped from him, along with the heavyweight championship. Richer than he had known how to dream of riches, Foreman felt lost.

He consented to a boxing burlesque for the glory of the American Broadcasting Company and took on five mediocrities in a single afternoon at Toronto. He outmuscled everyone, but as Joe Louis remarked after one of his own poorer efforts, "Nobody got hurt but the customers."

Finally, after a fifteen-month lay-off from serious boxing, Foreman knocked out Ron Lyle in Las Vegas last January. Lyle hurt Foreman in the first round and knocked him down twice before Foreman clubbed him senseless in the fifth.

Now . . . Foreman tried to explain where he was going. The problem was he couldn't be sure.

"After Zaire," he said, "Ali looked me in the eye and said, 'I'll give you a chance to get the championship back. You come ahead of Frazier and Norton.'"

"And?"

"He hasn't fought me." Foreman . . . stands six feet three, and his arms are so long that his reach measures seventy-nine inches. He smiles, mostly to himself. "I guess he was lying."

"Do you feel bitter?" I said.

"I don't get bitter. I hate not being heavyweight champion, but I got other important things, too. My reading. I can't maybe explain all of Nikki Giovanni's poetry, but I look at her face and I associate that face with the poetry and I understand. My religion. I believe in God. I love to read Matthew and Isaiah. . . . I'm not bitter, but I want that championship back."

George Foreman grew up in a matriarchy, in a slum so deprived that by 1959, only two families in the ward owned television sets. He was one of seven children, and he recalls that his great early delight was standing on a porch looking through a window at a Western movie on one of the television sets. Westerns were his favorite. The cavalry charges thrilled him, the movie soldiers riding bravely, firing blanks, and waving flags furnished by the prop department of Republic studios.

The one dream he remembers was wanting to be a defensive tackle. His school years at E. O. Smith Junior High were disastrous. "You hear about them integrated and partly integrated," he says. "E. O. Smith was unintegrated. All black. The way I was, to learn, I had to get the attention of the teacher, and there were other kids who were always better at that, so I didn't get the attention of the teacher, and I didn't learn. That took care of football. I dropped out in the ninth grade."

His diet was shocking. In such relatively affluent ghettos as Harlem and Watts, families serve dinners of chicken necks and chicken backs. Foreman remembers dinners of chicken feet. "I ate the toes," he says. There was no money, no food, no hope. He took to the streets.

He learned to rob, and when he had stolen money, he learned to spend it on cheap wine. He didn't like what he was doing, and wine drunks beat off reality. But then, sober, he would have to rob again.

By sixteen, George had become a chronic offender, and his future seemed reduced to a single word. Prison.

I knew a lady once who took her troubles into deep therapy and emerged three years later with an odd statement. "I've learned to believe in magic moments," she said.

"Merlin is dead," I suggested.

"I believe in magic moments," she said. "They're what life turns on."

Suddenly and quite magically, George Foreman, the delinquent alcoholic of sixteen, decided to . . . join the Job Corps, one of the social-welfare programs born of the Kennedy-Johnson years. There he met whites for the first time. "I had a mythology about whites," he said, "and the whites had a mythology about us. And we found out, whites and blacks, not all of us, but some, that we weren't so damn different. And I learned to work, clear land, and make a living, and I flew in an airplane, and they were always kidding me. 'Big George. Big George. You're so strong you ought to be a fighter.'"

He began boxing and within three years won the Olympic heavyweight championship at Mexico City. That summer other black medalists raised clenched fists as a symbol of black power. George Foreman, the heavyweight champion, proclaimed his victory by waving a tiny flag in the ring.

"The Job Corps made me a patriot," he said, "but people don't understand everything about that flag. I was holding it up because of what the Job Corps did for me, but I was also holding it up because I was crazy about flags. Remember, that's what I saw the cavalry wave in those old movies on television in the Fifth Ward."

George was restless on Stage Three at NBC. The actors worked for a few minutes, broke, and played the same scene again. They broke once more. . . .

Foreman played himself in a role that would not have challenged Paul Robeson, and he knew his lines. . . . More breaks. More retakes. Lunchtime.

"This," George Foreman said as actors fled for the commissary, "motivates me to go back to training. All these breaks. This is not a challenge. Fighting is. I work out in Livermore, near San Francisco. I was going to go back to working on the thirteenth, but why mess with luck? I'm starting on the fourteenth. . . .

"I got to be champion, and I bought three homes and a batch of cars, and I took the $56,000 Rolls back to the Fifth Ward, and somebody came up and said, 'Champ, now that you've made it, why don't you dump this thing and get a classy car, a Caddy.' . . .

"After I lose, I'm up in Vegas, and a couple of guys see me. They're driving a pimp's car. A '61 Chevy with pink velvet interior. They wave, and I wave back, feeling like a big man. Then one of them says, 'I hope Ali whips your ass again.'

"I was a difficult guy when I was champion. Arrogant. I can beat Ali; I mean next time, he's going to beat himself. When I get to be champion again, I'm not going to be difficult. I'm going to remember all these months. Next time I'm champion, I'll treat everyone as though I were just a contender, say No. 5."

Technically Foreman is attempting to alter his style. For all his slugging power, he has tended to punch somewhat wide. A straight line and a tight hook are the shortest distance between points, and Dempsey is said to have possessed knockout power with a six-inch punch. Toward tightening his blows, Foreman has engaged Gil Clancey, a boxing scholar, as his new trainer.

Foreman's graceless performance against Ron Lyle could have been a symptom of rust, or an uncertain moment in transition, or the simple result of getting slugged hard as hell in the first round. But also it might mean, as in the case of Sonny Liston, that one whipping by Ali forever snapped something in the psyche. . . .

I asked Foreman how he stood with that partner of every champion, the Internal Revenue Service.

"I'm not going to tell you where I keep my money," Foreman said.

"But you're okay?"

A small, warm smile. "IRS is the real undefeated heavyweight champ. They show you the left. You never see the right. They'll take everything, even your tears."

He grew serious. "Yes, I'm all right, and I can't complain about taxes. The Job Corps made me human, and income taxes supported that."

"My taxes," I said.

"Thank you very much," George Foreman said. The actors drifted back to Stage Three. I thought of the chicken feet and the $5.5 million purse and Nikki Giovanni's *The Women and the Men,* and I wished Odets could have met George Foreman and visited the Fifth Ward in Houston, Texas. I'm no critic, but that could have inspired one hell of an honest play.

36

Aspects of the Game

Sports Illustrated, August 16, 1976

I traveled the country for months during that distant summer.
All and all, baseball was doing fine.

Vandals had set fire to the grass. No one knew how they had gotten wet spring grass to burn or why anyone wanted to fire a soft suburban meadow, but there the ball field lay, grimy with ash on the eleventh day of spring.

"It's all right," the boy said. "We can play anyway."

I was wearing red sneakers, a gift Lou Brock had offered along with a lecture on quickness and traction and stealing bases. Brock's autograph is stitched near the instep, and someone, noticing the name as I loped through a softball game, once said, "Them sneakers have never moved so slow." Still they are my present from a superb big leaguer, and so a kind of totem. I didn't want them dirtied with black ash.

"We'll get messed up," I said. "We can try again next weekend."

"We don't have visitation next weekend. Come on. Just pitch a few," he said. Then, seductively, "After that, I'll pitch, and you can hit."

His name is Roger, and he has a sturdy twelve-year-old body and a passionate excitement at being alive. "I'm studying the Renaissance," he announced recently as I was preparing papers for a tax audit.

"Good," I said. "The Renaissance. . . . Who was Michelangelo?"

"Wait," Roger cried. "Don't give me the answer. I know. Michelangelo put statues in the gardens of the Medici."

So, though we don't live together anymore, we can talk about the Renaissance. And we can play ball.

He hits left-handed. We started working on that nine years ago, and now as he took an open stance, he chattered directions. "Don't throw too hard. I haven't started working out yet. Don't throw curves. Let me get my swing grooved. Okay. Come on."

I began to throw high pitches at medium speed. Roger lunged. Four years with the Little League in Ridgefield, Connecticut. Four seasons under coaches who work for IBM or sell insurance or pilot 727s, and nobody has taught him—or been able to teach him—that a good hitter does not lunge.

"Keep your head still," I said.

The boy's mouth tightened. He had not come to learn. He wanted to show me how far he could hit my pitching, swinging his own metal bat in his own way.

Very well, young man, I thought. Today in the April cold, you'll get a lesson whether you want it or not. Subject: He who lunges never hits .300.

I threw hard with an easy motion. Roger swung late. I threw easily with a big motion. He swung early. I tried to jam him, but the ball drifted inside toward his knees. Roger made a graceful arching leap. The ball skidded to the backstop. He lay face down, shaking on the earth.

I hurried to him. "Sorry. Sorry. You all right?"

He rolled over in the ash, blackening his jacket. He was shaking with defiant young laughter. "You couldn't hurt me," he said.

We grinned, and at once the lesson was done. He had earned the right to pitches he could hit. Roger began scattering line drives. Roger looped a fly to center. There was no one to retrieve the ball but me. He bounced sharply through the middle. Another chore for an aging, chilly right-hander. He lashed a high inside pitch clear to a ditch at the border of right field.

"Now we'll just play pepper," I said when I returned with the ball.

He insisted on borrowing my bat. Thirty-two ounces. A fat-barreled Ron Santo model. Either Roger did not know the rules of pepper, or he did not know how strong he has become. We stood thirty feet apart. I made a pepper toss. Roger whipped the big bat. The blackened baseball hurtled at my nose. I threw a glove up, deflected the ball, and stumbled. Sitting on the charred grass, I remembered a transcendent reality of baseball. The ball is hard. It is something to fear. Forty years ago I learned that from my father in Brooklyn fields that have vanished under high-rises. Seventy years ago he learned that from his father on fields that have disappeared under slums. And now my son, in careless, innocent excitement, has reinforced a family lesson as old as the century.

Roger came toward me slowly. The Ron Santo model seemed almost as big as he. His face was white. "Dad, I didn't mean to hit a liner at your face."

Getting up, glad to still have my nose, I fall back on an old Wayne-Bogart gambit. "Gosh, kid, I didn't know you cared."

"Sure I care," Roger said, and he put an arm around my waist. We started hiking to a distant house where splits of maple crackled in a fireplace. There we could sit before the fire and talk baseball.

What would I tell him? Of Stan Musial, most gentle of athletes, whose swing was like a viper's lash? Or of the day when Early Wynn brushed back Mickey Mantle, who bounced up and hit a single? Wynn was so furious that before he threw another pitch, he went into a careful pickoff move. Then he hit Mantle with his throw, knocking him to the ground alongside first base. "That SOB is so mean he'd like to knock you down in the dugout," Mantle complained. Or about Victor Pellot Power of Arecibo, Puerto Rico, whom the Yankees traded in 1954 for announced reasons that are not worth remembering? The real reasons were that Power was black and Latin and reputedly liked the company of white women. When I saw Power in the hilly Puerto Rican town of Caguas several weeks ago, he demonstrated that the Yankees had been correct. He liked white women well enough to have married a compact, smoldering blonde whose name is Ada. But in between, while the Yankees employed Joe Pepitone, erratic, libertine—but white—at first, Power, a solid .285 hitter, was indisputably the best fielder at that position in the American League. Seven times he won the Gold Glove.

Or would I merely tell him about my father, a teacher and an editor, who hit a baseball hard? Two months before his heart stopped, he was lining high drives to center on Monhegan Island off the coast of Maine. He was fifty-two and I was twenty-four, but I could not hit a ball as far as he. No power. He had hoped I would grow taller and stand someday beside Jake Daubert and Zack Wheat, the heroes of his own sandlot days. Then he was dead, and the people who admired his eidetic memory and his understanding of the Renaissance told me how fine it must have been to grow up at his side and to talk seriously with him about serious things, such as the gardens of the Medici. I don't believe we ever did. We talked seriously (and joyously) about baseball. That was a serious thing, and that was enough.

You learn to leave some mysteries alone. At twenty-eight I was susceptible to suggestions that I explain—not describe but explain—baseball in America. I published in small quarterlies. I addressed a Columbia seminar, and I developed a showy proficiency at responding to editors who asked me to "equate the game in terms of Americana."

Such phrases now bang against my brain like toothaches. I never look at the old pieces anymore, but I remember some generalizations I drew:

Baseball is not played against a clock. (But neither is tennis, golf, or four-handed gin rummy.)

Baseball rules have barely changed across generations. (Neither have the rules of water polo.)

The ball field is a mystic creation, the Stonehenge of America. That is, the bases are a magic ninety feet apart. Think how often a batter is thrown out by half a step, compared to instances when he outruns a hit to shortstop. But artificial surfaces have lately changed the nature, if not the dimensions, of the diamond. A ground ball at Riverfront Stadium moves much faster than the same grounder bouncing on the honest grass of Wrigley Field. Yet at last look, baseball in Cincinnati seemed to be surviving. Batters there are also thrown out by half a step.

Suppose the bases had been set eighty or eighty-six feet apart. The fielders simply would have positioned themselves differently, and a ground ball to short would still be a ground ball to short, 6–3 in everybody's scorebook.

I do believe this: baseball's inherent rhythm, minutes and minutes of passivity erupting into seconds of frenzied action, matches an attribute of the American character. But no existential proclamation, or any tortured neo-Freudianism, or any outburst of popular sociology, not even—or least of all—my own, explains baseball's lock on the American heart.

You learn to let some mysteries alone, and when you do, you find they sing themselves.

A TOWN WHERE SOMEONE DRIVES A KAISER

Alongside the two-lane blacktop that crosses northeast Oklahoma, the land rolls bare and poor. Outside of villages called Broken Arrow and Chouteau lie shacks and rusty house trailers where survivors of the Cherokee Nation live in poverty. This is not farming country. It is hard, red, intractable soil that we have abandoned to the Indians.

Then, as the road crosses into Arkansas and into the village of Siloam Springs, a wonder of pastureland abruptly appears. Siloam Springs is Wally Moon's domain. Wallace Wade Moon, late of the St. Louis Cardinals and the Los Angeles Dodgers. Now head baseball coach at John Brown University. Enrollment: 550. Team batting average: .362.

On the telephone Moon said he had a few more minutes of desk work to do before he could meet me. Waiting for him, I asked the lady behind the front desk of the East Gate Motel to explain the relative prosperity of Benton County, Arkansas.

"It's a little embarrassing," she said. Behind her spectacles, her eyes were pale and pleasant.

"How so?"

"Chicken droppings," the lady said. "I guess that's the best way to put it." Then she explained. Northwest Arkansas had been as poor as northeast Oklahoma until after World War II, when some men decided to try chicken farming in the Ozark foothills. "That went pretty good, you might say," the lady continued, "but it sure left a lot of chicken droppings. They smelled. So the farmers spread the stuff across the fields and hills, and after a few years the soil got a darn sight richer. Real good grass grew. After that, some other people brought in cattle, and the cattle grazed good and times got even better. Not that we don't have some poor, but Benton County's doing fine right now.

"Truth is"—the lady's eyes darted to make sure we were alone—"the economy here is built on chicken . . ."

"Yes, ma'am," I said.

Moon had talked rather less of chickens and more of a high sky and gentle streams when we had shared dinner after an old-timers' game the year before. Moon, outfielder and batsman, played twelve Major League seasons during the 1950s and '60s. He wore his hair short and his thick black eyebrows met, and he had the look of a Confederate cavalry captain. But he was a decent, tolerant man, with a master's degree from Texas A&M, wholly dedicated to squeezing a base hit out of each turn at bat.

The Cardinals called him up in 1954, just as they were selling Enos Slaughter, a portly, combative legend, to the Yankees. Two days before Moon broke in, the *St. Louis Post-Dispatch* published a front-page picture of Slaughter weeping with grief into a large white handkerchief.

Moon came from Arkansas delta country, and the first time he saw a Major League game, he was playing in it. The fans in St. Louis were, at best, belligerently neutral. They loved the legend Moon had been hired to replace. In his first time at bat in his first Major League game, Moon pulled a home run over the right-field pavilion of old Busch Stadium and into Grand Boulevard. That year Slaughter batted .248 for New York. Moon hit .304 and became Rookie of the Year.

Five years later with the Dodgers, he perfected his opposite-field stroke. The Dodgers played in the Los Angeles Coliseum then, and the left-field screen, the players said, was only a medium spit away from home. Moon hit nineteen home runs, most of them to left, tied for the league lead with eleven triples, and hit twenty-six doubles, and a Dodgers team of shreds and patches established itself in Los Angeles by winning the World Series from the White Sox.

When Moon's skills eroded, he and his wife, Bettye, debated city and country life. They had five children, and he could earn more money in a city. But Wally remembered the good days with his father, Bert, hunting and hiking through the woods of Benton County. There was an offer to try Benton County again as head coach at John Brown, a small Christian Evangelical school.

The Moons live in a rambling ranch set on two hundred acres three miles east of Siloam, a town with an artists' colony, no daily newspaper, a little light industry, and springs that were once thought to possess medicinal properties. A giant red oak towers over Moon's house, and inside there is a cheerful babble of children. Wally Joe, husky and twenty-three, writes free-form poetry and studies toward a master's degree in physical education. The four daughters, ages twelve to twenty, are bright, mannerly, attractive. Their interests range from baton twirling to Clementi piano sonatas. Moon said grace, and we dined sumptuously on Arkansas grass-fed beef. Then, in the old-fashioned way, the ladies went about their chores, while Moon and I retired to a sun-room crowded with pictures and trophies. On one wall Moon glowers from an old *Sports Illustrated* cover that has a caption announcing: "The Spirit of the Gashouse Gang."

"Actually, the spunkiest guys of all were those 1959 Dodgers," Moon said. "Not the best. Some of the old Brooklyn Dodgers on the way down. Fellows like Koufax and Drysdale on the way up. But I never played on a club that wanted to win more." He had admired Walt Alston, Moon said, and he had roomed with Koufax and told Sandy that he was tipping his pitches. But those were old times, and Wally had a new story to tell.

"Do I look tired?" he said.

"You sound subdued."

"We had a tournament double-header across the mountains in Pine Bluff yesterday. We had to win both games, and we won them big, 13–4 and 24–8. When we finished, it was 8:20 and only one restaurant in town was open. Only one waitress was working there. By the time we all got fed, it was past 11. There's no team bus. We have no budget for that. We travel in station wagons and cars. I was driving the lead car, and coming back across the Ozarks, we hit fog. I got home, still in uniform, at 5 a.m."

The John Brown Golden Eagles have names like Chuck Gardner, Dale Hatcher, Dave Stockstill. They come from towns like Texarkana, Texas; Paducah, Kentucky; and Hurley, Missouri. To a man, they played Little League ball and enjoyed it. To a man, they ache to play in the Major Leagues. "I'm not looking for a bonus," one of Moon's best players said. "If I had the money, I'd pay *them* to sign me."

Most of the players are on scholarship. They address Moon as "Coach," often in the deferential way a man in pain says, "Doctor."

276 | Part 4

Coach Moon imposes rules. No beanballs. Bench-jockeying is permitted but within limits. Moon is a devout Methodist, and none of his players "may blaspheme the name of the Lord."

"As a coach, my strongest point is batting," Moon said. "I teach them to hold their heads still and keep their bats back. Strike zone? They're not ready for that yet, and I don't believe in teaching too many things at once. Just develop a quick, compact swing. If I have a weak point, or a point where I lack confidence, that would be pitching." He looked across a darkening field.

"You're still learning baseball, aren't you?"

"I'm still learning, and I'm forty-six. Man, this is a difficult sport to learn."

The next afternoon John Brown played a twilight game against the University of Tulsa, which has a student body of six thousand. The Siloam Springs ballpark has been leveled in a glade, and as game time approached and the Franklin Electric plant and the Ace Plastics factory closed, pickup trucks and motorbikes and Chevrolets and Fords filled the lot behind center field. There is no admission charge to watch the Eagles. Minor league ball is gone forever from Siloam Springs. John Brown University is the town team.

The Eagles use aluminum bats, which Moon says saves $300 a year. They take batting practice without a cage. There is no budget for a batting cage either. The infield is dirt, not grass. "What's the name of this ballpark?" I asked Moon.

"It has no name. We call it 'the field.'"

The fans sat in wooden bleachers and on grassy banks. "A kind of Greek theater," Bettye Moon says. Two Major League scouts sat among the crowd. Both Fred Hawn of the Cardinals and Milt Boiling of the Boston Red Sox had come to see Moon's shortstop, Chuck Gardner, a junior who was batting .443.

The Eagles warmed up smartly with quick infield play. The outfielders, particularly Randy Rouse, showed strong young arms. Moon started Ron Rhodes, a junior left-hander who had won eight straight games, and his team jumped ahead when Gardner doubled home one run in the first inning and two more in the second. But Tulsa came back when Bruce Humphrey slammed a 380-foot home run over the cyclone fence in center field, and Tulsa kept coming.

These teams were good. Unlike college teams in the northern tier of states, they start working outdoors in February. Each club had already played forty games. But they are collegians, and collegians make mistakes. By the last inning, Tulsa had drawn ahead, 6–5. Gardner led off with a single, a murderous drive that hurtled past the pitcher's left ear. A sacrifice moved him to second. He was the tying run. Then Rouse grounded to shortstop, and Gardner tried to go to third.

That never works. The rule is as old as baseball. A runner cannot advance from second to third on a ball hit to the left side of the infield. Gardner was out by ten feet, and when Dave Stockstill blinked at a fastball, knee high on the outside corner, the Golden Eagles had been beaten.

Moon's lips were pressed together. He does not like to lose. "You can never advance on that play, Wally," I said.

He shook his head and spat, then looked less fierce. "But the kid wanted to score so damn bad."

Lightning interrupted the next day's workout, and a siren wailed steadily in downtown Siloam Springs. "That's a tornado alert," Moon said. "Don't worry till it warbles. A warbling siren means a funnel's been sighted." We repaired to the Quonset hut that is Moon's clubhouse, and he began to tell his twenty-four players about the previous day's game.

He had spoken privately with Gardner, and now he had more general things to talk about. "My analysis is that we got beat because they wanted to win more than we did," he said. "It wasn't a tournament game for us. We had a hard trip the other day. But that doesn't make any difference. No matter how you feel, when you walk through that gate and onto the field, you've got to kick yourself in the butt. Here or in the Majors. I can tell you from personal experience that across a Major League season your butt ends up pretty sore. But you've got to do it.

"Now, Ron," he said to Rhodes, "you remember when first base was open and I went out to the mound and told you to pitch around the hitter?"

Rhodes nodded gravely.

"In the Majors I would have told you to deliberately walk him. That was the play. But we're here to learn, and I want you to learn what I mean by pitching around a hitter.

"In that situation, with a runner in scoring position, the hitter is eager. Start him with a fastball all the way in on his belly. He's so eager he may swing, but he's not going to hurt you off a pitch like that. Then when you curve him, get it in the dirt. Not just low. In the dirt. He's still eager. If he walks, you aren't hurt, and if he swings at a bouncing curve, you aren't hurt either. But you gave him a pitch he could hit, and he hit it and it scored a run, and that's what we lost by. One run.

"For you hitters, look at that situation in reverse. Control your eagerness. That's a mental discipline. There's a lot of mental discipline in the game. But you've got nothing to be ashamed of. Tulsa is a good club. They wanted the game more than you did, and they got it."

Rain beat fiercely on the iron roof. "Do you have any questions?" Moon asked me.

"I'd like to ask how many of you gentlemen hope to play in the Major Leagues?" The boys, eighteen to twenty-one years old, looked at one another. Then slowly, shyly, all twenty-four of the Golden Eagles raised their hands.

"How many have a chance?" I asked Moon after the players had left.

"Probably none," Moon said. "The shortstop is good, but he's twenty-one years old. I've seen another college shortstop just about as good, and he's eighteen. A big three years. Then you figure beyond all the college shortstops, there are all the boys already in the minors playing 140 games a year, kids from all over the country and Latin America, and you realize what the odds are against Chuck Gardner. He'll play minor league ball. So will a few of the others. But most of them will go on from here to teach and coach. I want them to enjoy the game, but I want them to learn technique and conduct and discipline as well." Moon stood up. "Maybe they can pass on what I give them to others."

We went to a Rotary meeting then. We stood to pledge allegiance, and we sang "America the Beautiful" under the fervid conducting of a doctor named John Moose. I remembered morning chapels in my grade school and how every afternoon we played baseball on a gravelly field and how we sometimes admitted that our dream was to play baseball in the Majors. (None of us did.)

For all the fresh, clean-shaven faces of Moon's Golden Eagles, the trip to Siloam Springs was like a voyage into the past. Leaving town I saw a sign that read:

GUITAR LESSONS
PIANO TUNING
GOSPEL PIANO

Then I passed someone driving a yellow Kaiser car. I believe they stopped making Kaisers in 1955.

THE FRANCHISE BUSINESS

The man who owns the Dodgers did not like *The Boys of Summer*, a book I wrote celebrating baseball, life, the courage to be new—and certain men who spent a decade winning pennants for the Brooklyn Dodgers. A Los Angeles morning had broken summery and dense, light smog hovering under a yellow sky, after a night when the Dodgers defeated the Cincinnati Reds 5–0. Walter Francis O'Malley—a compelling seventy-three-year-old paterfamilias who mixes Quaker parsimony, pagan ferocity, and Irish-Catholic charm—looked up darkly from sheaves of correspondence. He did not say, "Hello." He did not say, "How are you?" Instead he growled in a Tammany bass, "This time are you going to write something positive?"

At such moments, I long to utter an infinite retort, at once deflating the critic and placing my published work beyond criticism lower than Ruskin's. But I am not any good at that. I am good at making plodding responses and later getting angry.

"It sold some copies," I said.

O'Malley waved his cigar as though it were a scepter. "Several stories involving Fresco Thompson and Buzzie Bavasi were unfortunate," he said. "They were so unfortunate that I asked my son Peter what in the world has gotten into our Brooklyn friend."

Ah, but we argued long ago in Brooklyn, too. O'Malley is a consistent man, and he has consistently believed that the first function of the sporting press is to sell tickets to Dodgers games. I looked out a window. Dodger Stadium, loveliest of ballparks, had been swept and scrubbed clean of the litter and gum deposited by 52,469 customers the night before. "What a pleasant office you have," I said.

"Not so pleasant," O'Malley said. "Outside my window there's a groundskeeper standing in center field with a hose, and I wonder, if he's going to use a hose, why the hell did I put $600,000 into an underground sprinkler system?"

"Why does he use a hose?"

"Because we brought him out from Brooklyn, and he used a hose there," the owner of the Los Angeles Dodgers announced impatiently.

O'Malley and I go back four decades, not only to a single borough but to a single neighborhood and a single private school. "You know," O'Malley said, mingling sentiment and blarney, "I take pride in being the man who handed you a diploma when you graduated from Froebel Academy. You certainly looked at things more positively then."

Like Joseph Kennedy or FDR, O'Malley is an indefatigable one-upman. Like them, he is a master of his trade. That trade is Major League baseball.

"You want to know about our success out here," O'Malley said. "First, we're not a syndicate. The Dodgers are a family corporation. Second, we don't have absentee ownership. Third, the chairman of the board, with whom you're sitting and who isn't getting any younger, comes to work at 8:30 on the morning after a night game. When the board chairman shows up that early, the rest of the staff tends to do the same."

O'Malley approaches me with suspicion because I write, as I approach him carefully because he criticizes. Still, Fred Claire, the Dodgers' vice president for public relations, set up a schedule of interviews that taxed my ability to assimilate and caused one cassette recorder to expire.

Al Campanis, the vice president of player personnel, opened a drawer and showed me his private treasury. Fourteen transcriptions of Branch Rickey on baseball. No one studied baseball more passionately than Rickey, and every Dodgers employee now hears, directly or indirectly, from the source.

"We wouldn't want this stuff to get around," Campanis said. Then, with a Byzantine flourish, he showed me some extrapolations.

"Thou shalt not steal," Rickey said. "I mean defensively. On offense, indeed thou shalt steal and thou must."

Amid such platitudes lies baseball gold. According to Rickey, the change of pace is a magnificent pitch. Instruct young pitchers in the art of changing speeds. But first let them master the fastball and control. Teach changing speeds in Double-A or Triple-A. On tape Rickey suggests that they will have gained confidence and sophistication at that level. Look for ballplayers who run and hit with power. Neither speed nor distance hitting can be taught. Consider the present and, simultaneously, plan for the future. Luck is the residue of design. Once Rickey assembled his staff and cried out in the voice of Job, "I stand on a cliff. On the edge of an abyss. I lose my footing. I stumble toward the yawning gates of hell. One man can save me. Only one. I ask each of you, who is that man?" This meant the Dodgers' bullpen was uncertain, and Rickey wanted a consensus on the best minor league reliever to call up. His name was Phil Haugstad. He won none and lost one.

In the dugout Walter Alston reviewed his twenty-two years of Dodgers managing. "We've had three eras out west," he said. "Carl Furillo, Duke Snider, and the rest were past their prime when they got to Los Angeles. Wally Moon helped the club. Next, there was a fast team. It had fine pitching with Sandy Koufax, whose perfectionism I admire. Now this good team—Steve Garvey, Ron Cey, and Davey Lopes. How long will I keep managing? It's always been a one-year contract. I wouldn't stay any place where I wasn't wanted. I can teach school, you know. Used to do that in Ohio. But I'll make my decision next October. I make it every October. Meanwhile, I have a delightful job."

Dixie Walker, the batting coach, instructed Steve Yeager, a good young catcher, with side comments to a relief pitcher and me. As a batting-practice pitcher threw, Walker chattered caressingly: "Think opposite field, Steve. Think other way. They're going to give you outside sliders, Steve. No one can pull them. Don't worry about the other, the inside stuff. Your hands are so quick, you'll pull everything there, the way Babe Ruth did. I played with Ruth."

Yeager popped three outside fastballs to right. Walker winced. Then he said, "I can't push him more. Ballplayers have changed. On the old

Tigers, nobody told you anything. Only Charlie Gehringer—he wasn't a coach but a player—said I should go the other way."

"You think this guy is working?" the pitcher said.

"I think so," Walker said. "But if I push him too hard—it's this new generation—he'll work against me. Against you."

Tom Lasorda, the third-base coach, discoursed on imposing team spirit. "You know, there are guys like Bill Russell, our shortstop, who will get down on their knees at parties and say, 'I'm a Dodger. I love the Dodgers.'" Lasorda gazed into a glass of soda water. "I love the Dodgers. Cut my own veins, I'll bleed Dodgers blue."

Steve Garvey, the first baseman, offered his theory on California crowds. "Friday night they're mad. They've worked a long, hard week. Make some errors early on a Friday night, and the people at Dodger Stadium crucify you. Saturday is date night. Medium. Sunday is easy. You can play real bad, but the fathers are out here with their sons. Nobody boos." Garvey touched his chin. "Monday and Tuesday nights you get the people who know baseball."

Dusty Baker, an outfielder fairly fresh from Atlanta, discussed a difference between the Dodgers and the Braves. "In Atlanta, you *hoped* to win. Out here, it's expected."

I had come to Los Angeles to consider the Dodgers for three days. I stayed for five. On each of the first two nights they drew over fifty thousand as they split a series with the Reds. Then the Braves flew in. Andy Messersmith had not begun to win, and the Braves were playing the dreariest baseball extant. Still, Dodgers crowds hovered around thirty thousand. Friday night brought the Houston Astros and Cap Night. Buy a ticket and you get a baseball cap worth about a dollar for free. Once again attendance soared over fifty thousand.

The Dodgers are contenders, as they have been through most of Alston's three generations of Los Angeles teams. They run well, play tight defense, gamble, hit to right, but it would be stretching things to claim that they look as strong as the Reds. Quite simply, the Dodgers, a good team, are this: the most valuable franchise in baseball.

The Dodgers win games. They make money. They are a rousing team to watch, and that all leads back to the seventy-three-year-old man sitting in a glass-walled office and glowering at a distant figure costing him money behind a hose.

I don't think the Brooklyn Dodgers, a glorious and profitable franchise, should have been moved eighteen seasons ago. A strong commissioner would have vetoed the transmigration as contrary to the best interests of baseball. The West then could have opened logically, with nascent franchises wriggling toward victory in San Francisco and LA. I don't blame O'Malley, a graduate of Culver Military Academy and the University of Pennsylvania and once a hustling lawyer, for trying to move above the American middle class. Ford Frick, the commissioner in 1957, was all elocution and putty. Frick is a pleasant, pensioned fellow who these days likes to discuss the sport of curling. Sweep, sweep, Ford Frick. Walter O'Malley, conniving, serious baseball man, one word is owed to you and your Los Angeles success. Congratulations.

"We have been fortunate, obviously so," O'Malley said. "We hoped we knew what fans wanted in a stadium. Good parking. We could still have done more there. Reasonable prices. We held the line, not increasing prices at all for eighteen seasons. Last year because of the free agency potential and this endless inflation, our top seat went from $3.50 to $4.50. We try to keep within the image of baseball as a daily event, so a fellow can afford to bring his wife or kids or grandparents. Our demographic image is the best in sport. I see them coming in with canes, walking sticks, and wheelchairs, and I see the middle generation, and I see the kids. Everybody's getting a reasonably priced evening's entertainment. The kids mean that we're building future fans.

"We've stayed in contention. That's all anyone can do. Injuries. We had a lot of injuries in 1975. Suppose the Reds lost Bench and Morgan? We stay in contention, and we're the only team that ever did—or ever will—fly the World Series flag on the Atlantic and the Pacific Coasts."

He looks very much as he did twenty years ago. Round face, round spectacles. Dark hair. The same incredible alternation in expression between patriarch and trial lawyer.

"If they had built you a ballpark in Brooklyn, would you have stayed?"

"I've got to correct you there. You're falling into the same trap the others have. A boy from Froebel Academy should know better than that." The cigar waves. O'Malley shakes his head.

"I never asked them to build me a new park in Brooklyn. I said we would build it on taxable land with our own money. We had a site at Atlantic and Flatbush Avenues where the subways intersected. There's no place back there big enough for many parking lots, so my thought was that you'd dock your car in any subway station and come to the ballpark for 15 cents.

"Now there was a thing in New York. Bobby Wagner was the mayor. A nice man, not very strong. I knew his father, the senator. Robert Moses was the real power in New York.

"We had a site, and a sports authority was set up to condemn the land we needed, but Moses blocked us. He had a site of his own bounded on one side by water, on another by a cemetery, on a third by a slum, and on the fourth by a parkway, which meant that everyone going to our games was going to have to pay out to the toll booths on the parkway that Moses had built. I couldn't see us drawing many people from the water or the cemetery. We had to come out here. We had ambitious plans for Brooklyn. We were toying with a domed stadium. We were looking ahead to pay television and hoping to get some financing that way, but they wouldn't give us the land we needed to do it.

"The writers have been snowed under by a theory that this LA thing was a big giveaway. This park was built for about $20 million, and it didn't cost the taxpayers a dime. If you want to consider the difference between private enterprise and socialism, look at our park here and the one the city of San Francisco built. Public monies were wasted out there in the cold and wind of Candlestick Point.

"We pay the County of Los Angeles more than $1 million in real-estate taxes. They write we've got the oil and mineral rights to our land, and that's so much bunk, too. If someone struck oil back of second base, the oil would belong to the City of Los Angeles."

He turned and gestured toward the hills behind center field. The terrain was once arid, but now Chavez Ravine has evergreens and desert plants. "When he was working here, Buzzie Bavasi asked me why I was spending all that money landscaping when we play six nights a week and nobody can see the hills after the sun sets. I told him I was doing it for our Sunday afternoon customers. You won't believe it, but growing things are important to me.

"We took a chance. They told us Los Angeles was not a baseball town. We had a short lease on the Coliseum, then we were at the mercy of the city council. I think we won there by a single vote. Otherwise we might have been playing in the street.

"Even my son asked me why I was taking the risk of putting so much money into the ballpark. I told him, 'Peter, after I'm gone—and maybe after you are, too—this ballpark will remain, and it will be a monument to the O'Malleys.'"

Outside in a corridor I passed Peter O'Malley, a six-foot-two graduate of the Wharton School of Finance who has run the Triple-A franchise at Spokane and now is president of the Dodgers—under the chairman of the board.

"How'd it go with Dad?"

"He doesn't know how to be dull."

"Where are you coming from?"

"Houston."

Peter O'Malley shook his head. "That's scary what's happened down there. Is it true the Astros' operation is $33 million in debt?"

The Houston Astros, formerly the Houston Colt .45s, have played under six managers and four general managers since they were organized in 1962. That was the year the Mets lost 120 games for Casey Stengel.

In 1963 the Astros brought up a promising first baseman named Rusty Staub and a good-looking outfielder named Jim Wynn. They subsequently traded both. In 1964, when the Mets lost only 109, the Astros found an aggressive young catcher named Jerry Grote. He later went to New York. In 1965 the Astros started a swift young second baseman—Joe Morgan—and had a pitcher with a forkball named Dave Giusti. Giusti has since become a star at Pittsburgh, and last year Morgan won the Most Valuable Player Award. He was playing for the Reds. The Astros have traded Cesar Geronimo and Jack Billingham to Cincinnati, John Mayberry to Kansas City, and Mike Cuellar to Baltimore, where he won the Cy Young Award.

Beyond such oafish deals lies an eerie death book. Jay Dahl, a Houston pitching prospect of great promise, died in an auto wreck eleven years ago. Jim Umbricht, another pitcher, died of cancer at the age of thirty-three. Twenty-nine-year-old Don Wilson, who had pitched two no-hitters, was found dead in a car beside his Houston home in the wretched morning hours of January 5, 1975.

After this mix of error and disaster, the Astros are now bankrupt and for sale. This year the team is in the hands of the creditors.

"I'd like to own a ballclub," I told Sidney Shlenker, a thirty-nine-year-old Houston entrepreneur who is the caretaker president of the team. "Thing is, my check would bounce."

Shlenker, a large, amiable man, smiled. "The way things are going around here, a bad check would be better than none at all," he said.

Last season the Astros finished forty-three and a half games behind the Reds, drew 858,002 people, and lost money. "When you get to Houston, look up a fan called Herschel Maltz," Wally Moon suggested in Siloam Springs. "He played ball with me at Texas A&M. A nonhitting Jewish first baseman."

At lunch, Maltz—now president of Century Papers, Inc.—confirmed that he was a first baseman, nonhitting, and Jewish. "But I had a good glove," he said. "Real good. Did Wally happen to mention that?" Then Maltz talked about Houston's continuing economic boom with a quiet, drawling pride.

"About the ballclub," I said.

"I'm turned off," Maltz said. "I used to go to forty games a year. I'd take customers. This year I haven't been to the Dome once. You know, I've been thinking that maybe they ought to change the rules of baseball. Give it a quicker pace, make it more lively, like football."

"Make it more lively" is a euphemism for "win the pennant." There were no yawns last October in Boston or Cincinnati. Bringing a contender into Houston is the weighty task of Talbot Smith, an intense, precise, bespectacled man of forty-two who resigned as executive vice president of the Yankees to become general manager of the Astros last August.

"I come from New England, and I don't dislike the East or even New York City," Smith says. "We had a comfortable place out on Long Island. I certainly wouldn't have left that and the Yankees if I didn't think there was a challenge here that I could meet in the foreseeable future."

When, then, will the Astros bring a pennant race to their Dome?

Bill Virdon, the field manager, speaks: "It doesn't just depend on us. We're in the same division as the Dodgers and the Reds. How fast we can be competitive depends on what they do as well as what we do."

"We aren't trading away any more young talent," Smith says.

"Right now we're trying to get them to play hard, exciting baseball," Virdon says. "Frankly, I don't see us competitive with the Dodgers and the Reds until the latter part of next season at the earliest. But that's possible. I'm shooting for it. And we're not finishing any forty-three and a half games out this year."

Texas was a promising land for Major League baseball when the Houston franchise was organized. The state was the birthplace of men who rose to baseball's pantheon, among them Rogers Hornsby and Tris Speaker. All by itself, Texas once supported a minor league. (Well, almost. Shreveport played in the Texas League, too.) The old Houston Buffs were a top Cardinals farm. Dizzy Dean began building his legend there.

"The Buffs were good and sometimes very funny," says Clark Nealon, a Texas newspaperman for forty-five years. "They once had a right fielder named Nick Cullop, who played beside a fine center fielder, Hal Epps. Epps had one problem. Going for a fly he never shouted, 'I got it!' or, 'You take it!' He said he couldn't run and holler at the same time. One night after a rainstorm, Cullop and Epps collided under a fly. Cullop ended on top with Epps lying face down in a mud puddle. 'You can't say, "I got it." You can't say, "You take it." Now we'll see if you know how to say, "Help!"'"

Judge Roy Hofheinz, a bulky, aggressive Texas politician, won a Major League franchise for Houston with the promise of a domed stadium. Hofheinz's Astrodome, which opened in 1965, is described in a brochure, with characteristic understatement, as the Eighth Wonder of the World. Some measure of Hofheinz's business acuity came out of an early controversy involving the playing surface of the Dome. Originally, the field was sodded, and the roof was made of 4,596 translucent plastic skylights that were scientifically designed to let in enough sunlight to keep the grass growing. Unfortunately, all that translucence created a creamy backdrop against which it was nearly impossible to follow the

flight of a fly ball. Hofheinz had the Lucite darkened and began negotiating with representatives from Monsanto to install artificial grass.

"We're thinking in terms of $375,000," a man from Monsanto said.

"You must be clairvoyant," said Hofheinz. "$375,000 was exactly what
I had in mind to charge you for promotion for using your product
in the Dome. Take our name. Call it AstroTurf if you like." The compromise gave Hofheinz what he wanted: an AstroTurf field for free.

The Dome cost $38 million, which Hofheinz financed largely through
$31.5 million in bonds issued by Harris County, Texas. (The current
lease costs the Astros $750,000 a year.) Then he built four hotels
near the Dome, a convention center called Astrohall, and an amusement park called Astroworld. The whole conglomeration was named
Astrodomain.

The hotels were empty too often. The amusement park lacked the
sparkling Disney touch. People came from fifty states to see the Dome.
They arrived as tourists and did not become baseball fans. The team
kept trading its best young talent, attendance slumped, and on the
fringes of Hofheinz's domain, one could begin to hear the insistent
whisperings of creditors.

Six years ago Hofheinz suffered a stroke. He now sits in a wheelchair, huge and bearded like Orson Welles, with his empire suddenly
revealed as a fiscal ruin. The four hotels and the convention center
have been sold. The amusement park has been leased to Six Flags
Over Texas. What remains of Hofheinz's Texas dream is a ballpark
owned by the county, a ballclub with some potential, and a debt that
Shlenker concedes is "more than $30 million."

Along with empty seats, I saw good baseball at the Astrodome. The
Astros played the Phillies tough in two of three games. Cesar Cedeno
in center is a superb player. James Rodney Richard, the six-foot-eight
right-hander, throws smoke. Roger Metzger, the shortstop, is fine.
Greg Gross in right will get his hits. Virdon has his athletes working;
they didn't beat the Phillies, but they played them, in Virdon's term,
competitively.

But it is premature to assert that the Astros' luck has turned. Smith
has introduced a promotion called the Foamer. On Foamer Nights, a
large bulb near a digital clock behind right field lights up during each

even-numbered minute. Should an Astro hit a home run when the light is on, management buys free beer for every adult in the house for the rest of the evening. For a chaser one night during the Phillies series, Smith threw in an extra freebie: if Mike Cosgrove, the Astros' pitcher, struck out Mike Schmidt when the light was on, there also would be free beer for everybody.

At 9:12 Cosgrove got two strikes on Schmidt. He gazed endlessly at catcher Cliff Johnson for a sign. The 17,338 fans made a rising inchoate noise. Finally, with the light still on, Cosgrove threw an inside fastball. Schmidt missed it. The crowd made an animal roar. Suddenly, all over the Dome grown men sprinted up the aisles. The place seemed to empty in seconds as the fans scampered toward refreshment stands.

In the sixth, with the Phillies leading 2–1 and men on first and third, Cosgrove walked the Philadelphia pitcher with two out. That base on balls led to an insurance run for the Phils.

Smith assumed a look of resignation. "When it didn't make any difference, he strikes out Schmidt and costs us $5,000 in beer. Then with the game in the balance, he walks the pitcher." Smith laughed to himself and said, "We're turning a corner, but we haven't turned it yet."

Some Houston business people claim that if Hofheinz had not been stricken, he might have rescued his empire. Interest on a $30 million debt demands respect—or awe—and I am even less qualified than the former comptroller of New York City to comment on multimillion-dollar juggling.

But Houston's baseball disaster is something more than money. Caught in his measureless Texas dreams, Hofheinz did not pay enough attention to his franchise. Baseball is competitive on the field, and baseball is competitive in the front office, and perhaps while Hofheinz mused about Astroworld, Tom Yawkey of Boston was talking to the scout who signed Fred Lynn.

No one has accused Walter O'Malley of dreaming small, but like every successful baseball executive, he keeps his focus. The diamond and the team. The team has to win or come close.

Judged against an insurance company, a Major League franchise is a small business, and a big-league franchise makes a weak base on which to build a financial empire. But looking after a franchise, with its farm teams, its scouts, its public relations, and all the rest, is a full-time occupation for any executive.

The Dodgers are not for sale. "Does anybody ever try to buy them?" I asked O'Malley.

"About once a week," he said.

Peter O'Malley elaborated, "I'd say we average two serious offers every year."

Playing in the Eighth Wonder of the World, the Astros are for sale. At last report, the message from Texas was brief: no takers.

37

A Baseball Sketchbook

Sports Illustrated, August 23, 1976

Artie Wilson's Major League record appears in a most abbreviated form in my copy of *The Baseball Encyclopedia*, which contains an extensive array of statistics on virtually everyone else who has ever played in the big leagues. The abridgement of Wilson's record was intentional but not malicious. To qualify for a full listing in the 1974 edition of the encyclopedia, a player had to have at least twenty-five Major League at bats; Artie Wilson had only twenty-two for the 1951 Giants. The cursory way in which Wilson is treated says a great deal about the incompleteness of what is supposed to be baseball's basic reference work. But it says even more about the game itself, which prevented Wilson and generations of players like him from qualifying for the encyclopedia because of a single and, indeed, malicious reason. Artie Wilson is black.

When you dig further, the records on Wilson still yield only a fraction of his truth. He played shortstop, second, and first with the Giants; appeared in nineteen games, and hit .182. Officially Wilson was thirty during his only Major League season. Some suggest he was four years older. Whatever, his skills had long since been eroded by having to play professional baseball eleven months a year.

Monte Irvin, who was thirty before he was allowed to begin his brief, brilliant big-league career, says, "Artie was one of the greatest shortstops anybody ever saw. In the old Negro leagues we called him the Octopus, because it seemed as though he had eight arms. He had tremendous range, wonderful speed, a super arm. Besides that, he was a first-rate pinch hitter. But by the time they let him join us on the Giants, he simply wasn't the player we'd known."

You find Wilson these days among the damp green silences of Portland, Oregon, where Artie's minister, the Rev. Thomas L. Strayhand, says there are no racial problems of any kind. Pastor Strayhand smiles slightly. "That's because there aren't enough of us blacks here for them to notice."

Wilson sells Chryslers for a company called Gary-Worth, and during our three days together he managed to mention in his quiet, relaxed way all the merits of a model called the Cordoba. Artie is a hard-working auto salesman, and yes, I would buy a used car from that man. But mostly we talked baseball, which Wilson looks back on with a warmth that others focus on old romances.

"Oh, but I loved playing the game," he said in the tidy living room of his two-story frame house in northeast Portland. "I loved it as a little kid 'round the sandlots in Birmingham, and I loved it playing for the Acipco cast-iron pipe company. Say, you know I played against Willie Mays's daddy back then? Cat Mays played for Westfield in the Tennessee Coal and Iron League. And I loved it with the Birmingham Black Barons. We used to have an All-Star Game in the colored league. I was the starting shortstop most of the years I was playing for Birmingham. Except 1945. That year they had Jackie Robinson take my place."

"I never thought Robinson had a big-league shortstop's arm," I said.

"Right," Wilson said, "but Jackie cheated. He studied the hitters good and made up for the arm by playing position. He knew where they'd hit the ball. For the Giants, Alvin Dark done the same thing. There wasn't nobody who saw me and Jackie in 1945 who wouldn't tell you but one thing. I was the best shortstop. There isn't nobody with intelligence who wouldn't tell you something else. For integrating baseball, Jackie was the best man."

What Artie loved most was his one season in the Major Leagues playing for Leo Durocher. "Leo had the greatest tricks," he said. "He'd carry a rubber cigar—he didn't smoke—and he'd come up to some rookie and say, 'Hey, gimme your matches.' Twenty minutes later he'd be asking the kid what he was doing in the Thunderbird Club last night. The rookie wondered how Leo knew where he'd been drinking. Leo had looked at the matches, that was how. But after a while the rookies got smart. You can't stay dumb forever. They stopped carrying matches and bought cigarette lighters. Then Leo would come up with something else. No way you could get ahead of that guy."

Artie, a trim man with a pencil mustache and a soft tenor voice, and his wife, Dorothy, put two children through college, which meant he always had to supplement his income by playing Caribbean winter ball. "The guys I knew in baseball," Wilson said. "Luis Tiant's father was on the New York Cubans. Best left-handed pickoff move I ever saw. Silvio Garcia, an infielder. Durocher said he'd have been worth a million if he was white. Luke Easter. They spoiled him up in Cleveland by getting him to pull. If they'd left Easter alone, he'd of hit 'em 450 feet to any field. When I was finishing in the Pacific Coast League, I played for Charlie Dressen. He was a sharp one, almost like Durocher. But not quite. Leo was off there by himself.

"One time with the Giants, Leo came into a Pullman car where a bunch of his players were shooting craps. Leo took off his jacket, got down on the floor, and in half an hour had every dollar in that Pullman. Then he stood up and told the players, 'You've already been taken to bed. Now it's time for you to go to sleep.'"

The memory made Wilson laugh softly in delight. He grew up in black poverty outside of Birmingham, but he says neither poverty nor segregation bothered him when he was a child. "I didn't know nothing else, and I was happy long as I could get into a game. For a baseball, we'd find an old golf ball somebody had hit out of bounds. We'd wrap some string around it tight and have our ball. For a bat, we'd saw down a tree branch. When I needed a buck or two for sneakers, I shined shoes.

"Later I got a job cutting pipes and playing ball for the Acipco Company, and one day I got careless in the factory and lost part of my thumb." He showed me his right hand. The thumb was cut off at the knuckle. "Didn't hurt much, and I just had to adjust my throwing a little. I pitched once in a while. In the colored leagues you had to play every position. After the accident, I could make my fastball move better.

"With the Black Barons we had an owner who ran a funeral parlor in Memphis. He paid us regular. We went from town to town by bus, and I got so I slept better sitting up in a bus than in a bed. Then Abe Saperstein got the club and took us out barnstorming, and we won nearly every game we played. When we got to San Francisco, Abe wanted to take us to DiMaggio's restaurant on Fisherman's Wharf. Then he got the word. A colored ball team wasn't welcome. I think that got me as mad as anything ever did."

Integration moved slowly. First Robinson. Then Larry Doby. Then Dan Bankhead. It was 1960 before the Majors were truly open.

"But the years you were excluded from organized ball?" I asked.

"You're thinking now, not then. Then, like I say, I was just happy to be a professional baseball player anywhere."

Wilson drove me about Portland, soft-selling his Cordoba, pointing out the Civic Stadium, where the Portland Timbers were playing soccer, and the Columbia River, crowded not with salmon but with freighters. "Rains a lot here and it's cool, but it's been my home for twenty-two years now," he said. "You have any plans for tomorrow?"

"No."

"Well, if I'm not intruding on you and interfering with your sleep, I'd like you to be my guest at church." It was a hesitant, strangely poignant invitation.

"Thanks," I said. "Appreciate that." Then, musing aloud, "Is your church integrated?"

"Of course it's integrated," Wilson said.

I attended Sunday School class at the Allen Temple Christian Methodist Episcopal Church, where we read Corinthians and men debated whether sin began with taking a drink or getting drunk. The issue still lay in doubt when services began. The congregation sang *Come, Thou Almighty King.* Wilson, the finance chairman of the church, supervised the passing of collection plates. Pastor Strayhand preached and chanted on life's decisions. After services, scores of people came up to shake my hand and bid me welcome. All of them were black.

At dinner Wilson said, "You remember when you asked if my church was integrated?"

"You told me it was."

"What I meant was that God don't know no color."

Then we were back to baseball again. Artie asked me what was happening in Seattle.

"Well, they have their dome, Danny Kaye and Les Smith have the franchise, and for the first few years the team there will be terrible."

"Is there any chance they might hire Leo to manage?"

"Depends on Durocher's health and how he's been getting along with Kaye. What makes you ask?"

The soft voice grew even more quiet. "I know a lot about the game. I can teach good. I'm fine selling cars, but I was just thinking that maybe if Leo got the managing job he might just happen to remember me."

The old Negro All-Star shortstop looked out a restaurant window into twilight. "My children has grown fine," he said. "My wife's a lovely woman. I'm at peace with myself. But I didn't just love *playing* that game. I loved being around baseball. The big leagues is the greatest baseball in the world.

"I don't miss nothing, and I don't resent nothing, 'cept bein' turned away at DiMaggio's. But now at my age, if Leo got Seattle and hired me as one of his coaches, I could help him and be back in the Major Leagues again.

"I'd pray for that," Wilson said without sadness, "'cept you just shouldn't ask the Lord for too much."

THE COUNTRY OF THE POOR

The president of the Eastern League, a round-bellied, hearty, country-slick New Englander named Paul Patrick McKernan, spends his winters teaching current events at Nessacus Middle School, outside the valley town of Pittsfield, Massachusetts. "I have a wife and four children," McKernan said in the league office, which is the sun-room of his house. "Whatever you hear about a great American baseball boom, it doesn't apply here. The minors are a depressed area."

I have seen a list of salaries paid to Major League baseball players during the 1975 season. These were not press-release exaggerations or newspaper guesses but figures printed in a private analysis called "Salary vs. Performance." You can find copies within a locked cabinet in any Major League office.

There are few surprises at the top. Excluding attendance bonuses and the variety of fringe benefits that Catfish Hunter worked into his contract with the Yankees, Dick Allen's salary led the Majors. The Phillies paid him $250,000. Then came Henry Aaron at $240,000, Johnny Bench at $190,000, Lou Brock at $185,000, and Willie Stargell at $181,000. Although Aaron is the only lifetime .300 hitter in the bunch, every man here has been a superstar. Every one of them has been able to argue that he put customers in the park.

The highest-paid pitcher was Ferguson Jenkins ($175,000), who is not really that good anymore, but the Texas Rangers were desperate when they signed him three seasons ago. Then came Tom Seaver at $170,000, Luis Tiant and Gaylord Perry at $160,000, and Steve Carlton and Don Sutton at $155,000. (On the advice of his tax people, Hunter has limited his straight salary from the Yankees to $100,000. He will get deferred income for many, many years.) They compose a pitching staff most managers could tolerate.

I found the wages of lesser players truly startling. Fritz Peterson, an ordinary left-hander, earned $66,000 in Cleveland. His earned run average was 3.95. Bob Bailey, who began as a wunderkind and grew up to be only a journeyman, earned $72,000 at Montreal. The average salary for Major League pitchers in 1975 was $51,000. The average for players at other positions was $55,000.

If you follow a basic law of economics—you can't pay what you don't have—these numbers indicate overall fiscal soundness in the Majors. Add broadcasting contracts worth $50.8 million this season and attendance that has been running about 10 percent ahead of the previous best year, and big-league baseball assumes an emerald glow of affluence.

But travel to Pittsfield through the rolling Berkshire hills, and you find yourself in the country of the poor. Early this season, when the Berkshire Brewers, Pittsfield's team, led the Double-A Eastern League, a night game drew only 110 fans. Later the management imported Bob Feller, Rapid Robert when nicknames were in flower and the hardest thrower of his time. At fifty-seven, Feller has become a fine showman, and he presented a splendid pregame pitching exhibition. The attendance at Wahconah Park was 351.

Pat McKernan sits up late analyzing what besets his minor league, but in Pittsfield one obvious and unconquerable monster stands against the sky. It is the master antenna for the local cable television company.

On certain evenings when the Brewers are at home, so is almost everyone else in Pittsfield. On one channel they can watch the Yankees. A second brings them the Mets. A third carries New England's summer demigods, the Boston Red Sox.

Berkshire County in western Massachusetts mixes low hills, three-thousand-foot mountains, small farms, upland meadows, swift-running brooks. It is most famous now for Tanglewood, the Boston Symphony's summer retreat, where a performance of Beethoven's Ninth draws fifteen thousand listeners. But while Tanglewood is relatively new, local baseball tradition goes back almost to Beethoven's lifetime. One hundred fifty years ago children played games similar to baseball in the Berkshire fields, and in 1859 Amherst and Williams played the first intercollegiate game at Pittsfield. The curveball had not yet been invented. Amherst won 73–32.

In October 1969 McKernan bought an Eastern League franchise for $1,000, and in December he concluded a working agreement with the Washington Senators. The Senators, nobody's first choice, offered the only deal he could get.

Under a standard Double-A working agreement, the Major League club supplies uniforms, a minimum of nineteen players, a trainer, and a manager. Double-A salaries run from roughly $2,500 to $8,000 per season. The local owner pays $150 a month toward the salaries of the nineteen athletes. The big-league club makes up the difference and pays the trainer and the manager in full. The parent club also selects the team and shuttles players in and out at will.

"So you don't control your product," McKernan said. "But I thought I had a chance. I was a manager-type in college, and I did some sports-writing in Batavia, New York. I figured that I knew baseball and I knew this town.

"I was not only the president of the Pittsfield Ball Club. In the beginning I was the sole employee. Then volunteers began to help. I started speaking. I sold some tickets. I sold some ads for the next season's program. Renting a bus was a big expense, so I went to a bank and borrowed money and bought a 1950-something-model bus that still ran well. The bank wasn't difficult. They knew me. The bankers wanted baseball here. If anything went wrong, the bank had the bus.

"We have seventy home dates, and I tried to come up with seventy promotions. All kids in free. All right. Some of them bring parents. The parents pay. Then once you've got people inside, you're selling them franks and Cokes and beer.

"In the four years I kept the team we always drew between forty-four thousand and fifty thousand fans a season. That averages out to better than five hundred a night. I never touched a dime of my own money, and the team itself never lost money—except sometimes I couldn't pay myself any salary.

"Then last year the league presidency opened. I wanted it, so I had to sell the club. Forget *The Sporting News*. I took an ad in the *Wall Street Journal*. It went like this:

DID YOU EVER WANT TO OWN A BASEBALL TEAM?
NOW'S YOUR CHANCE

"I listed my phone number, and I got forty responses. I sold the team for $45,000."

McKernan sipped a soft drink. "I made money with the team and I enjoyed it, so I have no sour grapes, but what do the big boys like Bowie Kuhn tell you they pump into the minors?"

"The figure they claim is $36 million annually."

"Well, in the Eastern League it costs the Major League clubs with farms $80,000 to $125,000 to support a franchise. But look what they get. We provide them with a training ground. They get to see if their prospects can play under hard conditions, after tough bus rides, day games following night games, under lights that may not be the greatest. We play 140 games, so they find out which kids have the stamina, who can play night after night after night.

"They could help us by giving us some continuity, by letting kids play in the regions where they grew up. They actually resist that. They say that playing before home folks puts too much pressure on a boy. A lot of Pittsfield people look at the Brewers as a bunch of visiting Californians who won't be around here next year. They'd rather watch local kids playing American Legion ball. And the Major Leagues could also stop televising us to death.

"Go look around the ballpark. They've got some talent. The manager, John Felske, is a fine guy. And remember this—I'm only thirty-five years old. I expect to get in the Majors someday myself. And then I'll remember—I hope I'll remember—the way things are out here among us poor people."

John Felske, the manager of the Brewers, is a powerful six-foot-three native of Chicago whose Major League career spanned three seasons and fifty-four games. He is authoritarian without being cruel, organized, precise, and convinced that baseball must be a discipline before it can be fun. Terry Ervin, one of Felske's outfielders, had just been suspended for bumping an umpire, and Felske made sure that Ervin did not draw meal money during his suspension.

"I don't get paid?" Ervin asked.

"That's what suspension means. You don't play and you don't get paid," said Felske.

"Then why do I have to show up at the ballpark?"

Felske rubbed a strong hand through his sandy hair. "When you're suspended, we don't even have to give you meal money, and we're not going to. I want you at the park because I want you to be working out."

"It ain't right, having to work out without getting paid," said Ervin.

"Think of that before you bump an umpire again," Felske said coldly.

Felske is thirty-four and has seen some boyhood Chicago friends go to prison. "I don't make a big thing of it," he says, "but we can all go wild as kids. My baseball career has kept me from making really wrong turns. I've made mistakes, like telling off Leo Durocher. That got me off the Cubs in twenty-four hours. But nothing disastrous, and my little kids are coming along fine."

Felske has a strong, pragmatic intelligence, and through twelve years as a catcher in organized ball he has mentally recorded managerial excesses. Once he played under Pete Reiser, an outfielder of infinite talent who destroyed his career by running headfirst into walls. By the time Felske played for him, Reiser was a sour man who ragged his players constantly. After one particularly unpleasant session, Felske went out and got the hits that won a game.

"I only was on you because it makes you a better ballplayer," Reiser said later. Telling the story, Felske smiled a hard smile. "Reiser got on me because he was a disappointed man. Both of us knew that, but I just walked away."

At Palatka, Florida, Felske played for Hal Jeffcoat, who spent twelve years in the Major Leagues. The Palatka club was a loser, and before that season was through Jeffcoat quit. He immediately called a team meeting.

"Before I go, there's just one thing I want you all to understand," Jeffcoat said. "None of you SOBs will ever make the big leagues."

If you play for Felske, you make practice on time or you pay a fine. You work out hard and play hard, or else you are benched. You find the manager present at the ballpark and absent from team parties. ("I can manage the ballplayers. I don't know about the wives.") But if you extend yourself, you'll be encouraged, not humiliated, and if your joy is playing recordings of Jethro Tull full blast on the team bus, you'll be tolerated, if not endorsed. "All I can say," Felske shouted over a Tull tape during a road trip last June, "is that it's a good thing for you guys that we don't have a fine for lousy musical taste."

Felske's best prospect and most delicate problem is a bespectacled outfielder–first baseman named Danny Thomas, who was batting .368 when I reached Pittsfield. He had hit sixteen home runs, and he was making diving backhand catches that showed perfervid competitive intensity.

A year ago at Reading, Pennsylvania, an umpire named Greg Henley called a questionable double play against the Brewers. The Reading second baseman caught the shortstop's toss, dropped it, recaught it at his knees, and threw to first. Had he retained possession at second base? Was the lead man out?

Henley thought he was. Thomas disagreed. After the game Thomas waited for Henley to dress. Then outside the ballpark he crashed a right into the umpire's face. McKernan suspended Thomas for the season.

Some Milwaukee officials wanted Thomas released at once. Uncontrollable hotheads make poor prospects. But Felske asked for another chance to work with Danny. The two have since held searching talks on youth, wildness, and throwing away a possible Major League career through insensate rage.

Now the Brewers were playing the West Haven Yankees in the close and exciting second game of a double-header. The Brewers moved ahead. West Haven stole the lead. The Brewers tied the score, and when the game went into an extra inning, Felske sent for Lee McLaurine, a small relief pitcher who had not given up a run all season.

With one out, the Yankees' Dennis Irwin walked. Dennis Worth lined a single to center. Brewers center fielder Kenzie Davis threw out Irwin at third. Both teams play hard, aggressive baseball, and Worth went to second on the throw. Garth Iorg singled to left so sharply that Worth had to stop at third.

Two out. Two on. Tie game. Pete Ward, the Yankees' manager, thought briefly of pinch-hitting for Mike Fischlin, his shortstop who was batting .198. For no reason Ward could later explain, he decided to let Fischlin hit.

McLaurine threw a breaking ball, and Fischlin looped it 135 feet down the first-base line. Brewers second baseman Neil Rasmussen ran and ran and dived and caught the ball one-handed. He fell hard on his left elbow, and the ball popped out of his glove. His momentum had carried him yards into foul territory. Not he, or Thomas in right, or first baseman Dave Lindsey moved to retrieve the baseball. They all assumed Fischlin's pop-up was foul.

But Henley, still umpiring in the Eastern League, was gesturing that the ball had been fair at the moment that it touched Rasmussen's glove. The Yankees kept running. The ball lay on the grass in foul territory. Worth scored. Iorg scored. Fischlin scored. You could not charge the second baseman with an error for his impassioned try. Fischlin had put the game out of reach with a 125-foot home run.

Three or four Brewers, none of them Thomas, stormed toward Henley. Felske, a big sandy-haired bear, sprinted from the dugout. He shoved several Brewers aside before they came close to the umpire. McLaurine, his game lost, his perfect ERA ruined, screamed in scarlet rage. Felske grabbed McLaurine's uniform and spun the pitcher ten feet away from Henley. Then, with his players blocked by his body and his authority, Felske lectured Henley until he ran out of words.

After the 9–6 defeat, most of the Brewers showered, dressed silently, and departed. After a while only Felske, McLaurine, Thomas, and I sat with our beers in the old wooden clubhouse. By now McLaurine's usual genial personality had returned.

"You know, I got so mad out there I was actually going to take a swing at Henley," he said.

Thomas, last year's Reading wild man, sat up straight. "Lee, don't you ever do that," he said. "Curse, if you got to. Throw your cap. Kick dirt. But never hit an umpire. It just isn't worth it. Think about it, will you? It just doesn't make any sense."

Felske gazed at me across a beer can. I have never seen a manager's face shine with greater pride.

It did not matter to John, but it did to me, that for the most exciting game I'd seen on any level all year, only two hundred people had sat in the grandstands of Wahconah Park.

NOT QUITE GALAHAD

Outside the multipurpose stadium in St. Louis, in the vaulting shadow of the Gateway Arch, a hulking statue purports to represent Stan Musial at bat. It is a triumph of ineptitude over sincerity.

St. Louis baseball writers who watched Stan Musial play baseball for almost a quarter of a century engaged a sculptor named Carl Mose to cast Old No. 6 in bronze. Then someone composed an inscription for the pedestal:

HERE STANDS BASEBALL'S PERFECT WARRIOR;
HERE STANDS BASEBALL'S PERFECT KNIGHT.

The shoulders are too broad. The torso is too thick. The work smacks of the massive statuary that infests the Soviet Union. It misses the lithe beauty of The Man.

"I saw the sculptor when he was working on it," Musial said. "I told him I never looked that broad. He said it had to be that broad because it was going to be against the backdrop of a big ballpark. He missed the stance, but what kind of man would I have been if I'd complained? The writers were generous to put it up. The sculptor did his best. Look, there's a statue of me in St. Louis while I'm still alive."

A pregnant woman, armed with an autograph book, charged. "Write for my son Willie," she commanded. Musial nodded, said, "Where ya from?" and signed with a lean-fingered, practiced hand.

"Thank you," the pregnant woman said. "Willie is coming soon. After he gets here and learns to talk, I'm sure he'll thank you, Mr. Musial."

Inside the round stadium, the Cardinals were losing slowly in the wet Mississippi Valley heat. The final score would be Cincinnati 13, St. Louis 2. We had left after the fourth inning, when baseball's perfect knight passed his threshold of anguish over the bad game being played by the home team.

To reach most old ballplayers, even millionaire old ballplayers like Hank Greenberg, you simply call their homes around dinner time. A pleased, remembered voice comes through the phone. "I had a good day playing tennis. How've you been? Who've you been seeing lately? Say, if you're ever in town, come over and we can talk about the old days."

To reach Musial, you call the office of the resort and restaurant corporation called Stan Musial & Biggie's, Inc. When I did, a secretary said crisply but politely, "I'm sorry, but Mr. Musial is on a goodwill tour of Europe. He'll be back briefly in two weeks. Then he's flying to the Montreal Olympics. We'll try to fit you in, but could I have your name again, and could you tell me what this is in reference to?"

It was in reference to one thing. Stan Musial, neither a perfect warrior nor any sort of knight, is my particular baseball hero. I once heard a teammate who knew him well call him a choker. "Considering his ability, he didn't drive in enough runs," the man said. Musial heard about that remark but would not stoop to make a response. During his twenty-two years with the Cardinals, Musial batted in a total of 1,951 runs. That is the fifth-highest total in the history of the Major Leagues. According to Jackie Robinson, Musial remained passive in baseball's struggle to integrate itself. "He was like Gil Hodges," Robinson said. "A nice guy, but when it came to what I had to do, neither one hurt me and neither one helped." But four years ago Musial worked quietly for the election of George McGovern as president. He is a political activist, and on racial questions he favors the men whom Robinson almost certainly would have preferred.

Musial is a man of limited education, superior intelligence, a somewhat guarded manner, a surface conviviality, and a certain aloofness, because he knows just who he is. Stan Musial, Hall of Famer, great batsman, and, thirteen years after he last cracked a double to right-center field, still an American hero.

We were rambling about baseball in one of his offices in St. Louis when my wife, who can be more direct than I, interposed five questions.

"By the time you got to be thirty-five," she said, "and your muscles began to ache, did you still enjoy playing baseball?"

Musial nodded, touched his sharp chin, and said, "I always wanted to be a baseball player. That's the only thing I ever wanted to be. Now figure that I was in the exact profession I wanted, and I was at the top of that profession, and they were paying me $100,000 a year. Yes. I enjoyed playing baseball very much right up to the end of my career."

"About politics?" Wendy asked.

"I'm a Democrat. Tom Eagleton, the senator, says he remembers sitting in my lap when he was a kid visiting our spring-training camp years ago."

"What do you think of Jimmy Carter?"

Musial laughed to himself. "I'd have to say he's very unusual for a candidate."

"You worked for Lyndon Johnson?"

"He asked me to run his physical-fitness program, and I did. I believe in physical fitness. I'm fifty-five years old, and I still swim two or three hours every day."

"But didn't you find Johnson vulgar?" Wendy said.

Musial looked impersonally at me, then at my wife. "No," he said, "because we only talked politics."

If I read him correctly, Musial had said in quick succession that Wendy's first question was naive, that Carter was the prince of peanut growers, and that Johnson would have sounded obscene in a roaring dugout. Just as he hit home runs without seeming to strain, Musial had implied all these things without a suggestion of rancor.

People were always mistaking his subtlety for blandness. An agent employed by both Musial and Ted Williams once said to me, "If you want to make some money selling articles, stick with Williams. The other feller's nice, but there isn't any electricity to him." Then one of the editors at *Newsweek*, where I was working, directed me to prepare a cover story on Musial. "Pick up the Cardinals out in Pittsburgh," the editor said, "and make Musial take you back to Donora. It'll work well, putting him back on the streets of the Pennsylvania factory town where he grew up."

At Forbes Field, Musial said that he was driving to Donora the next day and I was welcome to ride along with him—provided I promised not to write about the trip.

"Why not?"

"I promised someone I'd visit sick kids in the hospital. If you write that, it'll look like I'm doing it for publicity. And my mother lives above a store there. That's where she wants to live. We had her in St. Louis, but she missed her old friends, so she went back home and found a place she liked. No matter how you write that, the magazine will come out with a headline: 'Stan Musial's Mother Lives Above a Store.'"

"Well, I have to come back with a story."

"We'll spend some time and maybe come up with something," Musial said.

We talked batting for three days. To break a slump, he hit to the opposite field. He remembered a day at Ebbets Field when he had gotten five hits, all with two strikes, and he remembered a year when he suffered chronic appendicitis and played 149 games and hit .312. He remembered the double-header at Busch Stadium when he hit five home runs. He could even recall the different pitches that he hit.

"Do you guess at the plate?" I asked.

The sharp-featured face lit. "I don't guess. I know." Then Musial spun out a batting secret. He had memorized the speed at which every pitcher in the league threw the fastball, the curve, the slider. He picked up the speed of the ball in the first thirty feet of its flight, after which he knew how the ball would move as it crossed home plate.

About eighty pitchers worked in the National League then. Musial had locked the speed of about 240 different pitches into his memory. I had asked the right question, and Musial responded with a story that was picked up by a hundred newspapers.

They oversimplified, as newspapers often do. Even if you can identify a pitch thirty feet away, you are left with only a tiny fraction of a
second to respond. Musial's lifetime batting average of .331 was not the
product of a single secret. It was fashioned of memory, concentration,
discipline, eyesight, physical conditioning, and reflexes.

Going for his three thousandth hit, Musial neglected to concentrate
and took his stride too early. But he kept his bat back, as all great hitters do. On sheer reflex, he slugged a double to left.

Now in his office, Musial looked much as he had fifteen years before.
The same surprisingly thin wrists. The same powerful back. A waist-
line barely thicker than it had been. The deceptive self-deprecation
also persists.

"I'm semiretired," he insisted, but twice he politely broke off our
interview to take business calls. Stan Musial & Biggie's, Inc., a family-
held company, owns two Florida hotels and a restaurant and a hotel
in St. Louis.

"Are you a millionaire like Hank Greenberg?" I asked.

"Just write that I'm not hanging for my pension. A long time ago I
knew I couldn't hit forever, and I knew that I didn't want to be a coach
or manager. So Biggie Garagnani, who died young, and I started the
restaurant in 1949. Biggie knew the business, and I knew that just my
name wasn't enough. I put in time. I like mixing with people up to a
point, and my being here was good for business. I still walk around in
the place six nights a week when I'm in town. So while I was playing, I
was building a permanent restaurant business, and that just led naturally
into the hotels. What's my title? President of Stan Musial & Biggie's, Inc."

Unlike many self-made men from poor backgrounds, Musial is a
liberal, and his liberalism seems to deepen as he ages.

"I don't think Polish jokes or Jewish jokes or black jokes are really
funny," he said. "My dad came out of Poland and worked like hell all
his life. What was funny about that? Pulaski came out of Poland and
helped out in the American Revolution. Was that a joke? I've just come
back from Poland, and I enjoyed the country, the people, and seeing
them work hard building high-rises. Some of them knew me. I brought
my harmonica along and played a little."

"Polish songs?"

"Yeah. Like 'Red River Valley.'"

At the park, fans flooded toward his box, demanding autographs and making it difficult to study the game. Musial singled out Pete Rose for praise and said he felt embarrassed that so many Major Leaguers were hitting in the .200s. "There's no excuse for that. You know why it happens? They keep trying to pull everything, even low outside sliders. You can't do that. Nobody can. If you're a Major League player, you ought to have pride. Learn to stroke outside pitches to the opposite field. That's part of your job. A Major League hitter is supposed to be a professional."

"Do you miss playing?" I said as Rose rapped a single up the middle.

"No," Musial said. "Nice stroke, Pete. I quit while I still enjoyed it, but I put in my time. I like to travel now but not with a ballclub. Have you ever seen Ireland? Do you know how beautiful it is?"

After the game, we drove back to Musial's restaurant, and a crowd surrounded him in the lobby. He said to each, "How are ya? Where ya from?" One fiftyish man was so awed that he momentarily lost the power of speech. He waved his arms and sputtered and poked his wife and pointed. Musial clapped the man gently on the back. "How are ya? Where ya from?" Musial said to him again. The man looked as if he might weep with joy. At length he recovered sufficiently to say a single word, "Fresno."

"Does this happen all the time?" I asked.

"Isn't it something?" Musial said. "And I'm thirteen years out of the business. You know what Jack Kennedy said to me once? He said they claimed he was too young to be president, and I was too old to be playing ball. Well, Jack got to be president, and two years later, when I was forty-two years old, I played 135 games and I hit .330."

"Ebbets Field, Stash," I said. "They should have given you the right-field wall when they wrecked the place. You owned it, anyway."

"What do you think my lifetime average was in Brooklyn?" Musial said.

"About .480."

"It only seemed that way," he said. "Actually my lifetime average there was .360."

I can't imagine Galahad, the perfect knight, as a baseball hero. He was priggish and probably undersized. That doesn't matter. Having Stanley Frank Musial is quite enough.

38

Golden Triumphs, Tarnished Dreams

Sports Illustrated, August 30, 1976

Early Wynn won three hundred games, Roberto Clemente had three thousand hits, but their legacies have not matched their glorious records.

On January 19, 1972, Early Wynn, the pitcher, was voted into the Baseball Hall of Fame. Such tidings generally lead to a phone call from a wire-service reporter, who asks the player for a comment, and if you follow that sort of thing, you know what happens next. In a wash of sentiment, the player thanks mother, God, truth, justice, and the American way of life.

Early Wynn is not inclined toward sentimentality. Working through four decades in the Major Leagues, he had won three hundred games, and he had intimidated generations of American League batters with the best knockdown pitching of his time. He knew he deserved to be in the Hall of Fame.

The telephone rang. It was an enthusiastic young man from a wire service. "Naturally, I'm happy, and so is my wife," Wynn said. "We have had a long wait. . . . I don't think I am as thrilled as I would have been if I had made it the first time. I would have liked to have joined Stan Musial and Ted Williams and Walter Johnson as players who gained the honor the first year they were eligible."

A few weeks later, during a private conversation when he was less concerned with keeping in baseball's good graces, Wynn told me, "Hall of Fame? Hell, it's a Hall of Shame. I should have been voted in three years ago." He pulled the cork from a bottle of rare, old Canadian whiskey. He took a drink.

That summer Wynn managed Orlando, the Twins' farm team in the Class A Florida State League. It pleased him to work in the Minnesota organization under Calvin Griffith, because Calvin's uncle, Clark Griffith, had brought Wynn into the Majors in 1939. Early took a few days off to attend the induction ceremonies at Cooperstown that August and did make a few sentimental comments in a speech. That may have been an error. Griffith fired him from Orlando in November, making Wynn the only man I know of who was trumpeted into the Hall of Fame and bounced out of a managing job in the same year.

Baseball offers a full quota of absurdities. In the low minors, where players are supposed to be learning, you find one man, the manager, charged with teaching twenty different apprentices. In the Majors, where players are supposed to be fully skilled, you find special coaches for pitching, catching, and even base running. The big leagues have expanded chaotically, and clubs that might have become intense and profitable rivals—Oakland and San Francisco, for example—play in different leagues. It is tempting to regard Wynn's dismissal as one more instance of baseball's thoughtlessness. Some, knowing the Minnesota organization, suggest that Griffith simply wanted to find someone else who would manage for $500 less. I suspect other considerations were involved. Wynn is a fierce, direct man who can take a drink. Don Newcombe took a drink, too, and he told a Senate subcommittee last March that whiskey had cost him his career, his first marriage, all his investments, and his home. The difference is the classic borderline between drinking and alcoholism. Wynn could mix hard stuff with wine, drink throughout an evening, run at eleven the next morning, and pitch a shutout. Newcombe said that after his best season, 1956, when he was 27-7, he went to Japan with the Dodgers "and was so constantly drunk that [he] was unable to pitch a single game on the trip." (Newcombe is no longer an alcoholic. He says he promised in 1966 on the head of his oldest son never to drink again. He has kept his promise.)

To Wynn, convivial gatherings were a delight of big-league life. He went to parties and he gave parties—gay, raucous evenings rich in baseball talk and needling—and with a single exception, he never overestimated his capacity. One night, when he was pitching for Cleveland, he visited Bill Veeck, who owned the Indians. Martinis preceded dinner; stingers followed. "Curiously, I don't remember exactly what we served next," Veeck says, "but I do recall that at 4:30 in the morning I was mixing grasshoppers. Then it struck Early. He was scheduled to pitch the next day, and here he was drinking late with the boss."

"I better go home," Wynn said. "One o'clock game."

"It's too late to worry about sleep now," Veeck said. "You better just keep going."

Wynn reached the ballpark at eleven, put on a rubber jacket, and began to run. He sweated, showered, and went out and pitched a shutout. "Then the reporters came," Veeck says, "and Early answered all their questions. He got somebody with the knuckleball. Someone else was fooled by a high slider. He did just fine until the last reporter left the dressing room. Then he fell over on his face."

There was nothing bland about Early, nothing subdued, nothing cautious. He didn't like hitters, and he said he didn't like hitters. He knocked them down. "Why I should worry about hitters?" Wynn said. "Do they worry about me? Do you ever find a hitter crying because he's hit a line drive through the box? My job is getting hitters out. If I don't get them out I lose. I don't like losing a game anymore than a salesman likes losing a big sale. I've got a right to knock down anybody holding a bat."

"Suppose it was your own mother?" a reporter said.

Wynn thought briefly. "Mother was a pretty good curveball hitter," he said.

That was humor, but at Yankee Stadium I saw Wynn brush back his son. Joe Early was a tall, rangy boy who was visiting at his father's place of business for a day, and Early volunteered to throw a little batting practice. Joe Early hit a long line drive to left-center. The next pitch was at his cheekbone; it sent Joe Early diving to the ground. "You shouldn't crowd me," Wynn said with a certain noncommittal tenderness.

Wynn learned rope tricks and played supermarket openings. He began a newspaper column and within a month had attacked general managers for their penury and *The Sporting News* for publishing too much gossip. Air travel bothered him, so he took flying lessons and purchased a single-engine plane. He bought a cabin cruiser and a motorcycle and a Packard and a Mercedes, leading Shirley Povich of the *Washington Post* to comment, "Early does not lack for transportation." Wynn simply seized life with his great hands, implacably determined to squeeze every ounce of living out of his time.

Despite that, his staying power was prodigious. He pitched for the Senators in 1939, moved on in 1949 to become a mainstay of the great Indians staff that included Bob Feller and Bob Lemon, and ten years after that pitched the White Sox to a pennant and won the Cy Young Award. He was a thick-chested, black-haired man with a natural glower, which he would direct at the batters like a death ray. He seemed indestructible. But in the early 1960s he began to suffer attacks of gout. On a snap throw to first, he strained muscles near his elbow, and the gout moved into his pitching arm. His legs were weakening. It was time to quit, but he wanted to win his three hundredth game.

"During those last years," says Wynn's wife, Lorraine, "when he'd come back from running, his legs would be so sore that we had to work out this routine. He'd lie down on his stomach, and I'd take a rolling pin and move it up and down over the backs of his legs. That was the only thing that seemed to relax the muscles."

The old fastball was gone, and it was not until 1963 (it took him three seasons to win his last sixteen games) that Wynn got his three hundredth. To do it, he had to pitch in pain and terrible weariness, but three hundred was the goal, and he got there. "Hell, I've lost more than two hundred," he said.

His rage to live persisted, and one night he asked if there were any interesting parties in New York. We tried one, which was dull, and another, which was worse. "Let's go down to the Village Barn," he said.

"That's way downtown," I said. "I haven't been there since college."

"I just want to see that place one more time."

The Village Barn was barren. It was getting very late. We had some drinks. "The hitters may not know this," Wynn said, "they aren't all that smart. But I know it. I can't get 'em out anymore."

"You're in your forties, Early, what did you figure? You knew this was going to happen."

His face assumed a look of inexpressible sadness. "But now it's happening," he said.

After retiring, he drifted through a predictable mix of baseball jobs: pitching coach, scout, minor league manager. But he never became a politic man. In 1969, when Billy Martin managed the Twins, a columnist's story enraged Martin. Three sportswriters, Red Smith among them, appeared on the field. Martin began cursing at the perfidy of the press. "Anyone who talks to any of those newspaper bastards is crazy," Martin yelled.

Wynn had known Smith for twenty years. He was also Martin's pitching coach. Before Martin's popping eyes, Wynn walked over to Smith and welcomed him warmly to the field. He was not Martin's pitching coach again.

I spent a week with Wynn in Orlando in 1972, riding buses through central Florida, working out with the team when he would let me, tasting life at the bottom of the minors. He seemed to be an excellent manager. Some of the players, notably pitchers, were awed, so Early took them to dinner or visited their homes. The Twins resisted the idea of supplying beer for the team bus. Early bought the beer out of his own pocket. "I sort of have to be head counselor," he said.

His pitching approach was unorthodox, because he believed in the high slider. Usually you throw the fastball up and the slider down.

Wynn explained how to use the slider high. "Start with a bad one that breaks wide. Bad pitch, but till it breaks it looks okay. The batter goes for it and misses, and you have your strike. Try with something else, the curve, or for me the knuckler, and you can get a second strike. Now throw a spinner—not a slider but a ball that spins and looks like it's gonna slide—just where you threw that first pitch. The batter thinks it will break wide again. He doesn't swing, and you've got called strike three. Of course, you've got to put something on the ball." He meant that the pitcher had to throw hard, but few of the young men on his Orlando staff were really fast. The team went nowhere, and Griffith fired Wynn as the manager.

Early handled a bat well enough to pinch-hit for Washington. He was a switch hitter who once batted .319. He was a scholar of the game, and whenever I have watched him teach, he has been both stern and patient. The knockdown pitch has been curtailed by a system of fines, but I don't think that's why nobody likes Wynn.

Baseball executives increasingly favor men who are corporate-bland. More and more Major League teams are run by syndicates, and syndicates prefer managers and coaches who do as they are told, salute the company president, and study statistics rather than spend spirited evenings talking baseball with the press. Veeck might have brought Early to Chicago this season, but Paul Richards, Veeck's manager, wanted to be his own pitching coach. Charlie Finley? Proud, independent field leaders are not to Finley's taste.

Wynn has found work in Florida as sales coordinator for Wellcraft, a boat manufacturing company, and flying south I expected to find him depressed, or at least subdued.

He lives in Nokomis, forty minutes south of Sarasota, and commutes to his office every morning. "The traffic," he said, his old rage still intact. "What the hell do government officials think about, if they do think? What do they think the west coast of Florida is, a slum? It was no secret that more and more people would be moving here. We knew it twenty years ago. Why haven't they put in first-class roads?"

We wandered outside the house that I had first visited in 1954. It had been in the country then. Now other houses crowded close. He started his boat and headed toward an inland waterway, once a blue corridor of beauty. There were little mangrove islands then, and channel markers with pelicans sitting on them. As the boat approached, the pelicans would suddenly fly off. Later we fished, and I caught a Budweiser can.

Now the inland waterway runs between huge condominiums with white concrete sun decks and yellow shuffleboard courts. "I didn't used to know what ecology meant," Wynn said as we cruised. "I sure do now. I guess while I was up there pitching, somebody forgot to put in zoning laws."

We turned around and docked and walked into his party room. Baseballs from fifteen of his greatest victories hung from the ceiling. He had placed his Cy Young trophy on one wall. From another wall, three men smiled out of an old picture: Stan Musial, Ted Williams, Early Wynn.

"The Hall of Fame," I began.

"Hartford, Alabama, that's where I grew up, and the biggest thing that happened in that town was a peanut festival. But we had baseball, and we'd ride mule wagons many a mile for a town game. They write that when I showed up at a pro tryout I was barefoot. I wasn't, but I was wearing overalls. It's a long way from Hartford, Alabama, to Cooperstown, but any man who wins three hundred Major League games ought to get voted in as soon as he's eligible. I mean, don't people know how much hard work that is?"

I said I thought I did and asked how he liked the job at Wellcraft. "Well, I've always been fond of boats," he said. He took out a catalogue, and then the fiercest competitor I've known in baseball set about selling me a cabin cruiser.

A light checking account blocked the sale, but this wasn't precisely like a Wynn ball game. I knew I could resist his will without getting a fastball fired at my head.

THE CHILDREN OF ROBERTO

On a Puerto Rican plain, beside Avenida Iturregui and a pleasant subdivision called Country Club, six hundred barren acres stretch under a pitiless sun. Part of the land is dry and caked, part is still marsh. This is Ciudad Deportiva (Sports City), one of the last dreams Roberto Clemente voiced before a DC-7, overloaded and undermanned, carried him to his death in the Caribbean on the night of December 31, 1972.

I suppose sociologists would find Clemente's dream naive. He wanted to build a Puerto Rican sports camp open only to the very poor, who would attend free of charge. He hoped that "every single child from poverty can learn to play sports and maybe make some success as [he] did." More than $800,000 has been collected for Ciudad Deportiva, and soon four years will have passed since Clemente's death. On the barren plain two bulldozers work at a languorous pace that would have been inimical to Roberto Clemente.

Certain rumors persist about the death of Clemente, neither a saint nor a tramp but a gifted ballplayer with a social conscience. "Bobby had a woman in Nicaragua," someone insists. "That's the real reason he took that flight." Another Puerto Rican suggests that the plane contained gold, or U.S. dollars, which Clemente was going to sequester beyond the grasp of tax authorities.

These are the facts. That November, Clemente had taken an amateur Puerto Rican baseball team to play a series of games in Nicaragua. He had liked riding in ox carts as a boy in Carolina, his home village, and in Nicaragua he saw ox carts again. He also met a hospitalized child without legs and asked why he had no artificial limbs.

"We don't have any money," the boy said. "Legs would cost $800."

"When I go back to Puerto Rico I will raise the money," Clemente promised.

Five weeks later Managua was literally flattened by six violent shocks. Howard Hughes flew away at the first tremor. In Puerto Rico, Clemente organized a relief campaign. He appeared on television and radio, pleading for money, morphine, sugar. Although his back ached, he helped load supplies on trucks in a staging area near Hiram Bithorn Stadium. Then word reached him that soldiers in the Nicaraguan army were stealing the supplies and selling them to earthquake victims.

Clemente remembered the ox carts and the crippled boy. He had recently lined his three thousandth Major League hit, a double, and he had a strong sense of his Latin fame. "If I go to Nicaragua, the stealing will stop," he said, beating a palm against his chest. "They would not dare to steal from Roberto Clemente."

A jet could have been used. The DC-7 was cheaper. A certified flight engineer could not be found to work on New Year's Eve. Instead, the third seat in the cockpit was occupied by an aircraft mechanic. Sixteen sixty-pound bags of sugar were hastily loaded through the plane's forward door in the last minutes. Were they properly lashed down? According to witnesses, one engine seemed to sputter when the plane went down the runway at 9:20 p.m. A trained engineer, studying the engine analyzers that show the condition of each engine on a small green tube, can make an instant diagnosis. If necessary, he shouts, "Abort! Abort!" A mechanic lacks the flight experience to make such a decision.

The plane took off. Another engine coughed. On a tape of the plane's radio transmissions to the tower you can hear the pilot say without panic, "This is NC 500 comin' back around." It is thought that the pilot, a man named Hill, banked the plane steeply. It could have been that the bags of sugar shifted. In the blackness, NC 500 continued to bank and then slipped sideways into twelve-foot waves at approximately 150 mph. The aircraft might as well have flown into a wall of concrete.

"It was so sad for all of us," said Luis Rodriguez Mayoral, a Pirates scout who guided me about his island. "In one year we lost two great heroes. Roberto Clemente and Don Pablo Casals. But do people remember? If they did, wouldn't Ciudad Deportiva be more than this by now?"

Latins have a gift for patient melancholy, but Mayoral brightened quickly. "I will show you, amigo, that there is nothing else sad about baseball on our island. Our island baseball is wonderful, ¿tu sabes?"

We drove Mayoral's Volkswagen through San Juan, on to a village called Guaynabo, then to Caguas, a small city located along a road lined by royal poincianas, a tree with rust-red flowers. We watched Little League ball in Carolina, now a suburb in the San Juan sprawl, and we saw amateurs play in Las Piedras (The Rocks), a town that did not even appear on my tourist map. I visited a saloon there called, for reasons nobody knows, the Guadalcanal Bar. Puerto Rican baseball is a joyous pastime played mostly for the wonders of the game.

"We have a problem," said Vic Power, the old Major Leaguer, as he studied fourteen-year-olds on a cloudy day in Caguas. "We have much participation. Too much participation. Too many dreams of the Major Leagues. I see a good player. I have to tell him it is 10,000 to 1 he will not make the Major Leagues. Sometimes I have to tell them it is 100,000 to 1, because if you are both black and Puerto Rican, they will not easily accept you. It will be very much more difficult."

Five years ago Power took an amateur team to Cuba, where Fidel Castro sought him out and spoke of having wanted to pitch in the Major Leagues. (Early Wynn and Fidel Castro pitching on the same staff? It's a good thing not every dream comes true.)

Power's memories of playing as a black are cold and somewhat bitter. "It was very bad when I got to the States," Power said. "I am strong and not afraid, but I do not want to be murdered. When I first came to Florida for training in Fort Myers, one night I was afraid to cross the street. Three white men stood on the other side. I could see from the way they held themselves that it would be bad if we came close together.

"The light was green, and they walked across the street. I stood in a doorway, and as you see, I am very black. I hoped they would not notice me. They did not. They passed. When the light was red, I went across the street.

"The policeman came from nowhere. He held my shoulder, and he had a gun, and he said I was arrested for crossing against the light. He took me to court, and the judge looked at me in a hard way. This is what I said: 'I am Puerto Rican and a ballplayer, and I do not know how it is in the continental states. I thought the green light meant for whites to cross and the red light meant black people could cross the street.'"

"What did the judge tell you?"

"He said he didn't believe me but that the case was dismissed and that I should never again appear before him in court."

Then Power told harder stories, most of them ribald and bellicose. He mentioned that Ted Williams liked him, and he was proud of that. When Jimmy Piersall had called him a black bastard, Power had recognized Piersall's intensity and his own strength and had withdrawn. And Early Wynn, oh, Early Wynn. He lived in Florida, but he was a very good pitcher.

When you are looking at a team you have not seen before, watch the shortstop, who must move laterally and charge slow, twisting ground balls and make the play. Neither fourteen-year-old shortstop playing in front of Power and me looked promising. Power agreed. We were not seeing the best of Puerto Rican games. "In New York, in what you call Spanish Harlem, do they still remember my Gold Gloves up there?" he asked.

The baseball cast is always changing, and in Spanish Harlem people now talk of Felix Millan and John Candelaria and Willie Montanez. "Sure, they remember your Gold Gloves," I told Power.

He beamed. "This team is called Café Crema after a big coffee company that gives the uniforms. It is not the best team, and Café Crema is not the best coffee. When you have lunch, order our other coffee, Café Rico."

Following lunch the next day, Mayoral drove me to the Country Club section for a Little League playoff. At Parque Angel Ramos two hundred people cheered and watched and listened to Carlos de Jesus broadcast over loudspeakers as the game developed before their eyes.

Country Club defeated Valle Arriba 9–0, and the Country Club short-stop, Jorge Burgos, played impressively.

In the fifth inning, with Country Club's victory already safe, a Valle Arriba base runner reached second. The next pitch bounded five feet from the catcher. The runner did not try to advance, but when I looked up, there was Jorge Burgos backing up third.

"Good play," I told the twelve-year-old after the game.

"Not a good play," he corrected me in Spanish. "Just the play you're supposed to make."

"Would you like to make the Major Leagues?"

"In my short life, I have accomplished little aside from baseball," he said. "So my answer is, yes, I would like to play there. But perhaps later, when I accomplish other things, my answer would be different."

When Guaynabo played Cayey in a game of two town teams, two thousand fans showed up at 9:45 p.m. at the modern ballpark in Guay-nabo. Guaynabo's uniforms were blue and white. Cayey wore faded red. Guaynabo was leading by two runs when a cloudburst struck. The home team's ground crew moved so slowly that the field was drenched. The fans chattered and applauded and sipped beer. The Cayey manager announced that he was protesting the game "because of Guaynabo's lazy ground crew." The fans hooted and laughed, and everyone went home.

Near the ballpark in Las Piedras, on the narrow road that twists toward Humacao Beach, a young man was playing pepper with his son. Their names were José Soto, junior and senior, and after Mayoral introduced us, Mr. Soto said, "Vic Power tells me my child's swing is so good I should not touch it."

"¿Tu eres de Nueva York?" the small boy asked me. Was I from New York?

"Yes."

Had I seen the Yankees? Would I watch him?

The father chattered like a salesman, and José Soto Jr., who is seven, swung wildly, then missed six ground balls out of eight.

"He moves well," I told the father.

"If you come back to Las Piedras," the senior Soto said, "understand you always will be welcome."

That night I attended a Bicentennial banquet at the Caribe Hilton sponsored by the Association of the U.S. Army. The room was thick with braid and brass, and the menu included such dishes as Yankee Pot Roast, Revere Cheese Pie, and Liberty Tomato. The guest of honor was an astronaut and Marine officer named Jack Robert Lousma, who piloted *Skylab* 2 and logged 1,427 hours in space.

Lousma presented the governor of Puerto Rico with a photo of San Juan taken from an altitude of 270 miles. Then he made a curious speech. It was strange and beautiful in space, Lousma said, and one thing he had noticed was that you could not see the boundary lines between countries. Nevertheless, none of us should forget the constant peril of Godless atheistic Communism. The military men, some of them Puerto Ricans but most of them continental Americans, cheered. "Our space technology benefits every single person on this island," Lousma said. The band played "Dixie." A hundred officers sprang to attention.

I don't think José Soto Jr. would have been able to make any more sense out of Lousma's speech than I did. Puerto Rico is not poor compared to Haiti, but the median income is $2,328 per person. In the barrios, the billions invested in space programs appear irrelevant.

Baseball came to Puerto Rico in 1900, introduced by occupying U.S. soldiers after the Spanish-American War. It is the single continental export almost every islander understands and watches and plays.

It would be hard to explain the federal budget to the Soto family, but our sense of baseball needs no explanation. For what that father and son were doing in a scruffy tropical backyard was the same thing that my son and I had done many months before on a blackened field, set among $300,000 homes, in the casual prosperity of Westchester County.

39

Walter O'Malley in the Sunshine

New York Times, January 9, 1978

This column ran on the front page of the first "Sports Monday," the New York
Times' *then novel weekday section devoted entirely to sport. Abe Rosenthal, the little
Napoleon who ran the* Times, *said the column "has got to get readers' attention."
O'Malley and Brooklyn did. Both still do.*

Winter has laid an icy hand on McKeever Place, back of the old left-field stands, and there is nothing much for city kids to do but watch the new snow blacken under soot. In colder winters long ago, a magic sounded. You threw a rubber ball against a dun-brick wall and calculated how many months and weeks and days would have to pass before Jackie and Duke, Furillo and Preacher, Campy and Pee Wee marched home again to Ebbets Field, like heroes.

Already the red-brick houses called Ebbets Field Apartments show dirt, disorder, and other symptoms of incipient slum. Where generations of baseball crowds sorrowed and exulted lies only another corner of the urban wasteland. It is almost eerie in the whistling cold. The soul of Brooklyn shriveled and was lost when a baseball franchise moved and the wrecking ball ravaged Ebbets Field.

"If we hadn't moved . . ." Walter O'Malley mused over a Lucullan luncheon at Perino's Restaurant on Wilshire Boulevard. "If we hadn't moved . . ." Maestro O'Malley played a thoughtful look at a crystal chandelier.

"Sir," said a captain. "We have fresh raspberries today, flown in from New Zealand."

O'Malley's round face assumed a more practical expression. "Say," he said, "are you getting the tab for this lunch or am I?"

Walter Francis O'Malley is a feisty, visionary, manipulative adventurer of seventy-four winters who feels that politicians and circumstances booted him and the Dodgers out of the borough of Brooklyn. In what remains of Brooklyn, feeling runs the other way. Benedict O'Malley deserted us. The issue—who rejected whom—is native more to divorce than to the sports page.

Some remember the Dodgers of the 1930s with affectionate giggles. Frenchy Bordagaray, a Brooklyn outfielder, once tried to score standing up and was tagged out.

"Why the hell didn't you slide?" asked Casey Stengel, the manager.

"I was gonna, Case," Bordagaray said, "but I was afraid I'd crush my cigars."

One thousand on the laugh meter. Zero at the box office. The Dodgers spent the Great Depression shuttling between fifth and seventh place, playing before crowds of 1,208.

"Larry MacPhail brought in some decent ballplayers at the end of the 1930s," O'Malley said. . . . "Won a pennant, but then he went off to war. Now the Brooklyn Trust Company, a client of mine when I was practicing law, had a note outstanding that the Dodgers would not repay. They asked me to look into it, and I smoked things out at once. The club would not repay because it couldn't. There was no capital. Dodger stock hadn't paid a dividend in a generation. Litigation persisted with the estate of a former owner. Even Ebbets Field was in hock to a life-insurance company. Things were so bad a 25 percent share of the team was practically begging. I obliged and bought in for $250,000."

Branch Rickey replaced MacPhail and passed a variety of miracles. He found Duke Snider, traded for Preacher Roe and Billy Cox, and integrated baseball with Jackie Robinson.

"A great baseball man," O'Malley pronounced at Perino's. "The greatest. But Rickey didn't have much organizational business sense. The contract he wrote for himself was unfair to every other stockholder." O'Malley's eyes turned gelid. "We had to get him out of there if the club was ever going to make money, and we got him out of there in 1950."

As Dodgers president and at length controlling stockholder, O'Malley played a multilevel game. To the press and public, he portrayed himself as a fan, and it is true that he likes to watch baseball games.

But the man within, the interior O'Malley so to speak, burned with dispassionate brilliance.

Bad weather hurt attendance. Twenty-five years ago O'Malley charted receipts and concluded that radio whets the appetite of the fan; television satisfies it. He tried to talk pay television with David Sarnoff but was dismissed.

He saw blocks of brownstone houses boarded up in Bedford-Stuyvesant. Customers, Dodgers customers, were moving away.

The team was winning. Everyone knew that. But a winning team was not enough for O'Malley. He wanted victories plus profits, plus opportunities for future growth. He saw himself wedged into an old ballpark in a declining neighborhood, and it had taken him so long to get to where he was, he'd be damned if he'd stay wedged.

The New Zealand raspberries arrived, outrageously pink for January.

"I believed in mass transit," O'Malley said, "so I wanted a new park over the Long Island Railroad station at the intersection of Flatbush and Atlantic Avenues. I envisioned a ballpark, which we would build, which would not have cost the taxpayers a dime, right in the railroad station to deal with the suburban thing, and with a break on pay television, I could have given Brooklyn fans a dome. But Mr. Moses, Robert Moses, insisted that we move to Gravesend, at a site he was peddling that lay between a cemetery and the sea. Los Angeles turned out to be more convenient."

If Robert Moses had been less rigid twenty years ago, if the mayor, Robert Wagner, had been stronger—imagine the continuity of things. The Koufax-Drysdale years. Maury Wills stealing bases. That string of great Septembers. And now Steve Garvey, who wears Carl Furillo's old number. The Dodgers in Brooklyn to this day.

The fancy deepens. Time suspends. Old Brooklyn, borough of steeples and stick ball, could be old Brooklyn yet.

But if you think that, then fancy has turned your mind to butter. Ballclubs don't save cities, or even neighborhoods. The Indians remain in downtown Cleveland. Around their park, Cleveland wastes away. The Tigers linger in Detroit, which someone calls no longer a city but a rim around a bomb crater. In its new veneer, Yankee Stadium is particularly irrelevant to the horrors of the South Bronx.

Had the Dodgers stayed in Brooklyn, justice would have been served, because the Mets and Los Angeles deserve each other. But Brooklyn today would still be a borough of decay. Buildings would rot. Rats would prowl within sight of Walter O'Malley's pleasure dome.

May the souls of Jackie Robinson and Gil Hodges shine on in their glory; may the urban planners go to work.

40

Some Modest Proposals

New York Times, February 13, 1978

It always seems to be stimulating to write about bare flesh. But sad to tell,
bright, sparkly Lee Arthur died in 1989 at the age of forty-nine.

Back in the primordial days of the women's movement, circa 1973, a
worldly interviewer startled me with a set of coy questions. "Do you
have trouble knowing what to do with your eyes in the dressing rooms?"
asked Miss Lee Arthur, who was employed by the sports department
of a Pittsburgh television station.

"No," I said, blinking. "Why?"

Miss Arthur, who liked to say she was both "a sports broadcaster
and a broad sportscaster," took a three-beat pause. "They get naked
in there, don't they?"

Her own eyes twinkled, and I had to confront two issues:

1. The right of access to news sources.
2. Sex.

These Gemini reappeared last week in papers filed by attorneys for
Commissioner Bowie Kuhn. Answering the complaint of Melissa Ludtke,
a reporter for *Sports Illustrated* who wants entry into clubhouses, Kuhn
conceded that baseball encourages "media coverage." But ballplayers
wander "naked and seminaked" near their lockers. Allowing women
access "would be offensive to applicable standards of decency."

Despite the centerfold appeal of bodies, the significant point is news,
not nudity. At long last baseball has conceded that it courts coverage.
It's time for working journalists, men and women, girls and boys, to
reimpose healthy terms.

The pantheon sportswriters—Ring Lardner, Heywood Broun, Damon Runyon—disdained the sights and smells of locker rooms. They were eloquent and droll, and they were rooted in the press box. About the time that Jackie Robinson exploded onto the baseball scene, a more sophisticated journalism hatched. What Robinson, Dixie Walker, Ben Chapman said, or refused to say, was as important as certain final scores. Sportswriters began to leave their press-box baronies. Locker rooms became extensions of the field.

When Bob Rush of the Cubs threw a fastball into Carl Furillo's brow, I visited the victim in the Dodgers' trainer's room. Seeing the ghastly results of a beaning is wholly different from reading a team physician's report, edited by a press agent. When a gossip columnist reported that Robinson intended to retire, I caught him between turns at bat. "I said 'maybe,'" Robinson said, "and besides, I was just feeling fed up." When an umpire complained that ballplayers were calling him "a fairy," I audited behind the Dodgers' dugout. None actually called the umpire gay. The ballplayers merely shouted that he was "an adagio dancer."

Schooled that way, I was dismayed by house reporting rules in other arenas. Hollywood columnists interviewed stars amid a gaggle of press agents, hired to put off controversy and truth. White House reporters submitted to restrictions on direct quotation, attribution, and access that would have been unthinkable at Ebbets Field. Neither Johnson nor Nixon could have survived a year under the scrutiny Charlie Dressen knew.

Then came television. Reporters and announcers were lumped together as "media." The promoters and the ballplayers who dominate the channels set self-serving rules. Trainer's rooms were declared out of bounds. Clubhouse lounges appeared, from which all reporters were barred. Finally, Billy Martin sounded his Bronx cheer. The whole damn Yankees were off limits for twenty minutes prior to every game. "Don't blame me," Martin said. "The players voted for it."

"Did you?" I asked a Yankees veteran.

"Is that what Billy said?"

"Yes."

"Then we did."

I heard no protest from television and too few from the press. TV announcers and sports promoters work for the same dodge. Grab a rating. Peddle a ticket. You sell news and you buy it. That's show biz, not the press. As much as in the 1950s, the working press—people who type stories for a living—is left to tell things as they are, accurately and grammatically.

When Kuhn concedes that baseball needs coverage, the press had better distinguish itself from television. Then demand sensible terms.

Trainer's rooms should be open, at least to one pool reporter. This prevents concealment of injuries, a practice with nasty implications where people bet.

Professional athletes should be available to reporters from their arrival at a stadium until they leave. Questions can be annoying, but a span of stadium duty seldom lasts eight hours. That's a reasonable stint for a $200,000-a-year outfielder.

A curtained area should be added to locker rooms, where robed athletes can be interviewed by reporters of the other sex.

Miss Ludtke remains slightly restricted. Covering the Yankees, she cannot catch Thurman Munson in the shower.

I remain slightly restricted. Covering Wimbledon, I cannot catch Chris Evert in the tub.

All parties, and the First Amendment, will survive.

41

The Joy of Bill Veeck

New York Times, April 3, 1978

Living most of his life with only one leg, Bill Veeck was a profile in courage.

First Bill Veeck was sitting in the wooden bleachers at Payne Field, chattering with customers. Then I found him drinking beer and swapping stories with scouts from a half dozen clubs. Early the next morning he stood near the backstop of a practice field, making his own judgment on a young right-handed pitcher. The complete owner, I thought, at home anywhere in baseball.

A fan collared me and said: "It was hot in the stands yesterday, and I had my shirt off, and suddenly Mr. Veeck was rubbing suntan oil on my back. When I get to Chicago, people are going to ask me if I met Bill Veeck. Met him? He rubbed oil on my back. How do you like that?"

Bill Veeck is president of the Chicago White Sox. The chief executive. I tried to imagine George Steinbrenner or M. Donald Grant sitting in the bleachers of their New York ballparks, oiling a stranger's back. That wasted fifteen minutes. "But you see," Veeck said, "my situation is somewhat different from theirs. I can't afford to lose a single fan, to sunburn or to anything else."

At sixty-four, Veeck is crinkly haired and youthful and full of purpose and alive with joy. He has saved the White Sox for Chicago. He has replaced infielders who couldn't scoop grounders and outfielders who couldn't catch flies with good ballplayers others overlooked. He has made Comiskey Park a carnival ground, with fireworks and community singing and, for a properly dramatic home run, bursts of the Hallelujah Chorus over the loudspeakers. He goes his open-collared, jubilant, irreverent way in a baseball era notable for syndication and paranoia. "It's supposed to be fun," he says. "First of all, the game is supposed to be fun."

A season ago detractors said the White Sox were destined for bankruptcy. The team, someone wrote, would be lucky to finish last in the American Association. Veeck was recovering from surgery on his neck. This after thirty-one procedures—progressive amputations, really—on his right leg, which was injured on the island of Bougainville during World War II. His indomitable cheer persisted, but he looked frail, and his voice was soft.

"We do have enough cash, at least for now," Veeck said, "and I'm not suggesting that we have a great team, but we're improved. Don't judge us too quickly. Wait." The White Sox broke well and held first place until the middle of August. They finished third and drew 1,657,135 fans, which was a record and slightly more than twice what the team drew before Veeck came home to Chicago in 1976. Surprise, even dismay, rose in certain baseball quarters.

Front offices are full of people babbling about the dignity of the game. They approach baseball as a state religion. Veeck's carnival style upsets them, and his candor makes their ulcers boil. Discussing Walter O'Malley once, Veeck said, "He has a face that even Dale Carnegie would want to punch." Most owners are resolute reactionaries. "If they ran Congress, Kansas and Nebraska would still be trying to get into the union."

The establishment response suggests that Veeck is only a carnival type, and something of a clown. There was an unseemly rush to bury him when the 1976 White Sox finished last.

"Innocently or not," Veeck said, as the 1978 White Sox were defeating Kansas City, "people have misinterpreted. I've never argued that promotion can do much if you aren't winning. That isn't the psychology of the fan. The fans identify with the home team. When the home team wins, they feel that they win, too. They get away from the galling losses of life. When the home team gets beat, they get negative identification, the same rich, fulfilling experience they get when they're three months late with payments to the Friendly Finance Company.

"What I do say is promotion plus a winning team breaks attendance records. So I have fireworks and special nights, and any fan who calls the office can get me. I answer my own phone. But first I need a team that plays competitively."

Veeck cannot bid against the richest clubs, but he has extemporized an approach to free agents. "Play for me for a year," he says in effect. "If it's a good one, then go and make a great deal somewhere else." This brought Richie Zisk and Oscar Gamble to Chicago last year. They've moved on. Now the Sox have Bobby Bonds. Veeck describes this system as "rent-a-team." While the rent-a-teams prosper, the Sox move toward a future when they will themselves have wealth.

Sitting with scouts after the game, Veeck remarked that he was pleased with the talent in his camp. "It's hard to guess our opening lineup," he said. "It was hard a year ago for different reasons, and I put $500 of my own money into a contest that we announced on the radio. Everyone was eligible, even Bob Lemon, the manager." On Opening Day, Veeck noticed Lemon smiling as he carried the lineup card to the umpire.

"What was that?" Veeck asked later.

"I got five wrong," Lemon said.

Room 148 of the Sarasota Motor Inn rang with laughter. Grinning, Veeck sketched out a trade or two some of the baseball men might want to consider.

Just consider, mind you. No pressure.

Then it was time to tell another story.

42

Public Relations

New York Times, July 31, 1978

Billy Martin died in an auto wreck on Christmas Day 1989. He was not wearing a seat beat. Billy never was a seat belt kind of guy.

Pete Rose is a line drive, and Ron Guidry is a snapping slider. But the manager, any manager, is words. They fool you sometimes, the clever ones, and Billy Martin is a very clever one. They rage and charm and bluster until you think the managers win and lose. But what they do is talk. Chatter is a manager's occupation.

It is seductive to write about managers. The rookie from Pocatello is mute without his bat. The veteran speaks clichés he hears on television. But the manager makes time to seek phrases. He has no batting average to fall back on. "If you want to chew the fat for ten minutes," says Sparky Anderson, a man who prizes candor, "I'll offer you an hour. Why? Because when you print what I say you're advertising my game, my team, and Sparky Anderson."

The mix of molten and gelid prose advertising Billy Martin eventually will ebb. Readers have been schooled in Martin's genealogy, his mother's marital history, and his own taste in friends. Essays on Martin's life force, his search for a father image, and his death wish have been thrust upon us. When he thought his Yankees time was at an end, we learn, he shuddered, cried, and trembled. I cannot recall another baseball farewell so lachrymose. Babe Ruth and Lou Gehrig went out of the arena more quietly to face death.

Drama shines here, but not drama to my taste. There are no heroes in the Yankees organization this season. Without heroes you cannot have tragedy, only pathos, and Martin has been too much the tyrant to be pathetic. He exaggerated his role, and he manipulated his athletes, and he cited Casey Stengel as his godhead. That is another instance of manipulation. Stengel understood and accepted baseball politics with maturity and great sophistication. Billy Martin is not the second coming of Stengel. Rather he is Leo Durocher born again.

Confronted with noisy, self-promoting, hyperactive men, you forget what a manager does and where he is limited. The manager is given a roster selected by others. That is a critical point. The front office presents a manager with its team. Managers always feel that the front office has miscalculated. They say, "Damn, but I've got to play their mistakes." Managers complain consistently and inevitably, the way Bolivian colonels plot.

The most difficult personnel task is handling ten or eleven pitchers. You set up a starting rotation, determine long relief and short relief, and see that everyone gets enough work but that no one is pressed to exhaustion. This job is so complicated that managers assign it to somebody else. Billy Martin gave the pitchers to Art Fowler. Stengel assigned his pitchers to Jim Turner. Even managers who used to be pitchers—Tom Lasorda, Bob Lemon—let somebody else determine pitching rotation.

Fortunate managers work with superstars. Because superstars are not always humble, this can be vexing, although it is not so vexing as having no superstars with whom to work. Sparky Anderson says: "I don't treat everybody equal. We've got three Hall of Famers on the Reds [Pete Rose, Joe Morgan, and Johnny Bench]. Anybody who wants equality will have to go somewhere else. He won't find it in Cincinnati." Mickey Mantle disdained conditioning. He liked to drink. Some nights he flouted basic training in front of Stengel. The manager muttered but always turned away before there was a confrontation. An ill-conditioned Mantle won ball games. Stengel accepted this reality. Major League baseball is no pursuit of Hellenic ideals.

It is antithetic to baseball tradition to regard managers as press agents, but every good manager is a flack. Stengel divided the press into categories. "His writers," the men who regularly covered the Yankees, benefited from frequent briefings, sly confidences, and boundless cordiality. Reading their accounts, you found Stengel always the genial hero. The good hometown press extended to the team. Other journalists—for magazines and small, far-off newspapers—were surprised when, on interviewing Stengel, they found a suspicious, crabby man. But Stengel tamed the primary press and made his critics sound like illegal aliens.

Finally, a manager runs a ball game. I list this last because running a game is not difficult for a qualified man. In the deep minor leagues you see managers directing teams with confident, aggressive styles. Determining when to send a runner or whether to play hit-and-run is a decision that hundreds of baseball men can make with roughly equal skill.

In a calculated way Billy Martin created a paranoid climate in the Bronx that worked well in the short run. He told his players that they were a band of brothers against the world. But the paranoia spread and grew and became not a contrived climate but a real condition. Martin prompted quarrels with local writers. He fought with his own players. The brothers became brothers-in-law. Finally he attacked his employer, reminding some of us of the way Leo Durocher had mocked Horace Stoneham. That cost Durocher his job in New York twenty-three years ago.

They said that Leo was good, that he'd be back running a pennant-winning club soon. He never was.

We are back to words. Words make a manager. Words can destroy him.

I hope now we can concentrate on the sliders and the line drives.

43

Jim Lonborg at Thirty-Seven

New York Times, April 2, 1979

Jim Lonborg belongs to a select group: gifted, college-educated pitchers.
Others include Orel Hershiser and Christy Mathewson.

He has been making these baseball voyages for sixteen seasons now, and he remembers the first Major League training camp he saw. "I was young and fresh and overflowing with enthusiasm," Jim Lonborg said. "I threw relentlessly on the sidelines. I listened to everything everybody said. But even then as a rookie with the Red Sox, I wanted someone to compete with."

"In what way?" I said.

"Conditioning," Lonborg said. "I wanted to be the best-conditioned athlete on the squad. I picked my man: Bill Monbouquette, who was supposed to be the Red Sox' hardest worker. I think I got him. I think I worked even harder than Bill."

Now Lonborg was coming off a day when he pitched three splendid innings against the Mets. He struck out four. The Phillies, Lonborg's third ballclub since those distant Red Sox days, were suddenly issuing raves. Jim will be thirty-seven on April 16, and that is how spring goes for veteran pitchers. Have a bad outing, and club officials say they knew it; you're finished. Have a good one, and the same officials say, "That's the best Lonnie has thrown in the last two years."

He sat in the sun at Jack Russell Stadium after a siege of sit-ups and push-ups and an exercise in which he chased ground balls thrown first to one side, then to the other. He was perspiring. "What else have you done this morning?" I said.

Lonborg has a lean, handsome face. His good looks and his rangy build remind certain fans of Gary Cooper.

"You mean aside from running?" Lonborg said. "I run two miles every morning."

Primarily Lonborg aspires to be a pitching artist, "an artist on that little mound of dirt." But his intelligence, his interests, his soft speech, and his gentle courtesy make a man who transcends mounds and diamonds. He is perhaps the only Major Leaguer who regularly attends concerts of the Boston Symphony. He discourses well on the works of Cheever or Fowles. Beneath his two-hundred-year-old home in Scituate, Massachusetts, he has amassed a connoisseur's wine cellar. He speaks with ease of vintages and bottlings. He and his wife, Rosemary, have adopted three children. Two are Korean. In addition they have one of their own and expect another baby early next month. "That's five," Lonborg says, "and I'm not even Catholic."

From the outside a ballplayer's life is a glorious and highly paid exercise in glamour. Short work hours. A game to play eight months a year that brings fame and presumably happiness. But within baseball you see a different and sometimes difficult existence.

Lonborg devotes himself most passionately to his pitching and his family. But there lies conflict. The Korean children, Nicholas and Claire, are becoming truly comfortable in New England. Jim and Rosemary feel that moving the family to Philadelphia this season would be a serious dislocation.

"I've liked being a Phillie," Lonborg said. "I had difficulties with Danny Ozark last year, and I let them get in the way of my pitching. I've benefited from perspective on that. Nothing should get in the way of my trying to be an artist on the mound. But with my family in Massachusetts I'd rather not be a Phillie anymore. I'd like to go back to the Boston Red Sox."

"I'll be seeing Don Zimmer in a few days," I said.

"He knows. The whole Red Sox front office knows already."

Both the Phils and the Red Sox are contending teams. Pitching is the lifeblood of contenders, so Lonborg works this spring in irony. The better he performs, the more the Phillies want to keep him. Pitching well, then, can mean an extended separation from his family. There is little glory and less glamour in a solitary life for a family man.

Lonborg's career mingles accomplishment and pain. He has always thrown a fastball that sinks—a "heavy ball," in the baseball argot. In 1967 he won twenty-two games for Boston and was 2-1 in the team's World Series loss to St. Louis. That winter, skiing near Lake Tahoe, he tore ligaments in his left knee. "The bindings then were less sophisticated," he said. "If it had been earlier in the day, and I were less tired, I could have gotten them to release. But it was late in the day, and as I recall, the night before I hadn't gotten much sleep." Afterward, compensating for the injured knee, Lonborg began to suffer shoulder pains when throwing. The Red Sox banished him to Louisville in 1970 and again in 1971.

"Some people might have quit right there," I said.

"The pain in my shoulder was depressing," Lonborg said, "but pain really has at least two aspects. First, there is the physical element. The shoulder hurt. But second, how do you react emotionally? I wanted to keep on playing baseball, and there was only one way. I had to set myself to pitch through pain."

He did, and does. He has won ninety-nine Major League games since returning from what ballplayers call "the bus leagues."

In these autumnal years his life is disciplined. After a season he rests his arm for a month. "In October I limit myself to heavy yard work." On November 1 he begins a Nautilus program "to condition my whole body." Then he throws lightly three times a week against his children's trampoline. In mid-January he throws to a young catcher in a gym. Early in February he comes to Florida. "For me, at least," he said, "pitching is a full eleven-month job."

"How long, Jim?" I said. "How many more years do you think you can go?"

"I've always believed I'd get a gut feeling when it was time to quit. Something will tell me, 'Buddy, this is it.'"

"And then?"

"Maybe broadcasting in the New England area. Maybe a career in business. I may fail at that once or twice or even three times. Eventually I'll succeed. I'm not concerned. I have a certain sense of self-esteem."

I don't know another ballplayer more entitled to that feeling.

[After baseball, Lonborg entered Tufts Dental School. He now practices in Hanover, Massachusetts, a few miles south of Boston.]

44

A Visit with Red Smith

Notre Dame Magazine, December 1979

The author visits his longtime friend at Martha's Vineyard and finds the columnist spry, polymathic, and concerned that the New York Times *will fire him.*

Tomorrow Red Smith would reach the age of seventy-four. He would be springy of step, ebullient with youth, and well-tuned to a world that is newly born each day. Still, he would be seventy-four years old.

"When is your deadline?" Smith asked.

The day had broken a cool autumn blue. I mentioned a target date.

"Maybe you'd better hurry," Smith said. "My contract at the *Times* expires in five weeks, and I haven't heard a word about renewal."

Paranoia is a classic affliction of writers. Somehow, you will not be allowed to finish a work in progress. If you do finish, a dozen critics will hurl typewriters at your head. Should the critics be kind, the public will ignore what you have written. "Hell," says one durable writer of my acquaintance, "I admit I'm paranoid, but what else can you be when they're persecuting you?"

One of Red Smith's charms, across the thirty years I've known him, has been an abiding, diffidently expressed confidence. Pressed once by an admirer who hailed him as a titan of the press box, Smith winced but then conceded, "I know I'm a pretty good speller." He has not seemed to perceive the world as freighted with enemies. Rather, his views of sport, prose, and himself suggest that he is working for an audience of friends. The people he writes for are literate. They know which base is second. They delight in his stories, jests, insightful reporting.

"You aren't serious," I said. "Your column is the best thing in the *Times*' sports section."

"You aren't the editor at the *Times*," Smith said.

The next day, as Smith entered his seventy-fifth year, I telephoned A. M. Rosenthal, a complex, gifted, unsentimental journalist who runs the *New York Times*.

"Not renew Red Smith's contract?" Rosenthal said softly, as though in shock. "His contract will never be over. Do you know what Red means to me? Personally? I get depressed sometimes editing this paper. But whenever I get down I say to myself, 'Wait a minute. I hired Red Smith.'"

The full name is Walter Wellesley Smith. The late Stanley Woodward, a sports editor of irresistible ferocity and brilliance, found a women's school named Walter somewhere and thus could claim that Red was the only man in history named after three girls' colleges. The claim goes undenied. Smith's style in writing and life is graceful and measured, sensible and joyous—culture without pomposity. He lost his first wife, Catherine, to cancer, and he himself underwent surgery two years ago for a dangerous growth deep in the gut. But he does not dwell on pain. I assume he can write a tortured sentence, but I cannot remember reading one.

At work, Smith avoids the terrible triad of sports journalism: shrillness (as in televised pro football), overstatement (as in Olympian battles under purple sunsets), and mindless emotionalism (as in the beatification of Thurman Munson). His eyes may mist, so to speak, for vanished friends, but he spares us shrieks, polemics, and grunting sobs.

An especially choice sample of Smith's style described the balance of power between the late Walter O'Malley, czar of all the Dodgers, and Bowie Kuhn, a pleasant, somewhat stiff attorney who has found gainful employment as commissioner of baseball. "When O'Malley sends out for coffee," Smith wrote, "Bowie Kuhn asks, 'One lump or two?'" Writers fifty years Smith's junior had spent a thousand words making that point less well.

It is an error to perceive Smith's civilized approach as mild. We were discussing one sportswriter who is gifted but so painfully self-important that he recently remarked, "I have perfected the magazine sports profile."

"Did you read his latest piece?" I asked.

"No," Smith said. "I didn't have the energy."

Once, when people at *Sports Illustrated* were altering his stuff, Smith commented, "They put words into my copy that I've spent my life not using."

"Such as?" I asked.

"Such as 'moreover.'"

Boredom is the leopard that stalks the stag. Sports patterns repeat. Athletes say similar things from one decade to the next. Today's champion may not glitter like yesterday's hero whom we remember in the soft focus of our own youth. Not long ago someone asked Smith if he was beginning to find baseball dull after a lifetime in the press boxes.

"Baseball," Smith said, "is dull only to dull minds."

By its terse eloquence, the comment leads one away from the core of Smith's indomitable enthusiasm. The source is not baseball, his favorite sport. We are considering a professional, not a fan. The source is the newspaper business. "I love the newspaper business," Smith says, "whether I'm writing sports or anything else." . . .

Red and Phyllis Smith own a colonial home in . . . New Canaan, Connecticut, but they take special pleasure in the cedar house they have had built near a Vineyard crossroads known as Chilmark. The house is airy and modern, without being extreme. It is secluded, but in minutes the Smiths can drive to fishing boats that ride out through Menemsha Bite, or to a sandy spit that commands head-clearing views, or to a promontory 142 steps above a sandy beach backed by changing cliffs of clay.

This windy day Smith looked ruddy rather than red. He describes himself as ill coordinated and four-eyed. He also says that he is prolix and maundering. Actually, he is only one of the above (he does wear eyeglasses). He wore a blue sweater and gray slacks as he approached the arrival gate, and his walk was quick. Though the red hair has gone white, his face retains a young expression and a look that suggests he is about to smile.

At the cedar house, he laid a fire on a white-brick hearth. He has been trying not to smoke for several years, but my pack weakened his resolve. His hands shook slightly as he lit up. "I attributed this to alcohol once," Smith said, "but there was a time when I couldn't drink a drop, and the shaking persisted. Turns out it isn't whiskey but senility."

He does not like to play the dean, much less the critic, but eventually he agreed to compare sports sections past and present. "There is truly a generally higher level of competence," he said, "than there was, say, thirty years ago. We had illiterates then who grew up from copy boy, if you'll pardon me." I pardoned him. Thirty years ago at the *New York Herald Tribune*, I drew $26.50 a week putting away Red Smith's mail.

"Actually, there aren't as many papers," Smith said, "so there aren't as many jobs for bums. On the other hand there's a spreading tendency on newspapers to use a magazine approach. Newspaper editors are developing a notion that everybody has watched every event. I appreciate depth in coverage, but a newspaper shouldn't abdicate who won and by what score.

"Then, even though the general level of competence is higher, I don't see anywhere a developing [Joe] Palmer, [John] Lardner, [Westbrook] Pegler, [W. O.] McGeehan, or [Frank] Graham."

It is hard to say exactly why. Television salaries attract some journalists before they learn really how to write. Educational standards have sagged, and it is possible to win a journalism degree at certain universities without studying the American and English stylists who developed the written language. (Let alone Vergil or Aeschylus.) More people attend more schools. Each may learn less.

When Smith graduated from Notre Dame as a journalism major in 1927, he was equipped with both a sure sense of sports and a classical background. "The only team I tried out for was track," he said, "and that mostly as a way of avoiding gym. I couldn't run fast enough for the half mile so I thought perhaps I could run long enough for the mile, and I competed in a freshman-varsity handicap. Soon I was last, about ten laps behind. Rockne coached track, and he said, 'All right. You can drop out now.' So I not only finished last, I didn't finish."

We began to play a game of capsule columns. I'd mention a name, and Smith would comment.

Sugar Ray Robinson: "At the St. Louis zoo in Forest Park, a black jaguar was the most beautiful thing I ever saw. I'd get in front of the cage some days and say, 'Good morning, Ray.' Robinson said I made him conceited when I wrote about him."

Frank Leahy: "I suppose he laid it on too thick. He made one of the seconding speeches for Eisenhower in 1956, and you thought he might really say, 'We've got to win this for the Gipper.' I took pleasure in needling him, but at bottom Leahy was sincere. I believe Frank always stood up when his mother entered the room."

Muhammad Ali: "In nineteen years, the act has never really changed. We've had telephone conversations where he's said, 'Do you have enough?' Whatever his positions, how can a guy in my business hate a subject that cooperative?" . . .

Eddie Arcaro: "He was the best at what he did, and he was always approachable, always candid. Most of the time that's true with the great champions."

Ernest Hemingway: "I . . . found him diffident, a little shy. He was a big, gentle guy with what seemed a very sweet disposition. After he won the Nobel Prize, he was quoted as saying that he used the first $25,000 to get even. I had the bad taste to ask him why he was broke. . . . He said that with his first successful book [*The Sun Also Rises*], he gave the royalties to the mother of his son. With the next [*A Farewell to Arms*], he gave the royalties to his own mother.

"Then he said, 'Red, a fellow's only got so many books like that in him.'" . . .

Gertrude Stein postulated that being an artist begins with recognizing one's limits. She said that when Picasso showed her his poetry. Smith does not compose sagas or novels, and his style shimmers like a bark at sea, rather than shattering waters like a Leviathan. Certain dogged plodders, confusing easy reading with easy writing, see Smith as an airy sort, more concerned with lightness of line than with depth of thought. But I know no one, Nobel laureates or Pulitzer poets, more serious about the craft of writing.

Smith came out of Green Bay, where his father ran a grocery, with ample native talent. His triumph is the way he developed the talent across five decades. He applied at the *Times* in 1927 but was turned down. He then worked at newspapers in Green Bay, St. Louis, and Philadelphia, hoping somehow to make New York. When Stanley Woodward finally brought him to the *Herald Tribune*, it was 1945, twenty-eight years after Smith's first newspaper job. His stuff had gotten better and better, but Woodward had to lie to *Tribune* brass about the new man's age. He shaved the honest total by five years.

The *Tribune* was getting what Casey Stengel so admired, one of them men with experience. Smith could and did and does write the hell out of a sports column. He also knew how to cover a warehouse fire. No one was better prepared, or more anxious to play the Palace. His *Tribune* columns attracted a syndicate of ninety newspapers. Then, after the *Tribune* died, the *Times* hired Smith in 1971.

"The one trouble with him now," insists a younger writer, who would be radical if he had the patience to read Karl Marx, "is that he doesn't challenge sport's fascistic values."

Ah, but Red challenges sham, pomposity, grandiloquence, self-righteousness, and the self-anointed priesthood of the arrogant. I believe those qualities sum up Mussolini.

Growing with each decade, Smith has lately become the most distinguished champion of the baseball players union. That issue, the players' right to share the giant jackpot, is as political as sports really gets these days. For all its commercialism, sport is not a political system but an art form. An American art form. "Slot 44" is neither fascist nor communist; it is a way of making several yards. Sparky Anderson, who barred facial hair in Cincinnati, was not attacking the New Left; he wanted Bench and Rose and Morgan to look well groomed. Smith does not confuse the demands of a head counselor with the fiats of a dictator. He is alert to real issues, such as players' rights, without finding sociology in a line drive.

He describes Chris Evert Lloyd and Jimmy Connors as they are (self-occupied is what they are, before anything else). He does not constantly try, as Hemingway said of Jimmy Cannon, to write columns that leave the English language for dead. His only demand is that the reader be able to think, which is probably the first demand he found at Notre Dame when he arrived there fifty-five years ago.

Newspaper libraries show no specific predecessor. Oh, Heywood Broun was literate and Pegler was irreverent, but both went global. Current sports pages are blank of an inheritor. Once I asked Smith if he had any superstitions, and he said immediately, "Only the Holy Roman Church." Seeking the source of such a response is as fruitless as analyzing laughter. You had better simply rejoice that the phrase is there.

One does not say that directly to Mr. Smith. He has lived a long time—he is twice a great-grandfather—but outbursts of praise make him uncomfortable.

Crisp Vineyard night was lowering on the cedar house. It was time, we all agreed, to open a bottle of wine.

45

My Movie Option: Eight Years of Strikeouts

New York Times, May 4, 1980

A seriocomic report on how Hollywood repeatedly misplayed the ball, dropped the bat, lost the glove, and never did make a movie out of The Boys of Summer.

On a late wintry morning in 1972, when early copies of *The Boys of Summer . . .* were appearing in stores, an agent called and reported that he had, as he put it, a Hollywood offer. He mentioned several figures and concluded, "So on the first day of principal photography, you get $100,000, plus you have points."

"Points?"

"A percentage of the profits."

"First day of principal photography?"

"That's when they start making the movie."

As I blinked, I saw the streets of El Dorado. "But we're going to pass," the agent said. "We think the book will move, and a better option deal will come along."

I still do not know whether one has.

I've been in the movie option business continually since 1972. Myself and the books are praised, coddled, and at length rejected. Each year I sign my name, and someone mails a check. But the movie never gets made. That is, the "first day of principal photography" never arrives.

Optioning a book—buying the movie rights for a finite period—is probably the prime source of stories for producers. "Just being published gives a book a kind of endorsement in a producer's mind," says Owen Laster of the William Morris Agency, "and if the book sells, so much the better."

An option is also, by movie standards, inexpensive. Some options sell for as little as $1,000. Occasionally an option sells for $50,000. The average, according to Mr. Laster, is under $10,000.

"How many books are optioned every year?"

"Well over a thousand," Laster says. "Obviously, only a small percentage get on screen, but your case, having a book under continuous option for eight years, is decidedly unusual. You have a very strong property."

In the words of Gay Talese, who was among those who assessed it, *The Boys of Summer* is "a work about youthful dreams in American towns and big cities decades ago, and how some of these dreams were fulfilled, and about what happened to those dreamers after reality and old age arrived. It is also a book about ourselves."

I had covered the Brooklyn Dodgers for the *New York Herald Tribune* when people like Carl Furillo and Jackie Robinson, Preacher Roe and Carl Erskine were in a prime of youth and pride and sinew. I watched them play baseball well, as they usually did, and badly. I barnstormed with them through the South, moving from integrated Pullman cars to Alabama streets, where blacks stepped into the gutter to let a white buck pass. I did this after a comfortable Brooklyn boyhood where I learned, mostly from my father, that you could enjoy Dodgers baseball and Paul Robeson's concerts equally, if with different sensibilities.

The book uses scenes from a Brooklyn childhood with the tumult of Ebbets Field and subsequent visits to thirteen athletes after they had crossed to fifty and beyond. Time runs against an athlete with malevolent swiftness. I find Carl Furillo working as a day laborer at the World Trade Center. Billy Cox tending bar in a fading village north of Harrisburg. . . . Roy Campanella crippled in a wheelchair. Jackie Robinson going blind. From publication day the book sold well. . . . *The Boys of Summer* ascended in a graceful climb to the top of the *New York Times* list of nonfiction bestsellers.

More Hollywood offers. I began to learn additional movie terms, such as "special effects" and "process shot." "These are techniques," the agent said, "that will make it look as though an actor can play shortstop." I learned that my role in the production would be minimal. Once I sold the option, the producer, not I, would be in command.

"They can shoot *Heidi* and call it *The Boys of Summer*," the agent said, "but the thing they have to do first is make the project bankable."

"Bankable?"

"A package that will attract the money to shoot the picture."

Traditionally, baseball movies are hard to bank. That is what producers say during our annual option negotiations. Also traditionally, they are terrible. Can you remember William Bendix as Babe Ruth? Bankable Bill swung a bat downward, as if it were a hoe. Gary Cooper as Lou Gehrig? A tall Little Leaguer.

Although *The Boys of Summer* is mostly about time, the protagonists are ballplayers, and I thought it would help if at least some of the actors played Sunday softball.

"No longer a problem," the agent said. "We have a good offer from a producer named Lee Mendelsohn. He'll do it as a documentary for television, not a theatrical."

"Theatrical?"

"That's what we call a movie that plays in theaters."

Mendelsohn mailed a check promptly and began telephoning to explain his approach. He wanted to fly a camera crew about, to work with the real ballplayers. What was lost in professional acting would be gained in vérité. He would cover the Brooklyn glory days with ancient film and fresh narration.

His option ran for a year, and as the months passed he called less frequently. Toward the end, I was placing calls to him, and one afternoon Mendelsohn spoke suddenly about divorce.

"There's not much divorce in the book," I said.

"Not the book. Me, I'm getting divorced. I am going to make *The Boys of Summer*, but first I want to make a documentary called 'Divorce Around the World.'"

When Mendelsohn's option expired, a Beverly Hills agent said *The Boys of Summer* would be hard to sell again. "With all the pain in the book," he said, "it's what we call a downer. That means it doesn't all work out happily."

"*Hamlet* is a downer," I said.

"If you're arguing that *Hamlet* is bankable," the agent said, "try to finance it without Olivier."

El Dorado faded (which we handled through special effects) until another producer appeared. He was a cheerful, sensitive fellow called Irv Wilson, and a dramatization not a documentary was the way to go, he said. After I deposited his check, Wilson called to ask, "What do you think of Ben Gazzara as Curl Furillo?"

"Can Gazzara throw?" I said.

"We handle that with process shots and special effects."

Wilson's passion for the book seemed pure, and when he left the company called Viacom for Universal, he renegotiated his option. Then he engaged Mark Harris to write a screenplay. Harris, a PhD who teaches English at Pittsburgh, had gotten his novel *Bang the Drum Slowly* to the screen, in the one baseball movie I found moving. But after all, am I a critic? And after all, how bankable is a PhD who can write?

Harris wrote a screen treatment and a draft of a screenplay, but at length Wilson made a bleak report. "There's a big black building here at Universal where the money guys work, and they don't want to go ahead."

"Why not?"

"I can't find out why not," Wilson said. "The guys in the black building won't tell me."

When I saw him next at the Beverly Wilshire, Wilson looked older. "You'll make the picture yet," I said. "Cheer up."

"It's not just that," Wilson said. "I've gotten divorced. I had a date the other night, and the girl set fire to the dash of my Mercedes. With these damn courts here, the car is all I have left." He sighed and grimaced. "I've got to get out of this crazy business. Have you ever heard of frozen yogurt?" . . .

After Wilson's options died, another producer appeared from another studio. Again I got to deposit a check. He was flying to New York, this man said, with a writer and a director, and he wanted only one thing from me. "Show us your Brooklyn."

That Brooklyn, if it existed, vanished twenty-seven years ago when my father died. But the producer was coming a long way for a short drive. Four of us rode past the apartments that weather where Ebbets Field had been, and the Beverly Hills people talked with great excitement about certain changes they planned to make the story bankable.

"For example, your first marriage ends, the Dodgers leave Brooklyn, and the *Herald Tribune* folds in the same year."

"Anything else?"

"Yes, one little thing. Instead of your father dying in 1963, he recovers. Then, when you go see the old ballplayers, you bring your dad along."

I would have liked that. My father would have liked that more. Numb, I rode in a rented car to Coney Island. We'd eat real Brooklyn hot dogs, someone said, to get a real Brooklyn feeling. I did not have to wait for this option to expire before I knew how it would end. After we ordered the frankfurters, I reached for my wallet. No one else moved. Could a producer who did not raise $5 to cover hot dogs raise $5 million to make a movie?

A few months ago, the director Joan Darling optioned *The Boys of Summer* for this year. I deposited her check and left a message of thanks with her service. She has not responded, which may be a good sign. Or maybe not.

With the *Kramer vs. Kramer* furor, I thought briefly that Mendelsohn, Wilson, and I might yet reach El Dorado with that special on divorce around the world. As I see the opening scene, a young women, played by Meryl Streep, reacts to a divorced man's insensitive passion by igniting the dashboard of his Mercedes or Pinto. The ex-wife (Streisand) then appears through the flames with her banker-lover (Redford). They extinguish the fire and repossess the car.

No?

Then I have a way to bring *The Boys of Summer* to the first day of principal photography. Cast Mary Tyler Moore as Carl Furillo.

Wrong sex? We change the plot. Prose isn't all that sacred.

Can Miss Moore play the right-field wall? How does she throw? Process shots. Special effects.

But why Miss Moore when Tony LoBianco may be available?

Come on people, Mary is bankable. Unless you learn to think that way, we'll never get *The Boys of Summer* to first base, and you know what happens then? We end up selling frozen yogurt in the Valley.

That is what the boys of Beverly Hills would really call a downer.

46

Lafleur (the Flower of Canada)

Sport, **December 1981**

*Probably the best and certainly the most graceful hockey player of his time leads
Team Canada on a world tournament played across the provinces. After a
hard final loss to the Soviet Union, he graciously answered all my questions
and served as my interpreter.*

To know or rather to experience Guy Lafleur, as it was my fortune to
do across the last few weeks of summer, is to know a breed of sporting
royalty that has all but vanished with the good and gentle kings of children's stories. On the ice, as Heywood Hale Broun observes, Lafleur
skims with the grace of a hunting sea bird. When Guy accelerates in
that magic, weightless way he has, his honey-blond hair catching the
breeze, the fans . . . become mute except for cries of adoration. "Guy,"
they chant. "Guy, Guy, Guy."

Away from hockey rinks Lafleur is recognized everywhere by children, groupies, and solid middle-class people, all of whom seem to
want a smile and an autograph. The strong, sensitive face grins at you
from advertising posters across that vast country that is Canada, where
Lafleur is regarded as a precious national asset, like the oil fields of
Alberta or the restaurants of Montreal. Such attention can warp a man.
It can make him feel more important than he is, feed the common
human inclination toward arrogance and self-absorption, and choke
off gentler tendencies toward kindness and humility. But Lafleur is
kind, considerate, and, in many ways, a humble man. All that spoiled
our two-week jet journey across Canada in pursuit of the Canada Cup
was the denouement. In the most important of eighteen games match-
ing national teams from six countries, Team USSR—playing practiced

rather than inspired hockey in front of their magnificent goal tender Vladislav "Stonewall" Tretiak—defeated, no, routed the gifted young men who played for Team Canada by 8–1.

Come into the Team Canada dressing room, in the catacombs within the Montreal Forum, and behold Guy Lafleur in that harsh moment of defeat—his defeat, his team's, his country's. No one here is hiding from reporters. No one is cursing life or weeping. No one bashes hockey sticks against the walls.

Lafleur is in a corner, pinned by a semicircle of Anglo and French journalists armed with writing pads and microphones. His voice is low but hardly broken. His English is a modulated baritone, touched with a soft French accent. He is wearing gray slacks but has not yet put on a shirt. I notice how subtly muscled this trim six-footer is and how he goes from English to French and back without a flutter in his poise. Somewhere, in Edmonton or Winnipeg, Lafleur had told me that he truly despises losing.

A radio man from Quebec puts a mike in Lafleur's face and asks a question in French. Lafleur, who knows that my command of French is limited to menus, translates. "He wants to know if we were beaten by the best hockey team in the world.

"The Russians," he says, "were the best hockey team in the world tonight." . . .

"How do you feel now, Guy?"

He puffs air, and the flickering smile returns. "Disappointed. Very disappointed. But not depressed. I think I have gotten my mind together and my game together for the National Hockey League season. I'm very sorry I did not play better tonight, but . . ." A shrug.

"Guy," the journalists clamor, almost like fans. "Guy." There are more questions on a defeat that galls him. He answers as politely as if he were sitting in a nineteenth-century drawing room.

Great hockey was, quite simply, a Canadian cartel until the Russians applied their patient discipline to mastering the game. During the late 1950s, the Soviets sent their first team to North America. It was good enough to match top amateurs but not teams from the NHL. By 1972 the Soviets barely missed defeating the best of the NHL, and four years later the Central Soviet Army team came here and wiped out everybody but the Canadiens (a 3–3 tie) and Philadelphia. At length, in 1979, the unthinkable became reality. The best of the Russians destroyed the best of the Canadians 2 games to 1, concluding with a 6–0 rout. Now in 1981, under better conditions for the North Americans, the Russians won the big game by a greater margin, 8–1.

Whether we like it or not, Russia, not Canada and much less the United States, is now the hockey capital of the world. The Soviets, wearing red jerseys marked with the Cyrillic letters CCCP, change personnel from year to year, but the results—except at Lake Placid—are a constant. They play a highly organized game emphasizing short, accurate passes—a kind of chess at high speed—devoid of high-flying skaters like Lafleur and magic stick handlers like Wayne Gretzky. The effect is an impersonal, efficient Big Red Machine.

Machine over man. Humorless types sealed off from us by walls of language, culture, paranoia, and bulky secret-service operatives. The North American style, with its glorious individualism and freelance play, is more exciting but, on the record, second best.

Pierre Elliott Trudeau was able to smile as he handed the Soviets the Canada Cup, but the smile was funereal and forced. You might have thought the prime minister had just lost an election.

As events came together late last summer, two crises intersected. One was Lafleur's. The other cut against all the legends of Canadian hockey.

After the 1979 series against the Soviets, the Canadians protested that their All-Stars had practiced so briefly as a unit that the games were not a fair test. There is truth in that assertion. Hockey is far more a team game than, say, baseball. The players have to know the skating patterns, the fakes, the moves, the so-called flow of all their teammates to reach an ultimate level.

In setting up this Canada Cup, Alan Eagleson, the energetic lawyer who runs the NHL players union, admitted he was looking for a tournament that Canada would win. He invited national teams from Finland, Sweden, Czechoslovakia, and the United States, in addition to the best Canadians in the NHL and the Russians.

The Canadian players were mailed special exercise programs in June. The players were required to try out—even stars like Steve Shutt failed to make the squad. Team Canada assembled at the beginning of August and was put through demanding daily drills on and off ice. "When you play the Russians," Team Canada coach Scotty Bowman said, "you have to play two games. Hockey and endurance."

Proceeds of eventually more than $1.2 million would go mostly toward hockey scholarships and the NHL pension fund. Each NHL player was guaranteed only $3,000 for abandoning his summer lay time for more than six weeks of rugged training and superswift games. (Imagine asking America's top baseball players to work six weeks for a few thousand dollars. At those rates, most would refuse even to belch at a charity banquet.)

There was initially some question as to whether Guy Lafleur would even make the squad. After dominating the NHL for almost a decade, Guy, approaching thirty, slumped severely in the 1980–81 season. Since 1974 Lafleur had scored fifty or more goals for six consecutive seasons. Across those six seasons, this lithe, strong man missed only six games. Then last year, he missed almost thirty. His goal scoring dropped to twenty-seven.

At his best, Lafleur skates like all the rest of us in our wild, midwinter-night dreams. He accelerates, or veers, or stops with absolute precision and a minimum of visible effort. He can forecheck until the man is forced to circle backward, often without the puck, which Lafleur, whose stick is as quick as his skates, has deftly swiped. He passes with perfect timing, sometimes behind his back while skating at full speed, and he can shoot. In top form, he seems invincible.

But in 1980–81, Lafleur slid from Olympus toward the mean streets that mortals walk. First came persistent tonsillitis that kept him benched for a month. Back in action, he caught a stick in the eye, tearing a membrane. He hurt his ankle, strained hamstrings, and was unable to play himself into shape.

Canadians openly wondered if the fabled Lafleur was wilting. That is, had the years of fame produced both mental and physical weariness, a kind of premature old age, banking the fire on ice that was

Lafleur? Guy himself remarked that he would like to get away from Earth a while in a Jupiter space capsule and sort things out by himself.

Late in March he almost got away from Earth forever. Driving home after a game and a few glasses of wine, Lafleur fell asleep at the wheel of his Cadillac Seville. The car collided with a road sign, and the post crashed through the windshield . . . and all but severed Lafleur's right ear. He awoke and sat motionless. He was aware of pain and blood but couldn't immediately realize that he had missed death by less than three inches.

The accident, which required only plastic surgery, sent rumors surfacing like bubbles in a swamp: Lafleur had been drinking too much all year. No, but he is a heavy smoker. His finances were in chaos as a result of disputes with the Canadian tax authorities. Lafleur could retire comfortably today; some minor disagreements with Canadian tax people remain. His marriage was foundering. No, or apparently no, but fame and its demands have made the marriage materially comfortable and emotionally difficult for Lise Lafleur. Numbers of Canadians suspected last spring that the Lafleur era was ending as surely as the age of Wayne Gretzky was about to begin. Moreover, it was the worst Montreal Canadiens season in memory. After Montreal was eliminated by Gretzky's Oilers in the first round of the playoffs, the team fired coach Claude Ruel—reportedly no favorite of Lafleur's—and hired Bob Berry from Los Angeles to start rebuilding the Canadiens' dynasty.

The season lost, Lafleur, urged by Eagleson and others, flew to Sweden to represent Canada in a world championship tournament. Tired and short of sleep when he arrived, he was rushed on the ice in a game against a Dutch team. An anonymous Dutch player knocked Lafleur senseless with a clean body check. After that, Guy did not play well.

"Looking at Lafleur," commented Anatoly Tarasov, the sage of Soviet hockey, "I see a young man old before his time, probably because he has devoted himself more to recreation and other such interests than to pure dedication to hockey, such as our Soviet players give."

Now, in September, could Lafleur and a well-trained, well-coached Team Canada take the Soviets? Was the flower of French-Canadian hockey prematurely wilted, like a fleur-de-lis suddenly shriveled? Those questions awaited answers as we flew across miles of Canadian soil to the oil-rich, modern frontier city of Edmonton.

I met Lafleur in a hotel lobby before Canada was to play the Finnish team in their tournament opener.

"I'd like to watch a few games," I said, "to get a feel of how you're playing before we talk. That way I'm less likely to ask dumb questions."

Lafleur grinned. "Oh, I'm not worried about dumb questions," he said. "I'm worried that I may give you dumb answers."

Scotty Bowman had put together an extraordinary offensive team for Canada. Gretzky centered a line for Lafleur and Gil Perreault. Behind them came the Islanders' Stanley Cup line of Bryan Trottier, Mike Bossy, and Clark Gillies. In back of them were such extraordinary players as Marcel Dionne, Rick Middleton, and Bob Gainey.

The Finns stayed within a goal of Canada for a period but for no longer. As the second period began, Lafleur captured the puck, whirled up ice, and stopped dead on his wing about twenty feet from the Finnish goalie. There he paused. A Finn moved. Guy faked a shot and in the same motion drilled a pass onto Gretzky's stick, at the far side of the goal. Flick. Another score. Lafleur's face lit up, and he clenched a triumphant fist at his young confederate's goal. The deluge followed quickly; Canada defeated the Finns 9–0.

Next came a more competitive game against Team USA. The Americans, all players in the NHL, tied the score at 3 in the third period before the Canadians scored five unanswered goals. Although the team's defense bothered certain observers, Canadian enthusiasts now created a new name for their national squad: Team Awesome.

Lafleur and I chatted at length in a Winnipeg hotel coffee shop, punctuated by six autograph interruptions and one bit of badinage with Wayne Gretzky.

"Are you enjoying this tournament?" I asked.

"Very much," Lafleur said. "Playing with Wayne, setting him up for goals. Sometimes that can be more enjoyable than scoring a goal yourself. I feel . . ." The words came slowly. "I've found the fun of hockey again, and I think I know how I'll feel if we beat the Russians."

"How?"

"As though I could skate two thousand miles."

He began to talk quite lyrically about his life. He was born in 1951 in Thurso, Quebec, a town along the Ottawa River where all the men work either in a furniture factory or at the Thurso Pulp and Paper Company. His father—Rejean, fifty-one—cycles to work at the paper company, where he is a welder. Guy has offered to buy his father a car, but the older Quebecois says no, a bicycle is still good enough.

Guy remembers a warm boyhood with his family and hours of joyous skating and games of boot hockey in the street. At Sainte Famille School he was neither the best student nor the worst, but he was without question the best hockey player the school had seen. When he was fifteen, a history teacher said, "Guy, one day you are going to be owned by your public."

Now he sips his coffee and offers me a cigarette. "At fifteen or sixteen when you hear that, you just laugh. But the teacher, Norman Chouinard, was right. It is tough on my family, my wife, my son Martin. They don't get as much attention as they should. I let Martin skate with me before the Canadiens work out, and he is always disappointed to see the other players show up. That means his time with his father is over.

"My father likes to hunt," Lafleur continued, "and one night in Boston I found I missed him, and I called. I made some arrangements with airplanes, and I got to Thurso at about four a.m. Then we went hunting for deer. We didn't get any, but my father and I enjoyed being together very much." . . .

"How do you feel about putting in so much hockey time for so little money?" I asked Lafleur. The question seemed to surprise him. "It is as my history teacher predicted. That has come true. I belong to the public, and that public wants me to play."

"And your family?"

He sighed, not so much with sadness but as a man sighs at the nature of things, a man who has come to terms with himself. "They, of course, would like me at home. But before my family, before anything else, comes . . ." He grappled for an English word and could not find it. "*Le devoir.*"

Literally that translates as duty: it is Lafleur's duty to play hockey. But if you had heard his intonation, you might have heard a word with overtones of religion and love: devotion.

Team Canada played a hard, exciting tie with a fast, young Czech team in Winnipeg and then defeated the Swedish team 4–3 in Montreal. In the last of the round-robin games, Canada defeated the Soviets 7–3, displaying remarkable firepower against the backup Russian goalie, a chunky blond named Vladimir Myshkin, who does not approach the greatness of Tretiak. Next, after Canada defeated the United States and Russia outskated Czechoslovakia in semifinal games, the Montreal Forum was sold out for the best of Canada against the best of the USSR.

The two anthems rang through the Forum, and the Canadians skated with such brilliant fury that time after time the Soviets were forced to ice the puck. But Tretiak stopped Lafleur, Bossy, and Trottier on hard shots. He made twelve saves in the first period. Mike Liut had to make only four saves for Canada.

The Soviets have a way of escalating their game, of playing each period harder than the one before. This can only be achieved after the most strenuous (and year-round) conditioning.

After a Canadian rush broke down four minutes into the second period, Sergei Makarov sped up his wing and passed the puck to Vladimir Krutov alone in front of Liut. Krutov lost the puck, retrieved it, and passed back to Igor Larionov, who beat Liut.

Gillies scored in a scramble, tying the game, but then the Canadians and Liut allowed two rather easy goals by Sergei Shepelev that put the Soviets ahead by 3–1. Then, escalating yet a few more notches, the Soviets put Canada to rout in the final period. Thousands left the Forum before the game ended.

We are conditioned in this era to worship Vince Lombardi and his curious dictum, "Winning isn't everything. It's the only thing." A generation earlier we were more intelligently critical when Leo Durocher expressed the same thought more directly: "Nice guys finish last."

We can admire what we know of Soviet hockey without really liking it. If the USSR is able to produce a band of cold-eyed winners playing and training under the Great System, so be it. I prefer a freer spirit like Guy Lafleur, to whom winning is not the only thing, or even close.

Here is my report from the Canada Cup: Lafleur is flying again— flying, I expect, into another smashing NHL season.

And, thank heaven, the Russians haven't taken up baseball.

47

Dodger Verities Span the Seasons

New York Times, October 6, 1985

A look at a powerful Dodgers team and a look back toward the man who laid the dynastic foundation: Branch Rickey.

At the very center, in the tabernacle so to speak, of the most success-ful and efficient baseball organization on Earth, you find not a com-puter but a shoe box. It is cardboard, blue and white, and somewhat battered. Al Campanis, the old NYU second baseman who is the Los Angeles Dodgers' vice president for player personnel, removed the shoe box from the drawer beside his desk and looked for an instant as archeologists must have looked when they first uncovered artifacts from Troy. He smiled, worked off some rubber bands, opened the box, and said quietly: "The Branch Rickey Tapes."

This has been a notably merry time for the Los Angeles Dodgers, Western Division champions of the National League, a civil and mostly youthful baseball team that few expected to contend for a pennant. The Dodgers finished fourth in 1984, and when they broke to a stag-gering start this season—sixty-two errors in the first two months—there was speculation that the Dodgers' dynasty, which can fairly be traced to the embattled Brooklyn team of 1947, was at length coming apart under the ubiquitous palm trees of Los Angeles.

Campanis is a feisty and vigorous sixty-eight, but sixty-eight still. When he flew off to Florida early this season to supervise arm rehabilitation for the right-handed pitcher Bob Welch, someone suggested that his true mission was to find himself a retirement home. This apparently was meant lightly. Campanis was not amused.

Manager Tommy Lasorda, just turned fifty-eight, is stirred by pro-found passions for pasta, baseball, and aspects of the Hollywood life. His capacious office, adjoining the Dodgers' clubhouse, beckons you with a full wall of Frank Sinatra pictures and half a wall covered by signed photographs of Don Rickles. (You can also discover autographed pictures from Carl Erskine and Van Lingle Mungo, but these are some-what harder to find.) Lasorda is a splendid raconteur, exuberant and funny, and his clubhouse language tends toward electric blue.

As with Casey Stengel before him, Lasorda's solid baseball back-ground is sometimes clouded by his comical routines. When the Dodg-ers were averaging fewer than three runs a game back in May, Lasorda's credentials as a reigning wizard came under challenge.

And more than any individual, the Dodgers' baseball system—the pride of an organization that has attracted more than three million fans to Dodger Stadium in six of the last eight seasons—was coming under question. The Dodgers seem to scout for prospects just a little bit better and harder than anybody else. Then when a young man is signed, they enroll him in their complex teaching and training struc-ture, broadly Dodger Tech.

The prospect works not only with a minor league manager and coaches but with nine roving instructors (including Sandy Koufax) who shuttle among the Dodgers' six farm teams all summer. He learns tradition, the high deeds of Jackie Robinson, Don Drysdale, and the others right up to Fernando Valenzuela. He is tutored in everything from sliding home properly to practicing civility toward the media. He hears of the mystique of Dodger Blue. When and if he settles into steady work at Dodger Stadium, he feels a sense of organizational pride, and if he is fortunate—as Steve Sax was this year—he gets to drape a gen-tlemanly arm around Suzanne Sommers on Hollywood Stars' Night.

It is a superb system—home-grown ballplayers, the Dodgers like to say—but it is threatened by the peripatetic ways of modern baseball. Three years ago the Dodgers lost both Ron Cey and Steve Garvey. . . . But spokesmen insisted, at least in public, that new home-grown slug-gers like Mike Marshall and Greg Brock would replace the missing power. The Dodgers finished first in 1983 but fell below .500 last year, and it began to seem to some that the Dodgers' system, superb as it once was, had at length become an anachronism.

Such speculation was pretty much buried at 9:10 p.m. (PDT) last Wednesday while the Dodgers were on their way to a 9–3 victory over the Atlanta Braves. Mariano Duncan, a bubbly, young Dominican shortstop, was batting, and the Dodgers' extraordinary sophomore right-hander, Orel Hershiser IV, was on first base. Both are products of Dodger Tech. Diamond Vision, a huge display board above the left-field pavilion, flashed word that Cincinnati had been beaten in San Diego. The Dodgers had clinched the Western Division championship. The crowd—Los Angeles baseball crowds are passive by New York standards—began to cheer. Encouraged by Lasorda, the Dodgers' players climbed out of the dugout and applauded the fans who were applauding them. Play stopped for three minutes. At first base Hershiser felt so moved that tears came to his eyes.

Near the dugout Mike Marshall, who had hit his twenty-seventh home run, said he wanted to dedicate this triumph to the Dodgers' fans "and also to all the people who picked us to finish fifth."

"The spirit of Branch Rickey still stirs in these offices," Campanis said, peering into his shoe box full of tapes. "We recorded some of Mr. Rickey's lectures when he was running the Brooklyn Dodgers in 1950, and I've had them transferred to cassettes." Campanis studied the cassette labels and read some titles aloud:

"Luck Is the Residue of Design." "Is What We Are Doing Worthwhile?" "Intestinal Fortitude." "The Cure Is Sweat."

"Do you have your coaches and scouts listen to these tapes?" I asked.

"Damn right. Every year. And I listen to them myself, too, about every six months. Mr. Rickey was the master, and he's still teaching all of us, thirty-five years after these talks were recorded."

This Dodgers team that Campanis, Lasorda, and the farm system have created is young, aggressive, generally fleet, and possessed of remarkable first-line pitching. You don't find outsized characters like Jackie Robinson or Duke Snider because the team is young and still developing and also because ballplayers in this era try to be more calculating with their public image than the free thinkers who ennobled Ebbets Field.

The catcher Mike Sciosia (pronounced So-sha) is a master at block-ing the plate and has hit almost .300 down the stretch. He is the team's player representative—there is no captain—so when we met for brunch the other day it seemed reasonable to tackle one of baseball's largest issues: cocaine.

"I'm actually glad you asked about that," Sciosia said. "Of course, we had the problem on our club with Steve Howe. Everybody on the outside seems to have a solution now, but nobody's asking the ballplayers." . . .

"It was a real problem," Sciosia said, "but that doesn't mean there's any magical cure. I favor a combination of approaches. You hear about testing. The testing for cocaine is not always accurate, and besides it doesn't hit the problem at its source. First we need positive peer pres-sure, applied by team leaders all through baseball. Cocaine just isn't acceptable. Don't think you can handle it, because you can't. Second, education and the long-term effects of the stuff. What it does to you, your family. How hard it is to kick. That sort of thing. Then we'll have to see how testing works in."

Sciosia plunged into a fruit salad and started talking about his development from big and strong and raw into a polished player. Roy Campanella, who still works for the Dodgers, used to drive his battery-powered wheelchair onto a field in Vero Beach to work with Sciosia behind a plate. (Almost every time he did, someone shouted, "Hey, Campy! Don't get a flat.")

"I learned from Roy, and then I learned from Del Crandall when Del managed me at Albuquerque," Sciosia said. "Aside from the tech-nical things, you really have to think. Who the hitter is. What he expects. What he doesn't expect. You want to plan three or four or five pitches ahead."

"About plate-blocking," I said.

"You can't practice it," Sciosia said. He grinned. That is one of his favorite small jokes. "An older catcher like Gary Carter of the Mets, who has a bad knee, may give up plate-blocking, figuring he'd rather stay in the lineup. I'm not at that point yet." Indeed. He is really the finest plate-blocker in all baseball, big and fearless and tough.

Tall, blond-mustached Jerry Reuss is thirty-six and, with Bill Russell sidelined by an eye affliction, a dean of the Dodgers in the playoffs. Reuss is also a pitcher in transition. Over the past five years his fastball and hard, low slider gave him the best earned-run average in the Major Leagues (an aggregate 2.87). But surgery on his left arm has forced him to convert himself into a finesse pitcher. We met in a hotel room in Houston, where Reuss . . . traced transitions on the Dodgers, since he joined them in 1979, with great insight and skill. He was a math major in college long ago, and he speaks polysyllabically and with great precision.

The last world championship Dodgers team (1981) was "diverse, strong, developed." It starred players like Steve Garvey "who cultivated catching everybody's fantasy." At that time Tom Lasorda had to "motivate the veterans." Now with a younger team, "he has to educate as much as motivate."

"The Steve Howe situation was a serious distraction," Reuss said. "Almost everybody liked Steve, but drug addiction is a nasty disease. One makes a decision, I believe, to give in to it, and nobody much liked that or all the questions about it all the time.

"I don't see drugs as a baseball problem. It's a problem throughout society. You can say that baseball is a microcosm of society, but in the sense we are segregated by fame."

"With the strike and drug stories," I said, "this hasn't been much of a year for the image of ballplayers."

"We make large amounts of money," Reuss said, "and people resent that. They're not aware of the pressures, the physical pain, and the emotional stress that go with our careers."

Reuss had long received letters from fans asking for autographed pictures. Three years ago he conceived an interesting plan. He now sells autographed pictures, with most of the proceeds going to the Cystic Fibrosis Foundation. "That way," he said, "the club is happy, the fans are happy, the charity is thrilled, and I'm giving something back to the country." Jerry Reuss, left-hander in transition, is also honorary chairman of the Los Angeles Chapter of the Cystic Fibrosis Foundation.

If Ring Lardner would have trouble recognizing Sciosia and Reuss as ballplayers, Orel Leonard Hershiser IV might have inspired him toward a departure in the short-story form.

Hershiser is tall (six feet three), bespectacled, and in civilian clothes has the look of an English instructor at a small midwestern college. "So," I said, when we met while waiting for a charter flight in Houston, "you're Orel Hershiser Fourth."

"Yes," he said, "and my father is Orel Hershiser Third, and my son is Orel Hershiser Fifth."

Dr. O., as some Dodgers enthusiasts call him, has become a splendid pitcher at the age of twenty-seven with a commanding sinker, a fine curve, and a good change of pace. In two Major League seasons, he has thrown a three-hitter, four two-hitters, and two one-hitters.

"Do you think about a no-hitter?" I said.

"Only every time I go out to the mound."

In spring training, when Lasorda was motivating his players, he called a meeting and launched an impassioned speech. "If the president of the United States called," Lasorda said, "and told me I had to take twenty-five guys to Nicaragua to fight for the United States, I'd take the twenty-five guys who were going to play for me."

"You better make that twenty-four, skipper," Hershiser said, deadpan, "and one conscientious objector."

Hershiser's father bought into a variety of printing businesses, and the family lived variously in Buffalo, Toronto, and Cherry Hill, New Jersey. After graduating from Bowling Green, where he did not make the baseball team until he was a junior, Hershiser was drafted in the seventeenth round. He spent five seasons in the minor leagues. "Discouraging?" I asked.

"Being down there and being broke? It wasn't discouraging," he said, "because I always felt I was moving on an upward plane. I wasn't that broke, because my parents sent me enough money to see that I ate properly."

"And now," I said, "You have an agent."

Hershiser grinned. "Agent?" he said. "Agent? That sounds a little sleazy. I have an attorney. And doesn't that sound as if there was some morals there?"

He is consistently droll off the mound and consistently rugged on it. Lasorda has nicknamed this tall and academic-looking fellow "Bulldog."

I watched the Dodgers split a pair with Houston. Then they swept the San Francisco Giants, a team of shreds and patches, before clinching the division championship during the game with Atlanta that boosted Hershiser's record to 19-3. They get good power hitting from Pedro Guerrero, Mike Marshall, and, occasionally, Greg Brock. They have speed in Steve Sax and Mariano Duncan, solidity in Sciosia, brilliant starting pitching, and a so-so bullpen. "Not the greatest team I ever managed," Lasorda said, "but the greatest bunch of guys."

How does this Dodgers team stand up against the storied Dodgers club of thirty years ago that brought Brooklyn its only World Series victory? The starting pitching is better. Among the position players my guess is that only Guerrero in left field would have made the starting lineup, and I'm not even sure about that.

Sandy Amoros saved the 1955 World Series for Brooklyn with his famous running catch of Yogi Berra's drive down the left-field line. Amoros could catch the ball because he was left-handed and was able to reach toward the line with his gloved right hand. Guerrero, who is right-handed, would not make that play.

"But he doesn't have to," insisted Fred Claire, the Dodgers' executive vice president. "He hits a three-run home run in the third inning that puts the game out of the Yankees' reach."

When it was time to go, Hershiser said: "What's this? You're leaving us? You won't write in your hotel? You have to be home? In a certain room, looking at a certain picture?"

"That's right, Orel. Not only pitchers are neurotic."

Then Reuss gave me a picture with a warm personal inscription and to my inexpressible delight reached into his locker, produced my most recent book, and asked me to inscribe it to him.

I had come to Los Angeles with aspirations toward journalistic neutrality. Now a Major Leaguer, a Dodger, had asked me for an autograph.

Can you imagine what that does to journalistic neutrality? Go, Orel. Go, Jerry.

Go, Dodgers!

Part 5

A New Millennium

48

Joe Black, 1924–2002: Hard Thrower, Soft Heart

Los Angeles Times, May 18, 2002

An affectionate farewell.

We were riding a slow train somewhere between Mobile and Montgomery in the old racist South, "the Hookworm Belt," as the great sports editor Stanley Woodward described it. Joe Black was a twenty-eight-year-old Dodgers rookie who would have been a big leaguer years before, except for his color. Now he was telling me stories about life in the Negro Leagues, using a kind of *Amos 'n' Andy* drawl. After a while he said, "You're with a big paper. Does the manager tell you if he's gonna keep me?"

I was young enough and brash enough to be blunt: "You really want to make this ballclub, don't you?"

Black looked at me clear and straight. The drawl vanished. "If I could express myself as well as Shakespeare, I still couldn't tell you how much I want to make the Dodgers," he said.

So began a friendship that ran for fifty years and ended in the only way it could end, with a departure. Joe Black, who died Friday of prostate cancer, was more than the first black pitcher to win a World Series game. He was a psychologist, a humanist, a businessman, and across his seventy-eight years a magnificent advertisement for America.

He did make the Dodgers, and in that first season, 1952, he won fifteen games and saved fifteen more for a club with somewhat shaky pitching. That brought the team a pennant. On the last day of the season, a friendly case arrived in the press box at the top of Ebbets Field. It contained one bottle of Scotch whisky for each sportswriter who had regularly covered the team.

"I know I threw the pitches," Black wrote in a cover note, "but the stuff you fellows wrote sure helped." You may have anticipated the brand of Scotch Joe sent. It was Black & White.

The great reliever started three games against the Yankees in the World Series, posted a 2.53 earned-run average, but was beaten on short rest in the seventh game.

That winter we worked out together, and he told me more than once that his pitching success was really simple. "They've got people here in Brooklyn who can think," he said. "They say throw high, I throw high. They say throw low, I throw low." He left out this: he threw 97 mph, and in his great 1952 season he could throw a ball that hard over a matchstick.

He kept his arm loose by throwing a rubber ball. I became his off-season catcher in a small YMCA. The experience, catching that midwinter smoke, remains vivid as an electric shock.

He never again matched '52, and after his career wound down in 1957, he became a schoolteacher back home in Plainfield, New Jersey. . . . One day, he brought a bedraggled school baseball team to Yankee Stadium, and Casey Stengel came out of the dugout to shake his hand.

"Case," Joe said, "these are good kids, but they've lost their last eleven games. What do you think I ought to teach them?" Stengel did not hesitate. "Teach 'em to lose in the right spirit," he said.

The Greyhound Corporation offered Black ten times his teaching salary to become a vice president for marketing. Part of the job, to be sure, was the high-level selling of bus tickets to African Americans. But also—Joe made sure of this—it was articulating ideas about blacks and whites in our society. Here are some of the things he said:

To exalt a special language for black Americans is a kind of bigotry. "What is our language? Fo'teen for fourteen? Pohleeze for police? Any man, white or black, who says white people have to learn 'our' language is insulting. What he's saying is that every other ethnic group can migrate to America and master English. But we, who were born here and whose families have lived here for so many, many years, don't have the ability to speak proper English. Wear a dashiki or an

African hairdo, but in the name of common sense, learn the English language. It is your own."

When Martin Luther King was shot, Black flew to Atlanta to help with the services. So did Sammy Davis Jr. Afterward, Joe found himself clearing a path for Davis through a gathering of poor Atlanta blacks.

"My people, my people," Davis cried, throwing out both hands in deep emotion.

"Some," Black said, "are your people. Our people. Some will steal the rings off your fingers. Stay close and keep your hands in your pockets, Sam."

Like his life, Joe Black's words spoke banners.

49

Scorecard: Mind Over Batter

Sports Illustrated, December 8, 2003

No one had a better head for pitching than Warren Spahn.

Warren Spahn seldom forgot a name, a face, a batter's tendencies, or an insult. More than once he recalled the trauma of his Major League debut as an obscure twenty-year-old left-hander with the wartime Boston Braves. It was 1942, and Casey Stengel, managing Boston to a seventh-place finish, summoned Spahn from the bullpen to face the Dodgers' Pee Wee Reese. "Kid," Stengel said, "this hitter has been beaned and got his skull broke. I want you to throw your first two pitches at his head."

Spahn was a magnificent competitor, but he was also a sportsman. He threw two fastballs shoulder-high inside, neither near Reese's head, then walked the Brooklyn shortstop. Stengel made his bent-legged way back to the mound. "Yer outta the game," he said, "and when you get to the dugout, keep walking till you reach the clubhouse. There's gonna be a bus ticket there back to Hartford. You'll never win in the Major Leagues. You got no guts."

Proceeding with this narrative long afterward, Spahn uttered a put-down for the ages. "A few years later," he said, "after I won the Bronze Star during the Battle of the Bulge . . ."

Nor did Spahn's story finish there. Stengel moved on and won five World Series for the Yankees. Spahn would go on to win 363 games, more than any other left-hander. The two crossed paths again, in 1965, when Spahn's pitching days were almost done and Stengel was managing the Mets into the cellar. Spahn was pounded in a few starts, and Stengel complained, "The hitters jump on him so quick, I can't get him outta there fast enough." Summing up not so long ago, Spahn said, exercising his fine and occasionally malicious wit, "I pitched for Casey Stengel both before and after he was a genius." . . .

Spahnie's study of pitching was as profound as that of the immortal Christy Mathewson. "Home plate is seventeen inches wide," Spahn liked to point out. "All I asked for were the two inches on each corner. The hitters could have the thirteen inches in between. I didn't throw there." He was very fast when young but evolved into a master of the slider and the changeup. "Batting is timing," he said. "Pitching is upsetting timing."

Few who saw Spahn will forget the arcing grace of his windup. His strong arms pumped far back, and as he rocked, his right leg kicked high before he threw. His motion was unique and fluid, a sort of pitching equivalent to Stan Musial's swing. "Musial was the hardest man to fool," Spahn said. "He had an average of .314 against me, but I never brooded when Stan hit me. The time to worry was when some .250 hitter knocked my cap off with a line drive."

Like many good soldiers, Spahn didn't like to discuss his wartime adventures, much less dwell on how he won his medal. When I asked about his battlefield promotion from enlisted man to lieutenant, he said lightly, "Hell, in the Bulge they were running out of officers."

He went on, "After you've tried to sleep in frozen tank ruts within the range of Nazi guns, every day you get to play baseball is a breeze."

During a recent gathering in Cooperstown, I introduced him to my wife and said, "After a game Mr. Spahn remembered each one of the 125 pitches he had thrown, where it was, what it was, and the sequence."

The praise made Spahn uncomfortable. "That's nothing special, Mrs. Kahn," he said. "After all, pitching is what I did."

50

A Few Moments with TSW

Boston Red Sox Magazine, June 2007

Mr. Williams shows his style, his temper, and in the end some welcome warmth.

The Dodgers, the real Dodgers, the Brooklyn Dodgers, were rising out of decades of mediocrity and becoming a winning team. Brooklyn was only a borough, not a city, and a common butt of cliché comedians' humor. So the rising of the Dodgers possessed great importance for us. Did something dramatic happen in 1941, say a tall, skinny outfielder hitting .406? Not bad, we said, but no big deal. Rogers Hornsby, the St. Louis Rajah of our league, the National League, once batted 18 points higher, .424. The big Brooklyn news in autumn of '41 was that the Dodgers won a pennant for the first time in twenty-one years. Reiser, our super-rookie, led the league in triples, runs scored, and batting (.343).

With time came more sophistication. We didn't actually see much of such American Leaguers as Ted Williams, or Hank Greenberg of Detroit, or even Joe DiMaggio of the primordial Bronx, but we learned from box scores that these were imposing athletes and would have been in any time, in any league. . . .

With peace, even in Brooklyn we joined a nationwide debate. Who was the best all-around hitter in the game, Ted the Thumper—the Fanueil Flash—or Stan "The Man" Musial of St. Louis? In retrospect the question is simplistic. Which ballpark, who's pitching, and what's the game situation are all factors that make a single answer somewhat silly. For two seasons, as a visiting player at Ebbets Field, a total of twenty-two games, Musial batted over .500, including one game where he went 5-for-5 all with two strikes. I don't imagine there has ever been a better hitter than Musial in Brooklyn, but he didn't hit that phenomenally anywhere else.

"The only time I went head to head with Ted," Musial told me recently, "was in the 1946 World Series where the Cardinals played the Red Sox. Williams hit .200. I hit .222. Between us we were one .400." . . .

In 1955 Ralph Graves, the gifted articles editor at *Life* magazine, asked me to write a story about Billy Klaus, a journeyman shortstop whose exciting play, Ralph said, could very well lead the Red Sox to a pennant.

I picked up the team in Detroit and asked Williams near the batting cage if we could talk about Klaus.

"Tomorrow," Williams said, in a voice that carried to Kankakee. "Right here. One o'clock."

I appeared dutifully and said that I'd been reading that Billy Klaus was a sparkplug.

"Fiddlesticks," Williams said in coarser English. "There is no such thing as a sparkplug on a Major League team. You musta been reading *them*!" A large, disdainful gesture indicated the Boston baseball writers, who were gathered in a silent semicircle perhaps fifteen feet away.

"Klaus had an ordinary year last season in the minors," I said. "Maybe even a bad year. How do you explain going from a bad year in the minors to a fine year in the Majors?"

"Who you asking?"

"You."

"Mister"—now the voice surely reached Oahu—"I can see you don't know very much about baseball if you're asking me about a bad year. Because old TSW, he don't have bad years. You see those guys [the Boston baseball writers]? They'd all give their right arm for me to have a bad year. But it don't happen, and it never will. Because TSW, he don't have bad years." Williams slammed his bat fiercely to the grass, and it came pinwheeling back to him. He caught it deftly, and then he walked away.

A few minutes later a veteran Boston baseball writer—one of Williams's Knights of the Keyboard—approached me and said, "He only did that so you would knock us in a national magazine. But if you print what he said, I promise you this. No Boston baseball writer will ever speak to you again."

Of course I printed Williams's words, but until now they have not seen the light of day. The '55 Red Sox swooned, eventually finishing fourth, and Ralph Graves at *Life* told me he could not run my story. "We only have room for real contenders," said Ralph, who is a Harvard man.

My path next crossed that of Williams in the mid-1980s, when a publisher asked me to write about Joe DiMaggio and Marilyn Monroe. I began by mailing questionnaires to DiMaggio's contemporaries, with Williams high on the list. His response came back quickly and in longhand.

"Joe DiMaggio is a fine guy," Williams reported, "and by the way I've read *The Boys of Summer*. You have written one great book." Better hitter, Williams or Musial? Don't ask me. (No sane person would want to pitch to either.) But I will say this. I've never met a better literary critic than Ted the Thumper from old Fanueil Hall.

51

Clem

An Original Story

Before he became an established Brooklyn Dodgers pitcher in 1951, Clem Labine's long baseball career included stints at Newport News, Greenville, Asheville, Pueblo, and St. Paul. Extended stays in what were then called the bush leagues were common when Major League teams ran extensive farm systems and controlled as many as six hundred ballplayers in what some reporters called chain gangs. "One thing you had to learn," Labine recalled, "was how to sleep sitting up on a bus."

On the pleasant March evening in 1952 when I began covering the Brooklyn Dodgers for the *New York Herald Tribune*, there were no comets seen. This would be one of the great voyages of my life, but for all I could tell, the universe was uninterested. And the ballplayers didn't appear to care, either.

Back then no fewer than nine New York–area newspapers assigned reporters to cover the team. Add visiting columnists, and you usually had about one sportswriter interviewing and typing for every two athletes hitting and throwing. The appearance of one young writer more or less did not make much difference in the Dodgers' scheme, which at the moment seemed cursed by Satan.

In the last inning of the last game of the 1950 National League season, the Dodgers lost the pennant to Philadelphia when a Phillies outfielder named Dick Sisler sliced a short, opposite-field home run into the second or third row of seats behind left. In the last inning of the last game of the 1951 National League season, the Dodgers lost the pennant to the New York Giants when Bobby Thomson hit a line drive into the lower left-field seats, a hard wallop but not a home run in many ballparks of the time, other than the horseshoe-shaped Polo Grounds.

I don't know of another instance where a big-league team lost successive pennants on successive closing days. All the Dodgers felt this was a question about the team's collective courage. In the characteristically rough and coarse baseball humor of the time, Sal Maglie, the great Giants pitcher, went around asking, "What do the Dodgers and [famously gay entertainer Lee] Liberace have in common?"

After a moment, Maglie answered his own question. "They both choke up on the big ones."

So there I was, standing in the lobby of the McAllister Hotel in Miami wondering if I was worthy of a big-league assignment. And there the Dodgers walked about toward restaurants and bars, wondering on some level why they couldn't win a bloody pennant.

Someone called my name, then said, "I'm Clem Labine." I found myself looking at a sturdy six-footer, with a strong-jawed, handsome face. Down the final stretch of the previous season, Brooklyn's Satanic Bobby Thomson season, he had been the best of Dodgers pitchers. He was twenty-five year old. I was twenty-four. "Are you free tonight?" Labine said.

"I'm free until April, Mr. Labine."

"It's Clem. Would you like to go to a movie? A picture called *Moulin Rouge* is playing down the street. It's about the French painter Toulouse-Lautrec."

I suppose I blinked. On my first night with a ballclub I did not expect to hear a Major League pitcher mention serious painting. Clem blinked back. He did not want to appear pretentious (or even worse, in those distant big-league days, intellectual). "I only know that," he said quickly, "because my family is French."

He paid for my ticket, 25 cents, a debt that became a running joke between us for fifty years. Then we watched in wonder as José Ferrer played the dwarfed Lautrec, Zsa Zsa Gabor performed beautifully as Jane Avril, and the movie starred the paintings, the Lautrec paintings, where harlots, performers, and colors brightened our night.

At drinks afterward we got around to pitching. Labine came from a blue-collar Rhode Island family. His father was a weaver, and he never went to college, but he possessed a remarkable analytical mind. He could make a sinker snap and buzz and a curveball snarl with menace. More than that he understood the physics, the aerodynamics, of pitching. Yes, he conceded, painting intrigued him, particularly Impressionist work. He liked narrative poetry, the works of Robert W. Service, and hey, this was too much about him. Where was I from and had I played a little ball myself?

"Brooklyn, Clem. I could play a little, but nothing like you."

"I'll bet you were better than you say, and I'll just guess you were Phi Beta Kappa."

"Better at poetry. Never finished college. I've done some dumb things."

"Me, too. I volunteered in the war, and I became a paratrooper."

"Why would an intelligent guy like you want to jump out of airplanes?"

Labine paused and grinned. "I was eighteen years old."

Such is the stuff of friendship. From that night through 1962, when Labine's career wound down, I saw Clem pitch in more than one hundred big-league games. Numbers, which seduce so many current baseball reporters (it is easier to write stats than it is to write well), don't tell much. Labine, Clement Walter, 13 years pitched, 77 games won, 56 games lost, World Series, 2 victories, 2 defeats. Against this, consider the comment of E. J. Buzzie Bavasi, the Dodgers' general manager for almost twenty years. "Along with Jackie Robinson," Bavasi says, "Labine was the best competitor I ever saw."

By choice Labine primarily was a relief pitcher. He said he liked the challenge of walking into a jam. But he could start as well, and he sometimes remarked that he had thrown the two least-remembered shutouts in the annals. On October 2, 1951, in the second game of a three-game playoff, he shutout the Giants, 10–0, at the Polo Grounds. The game was close early. It turned when Labine struck out Bobby Thomson with the bases loaded on a fierce hook. But the next day Thomson hit his famous homer off Ralph Branca, and the memory of Clem's shutout faded quickly. Five years later on October 9, 1956, Labine shut out the Yankees, 1–0, across the ten innings of the sixth game of the World Series. But the day before, Don Larsen had pitched his perfect game against the Dodgers. To most, Labine's second great clutch shutout was an anticlimax.

He was a proud feller with an artistic bent—he would later design men's sportswear—and that combination produced torrents of envy within Dick Young of the *Daily News*, a talented reporter and one of the meanest men I've come across. Young filled his columns with scorn for the great reliever, questioning Labine's courage and even his manhood. Clem took it in silence for a long time.

But at length Labine approached Young. He was carrying a roll of tape. "I'm bigger than you, so a fight wouldn't be fair," Labine said. "I'm going to have the trainer tape my right arm behind my back. Then we'll go at it. I think the fight might be even if I only had one arm to swing."

Young fled.

After brief terms with the Tigers and the Pirates, Labine retired to Woonsocket, Rhode Island, where he worked as a designer and plant manager for Deerfoot Sporting Goods. When *The Boys of Summer* was published in 1972, Clem sent me a blue-and-white warm-up jacket, with the title of the book appearing in script on the back and my first name, also in script, written over the heart. Only a few years later, Deerfoot folded, overwhelmed by cheap imports from Asia. Moving on, Clem was soon placing commercial mortgages for a bank.

With the years, he had become acquainted with sorrow. His first wife died of breast cancer, leaving Clem not only with tragedy but huge bills an insurance company refused to pay on the grounds that the cancer treatment was experimental. Clem sold his house, paid his debts, and moved into a condo. His son, Jay, joined the Marine Corps during the Vietnam War. Three months later in the Mekong Delta, a land mine blew away one of Jay's legs.

Clem declined to yield to despair. He got married again, this time to a charming girl from Providence. "I didn't even know he'd been a pitcher," Barbara Labine says. "I came from a fine Italian family. We didn't listen to baseball on the radio. We listened to opera."

We would meet annually at Cooperstown in high summer, gathering at the mansion of our late friend Walter Rich. We were joined on various occasions by George Pataki, Tip O'Neill, and George W. Bush. They were all fine baseball fans and loved to hear Clem spin out his stories or lecture in his unpretentious way on the art of pitching.

"Most people are high-ball hitters," he might begin, "because our eyes aren't in our knees."

When the revels ended in the summer of 2006, I reached for a final Scotch.

"You don't need that," Clem said. "You're driving home."

Cooperstown is only two hours away, but the road is a winding, narrow blacktop. "I'd say I can handle it, Clement."

"Don't drink that Scotch," Labine said, "and next year we'll get the wiffle-ball set, and I'll throw you a high change."

There is no easier pitch for me to hit. I put down the glass. But I never did see that change. On March 2, 2007, in the fullness of his eighty years, Clem died. He had been coaching the winning team in a Dodgers fantasy camp when a stroke brought a well-lived life to a close.

I will not have another friend like Clem, but to surrender to despair would be a disservice to all that he believed. I have before me the *Boys of Summer* jacket he designed. Within I have my memories. Now that Clem is gone I remember him in words first spoken by Socrates.

To a good man no evil can come, either in life or after death.

[End it . . . RK]

Nonfiction

Into My Own (2006)
Beyond the Boys of Summer (2005)
October Men (2002)
The Head Game (2000)
A Flame of Pure Fire (1999)
Memories of Summer (1997)
The Era (1993)
Games We Used to Play (1992)
Joe and Marilyn (1986)
Good Enough to Dream (1985)
A Season in the Sun (1977)
How the Weather Was (1973)
The Boys of Summer (1972)
The Battle for Morningside Heights (1970)
The Passionate People (1968)

Novels

The Seventh Game (1982)
But Not to Keep (1978)